Nuclear Weapons and Arms Control in the Middle East

CSIA Studies in International Security

Michael E. Brown, Sean M. Lynn-Jones, & Steven E. Miller, series editors
Teresa Johnson Lawson, executive editor
Center for Science and International Affairs (CSIA)
John F. Kennedy School of Government, Harvard University

Published by The MIT Press:

The International Dimensions of Internal Conflict, Michael E. Brown, ed. (1996)

Avoiding Nuclear Anarchy: Containing the Threat of Loose Russian Nuclear Weapons and Fissile Material, Graham T. Allison, Owen R. Coté, Jr., Richard A. Falkenrath, & Steven E. Miller (1996)

The Arms Production Dilemma: Contraction and Restraint in the World Combat Aircraft Industry, Randall Forsberg, ed. (1994)

Shaping Europe's Military Order: The Origins and Consequences of the CFE Treaty, Richard A. Falkenrath (1994)

Published by Brassey's, Inc.:

Damage Limitation or Crisis? Russia and the Outside World, Robert D. Blackwill and Sergei A. Karaganov, eds. (1994)

Arms Unbound: The Globalization of Defense Production, David Mussington (1994)

Russian Security After the Cold War: Seven Views from Moscow, Teresa Pelton Johnson and Steven E. Miller, eds. (1994)

Published by CSIA:

Cooperative Denuclearization: From Pledges to Deeds, Graham Allison, Ashton B. Carter, Steven E. Miller, and Philip Zelikow, eds. (1993)

Soviet Nuclear Fission: Control of the Nuclear Arsenal in a Disintegrating Soviet Union, Kurt M. Campbell, Ashton B. Carter, Steven E. Miller, and Charles A. Zraket (1991)

Nuclear Weapons and Arms Control in the Middle East

by Shai Feldman

CSIA Studies in International Security

with cooperation from the Jaffee Center for Strategic Studies
Tel Aviv University

The MIT Press
Cambridge, Massachusetts
London, England

Library of Congress Cataloging-in-Publication Data

Feldman, Shai, 1950–
Nuclear weapons and arms control in the Middle East / by Shai Feldman.
p.   cm.—(CSIA studies in international security)
Includes bibliographical references and index.
ISBN 0-262-06189-9 (alk. paper).—ISBN 0-262-56108-5 (pbk.: alk. paper).
1. Nuclear arms control—Middle East. 2. Nuclear nonproliferation. 3. Security—
International. I. Title. II. Series.
JX1974.74.M627F45   1997
327.1'747'0956—dc21   96-44081
                                                                CIP

10 9 8 7 6 5 4 3 2 1
Printed in the United States of America

Contents

About the Author

Shai Feldman is a Senior Research Fellow at the Center for Science and International Affairs (CSIA) at Harvard University's John F. Kennedy School of Government. For the previous decade and a half, he was a Senior Research Associate at Tel Aviv University's Jaffee Center for Strategic Studies where, since 1989, he directed the Project on Regional Security and Arms Control in the Middle East. Educated at Hebrew University in Jerusalem awarded the MA and PhD by the University of California at Berkeley, Dr. Feldman has written extensively on nuclear proliferation; Israeli national security, domestic politics and defense policy; and U.S. foreign and defense policies in the Middle East. He is the author of *Israeli Nuclear Deterrence: A Strategy for the 1980s* (New York: Columbia University Press, 1982); and *The Future of U.S.-Israel Strategic Cooperation* (Washington, D.C.: The Washington Institute for Near East Policy, 1996). He co-edited, with Ariel Levite, *Arms Control and the New Middle East Security Environment*, Study No. 23 (Tel Aviv University: Jaffee Center for Strategic Studies, 1994); and edited *Confidence Building and Verification: Prospects in the Middle East*, Study No. 24 (Tel Aviv University: Jaffee Center for Strategic Studies, 1994). With Abdullah Toukan of Jordan, he recently wrote *Bridging the Gap: A Future Security Architecture for the Middle East,* under the auspices of the Carnegie Corporation's Commission on Preventing Deadly Conflict.

In memory of

Aharon (A'rale) Yariv,
Shalheveth Freier,
and
Mordechai (Motta) Gur

Acknowledgment

Work on this volume has been conducted as part of the Jaffee Center's project on Security and Arms Control in the Middle East and would not have been possible without generous assistance by the Ford Foundation. The Foundation's grant funded the launching of the project, research for this book, and two international conferences — the Ginosar Conferences on Security and Arms Control in the Middle East. Travel to various seminars, conferences, and informal meetings that were attended by colleagues from Arab states was also made possible by the Ford Foundation. Other assistance dedicated to addressing the prospects for nuclear arms control in the Middle East was granted by the Ploughshares Fund. No words can describe my gratitude to Enid Schoettle, Steven Riskin, Shepard Forman, and Christine Wing at the Ford Foundation, and Sally Lilienthal and Karen Harris at Ploughshares.

I am also grateful to a number of Israelis who have helped shape this book. My colleagues at the Jaffee Center all read the first draft and provided numerous useful comments. I am particularly indebted to my friend and colleague Ariel Levite, now Deputy Director for External Relations at Israel's Ministry of Defense and a member of the Israeli delegation to the Arms Control and Regional Security (ACRS) talks, for his many suggestions.

Two distinguished Israelis also read the first draft of this manuscript and provided extensive important comments: Hanan Baron, former Senior Deputy Director General of the Ministry of Foreign Affairs and presently co-chairman of Israel's delegation to the ACRS talks, and the late Shalheveth Freier of the Weizmann Institute of Science, former Head of Israel's Atomic Energy Commission. I am very grateful for their willingness to contribute their time and intellectual energies so generously. Of course, I alone am responsible for any errors and faulty analysis contained in this book.

Many thanks are also due to the individuals who contributed to the collection of the data needed to write this volume. Danny Leshem, Sam Wiederman, and Yiftah Shafir have sorted, coded, and filed the data collected by the Jaffee Center's project. Avi Mualem, a student of the Middle East at Tel Aviv University, checked the transliteration of the many Arabic sources cited here. Above all, I am indebted to my former research assistant, Tali Shilo, whose intellectual and organizational skills were critical to every aspect of writing this book.

The final phases of work on this book were conducted during my first year as Senior Research Fellow at the Center for Science and International Affairs of Harvard University's John F. Kennedy School of Government. I would like to thank Graham Allison and Steven Miller for giving me the opportunity to bring this book to its final shape, and to Sean Lynn-Jones and Teresa Lawson for orchestrating the process involved in publication. Many thanks to Miriam Avins for doing a meticulous job in copy-editing the manuscript, and to Deborah Kamen and Dawn Opstad for excellent proofreading.

Finally, I would like to devote some words to three friends and mentors I lost within a year. All three were among the most distinguished of Israelis, much senior to me in age and rank. But I felt very close to each of them for many years, in mind as well as in heart.

In late 1977, I was fortunate to be the first young researcher hired by Maj. Gen. (res.) Aharon Yariv, the founder and first Head of what later became the Jaffee Center for Strategic Studies at Tel Aviv University. I have benefited enormously from his unique wisdom and energy, experience and expertise, and sense of balance and human compassion. Yariv was truly an intellectual leader — providing a strong sense of direction while encouraging a wide diversity of thought. He was also "an officer and a gentleman" — his high military rank never compromised his sensitivity to human suffering and his willingness to help. His death in early 1994 has left a huge void.

Equally sad was the death in late 1994 of Shalheveth Freier, a man I had known from childhood. As one of the founding fathers of Israel's intelligence community, its defense research and development, as well as its nuclear program, Shalheveth spent most of his life in the dark realm of the "highly classified." Thus, it will be many years — if not generations — before his full contribution to Israel's creation and survival becomes known. In later years, Shalheveth became a central architect of Israel's more forthcoming approach to nuclear arms control, designing Israel's Nuclear-Weapons-Free Zone (NWFZ) initiative. He combined unparalleled modesty, the best of German-

Jewish culture and education, and an uncompromising devotion to Israel's well-being. To those who were fortunate to have known him, Shalheveth has set very high standards. His presence in Israel's small arms control community is greatly missed.

In mid-1995 I lost another mentor — Deputy Minister of Defense Mordechai (Motta) Gur. Motta's imprint on Israel's history was considerable: he was a young battalion commander during the retaliatory raids of the early 1950s, the commander of the paratrooper brigade that waged the costly battle over "Ammunition Hill," which played a decisive role in the conquest of East Jerusalem during the 1967 war, and the Chief of Staff who rebuilt the Israeli Defense Forces (IDF) after the 1973 War. Motta was often misunderstood during his later quest for political leadership; his fate was finally determined by recurring illnesses that he endured for many years with enormous courage.

To me, however, Motta was above all a warm individual and a philosophical partner. His warm personality and ability to make human contact instantly were unique. In the best tradition of David Ben Gurion, Israel's founding father, Motta was both a defense hawk and a political dove. He was determined that to avoid war, Israel must combine robust operational and strategic deterrence with an effort to reduce its adversaries' motivation to fight by making every attempt to meet their priorities and concerns. Throughout the past decade and a half, he took deep interest in my work and in the impressions I gathered during my many travels abroad. His reactions affected my thinking on more than one occasion. I will sorely miss him.

Preface

This volume assesses the prospects that Middle East states might agree to apply some measures to arrest the spread of nuclear weapons. It examines the current state of nuclear programs in the region, the parties' perceptions of the danger entailed in nuclear spread, the approach of Middle East states to both arms control in general and to nuclear arms control, the implications of various items on the regional and global nuclear nonproliferation agenda, and the special role of the United States in the Middle East and its approach to the possible spread of nuclear weapons there. Efforts by external powers to prevent the spread of nuclear weapons in the Middle East are examined largely as they influence the positions adopted by the region's states. These efforts include unilateral export controls, such as those enacted by the U.S. Congress; multilateral export controls, such as those applied by the Nuclear Suppliers Group (NSG); and other external arms control agendas ranging from the May 1991 Bush Middle East Arms Control Initiative to the 1995 Nuclear Non-Proliferation Treaty Review and Extension Conference.

Chapter 1 outlines the practical-political and theoretical rationales for examining the prospects for arresting nuclear proliferation in the region. A main focus of the chapter is the changing political climate for arms control in the Middle East — the progress made in recent years in Arab-Israeli peacemaking and the evolution of the Middle East Arms Control and Regional Security (ACRS) talks. This evolving Arab-Israeli peace process makes it possible for the first time to consider seriously the application of nuclear arms control in the Middle East. At the same time, the nuclear issue has already become a major source of contention in the evolving ACRS talks. Another focus of this chapter is the lively scholarly debate on the consequences of nuclear proliferation. Due to the inconclusive nature of the debate on the consequences of nuclear spread, one cannot take a relaxed approach to the prospects of proliferation in the Middle East. Hence the importance of examining whether the region's states might adopt some measures to limit the spread of these weapons.

Chapter 2 analyzes the nuclear programs pursued by Middle East states, evaluating the likelihood that each of these programs might lead to the acquisition of nuclear weapons. The central conclusion of this chapter is that none of the region's Muslim states is close to possessing nuclear weapons. Unless fissile material is soon smuggled into the Middle East, there is still time to reverse the pursuit of nuclear arms in the region.

Chapters 3 and 4 examine how the region's states view nuclear weapons and their likely impact in the Middle East: what the nuclear-related threat perceptions of Israel, Iran, and the Arab states, and how do they intend to withstand these threats? The two chapters illustrate that the different strategic imperatives of Israel and the region's Arab and Muslim states have resulted in different approaches to the possible acquisition of nuclear arms. At the same time, most of these states, including Israel, express alarm regarding the perceived existence or the possible spread of nuclear capabilities in the Middle East. These fears may provide a basis for exploring the prospects for applying some nuclear arms control measures in the region.

Chapter 5 outlines the global and regional nuclear nonproliferation agenda. It presents the menu of nuclear arms control measures to which Middle East states must respond. Readers who are familiar with these measures may choose to skip this chapter.

Chapter 6 elaborates the nuclear nonproliferation policy of the United States and its approach to the spread of nuclear weapons in the Middle East. Particular attention is given to U.S. policy regarding Israel's nuclear potential. This analysis demonstrates that while the United States remains committed to preventing nuclear proliferation, the application of this policy has been compromised by competing considerations and interests. In the Middle East, Israel has been a "special case" in Washington's nuclear nonproliferation efforts for many years. Thus, the United States is unlikely to pressure Israel to dismantle its nuclear potential, and Arab efforts to induce such pressures are likely to prove futile. Hence, the Arab states have no alternative but to engage Israel directly in a discourse on preventing the spread of nuclear weapons in the Middle East.

Chapters 7 and 8 examine Israeli and Arab approaches to nuclear arms control, elaborating how their positions are reflected in initiatives proposed in multilateral organizations — primarily the UN — and in the ACRS talks. These chapters show that the gap between Arab and Israeli attitudes toward nuclear nonproliferation remains considerable.

Chapter 9 shows that efforts to link the adoption of measures to stem the spread of nuclear weapons to the prospects for conventional arms control in the region are futile. Since Israel and the Arab states have equally long lists of concerns in the conventional weapons realm, neither would benefit more than the other from creating such a linkage.

Conversely, Israel's small size and the heritage of the Holocaust makes it extremely sensitive to chemical and biological weapons. For this reason, Israel is unlikely to accept significant constraints on its nuclear potential until the threat of chemical and biological attack is removed. Appreciating this linkage, some Arab states continue to resist signing the Chemical Weapons Convention until Israel signs the NPT.

Since Israeli and Arab approaches to global and regional nuclear arms control remain divergent, the final chapter suggests the adoption of a number of interim nuclear arms control measures. These steps are designed to begin a process that would stem the further spread of nuclear capabilities in the Middle East until the political and security environment in the region permits more dramatic denuclearization measures.

Although this book addresses the Middle East at large and much attention is given to the nuclear programs and intentions of Iraq and Iran, it is written largely from an Arab-Israeli perspective. There are two reasons for this. First, for the past half century, this conflict has constituted the main axis and defining feature of Middle East politics. While other issues and conflicts also influence the behavior of the region's states — particularly in the Gulf area, where security is affected to a far greater degree by the capabilities and intentions of Iraq and Iran — the Arab-Israeli conflict continues to absorb much of the diplomatic and military energies of the Middle East.

Second, a number of Middle East states have chosen to define their approaches to nuclear weapons and to nuclear arms control primarily in relation to Israel's nuclear efforts and the positions it has adopted regarding the global nuclear arms control agenda. This approach was adopted publicly even by states whose nuclear activities were largely affected by other causes — notably in the case of Iraq and Iran, whose nuclear efforts seem to be largely driven by fears of each other's capabilities and intentions.

Among the Arab countries, particular emphasis is given to Egypt's approach to the nuclear issue because of Egypt's centrality in the Arab world as the largest and most populous of the Arab states, and also because for many years Egypt has been the spearhead of Arab diplomatic activity in the arms control realm. As will be shown, this centrality is reflected most clearly in the ACRS talks. Egypt is among the Middle East states whose approach to nuclear arms control is driven primarily by its Israel-related considerations and concerns.

A number of issues elaborated in this volume were also addressed in my first book, *Israeli Nuclear Deterrence: A Strategy for the 1980s* (1982). My views on some of these issues have evolved, especially regarding certain irreducible risks of nuclear proliferation. While my first book was written from the perspective of Israel's national security, this volume addresses the Middle East at large. I am hopeful that the two books will be seen as complementary, thus helping make knowledge in our field become more cumulative.

An important contribution to this book was made by the many discussions held during the two Ginosar Conferences conducted by the Jaffee Center's Project on Security and Arms Control in the Middle East. The talks delivered at these conferences are published in Shai Feldman and Ariel Levite, eds., *Arms Control and the New Middle East Security Environment* (1994) and Shai Feldman, ed., *Confidence Building and Verification: Prospects in the Middle East* (1994).

Equally important were the many informal discussions I held with scholars and officials from Arab states, mostly after the 1991 Gulf War. These exchanges took place in a large number of meetings, hosted by U.S., European, and Egyptian research centers and other nongovernmental organizations over the past five years. These meetings provided important insights into Arab and Israeli security concerns, their nuclear and non-nuclear threat perceptions, and the parties' approaches to nuclear arms control. Due to the sensitivity of these discussions, they are not cited in this volume as sources of specific insights and suggestions presented here. Wherever possible, an effort is made to anchor the insights gained in these meetings and conversations to open sources. But these informal exchanges were critically important in developing the arguments elaborated here and in guiding me through the multitude of media reports.

Nonetheless, there are clear limits to the data available for this study. Open sources on nuclear developments in the Middle East may provide misinformation and disinformation. Data and "assessments" placed in the public domain regarding the nuclear capabilities and designs of Middle East states are often driven by political and other motives. Similarly, statements and expressions cited as evidence of the parties' threat perceptions and approaches to nuclear arms control may be self-serving. Every effort was made here to reduce such exposure by avoiding unreliable sources and by cross-checking the more reliable data. But these are only partial remedies to a problem that cannot be entirely eliminated.

Nuclear Weapons and Arms Control in the Middle East

Chapter 1

Nuclear Arms Control in the Middle East: Why Now?

This chapter outlines the practical, political, and theoretical rationales for a fresh examination of the prospects for arresting nuclear proliferation in the Middle East. Progress in recent years in Arab-Israeli peacemaking has changed the political climate for arms control in the region. The evolving Arab-Israeli peace process makes it possible for the first time to hope for serious application of nuclear arms control in the Middle East. These are the subjects of the first part of this chapter.

Three Israeli-Palestinian agreements reached between September 1993 and October 1995 have already led to Israel's withdrawal from Gaza and the population centers of the West Bank and to the establishment of the Palestinian Authority in these areas. Due to the centrality of the Israeli-Palestinian dispute, these agreements have had a major impact on other dimensions of Arab-Israeli peacemaking: by October 1994, the Israel-Jordan peace agreement was signed. And, in early 1996, diplomatic efforts to resolve the Israeli-Syrian and Israeli-Lebanese conflicts were also accelerated. Altogether, these developments create a political atmosphere that is more conducive than ever before to enhancing regional security and to negotiating arms control in the Middle East.

The second section of this chapter elaborates the evolution of the Middle East Arms Control and Regional Security (ACRS) talks launched in early 1992. For the first time in the region's history, Israel, thirteen Arab states, and the Palestinians began to discuss possible approaches to security, confidence building, and arms control in the Middle East. The ACRS talks have laid the basis for implementing important regional confidence and security building measures (CSBMs) and have resulted in much progress toward a common approach to security and arms control in the Middle East, but after four years the talks have reached a deadlock. By early 1995, the gap in the parties' positions with regard to nuclear arms control blocked any further progress in the conceptual and operational dimensions of the ACRS process. The significance of the ACRS process justifies a detailed examination of this gap as well as an exploration of how the parties' different nuclear perspectives might be bridged.

The final section focuses on the scholarly debate regarding the consequences of nuclear proliferation. The effective deterrence that nuclear weapons provide can contribute to regional stability, yet the danger that these weapons would be misused — while often exaggerated — cannot be dismissed. Whether the overall effects of nuclear spread would be largely stabilizing or destabilizing is likely to depend primarily on the general political circumstances prevailing in the region when such proliferation takes place. This section argues that the inconclusive nature of the debate on the consequences of nuclear spread does not allow policy makers to take a relaxed approach to the prospects of proliferation in the Middle East. Hence the importance of examining whether the region's states might adopt some measures to limit the spread of these weapons.

The Political Context of Arms Control

Although the United States and the Soviet Union never engaged each other in war and maintained full diplomatic relations and other channels of communication with one another throughout the Cold War, their arms control negotiations resulted only in constraints on the strategic arms race (in the form of the SALT I, ABM, and SALT II accords): no meaningful *arms reduction* agreements were concluded before the late 1980s. The joint NATO–Warsaw Pact acceptance of the Helsinki Final Act in 1975 eventually led to important political changes, but only with the rise of Mikhail Gorbachev did the United States become convinced that the Soviet Union's intentions no longer posed a threat to U.S. security and survival, and that the Soviet leadership was sufficiently trustworthy to be engaged in serious arms reduction talks.

The U.S.-Soviet record shows that while a fundamental political change — one that changes the parties' overall threat perceptions — is not a prerequisite to the adoption of significant arms control measures, such a change must take place before arms reduction agreements can be concluded. Indeed, the 1987–92 U.S.-Soviet "disarmament race," which included the INF, START I, CFE, and START II agreements, shows that far-reaching disarmament measures can be implemented once a political conflict is resolved.

This argument is at least as valid for the Middle East, where for the past fifty years the Arab-Israeli dispute has spurred much of the quest for arms in the region. Israel has acquired weapons largely because it perceives that its security and survival are threatened by the region's states, which have rejected its existence and enjoyed a preponderance in most categories of potential national power. Similarly, some of the Arab states have worked to arm themselves due to their perception that their security was threatened by Israel's ever-growing military and scientific-technological capabilities and its propensity to expand. The rivalries in the Persian Gulf have been equally important in inducing the regional arms race. The quest for hegemony has led Iraq and Iran and the states they threaten — Saudi Arabia and the smaller Gulf states — to acquire ever-larger arsenals. The strategic importance of the Gulf region, and the resulting involvement of external powers, also induced a growing fear of "external intervention" there.

Thus, the prospects that Middle East states will become less motivated to acquire ever more destructive arsenals is tied to the extent to which they will feel themselves less threatened. Indeed, the connection between the prevailing political conditions and the arms race seems strongest in the nuclear realm. Since nuclear capabilities are often seen as instruments of "existential deterrence" — deterring threats to a state's survival — a more stable and benign political environment in which states do not perceive threats to their survival is bound to be more conducive to nuclear arms control.

A political resolution of the Arab-Israeli conflict might reduce Israel's perceived need to rely on existential deterrence and would diminish the motivation of some Arab states to continue to build their conventional arsenals. Were such a resolution to be accompanied by the application of a wide array of bilateral and regional confidence and security building measures, the parties' need to field large standing forces to hedge against a surprise attack would also diminish.

Similarly, if the important countries in the Gulf region — Iraq,

Iran, Saudi Arabia, and Kuwait — no longer viewed one another as threatening their security and survival, their quest for ever more sophisticated weapons might lessen, and this might reduce their concern that they might be harmed by arms control measures. Thus, the possibility that these countries could be persuaded to join an effective arms control regime is tied to the prospect of achieving stability and confidence building in the Gulf area.

There are additional important links between peace and arms control. As the U.S.-Soviet experience demonstrates, a fundamental change in the political climate is needed for the parties to accept the intrusive verification measures that allow arms control accords to be effective. For example, Mikhail Gorbachev's willingness to drop the Soviet Union's long-standing objection to on-site inspections paved the way for a wide array of NATO–Warsaw Pact arms control and confidence-building agreements.

Generally, states tend to regard effective verification measures — particularly on-site inspections — as an infringement of their national sovereignty and as a threat to expose their strengths and weaknesses. As long as a high state of conflict prevails, concern that sensitive data might be compromised leads states to reject such inspections. In addition, on-site inspections and other regional verification and confidence-building measures are resisted by some Arab states on the ground that these interactions would imply a normalization of their relations with Israel. These states have refused to contemplate such normalization until all territorial disputes with Israel are resolved.

Once an Arab-Israeli peace is obtained and stability in the Gulf region is achieved, the region's states might become less sensitive to the political implications of mutual on-site inspections; this would improve the ability to verify compliance with arms control agreements. Thus, the ability to implement a wider arms control agenda in the Middle East — embracing conventional as well as nonconventional arms — will continue to be tied to the progress of Arab-Israeli and regional peacemaking.

This relationship makes the gains achieved by the mid-1990s in the Arab-Israeli peace process particularly significant. Since the Israeli-Palestinian dispute is a central pillar of the Arab-Israeli conflict, the dramatic progress toward a resolution of this dispute in 1993–95 has transformed the political discourse in the Middle East. Major achievements include the Israel-PLO Declaration of Principles concluded in Oslo in September 1993; the agreement signed in Cairo in May 1994 on Israel's pullback from Gaza and Jericho and the establishment of a Palestinian Authority in these areas; and the Israeli-Palestinian agreement signed in Washington in October 1995, providing for Israel's withdrawal from all other major population centers of the West Bank. The elections to the newly created Palestinian Council, held in the West Bank and Gaza in January 1996, were another important milestone on the road to a resolution of the Palestinian-Israeli conflict.

These developments in Israeli-Palestinian peacemaking affected other facets of the Middle East conflict. In October 1994, the Israel-Jordan peace treaty was signed in Washington; low-level relations were established in 1994–95 between Israel and a number of Maghreb and Persian Gulf states. Of course, this progress could not have taken place without the earlier breakthroughs achieved in Arab-Israeli negotiations: the 1974–75 Israeli-Egyptian and Israeli-Syrian disengagement agreements, the 1978 Camp David accords and the Egypt-Israeli peace treaty signed in 1979, and the bilateral and multilateral Arab-Israeli negotiations launched in Madrid in late 1991 and in Moscow in early 1992.

In late 1995, following the assassination of Israel's prime minister, Itzhak Rabin, diplomatic efforts to resolve the Israeli-Syrian dispute were accelerated. Should these negotiations succeed and lead to an Israel-Lebanon agreement as well, peace will have been established between Israel and all its immediate neighbors. Thus, the political context of a possible Arab-Israeli arms control process will have been completely transformed.

Indeed, such a change would be even more dramatic than the change witnessed earlier in U.S.-Soviet relations. This is because the parties to the Middle East conflict have repeatedly engaged each other in warfare over the past five decades, at a significant human cost. Moreover, while the United States and the Soviet Union maintained embassies in each other's capitals throughout the Cold War, during most of this period the Arab states did not engage in any open relations or overt communication with Israel. Hence, the recent developments in the Middle East imply a transformation in the nature of the personal, political, and international discourse in the region.

Much of the progress in the Middle East can be attributed to three related earlier developments: the end of the Cold War, the breakup of the Soviet Union, and the 1990–91 Gulf War. The end of the Cold War and the breakup of the Soviet Union eliminated the strategic umbrella previously provided by Moscow to the more radical Arab states, including Syria. This loss limited the ability of Syria's President Asad to block Jordan and the Palestinians from joining the peace process, and finally led him to conclude that negotiations remained the only avenue open to achieve Syria's strategic, territorial, and political objectives.

The impact of military technology and the strength of Washington's commitment to Israel were demonstrated once again during the Gulf War; this must have reinforced Asad's conclusion that Israel cannot be defeated militarily and must be accommodated politically. He was also probably persuaded that with the demise of the Soviet Union, the Middle East negotiation process was the only way to protect Syria against possible aggressive Israeli designs. In turn, Syria's new approach allowed the Palestinians and Jordan greater room to maneuver.

The end of the Cold War ended the superpower competition that both fueled much of the arms race in the Middle East and prevented the then-major arms suppliers — the United States and the Soviet Union — from cooperating to arrest the proliferation of weapons in the region. Meanwhile, the Gulf War increased the awareness of the region's states and some of their external suppliers of the dangers associated with an uncontrolled arms race. Thus, an international and regional environment that is more conducive to arms control has gradually emerged.

While this new environment is encouraging, the resolution of the Arab-Israeli dispute would not necessarily relieve all perceptions of existential threat in the region. Indeed, some of the region's conflicts might be exacerbated once Arab-Israeli peace is achieved, since the Arab-Israeli conflict would no longer serve to unify the Arab states.[1]

Interest in nuclear weapons may remain where strategic deterrence might still seem relevant, primarily in the context of the relations between Iraq and Iran. Indeed, it seems unlikely that the pariah states of the Gulf subregion could be incorporated soon in the new Arab-Israeli "arc of hope." Given the strategic interactions between the two subregions, continued conflict in the Gulf subregion could limit the possibility of arresting the proliferation of arms in the Arab-Israeli conflict area.

The Multilateral Arms Control Talks

The seeds of confidence-building and arms reduction measures in the Middle East were planted after the 1991 Gulf War. In January 1992, a multilateral conference was held in Moscow to address region-wide problems of the Middle East. At this meeting, Israel and 13 Arab states agreed to create a working group on Arms Control and Regional Security (ACRS). Like other working groups launched by the Moscow conference, the ACRS talks were intended to complement the bilateral Arab-Israeli negotiations initiated at the 1991 Madrid Conference and to improve the climate for resolving the core issues in these negotiations. Specifically, the ACRS process was designed to reduce the likelihood and consequences of violence and war and to promote strategic stability in the Middle East.

The initial round of the ACRS talks, held in Washington in May 1992, was plagued by fundamental disagreements, primarily between Israel and Egypt. Egypt gave the highest priority to arresting nuclear proliferation in the Middle East, focusing on Israel's nuclear weapons first. Conversely, Israel stressed the deep distrust prevailing in the region and the importance of dealing with conventional weapons, with which all Middle East wars have been fought.[2]

The second ACRS working group meeting, convened in Moscow in September 1992, attempted to settle these conflicting agendas by adopting a U.S.- and Russian-proposed compromise that incorporated both priorities.[3] In effect, the American and Russian cosponsors suggested a joint effort to define long-term objectives ("a vision") for the process, but argued that progress toward the realization of these goals must be built "brick by brick" through the gradual growth of mutual confidence.[4] Thus, the importance of early implementation of regional confidence-building measures was stressed. The parties were requested to indicate their attitude toward a long list of CSBMs submitted by Russia and the United States.[5]

At the closing of the Moscow talks, the participants agreed to provide alternative definitions of the long-term objectives for the process, as well as lists of CSBMs that might be implemented initially.[6] Thus, between September 1992 and May 1993, Israel and Jordan launched internal efforts to define ultimate purposes for the region's arms control process.[7] Egypt already had such a definition in the form of the April 1990 Mubarak Initiative, which called for the transformation of the Middle East into a Weapons of Mass Destruction–Free Zone (WMDFZ). Variations on this theme were also expressed in a paper distributed earlier by Nabil Fahmy, the head of Egypt's delegation to the ACRS talks.[8]

Following complex internal negotiations during late 1992, the Israeli government produced a document defining its approach to the objectives of arms control in the Middle East.[9] The essence of the approach was made public in a speech delivered by Foreign Minister Shimon Peres on January 13, 1993, to the international conference convened in Paris to sign the Chemical Weapons Convention. In effect, Israel adopted the substance of the Mubarak Initiative but made it clear that the establishment of a WMDFZ in the Middle East would require the prior achievement of a stable and durable peace and the application of mutual verification measures.[10]

At the multilateral working group meeting held in Washington in May 1993, Israel, Egypt, Jordan, and Oman each presented their visions, and a number of proposals for regional CSBMs were discussed. Subsequently, the parties agreed in Washington that sub-working groups, each entrusted with a particular task, would hold intersessional meetings. External sponsors were nominated to escort the parties through the complexities of these tasks. The United States and Russia co-sponsored the effort to define the ultimate purposes of a Middle East arms control process and a set of declaratory confidence-building measures; Canada was asked to sponsor an examination of maritime confidence-building measures and means for avoiding incidents at sea; Turkey was nominated to guide the exploration of alternative methods for exchanging military information and providing prenotification of military exercises and large-scale military movements; and the Netherlands agreed to lead an examination of the utility and functioning of a regional communication network. All regional parties to the talks were urged to send to these intersessional meetings military officers who might be instructed by their governments to help implement CSBMs in the future.[11]

In July 1993, Egypt hosted the members of the ACRS working group for a workshop on verification.[12] This was the first meeting of its kind conducted in the region itself. The seminar included presentations and discussions in Cairo as well as a visit to the Sinai, where participants could ascertain the functioning of verification measures applied by the Multinational Force and Observers (MFO) as a result of the 1979 Israel-Egypt peace agreement.

In September 1993, a meeting on maritime confidence-building measures took place in Nova Scotia, and a seminar on crisis communication was conducted in the Hague. In early October, the first meeting on the exchange of military information was held in Turkey. During fall 1993, the parties involved were also invited to observe on-site inspections, conducted by the Conference on Security and Cooperation in Europe (CSCE), of a Royal Air Force base in Britain and a NATO military exercise in Denmark.

In mid-October 1993, meetings on the ultimate goals of the process and on declaratory confidence-building measures were held in Vienna. These were the only truly confrontational intersessional talks: Egypt's representatives stressed that priority should be given to nuclear arms control, while the Israeli delegates emphasized the need for political accommodation and for the evolutionary application of a confidence-building approach.

Earlier, as part of their joint agenda for negotiating the resolution of the Israeli-Jordanian dispute, signed in Washington in mid-September 1993, Israel and the Hashemite Kingdom of Jordan had agreed that the Middle East should be transformed into a WMDFZ. This document stated their "mutual commitment, as a matter of priority and as soon as possible, to work towards a Middle East free from weapons of mass destruction — conventional and unconventional weapons." It also stated that "this goal is to be achieved in the context of a comprehensive, lasting and stable peace, characterized by the renunciation of the use of force, reconciliation and openness." The formulation represented Jordan's willingness to meet Israeli concerns by agreeing to include conventional weapons within the definition of weapons of mass destruction. It also underscored the view of both governments that significant and meaningful arms control can only be achieved in the context of stable peace. Similar language was inserted into the peace agreement signed by the two countries in October 1994.

The next ACRS plenary meeting took place in Moscow in early November 1993. After a survey of the intersessional workshops, difficult negotiations regarding the future course of the process took place. Again, Egypt emphasized the need to implement nuclear disarmament; Israel stressed the importance of conflict-resolution and confidence building.[13] Tension rose as a consequence of the intensity with which these two principal parties adhered to their positions. Nevertheless, the Moscow meeting ended in an agreement to divide the future activities of the ACRS working group into two "baskets": the "conceptual basket" and the "operational basket." The conceptual basket would explore the possibility of reaching a consensus on principles to guide the future relations of the region's states; on the ultimate objectives of the arms control process; and on a set of declaratory measures that might provide the parties with effective mutual reassurances. The parties were also expected to define the region's boundaries; to articulate their threat perceptions; to elaborate generic verification methods; to design crisis- and conflict-prevention mechanisms; and to produce menus of confidence-building measures.

The operational basket was to suggest various practical mechanisms to increase transparency and reduce the danger of unintended escalation. These included maritime confidence-building measures and mechanisms to prevent incidents at sea; procedures for military-to-military contacts and the exchange of military information; arrangements for prenotification of major military exercises and movements; and the establishment of a regional communications network.[14]

In mid-January 1994, the parties to the ACRS talks met in the Netherlands to examine the issues involved in establishing a Middle East communication network. They agreed that this network would initially provide ACRS participants with an efficient mechanism for transferring messages relevant to the ACRS process and that until such a network could be located in the region, messages would be sent through the CSCE network "hub" in the Hague. The ACRS cosponsors regarded the establishment of this network as the first "flag project" of the operational basket.[15]

The first meeting of the conceptual basket talks took place in Cairo in early February 1994.[16] Prior to that, the head of Egypt's delegation to the ACRS talks, Nabil Fahmy, traveled to Israel to discuss the agenda for the Cairo meeting with his Israeli counterparts. The trip did not resolve the two countries' substantive disagreements, but did help to diffuse some of the tension.[17] The Cairo talks produced a first draft of a "Declaration of Principles" (DOP) on peace and security in the Middle East. The draft was modeled on the 1975 Helsinki Final Act and accommodated the parties' priorities by addressing their future political relations, the need to establish mutual confidence, and their commitment to arms reductions, including the transformation of the Middle East to a WMDFZ.[18] Yet the parties failed to agree on a number of formulations regarding some of the issues discussed; the delegations went home with a document containing alternative (bracketed) formulas that their governments were asked to consider further, with a view toward reaching agreement at a later meeting.[19]

The May 1994 meeting in Doha, Qatar, was the first ACRS plenary session to take place in an Arab country.[20] The participating delegations agreed to drop some of the political clauses of the draft document and they reached consensus on most other formulations. Reportedly, Saudi Arabia — somewhat surprised by the significant progress made at the Cairo conceptual basket intersessional meeting — was particularly adamant that human rights issues should be avoided and that the document would make no reference indicating an obligation to normalize relations with Israel.[21] Thus, it objected to a detailed elaboration of the future political relations among the region's states, arguing that this should be left to the bilateral track of the Arab-Israeli peace process.[22] Consequently, the delegations decided that the draft declaration would be discussed further at a subsequent conceptual basket meeting.[23]

The next meeting of the conceptual basket took place in Paris in mid-October 1994. It was primarily devoted to a discussion of the various parties' threat perceptions, with a view to examining how such threats might be mitigated.[24] Saudi Arabia had meanwhile changed its approach to the ACRS process and began to play a more constructive role in these talks, dropping some of the objections it raised at Doha.[25] While the title and resulting status of the DOP was changed to a less ambitious "Statement on Arms Control and Regional Security," agreement was reached regarding all subjects except the nuclear issue.

By the time of the Paris meeting, the global arms control agenda began to affect the ACRS process. The approach of the April 1995 Nuclear Non-proliferation Treaty (NPT) Review and Extension Conference led Egypt to insist that the ACRS statement include a clear stipulation that "all the parties in the region" should "adhere to the NPT in the near future." In contrast, Israel insisted that the document confine itself to a commitment to transform the Middle East to a "mutually verifiable" zone free of weapons of mass destruction. Compromise language proposed by U.S. delegates failed to bridge the gap between the two parties' positions.[26]

The first meeting of the ACRS operational basket was held in Turkey in April 1994. It further discussed the possible application of regional confidence building measures, including a proposal to hold a joint rescue-at-sea exercise in which Israel, a number of Arab states, and the U.S. Sixth Fleet would participate. The meeting also advanced an agreement on the use of the CSCE communication center in the Hague and on the establishment within two years of a Middle East Regional Communication Center in Cairo.[27]

These matters, including procedures for the exchange of military information and the prenotification of significant military exercises and movements, were further elaborated at the May 1994 ACRS plenary session in Qatar. Due to pressure applied by some delegations, the parties agreed to scale down the proposed joint naval exercise to a demonstration conducted by U.S. and Canadian naval units off the shores of Italy, to be observed by representatives of the ACRS participants.[28] The Israeli delegation invited representatives of all parties to the ACRS talks to visit Israeli Defense Forces (IDF) military bases.[29] Later, senior Israeli and Arab naval officers met in Halifax, Canada. The informal atmosphere there provided another useful opportunity to establish personal relationships and to discuss the participants' threat perceptions and security concerns.

In November 1994, the operational basket met in Jordan, at a resort located on the eastern shore of the Dead Sea. The Jordanian delegation, led by Abdullah Toukan, presented its proposal to establish a Regional Security Center (RSC) in Amman. The Center would have a wider role than the CSCE's Crisis Prevention Center (CPC) in Vienna, and would conduct joint studies of conflict management and resolution. Agreements were crystallized regarding the prevention of incidents at sea and with regard to cooperation in search and rescue operations. The parties also agreed to conduct a joint naval exercise to examine how some of the understandings reached might be implemented. In addition, the issues involved in the prenotification of major military movements and exercises were further elaborated.[30]

At the ACRS plenary in Tunis in early December 1994, Israeli and Egyptian delegations made some tentative efforts to accommodate each other's priorities on the NPT issue, but failed to agree on any formulation that might allow the adoption of the proposed statement (see Appendix 13). At one point the Israeli delegation suggested that the preamble to the statement include a nonbinding reference to the NPT as one of the global nonproliferation instruments that could be considered following the establishment of comprehensive peace.[31] In turn, the Egyptian delegation indicated a willingness to drop the word "immediately" from the proposed statement's reference to the parties' obligation to sign the NPT. Instead, it circulated a "non-paper" that would allow Israel to sign the NPT two years after the signing of peace agreements among Israel, Syria, and Lebanon. However, these steps were not sufficient to bridge the gap between the two parties' positions.

At the same time, the Tunis meeting made some progress in defining the region's boundaries. An Israeli draft on this issue was recognized by the participating states as "useful." In addition, the meeting made further progress in preparing the implementation of CSBMs in the Middle East, adding to the achievements made earlier at Doha and in a number of the operational basket meetings. Six states agreed to link themselves to the regional communication hub in the Hague and to relocate it to Cairo within two years. An understanding was also reached regarding the prospective establishment of a Regional Security Center (RSC) to be located in Jordan, with branches in Tunisia and Qatar.[32]

On the maritime front, memoranda of understanding were finalized regarding the prevention of incidents at sea and cooperation in search and rescue (SAR) operations, and a SAR exercise was scheduled to be held off the shores of Tunisia in March 1995.[33] Discussions were also conducted regarding a French proposal to use civilian satellite imagery for purposes of confidence building and verification in the Middle East.[34]

Further progress was also made at Tunis in establishing arrangements for the exchange of military information and for providing prenotification of major military movements and exercises. A working paper was accepted that stipulated that such exchanges would be made on a voluntary basis: the parties willing to engage in such exchanges would inform the ACRS cosponsors of their willingness and would then conduct the actual exchanges directly with one another.[35] Yet agreement on specific guidelines for such notifications was not reached. Discussions focused on a proposal to establish the movement of 4,000 troops and 110 tanks as a threshold for prenotification, and issues concerning the possible transfer of military data to states that are not party to the ACRS process were left unresolved.[36] Decisions regarding these matters were postponed to subsequent operational basket and plenary ACRS meetings. The Israeli delegation to the Tunis talks expanded its previous invitation to the ACRS participants to visit Israeli military and industrial-defense installations.[37]

The ACRS Talks at a Crossroads

The ACRS talks had not produced a single high-profile formal agreement by late 1994 but the array of activities conducted in their framework was unprecedented and extraordinary. Only a few years earlier, it seemed impossible that a large number of Arab states would be willing to engage with Israel in examining region-wide CSBMs. Moreover, the exercise itself was an important confidence-building measure, since it provided opportunities for a growing number of Israeli and Arab military personnel and government officials to interact informally and develop an understanding for each other's perceptions and security concerns. Thus, especially by the standards of the Middle East, the cumulative effect of these developments must be considered a dramatic breakthrough.

The ACRS framework has established itself as a serious venue for discussing and negotiating arms control in the Middle East. In addition, it has already had a modest but important impact on the bureaucracies of the participating states. Egypt's foreign ministry was the first of the region's states to develop a cadre of experts who have taken an active part in negotiating global arms control treaties. To varying degrees, the ACRS process has led other Middle East countries to appoint individuals and small governmental bodies to prepare for ACRS activities, creating small bureaucratic islands that have gradually developed more than a fleeting interest in arms control. Thus, for the first time, an embryonic arms control community has been created in the Middle East.

Yet the ACRS process suffered from serious weaknesses. First, the mechanisms established by the ACRS participants are voluntary — and hence highly reversible. Second, Syria and Lebanon remained outside the ACRS process and continued to insist that they would consider joining the multilateral talks only after a breakthrough in Israeli-Syrian and Israeli-Lebanese bilateral negotiations.[38] Third, some of the region's key sources of proliferation concerns — Iraq, Iran, and Libya — have not been invited to take part in these multilateral discussions. Thus, the gains made at ACRS in establishing the basis for a regional arms control process remain confined to only a part of the Middle East.

More important, by mid-1995 Egypt became increasingly frustrated by its failure, both within ACRS and during the extensive negotiations held prior to the April NPT Review and Extension Conference, to obtain an Israeli commitment to sign the NPT. Cairo saw little progress toward meeting its priority: arresting and eventually rolling back Israel's nuclear program. Moreover, in Egypt's eyes, the considerable gains made in establishing and elaborating an infrastructure for a CSBM regime in the Middle East met Israel's quest for region-wide political recognition as well as its emphasis on the need to implement CSBMs first.

Consequently, Egyptian officials indicated informally that if the impasse on the nuclear issue were not resolved, their government might lose interest in the ACRS process and would even reconsider its previous consent to locate the Regional Communication Center in Cairo. Fearing a collapse of the ACRS talks, the United States canceled a plenary session, originally scheduled to be held in September 1995 in Amman, that was intended to provide final approval for a wide array of regional CSBMs. By mid-1996, a new date for the convening of this plenary was yet to be announced, indicating that the ACRS process had become a hostage to the parties' competing approaches to the nuclear issue.

The Consequences of Nuclear Proliferation

The improved political climate in the Middle East has created an environment more conducive for nuclear arms control, while the deadlock reached in the ACRS talks over the nuclear issue makes it imperative to understand the gap between the parties' positions and to explore ways of bridging this gap. Moreover, the scholarly debate on the impact of nuclear proliferation indicates that the consequences of nuclear spread in the Middle East are unlikely to be all benign. This provides added rationale for examining the prospects that the region's states might agree to adopt some measures for halting the proliferation of nuclear arms in the Middle East.

THE STABILIZING EFFECTS OF NUCLEAR WEAPONS

In an earlier work, I portrayed the logic of nuclear deterrence from the perspective of a single small state seeking security and survival.[39] Effective deterrence requires robust capabilities and considerable determination. The outcome of deterrent confrontations is determined by the relative capacity to inflict punishment and the relative willingness to absorb it. Generally, and despite the clear constraints addressed below, nuclear weapons provide states with far more robust deterrence than conventional arms.[40] There are several reasons for this.

First, a state equipped with nuclear weapons enjoys a nearly unlimited capability to inflict punishment, since the amount of damage that can be caused by a small number of nuclear weapons is virtually unlimited. Nuclear weapons can cause significantly greater damage than conventional explosives because the blast-to-weight ratio of nuclear devices is about a million times greater.

Second, nuclear weapons leave far less room for misperceptions about the damage that can be caused. A simple extrapolation from the widely recognized horrors of Hiroshima and Nagasaki to today's far larger–yield nuclear weapons leaves little doubt that the use of any nuclear arms would be catastrophic. The 1986 nuclear accident at Chernobyl, whose disastrous effects were very modest compared with the expected outcomes of a possible nuclear weapons exchange, reinforced perceptions of the power of nuclear weapons.

Third, nuclear deterrence, unlike conventional deterrence, is not vulnerable to variations in states' sensitivity to costs. Conventional deterrence may fail because countries and regimes may be insensitive to the costs involved in the execution of a threat to use conventional forces. In contrast, it is difficult to envisage a regime so insensitive to costs that it might ignore credible threats to inflict nuclear punishment.

Fourth, nuclear weapons provide stable deterrence, because states possessing these weapons can feel confident that their nuclear arsenals will not be preempted. It is suicidal to make a preemptive nuclear attack unless such an attack can entirely destroy an adversary's nuclear arsenal; if even a few weapons survive the preemptive attack, the likely nuclear retaliation would be devastating. Unless a state stores its entire nuclear arsenal in a single exposed location, and unless its adversaries become convinced that it does not hide additional weapons, they cannot be confident that a preemptive strike would destroy all of the state's nuclear weapons.

The knowledge that their nuclear arsenals are largely invulnerable to a first strike should make states possessing such weapons self-confident.[41] In turn, this confidence should diminish their own propensity to act preemptively. Thus, overall regional stability should increase in areas where nuclear weapons have proliferated. In contrast, in the conventional realm, states are sometimes tempted to preempt, fearing that an adversary's first strike would decide the outcome of the confrontation, and assessing that a preemptive attack could avert these dire consequences. In addition, a failed preemptive attack with conventional weapons would not necessarily result in catastrophe. Indeed, due to the more limited risks involved in the conventional battlefield, states are far more willing to exercise violence, for offensive as well as defensive purposes.

Nuclear weapons provide several kinds of deterrence. They are particularly useful in providing states with effective "existential deterrence" or "general deterrence," the capacity to deter threats to the state's survival. Faced with the threat of destruction, a nuclear-armed state will have no reason to refrain from annihilating its attacker. That the potential attacker may also possess nuclear weapons would make little difference in this case, since the state's survival is already threatened. Thus, the widely shared view that nuclear deterrence is negated once adversaries acquire a countervailing capability is

add to p. 3 cite

erroneous: existential deterrence enjoyed by nuclear-armed states is insensitive to the possible acquisition of nuclear arms by potential adversaries.

Nuclear weapons also provide a measure of "residual deterrence" against more limited or specific challenges — against threats that fall far short of endangering the state's survival.[42] However, in contrast to the robust "existential deterrence" they provide, nuclear weapons produce far less effective "specific deterrence" of limited challenges.[43] Adversaries are unlikely to believe that the nuclear option would be exercised over relatively minor matters.

The outcome of "specific" challenges is determined by the parties' relative determination regarding the issue in dispute.[44] For example, the United States withstood Soviet challenges over Berlin and Cuba because it cared more about the matters involved. Conversely, the Vietcong and North Vietnam succeeded in challenging a nuclear-armed United States, and the Afghan Mujahedeen prevailed over a nuclear-armed Soviet Union, because the United States and the Soviet Union were not willing to sustain the costs that their local rivals inflicted upon them. In both cases, the two superpowers were also unable or unwilling to use nuclear weapons against their adversaries. Thus, nuclear-armed states can fail to deter non-nuclear adversaries if the contested issues are more important to the non-nuclear actors. The Vietcong, the North Vietnamese, and the Mujahedeen displayed more determination and a greater willingness to absorb costs, thus deciding the outcomes of the respective deterrent confrontations. This is consistent with a robust deterrence theory, one that predicts that deterrent confrontations will be determined not only by the parties' relative capacity to inflict punishment but also by their relative willingness to sustain such punishment.

This logic of deterrence operates in the Middle East. Israel's reported nuclear potential has provided an effective existential deterrence by suggesting to the Arab states that they cannot destroy the Jewish state without risking their own annihilation, an unacceptable price. In turn, this existential deterrence has contributed to Israel's cumulative deterrence, its desire that the Arab states come to see that Israel must be considered a permanent feature of the Middle East and should therefore be accommodated politically.

Indeed, the decisions of a growing number of Arab states to engage

Israel in a peace process would be difficult to explain without reference to Israel's perceived nuclear potential. These states might have considered other aspects of Israeli cumulative deterrence — its qualitative edge in the conventional realm and the support it received from the United States — as transitory. By contrast, Israel's reported nuclear potential could not be eliminated, even by an Arab acquisition of nuclear weapons. Indeed, Arab states may have estimated that if other elements of Israel's deterrence were to deteriorate, it would be compelled to make its nuclear potential all the more explicit.

Arab perceptions that Israel possesses a nuclear potential also provide it with considerable residual or specific deterrence. For example, during the 1990–91 Gulf War, Iraqi President Saddam Hussein was probably deterred from attacking Israel with ballistic missiles armed with chemical warheads not because he was certain that Israel would retaliate with nuclear weapons, but rather because he could not rule out this possibility. In this case the heritage of the Holocaust, which made Israel particularly sensitive to "gas warfare," coupled with a number of statements issued at the time by Israeli leaders and by U.S. Secretary of Defense Richard Cheney, made "specific deterrence" credible.[45]

The logic of deterrence will prevail as long as Israel possesses a nuclear potential. Thus, were Israel to withdraw from the Golan Heights as part of a peace agreement with Syria, Syria would be dissuaded from mounting a major assault on Israel not by any certainty that such an attack would trigger Israeli nuclear retaliation, but because it would be unable to dismiss the possibility that Israel's response might result in a spiral of escalation, eventually leading to the crossing of the nuclear threshold.

At the same time, the Middle East also bears witness to the fact that nuclear weapons provide only limited specific deterrence. Despite the perceptions that Israel was nuclear-armed, Egypt challenged Israel's holding of the Sinai during the 1969–70 War of Attrition. Syria and Egypt challenged Israel's occupation of the Golan and the Sinai by launching the 1973 War. The Lebanese Shi'ites challenged Israel's occupation of Southern Lebanon in 1983–85. The Palestinians in the West Bank and Gaza launched the *Intifada* against Israeli occupation in December 1987. Saddam Hussein fired his conventionally-armed ballistic missiles at Israel during the 1990–91 Gulf War. Consistent with deterrence theory, Israel's failure to deter these challenges was due to the challengers' higher determination, their greater willingness to sustain costs. In a number of these cases the challenge was too small to merit the potential costs of a nuclear response; other cases involved communal conflicts to which nuclear weapons are largely irrelevant.

Thus, while nuclear weapons do not protect states from all the threats they might face, they do provide effective existential deterrence: they avert threats to states' survival. They also contribute to cumulative deterrence by persuading adversaries that they should politically accommodate the nuclear-armed state. Under some circumstances nuclear weapons also provide a measure of residual deterrence against more limited challenges, since adversaries may not be able to exclude the possibility that their limited attack might escalate, leading to a nuclear catastrophe. Yet only more seldom do nuclear weapons provide effective specific deterrence against challenges that fall far short of threatening the state's survival; the outcome of such confrontations is largely decided by the relative determination manifested by the parties to the dispute.

THE DESTABILIZING EFFECTS OF NUCLEAR PROLIFERATION

Despite the possible contribution of nuclear weapons to deterrence, however, the consequences of nuclear proliferation in the Middle East and other regions are unlikely to be entirely benign. First, there is concern that the greater the number of states possessing nuclear weapons, the greater the probability that these weapons will be used. The focus of this concern is not the total number of nuclear weapons in the various states' arsenals but rather the number of "fingers on the button": how many different leaders can decide whether or not to use nuclear weapons. This danger will grow as additional states acquire nuclear arms, even though the global inventory of nuclear weapons is shrinking as the United States and Russia satisfy their INF, START I and START II commitments.

A second concern is that another use of nuclear weapons would legitimize their further use. A related fear is that the next use of nuclear weapons may lead to uncontrolled escalation. Thus, the damage caused by nuclear weapons in 1945 is said to have been limited only by the fact that the United States had exhausted its nuclear stockpile of two 14–23 kiloton bombs. In contrast, future nuclear states are expected to possess many more weapons of higher yield. A third reason why the acquisition of nuclear weapons by additional states is considered to be far more dangerous than the possession of these weapons by the original five nuclear powers — United States, the Soviet Union, France, Great Britain, and China — is that the dangerous consequences of these states possessing nuclear weapons were mitigated by the stabilizing effect of the post–World War II bipolar international system.[46] Bipolarity was stable in part because deterrence is most effective in bilateral contexts, between two states or two blocs. More generally, bipolarity made policy management easier because the system's clear divisions simplified calculations. But like most regions, the Middle East is multipolar, and the spread of nuclear weapons would likely result in much greater problems of policy control.[47]

Fourth, new nuclear states are expected to be more likely to use nuclear weapons than the original nuclear powers if they share a border with an enemy. For example, in the Middle East "the stakes involved are who is going to live on this one little strip of land next to the Mediterranean. Ultimately, national survival is at stake."[48] By contrast, it is asserted that the U.S.-Soviet nuclear balance was stable largely because the political stakes for the two superpowers were limited. This argument displays a measure of historical amnesia; a much stronger argument is that the dangers of U.S.-Soviet nuclear relations were somewhat mitigated because the two countries were not contiguous. Europe and the Atlantic and Pacific oceans provided an effective physical and psychological barrier between the two superpowers. Another mitigating factor may have been that the United States and the Soviet Union had never engaged each other in major wars.[49] By comparison, potential nuclear states like India and Pakistan have common borders and a record of past warfare, as do Iran and Iraq. Thus, it is feared that the proliferation of nuclear weapons in the Middle East — a region that has experienced recurrent warfare — could have particularly dire consequences.

The problem of territorial contiguity also has negative implications for crisis stability. Common borders would result in short warning times; this could heighten fears of a preemptive strike and could lead neighboring nuclear states to adopt dangerous "launch on warning" postures.

A fifth fear is that leaders of larger new nuclear states might attempt to exploit their larger territory to strike smaller nuclear states. This argument assumes that smaller states will find it more difficult to secure their nuclear weapons from an adversary's preemptive strike and that larger states may view themselves as better able to recover from a nuclear exchange. Variations of this argument were originally advanced in the U.S.-Soviet context and were later applied to the Middle East. Yet the size of a state's territory has little bearing on its ability to protect its nuclear weapons from an adversary's first strike. Clearly, a large state can more easily make its nuclear weapons invulnerable by dispersing them throughout its territory. But small states can also achieve such invulnerability through a combination of concealment, variation, mobility, and dispersal. For this purpose, the vast seas can be used; placing nuclear weapons on submarines and surface ships makes their destruction very difficult.[50]

A state's area is also largely irrelevant to its relative recovery rate. Indeed, the value of the concept of relative recovery rates is itself highly questionable: At the height of the Cold War it was feared that the Soviet Union's vast territory would allow its leaders to take greater risks, knowing that their country would be able to rebuild itself more quickly following a nuclear exchange, yet it was never clear why a leader would be comforted by the knowledge that his country would recover more quickly than its adversaries from a full-scale nuclear catastrophe. In any case, recovery rates are unlikely to be related to the size of territory possessed. Egypt, for example, is a vast country, but its important assets are centered in three locations: Cairo, Alexandria, and the Aswan Dam. Its greater territory does not make it less vulnerable than Israel, despite the latter's very small size.

A sixth source of nuclear alarm stems from the proposition that leaders outside the boundaries of the advanced industrial states are more prone to irrational behavior.[51] These leaders are said to be more likely to become prisoners of their rhetoric and to be guided more often by religious, ideological, or sectarian imperatives, making them less subject to rational considerations. It is sometimes asserted that even the knowledge that their adversaries might retaliate in kind would not deter such leaders from using nuclear weapons. Not much evidence was ever produced to support these propositions, and as recently as the First and Second World Wars, the leaders of today's advanced industrial states were willing to sacrifice millions of their soldiers and civilians in the service of various causes. Thus, the argument that new nuclear states may be led by "new Hitlers" seems to ignore the fact that Hitler himself ruled a nation that before and after was a symbol of rationality and progress.[52]

When applied to the Middle East, the "Third World irrationality" theme seems to derive its deductions about leaders' rationality from the extreme rhetoric they frequently employ. Such deductions reveal a tendency to apply criteria based on post–World War II Western political culture to other regions of the world, as well as a failure to understand the role of rhetoric in some non-Western societies. Consequently, the vast gap between the language utilized by leaders in the Middle East and their actual behavior is often overlooked. Their purposeful if not cynical use of extreme rhetoric, primarily as a tool for mobilizing domestic support, is largely ignored by Western observers. This has led to a failure to realize that the behavior of seemingly crazy leaders, such as Libya's Mu'ammar Qadhafi and the Iranian Ayatollahs, has been much more cautious than their rhetoric would imply.

The "Third World irrationality" theme has gradually disappeared from the discourse on proliferation, largely because liberal nuclear alarmists have increasingly recognized its ethnocentric basis. It has been replaced by a less offensive proposition that leaders like Saddam Hussein are more likely to miscalculate than their advanced-industrial counterparts. Yet past leaders of today's advanced industrial states have made as many gross miscalculations as have Third World leaders. Based on Barbara Tuchman's work, it is difficult to sustain the proposition that Third World leaders enjoy a monopoly on folly.[53]

It is true that Saddam Hussein made two enormous strategic errors within ten years: in 1980 he calculated that Iran could be defeated easily following the purges of its military command by Ayatollah Khomeyni's clerics, and that its leadership would capitulate following the conquest of western and southwestern Iran; in 1990 he failed to anticipate the U.S., international, and regional responses to his conquest of Kuwait. While there can be little dispute about the magnitude of the first of these mistakes — it is comparable to Japan's attack on Pearl Harbor and to Hitler's invasion of Russia — the second can be regarded as irrational only in retrospect. At the time, a number of prominent observers in the United States and elsewhere believed that a war in the Gulf would involve far higher U.S. casualties than were ultimately sustained. In addition, Hussein's original estimate of U.S. willingness to absorb such costs was not baseless. Indeed, President George Bush needed the UN's approval in order to gain the U.S. Senate's support for the campaign, and even then the Senate voted to authorize the use of U.S. forces against Iraq by only a very narrow margin (52–47).

Thus, while the premises leading Saddam Hussein to invade Kuwait turned out to be mistaken and resulted in war and defeat, his plans to manipulate the U.S. sensitivity to costs were not irrational. Moreover, Saddam's political survival demonstrates that he did not assume intolerable risks. In general, all states are prone to miscalculation and there is not much evidence that Third World regimes are more likely than more advanced industrial states to make such mistakes.

A seventh and related theme suggests that problematic civil-military relations in many new nuclear states will allow the military to assume control over nuclear programs and weapons. The dangers involved in this possibility were elaborated by Scott Sagan:

Professional military organizations — because of common biases, inflexible routines, and parochial interests — display strong proclivities toward organizational behaviors that lead to deterrence failures.... This organizational critique argues that professional military organizations, if left on their own, are unlikely to fulfill the operational requirements for rational nuclear deterrence. Second, such organizational behavior can be effectively countered only by tight and sustained civilian control of the military. Unfortunately, there are strong reasons to believe that future nuclear-armed states will lack such positive mechanisms of civilian control.[54]

The fear that nuclear weapons in Third World countries would be under insufficient civilian control is coupled with the concern that the professional and organizational biases of the top military command would lead it to ascribe war-fighting roles to nuclear weapons,[55] and that the military would argue for the use of nuclear weapons in a preventive war.[56] By contrast, civilian leaders are viewed as more likely to regard nuclear weapons primarily as instruments of deterrence.

Whereas civilians focus on war avoidance, it is feared that the military's "nuclear war-fighting" approach would increase the likelihood that nuclear weapons would actually be used.

An eighth concern is that the controls exercised by the leaders of new nuclear states over their weapons would be less tight than the "fail-safe" systems employed by the acknowledged nuclear powers, for two reasons. First, Third World states are technologically less advanced, so the command and control systems and mechanisms at their disposal would likely be less complex and sophisticated. Consequently, their nuclear forces would be more exposed to unauthorized use.[57] Second, given the modest size of the nuclear arsenals that new nuclear states are likely to possess, the need to ensure that their weapons will survive an adversary's first strike is expected to lead these countries to emphasize readiness at the expense of safety. For example, new nuclear states are less likely to separate warheads from their delivery vehicles. Lewis Dunn noted this problem in the context of the "force-building choices" that any new nuclear state will be compelled to make; he argued that "rational" nuclear force–building choices may lead to unstable regional strategic outcomes.[58]

Sagan made the same point from the perspective of organization theory, pointing to the disincentives to pursue safety at the expense of an organization's primary missions. He argued that if new nuclear programs were controlled by military organizations, less attention would be given to securing second-strike forces and reducing exposure to accidental use or other dysfunctions. Sagan emphasized that invulnerability is expensive, and would therefore threaten the military's desire to buy more weapons.

The evidence to support this proposition is inconclusive. For example, it seems that India has refrained from maintaining completely assembled warheads and that Pakistan stores and maintains its nuclear warheads separate from their delivery vehicles.[59] The United States and the Soviet Union followed similar policies when their nuclear arsenals were still embryonic. Thus, leaders of new nuclear states may be more aware and more sensitive to the consequences of the mishandling of nuclear weapons and less prone to sacrifice safety for readiness than Sagan and Dunn believe.

A related limitation attributed to new nuclear states is that they lack the "safety culture" that is embedded in the more advanced industrial states.[60] Dunn argues that new nuclear states "may pay less attention to safety, putting top priority on building the bomb," and Sagan lists many reasons to expect that new nuclear states would face much greater risks of nuclear accidents than the United States.[61]

A ninth and widely shared concern about new nuclear states is that they are more likely to experience greater domestic instability, and that nuclear weapons might be used in factional wars or a crisis of succession. Indeed, Saddam Hussein has used chemical weapons against Iraqi citizens — the Kurd population at Halabja — and in 1994, ballistic missiles were employed in Yemen's civil war.[62] However, it is difficult to see how nuclear weapons could be used in an internal struggle without inflicting unacceptable costs on the initiating party.

Some of the preceding arguments are based on questionable premises and reveal a measure of cultural paternalism among members of the U.S. arms control community. For example, outcomes are deduced from the premise that military organizations in Third World countries might be left on their own to deal with nuclear weapons,[63] while in fact, Third World leaders rarely permit their military organizations much latitude on any matter. Granting their militaries such freedom would present Third World leaders with a permanent threat of coups.

A more credible assertion is that, even if the degree of U.S.-Soviet nuclear stability could eventually be obtained in other regions, the transition from embryonic nuclear programs to secure, safe, and fully controlled nuclear capabilities would be extremely hazardous. New nuclear forces are likely to be most vulnerable to preemptive and preventive first strikes, and the mechanisms available to ensure their control and safety are likely to be rudimentary. This could lead new nuclear states to adopt dangerous "launch on warning" postures — at least during the first phase of deployment.

Equally convincing and disturbing is the fear that new nuclear powers would be in a better position to attack their non-nuclear neighbors with conventional forces, while holding other neighbors and outside powers at bay by the implied or explicit threat to use nuclear weapons against them. Indeed, it would have been much more difficult and hazardous to compel Saddam Hussein to withdraw from Kuwait had Hussein possessed operational nuclear weapons in 1990–91.

For the United States, wider nuclear proliferation would increase the likelihood of nuclear confrontations with new nuclear states. While such risks could be minimized by disengaging from certain regions, the United States has vital national interests at stake in the Middle East, particularly in the Gulf region. Thus, the level of U.S. involvement in the Middle East will remain high, while the risks of its involvement will grow exponentially once nuclear weapons proliferate.

THE LIKELY EFFECTS OF PROLIFERATION IN THE MIDDLE EAST

An assessment of whether nuclear proliferation in the Middle East would be likely to stabilize or destabilize the region depends upon whether the focus of inquiry is the possible contribution of nuclear weapons to a single state's security or the likely effects of nuclear proliferation on regional and global stability. Nuclear weapons can provide states with effective existential deterrence and, under certain conditions, they may also yield a measure of residual deterrence. Their overall contribution to a state's security may be considerable, particularly if the state perceives its survival as potentially threatened.[64] By contrast, there are a number of reasons to believe that the spread of nuclear weapons to additional states may threaten global and regional security more than their possession by the original five acknowledged nuclear powers. Most of these reasons, such as the irrationality attributed to Middle East leaders, are likely to prove less worrisome than some observers believe. Yet other risks — such as those associated with the lesser culture of safety ascribed to many Third World states — cannot be entirely ignored.

The inconclusive nature of this debate points to the possibility that whether the spread of nuclear weapons would have largely stabilizing or destabilizing effects in the Middle East would depend on the specific strategic and political circumstances prevailing in the region when nuclear proliferation takes place, as well as on the manner in which the spread of nuclear weapons might occur. A number of scenarios serve to highlight the main factors that will determine whether nuclear catastrophe can be avoided.

The dramatic changes in the Middle East have transformed it into an arena of struggle between two sets of forces: the "new" versus the "old" Middle East. The most salient expression of the "new" Middle East is the Arab-Israeli peace process encompassing the governments of Israel, Egypt, Jordan, Tunisia, Morocco, most of the Gulf states, and the Palestinian Authority. Yet the process is only one manifestation of a much wider phenomenon. It represents secular, pragmatic forces, determined to resolve conflicts peacefully and to improve the standard of living and the quality of life for the region's populations through economic development. In contrast, the "old" Middle East, represented by Iraq, Iran, and Libya, manifests internal as well as external aggression, political and religious fanaticism, and a willingness to inflict and sustain much punishment in the service of a great cause.

While the "old" Middle East continues to harbor aggressive designs, the "new" seeks arms control and regional cooperation in economic development and integration, environmental conservation, resource utilization, and refugee resettlement. Internally, the "new" Middle East is driven by the middle class, the business community, free enterprise, and an open media; the "old" Middle East is represented by the security services, the militaries, the planned economy, the government-run media, and the institutions of fanatic and violent religion.

Struggle between these forces take place not only between states but also within states. Examples include the civil war in Algeria, the violence exercised by the Gama'at Islamiyya in Egypt, the challenge that the Hamas and the Islamic Jihad pose to the Palestinian Authority, the threat presented by the Hizbollah to the sovereignty and integrity of Lebanon, and the challenge presented by the extreme right to Israel's elected government.

A triumph of the "new" Middle East would imply that the Arab-Israeli peace process would expand to encompass a resolution of the conflicts among Israel, Syria, and Lebanon as well. Such a development would be likely to lead quickly to the development of relations and interactions among Israel, most Gulf states, and a number of states in North Africa. It would also enable a web of agreements to be concluded in the framework of the Middle East multilateral talks, designed to address the region's pressing socio-economic problems. Finally, it would imply that religious fanaticism will be defeated where it has not yet triumphed — from Algeria to Egypt — and that the Islamist regimes in Iran and Sudan would be replaced by more secular forces.

In this more benign environment, the incentives for the further spread of nuclear weapons would be far diminished and the risks entailed in such proliferation would be relatively low. Under such circumstances, most dangers predicted by more alarmist analysis regarding the consequences of nuclear proliferation would be unlikely to materialize.

By contrast, a reversion to the "old" Middle East would imply the collapse of Arab-Israeli peacemaking; the breakdown of all attempts at regional economic cooperation and other multilateral efforts; the triumph of Islamists in Algeria, Egypt, and among the Palestinians; the strengthening of the Islamist regimes in Iran and Sudan; a significant weakening of the secular Ba'ath in Syria and the Hashemites in Jordan; an accelerated regional arms race; and a strong propensity among many of the region's states to challenge Israel, the United States, and everything else Western. While the introduction of nuclear weapons into such an environment would not necessarily justify all the anxieties of the nuclear alarmists, it would be difficult to be confident that none of the more dangerous possible consequences of nuclear proliferation would materialize. Moreover, the expectation that under these conditions nuclear spread might lead to extremely dire developments might induce some of the region's states to make every effort to prevent their neighbors from obtaining these weapons. Thus, states' propensity to take preventive and preemptive action would be considerable; repeated resorts to violence in a region where nuclear weapons are spreading might eventually result in catastrophe.

The rate at which nuclear proliferation might take place might also affect whether the consequences are stabilizing or destabilizing. Yet the paces of horizontal and vertical proliferation may have different consequences for regional stability. In general, a slower rate of horizontal proliferation — the spread of nuclear weapons to additional states — would be more stabilizing; the region's leaders, government officials, and military commanders would have more time to adjust to the constraints imposed by their neighbors' acquisition of nuclear arms.[65]

By contrast, slow vertical proliferation — the growth of a state's nuclear arsenal — may have some negative consequences. Although adversaries' incentives to attempt a preventive or preemptive strike will be minimal once a nuclear force of any size has been obtained, such incentives cannot be entirely ignored as long as the force structures involved are very small and extremely vulnerable. Thus, rapid vertical proliferation ensures that nuclear states quickly become immune to an adversary's first strike, and provides little opportunity for adversaries to initiate or anticipate preventive and preemptive action.

The rate of nuclear proliferation in the Middle East would be largely affected by whether nuclear weapons reach the region through indigenous production — based on the nuclear scientific and engineering infrastructures developed by the region's states — or through the illegal purchase of weapons or weapons-grade material, possibly from the former Soviet Union.

The indigenous development and production of nuclear weapons in the Middle East is bound to be slow (see Chapter 2). Indeed, based solely on such capabilities, it is unlikely that a new nuclear state would emerge in the Middle East before about 2005. By contrast, significant shortcuts, such as the illicit acquisition of fissile material, could provide one or more of the region's states with a nuclear capability almost overnight. If "nuclear anarchy" in Russia and other quarters of the former Soviet Union leads to instant proliferation, Middle East leaders would have a far more limited opportunity to adjust themselves to the new dangers and constraints imposed by the spread of nuclear weapons.

Given the inconclusive nature of the scholarly debate regarding the effects of nuclear proliferation, judgments about the possible consequences of their spread in the Middle East must take account of possible future strategic trends in the region and the pace and manner in which nuclear proliferation might take place. Yet it is impossible to predict how the struggle between the "old" and the "new" Middle East will be determined, and equally impossible to rule out the possibility of rapid horizontal proliferation and slow vertical nuclear spread. Given such uncertainties, it would be wise to examine the possibility that the region's states might adopt nuclear arms control measures that may help avert the more dangerous possible consequences of nuclear proliferation in the Middle East.

Conclusions

There are three main reasons for a new look at the prospects for nuclear arms control in the Middle East. First, the progress made in recent years in Arab-Israeli peacemaking has improved the political climate for arms control in the region. The evolving Arab-Israeli peace process makes it possible for the first time to consider seriously the application of negotiated nuclear nonproliferation measures in the Middle East.

Second, nuclear arms have already become a major source of contention in the ACRS talks. The historical significance of these talks — allowing Israel, the Palestinians, and thirteen Arab states to discuss for the first time alternative means for enhancing the region's security and stability — makes it imperative that a serious effort be made to explore how the present stalemate might be overcome.

Finally, research on the consequences of nuclear spread does not rule out the possibility that nuclear proliferation in the Middle East would be destabilizing or catastrophic. Hence it is important to examine whether the region's states might adopt some measures to limit the spread of nuclear weapons.

NOTES

1. Indeed, this process seems to be already in motion; since the 1990–91 Gulf War it appears that there is no longer even an illusion of region-wide unity in the Middle East.

2. Ori Nir, "Arabs demand to discuss control of nuclear weapons first. Israel and the U.S. object," *Ha'aretz*, May 13, 1992; and John M. Goshko, "Israeli-Arab Arms Control Talks End Here," *Washington Post*, May 15, 1992. See also Robert J. Einhorn, "Arms Control and Regional Security in the Middle East," *Policywatch*, No. 96 (Washington, D.C.: The Washington Institute, August 2, 1993). All translations from Hebrew sources are the author's.

3. "Multilateral arms control committee talks in Moscow ended," *Ha'aretz*, September 18, 1992; and Aluf Ben, "Summary of arms control talks: Compromise between Israel and Egypt," *Ha'aretz*, September 20, 1992.

4. Aluf Ben, "Arms control talks: Discussion of operating joint communication center in Gulf of Eilat," *Ha'aretz*, September 14, 1992.

5. Aluf Ben, "Cornerstone for building trust," *Ha'aretz*, January 26, 1993.

6. Aluf Ben, "Syria may participate in next meeting of arms control talks," *Ha'aretz*, September 27, 1992.

7. Ben, "Cornerstone for building trust."

8. Nabil Fahmy, "Regional Arms Control, CBM and Peacekeeping Requirements," Paper presented at the Ninth Regional Security Conference of the International Institute for Strategic Studies (IISS), Istanbul, Turkey, June 7–10, 1992.

9. Aluf Ben, "Jerusalem: Regional nuclear disarmament should be discussed only in the multilateral negotiations," *Ha'aretz*, January 5, 1993.

10. David Makovsky, "Peres to seek mutual verification of arms ban with Arabs," *Jerusalem Post*, January 13, 1993; Nitzan Hurewitz, "Peres proposes to the Arab states to establish a WMD-free zone in the Middle East," *Ha'aretz*, January 14, 1993; and Ben, "Cornerstone for building trust."

11. Aluf Ben, "Israel asked to react to proposal to freeze production of fissile material," *Ha'aretz*, April 4, 1993; Ben, "Israel and the Arab states will discuss confidence building measures," *Ha'aretz*, May 11, 1993; "Israeli sources: Progress achieved in the arms control committee," *Ha'aretz*, May 20, 1993; "Israeli sources: Arms control talks progressing faster than expected," *Ha'aretz*, May 21, 1993; and Ben, "Israel obtained all its objectives at the U.S. arms control meeting," *Ha'aretz*, May 23, 1993.

12. Aluf Ben, "Israeli representatives will participate in an arms control seminar in Cairo," *Ha'aretz*, July 9, 1993; and "Middle East arms control workshop opens," *Jerusalem Post*, July 12, 1993.

13. Aluf Ben, "Agreement in the arms control talks on establishing regional communication center for the Middle East," *Ha'aretz*, November 9, 1993; and Ben, "In the Role of the Bad Guys," *Ha'aretz*, December 30, 1993.

14. See Aluf Ben and Akiva Eldar, "Proposal to establish a communication and crisis management center for Middle East states will be presented at multilateral conference in Moscow," *Ha'aretz*, October 31, 1993.

15. Aluf Ben, "Agreement in the arms control talks on establishing regional communication center for the Middle East," *Ha'aretz*, November 9, 1993.

16. "Middle East arms control talks begin in Cairo," *Al Hamishmar*, January 31, 1994.

17. Aluf Ben, "Egypt and Israel trying to diffuse some of the tension in arms control talks," *Ha'aretz*, January 26, 1994.

18. Aluf Ben, "Arms control working group meeting will end today with joint declaration of principles," *Ha'aretz*, February 3, 1994; and Ben, "Draft declaration of principles formulated in arms control talks," *Ha'aretz*, February 6, 1994.

19. Aluf Ben, "Israeli delegation leaving today for Qatar to participate in multilateral arms control negotiations," *Ha'aretz*, May 1, 1994; and Ben, "Efforts to complete draft declaration of principles toward opening of arms control talks," *Ha'aretz*, May 3, 1994.

20. See Aluf Ben, "Israeli delegation leaving today for Qatar," *Ha'aretz*, May 1, 1994; and Ben, "Israeli delegation arrived for first arms control talks at Qatar," *Ha'aretz*, May 2, 1994.

21. "Qatar minister of foreign affairs: Israel should sign the nuclear nonproliferation treaty," *Ha'aretz*, May 4, 1994; and "Draft Agreement on Principles Rejected in Multilateral Arms Control Negotiations," *Ha'aretz*, May 5, 1994.

22. In the words of the head of the Saudi delegation, Prince Turki Bin Abdullah Bin Muhammad Al Sa'ud: "We categorically reject the political section of the project, which is aimed at normalizing relations between Arab states and Israel." See "Israeli and Arab delegations fail to agree; Saudis reject political section," Agence France Presse (AFP) news agency, Paris, in English, May 6, 1994. See British Broadcasting Company (BBC), Vol. ME/1991, May 7, 1994, p. MED/15.

23. "Draft arms control principles rejected," *Ha'aretz*, May 5, 1994.

24. Nitzan Hurewitz, "Arms control in the Middle East will be discussed in an experts' meeting in Paris," *Ha'aretz*, October 11, 1994.

25. Sharon Sade, "Defense sources: Saudi Arabia increased its involvement in arms control talks," *Ha'aretz*, October 6, 1994.

26. After the Paris meeting, representatives of the participating states conducted joint visits to nuclear facilities in Germany and defense facilities in Switzerland. See Sade, "Defense sources: Saudi Arabia increased its involvement."

27. Aluf Ben, "Israeli Delegation Leaving Today for Qatar," *Ha'aretz*, May 1, 1994. See also "Arms control talks: Government 'willing' to host regional security center," Middle East News Agency (MENA) from Cairo, in Arabic, February 4, 1994 (BBC, ME/1915 February 7, 1994, p. MED/15).

28. Sharon Sade, "Exercise of safety at sea in the framework of arms control discussions will be conducted in Italy," *Ha'aretz*, June 1, 1994.

29. "Israel Invites Arabs To Tour IDF Bases," Jerusalem Qol Yisra'el (radio) in Hebrew, May 3, 1994. See Foreign Broadcasting Information Service (FBIS), Vol. FBIS-NES-94-086, May 4, 1994, p. 19.

30. Sharon Sade, "Israel, Jordan, and Egypt will conduct a joint naval exercise to examine arms control arrangements," *Ha'aretz*, November 11, 1994.

31. See Sharon Sade, "Arab representatives will accept Ivri's invitation to visit IDF bases," *Ha'aretz*, December 16, 1994.

32. Sharon Sade, "Israel prepared to permit Arab representatives to visit defense installations," *Ha'aretz*, December 14, 1994; and Sade, "Arab representatives will accept."

33. Sharon Sade, "Jordan would like to host next meeting of arms control talks," *Ha'aretz*, December 18, 1994.

34. Sade, "Israel prepared to permit."

35. Sade, "Arab representatives will accept."

36. "Israel, Arab Nations Reach Tension-Easing Pacts," *Washington Post*, December 21, 1994.

37. Sade, "Israel prepared to permit."

38. See statement by Syria's Foreign Minister Faruq al-Shar' cited by Syrian Arab Republic Radio January 28, 1993 (BBC, ME/1599 January 29, 1993, p. A/13). Similarly, in Brussels in late 1994, al-Shar' said that a "substantial agreement in the peace process might bring Syria to join the multilateral talks." Guy Bechor and Aluf Ben, "Al-Shar': We proposed to renew the peace talks two weeks ago but Israel rejected the proposal," *Ha'aretz*, November 29, 1994.

39. Shai Feldman, *Israeli Nuclear Deterrence: A Strategy for the 1980s* (New York: Columbia University Press, 1982). The ideas in this book were the result of much discussion with my fellow Ph.D. student at Berkeley, Stephen Van Evera, now at MIT. These ideas were developed in Stephen Van Evera, "The Effects of Nuclear Proliferation" (unpublished manuscript, University of California, Berkeley, Department of Political Science, 1976); and Van Evera, "Nuclear Weapons, Nuclear Proliferation and the Causes of War" (unpublished manuscript, University of California, Berkeley, Department of Political Science, 1978); as well as in various drafts of Shai Feldman, "Israeli Nuclear Deterrence: A Strategy for the 1980s" (Ph.D. Dissertation, University of California, Berkeley, 1980).

40. Feldman, *Israeli Nuclear Deterrence*, pp. 32–43.

41. Steven Miller points out, however, that "the behavior of nuclear armed states has failed to conform to these predictions. The United States and the Soviet Union, for example, seemed to feel remarkably insecure during the Cold War, given their size, power and nuclear status.... Far from being insensitive to the military preparations of the other side, both countries were obsessed by them. By the standards of modern history, they spent unusually large shares of their national treasure on defense. And throughout the Cold War the United States and the Soviet Union opted for precisely the war-fighting nuclear doctrines that are regarded as unnecessary, inappropriate and destabilizing by most deterrence theorists." Steven E. Miller, "The Case Against a Ukrainian Nuclear Deterrent," *Foreign Affairs*, Vol. 72, No. 3 (Summer

1993), p. 71. While Miller's point is well taken, it is noteworthy that South Africa's inventory included only seven nuclear warheads and that both India and Pakistan insist that they do not possess assembled weapons. In this respect, a number of "new nuclear states" seem to conform much more closely to the expectations of nuclear deterrence theory than did the Cold War superpowers.

42. Kenneth Waltz argues that nuclear weapons "make the cost of war seem frighteningly high and thus discourage states from starting any wars that might lead to the use of such weapons." He further stresses that "nuclear weapons make states exceedingly cautious." See Kenneth N. Waltz, *The Spread of Nuclear Weapons: More May Be Better*, Adelphi Paper No. 171 (London: IISS, 1981), pp. 3, 5.

43. The terms "residual deterrence" and "specific deterrence" are closely related; both refer to the ability to deter less-than-existential threats. "Residual deterrence" is the caution induced by the idea of confronting any nuclear adversary. "Specific deterrence" is the ability to deter specific challenges.

44. See Feldman, *Israeli Nuclear Deterrence*, p. 31.

45. See Shai Feldman "Israeli Deterrence During the Gulf War," in Joseph Alpher, ed., *War in the Gulf: Implications for Israel* (Tel Aviv: Jaffee Center for Strategic Studies [JCSS], Tel Aviv University, 1992), pp. 184–209.

46. However, Scott Sagan argues that the possession of nuclear weapons by the five recognized nuclear powers was far more dangerous than most observers believe. See Scott Sagan, "The Perils of Proliferation: Organization Theory, Deterrence Theory, and the Spread of Nuclear Weapons," *International Security*, Vol. 18, No. 4 (Spring 1994), pp. 66–107.

47. "With clear dividing lines it was easier to calculate relative military advantage and the risks of action." Lewis Dunn, "The Nuclear Agenda: The Middle East in Global Perspective," in Shai Feldman and Ariel Levite, eds., *Arms Control and the New Middle East Security Environment*, JCSS Study No. 23 (Tel Aviv: JCSS, Tel Aviv University, 1994) p. 235. This point was made almost thirty years earlier in Stanley Hoffmann, "Nuclear Proliferation and World Politics," in Alastair Buchan, ed., *A World of Nuclear Powers?* (Englewood Cliffs, N.J.: Prentice-Hall, 1966), p. 107.

48. Dunn, "The Nuclear Agenda," p. 234.

49. See Feldman, *Israeli Nuclear Deterrence*, pp. 149–150.

50. Ibid., pp. 90–102.

51. This point was made in the 1960s and 1970s in Michael Mandelbaum, "International Stability and Nuclear Order," in David C. Gompert, et al., *Nuclear Weapons and World Politics: Alternatives for the Future* (New York: McGraw-Hill, 1977), p. 66; Raymond Aron, *The Great Debate: Theories of National Strategy* (Garden City, N.J.: Doubleday, 1965), pp. 61–62; and

Hoffmann, "Nuclear Proliferation and World Politics," pp. 89–90.

52. See Waltz, *More May Be Better*, p. 20.

53. See Barbara W. Tuchman, *The March of Folly: From Troy to Vietnam* (New York: Random House, 1984).

54. Sagan, "The Perils of Proliferation," p. 68. Sagan adds: "Two widespread themes in the organization theory literature focus attention on the major impediments to pure rationality in organizational behavior. First, large organizations function within a severely 'bounded' form of rationality: they have inherent limits on calculation and use simplifying mechanisms to understand and respond to uncertainty in the external environment…. Organizations are often myopic: instead of surveying the entire environment for information, organization members undertake biased searches, focusing only on specific areas stemming from their past experience, recent training, and current responsibility…. Second, complex organizations commonly have multiple conflicting goals and the process by which objectives are chosen is intensely political. Such a political perspective envisions apparently irrational behaviors as serving the narrow interests of some units within the organization, even if the actions appear 'systematically stupid' from the leadership's overall perspective" (pp. 72–73).

55. This point was made some fifteen years ago in Yair Evron, "Some Effects of the Introduction of Nuclear Weapons in the Middle East," in Asher Arian, ed., *Israel: A Developing Society* (Tel Aviv: Pinhas Sapir Center for Development, Tel Aviv University, and Assem, Netherlands: Van Gorom, 1980), p. 107. A response to this argument can be found in Feldman, *Israeli Nuclear Deterrence*, pp. 149–152.

56. Sagan argues that "preventive war is more likely to be chosen, however, if military leaders have a significant degree of influence over the final decision. While there have not been, obviously, any preventive nuclear wars among the new proliferants, the probability of such attacks will increase since civilian control over the military is more problematic in many of these cases." Sagan argues that Pakistan is a good example, but all of his confirmed examples of the Pakistani military's advocacy of preventive war are from before India detonated a nuclear device. Sagan, "The Perils of Proliferation," p. 82.

57. See Lewis Dunn, "Nuclear Proliferation and World Politics," in Joseph I. Coffey, ed., *Nuclear Proliferation: Prospects, Problems, Proposals*, Annals of the American Academy of Political Science (AAPS) No. 430 (Philadelphia: AAPS, 1977), p. 98. See also Feldman, *Israeli Nuclear Deterrence*, pp. 164–167.

58. See Dunn, "The Nuclear Agenda." Dunn asks: "For example, does [such a state] emphasize readiness, or does it emphasize safety? There is a trade-off between these requirements, since one effective way to have safe nuclear weapons is to keep them disassembled. But if they are kept disassembled, they would not be ready for use in a crisis or conflict…. At this force-building level, some countries in the Middle East have very good reasons to make choices that will be less, not more, stabilizing" (p. 235).

59. This assessment is based on informal conversations with analysts familiar with the defense postures of India and Pakistan. Unfortunately, open-source evidence to support these assertions is not available.

60. See Sagan, "The Perils of Proliferation," p. 94.

61. Dunn writes: "Consider how the Iraqis stored chemical weapons: they simply kept chemical agents in 55 gallon drums that were thrown around. At the very least, Iraq clearly had a very different safety culture." Dunn, "The Nuclear Agenda," p. 235.

62. See "Southern Scud attack on San'a reportedly kills more than 23 civilians," BBC, ME/1995 MED/1, May 12, 1994.

63. Sagan, "The Perils of Proliferation," p. 68.

64. Hence, it is hardly surprising that while the United States and Russia are reducing their nuclear arsenals dramatically, and while in the coming years France and Britain may also accept some limitations on their nuclear stockpiles, none of the acknowledged nuclear powers is likely to forgo its nuclear arsenals completely.

65. The danger that proliferation would follow the opposite path was termed by Steven Miller "the risks of 'instant' proliferation." See Miller, "The Case Against a Ukrainian Nuclear Deterrent," p. 72.

Chapter 2

Nuclear Programs

This chapter assesses current proliferation trends in the Middle East.[1] It provides a detailed analysis of the nuclear programs pursued by the region's states, and evaluates the likelihood that each of these programs might lead to the acquisition of nuclear weapons. The central conclusion of this chapter is that none of the region's Muslim states is currently close to possessing nuclear weapons. This means that unless fissile material is soon smuggled into the Middle East, there is still time to reverse the pursuit of nuclear arms in the region.

In recent years, concern about nuclear proliferation in the Middle East has focused primarily on Iran and Iraq. Iran has launched a major nuclear effort and Iraq has maintained the human infrastructure of its advanced nuclear program. There is also reason to believe that Iraq's motivations and determination to acquire a military nuclear capability have not diminished. It is far less likely that Libya, Algeria, Syria, or Egypt would obtain nuclear weapons in the foreseeable future. In the international community as well as in the Middle East, Israel is widely regarded as having already obtained an advanced nuclear capability.

While this chapter focuses on the evolving nuclear infrastructures of Middle East states, a second potential route for proliferation should also be acknowledged: the possibility that one or more of the region's states might import a "quick fix" nuclear capability. In the immediate aftermath of the breakup of the Soviet Union, this concern centered on the possibility that control over some nuclear warheads might be lost, creating the danger that they might be smuggled and sold clandestinely in the Middle East. Additional concerns focused on the possibility that deteriorating economic conditions in the former Soviet Union (FSU) could lead some of its nuclear scientists, engineers and weapons designers to seek employment among the region's states.[2] A more likely possibility is that reprocessed plutonium or enriched uranium would be stolen and sold to Middle East clients.[3] According to President Boris Yeltsin, by the early 1990s Russia possessed some 150 tons of plutonium and over 1,000 tons of enriched uranium.[4] Even optimistic assumptions about current accounting, safety, and security procedures in the FSU suggest that small amounts of such materials could be stolen and smuggled. This is particularly worrisome since only 10 kilograms of plutonium or 25 kilograms of enriched uranium are needed to construct a nuclear device.

While there is little credible evidence that substantial smuggling of fissile material from the former Soviet Union has occurred, by mid-1994 there was increasing evidence that such efforts were indeed underway. On May 10, 1994, 6 grams of plutonium were discovered near Stuttgart in southwestern Germany. On June 13, 0.8 grams of uranium enriched to 87.5 percent were found in Landshut. On August 10, some 580 grams of mixed dioxide (MOX) fuel were seized at Munich airport; its plutonium content was reportedly 300–350 grams, of which 87 percent was Pu-239. This unusually high concentration of plutonium would make the material weapons-grade, but the plutonium would need to be separated chemically from the other materials in the fuel.

On August 12, 1994, at the train station of Bremen, Germany, 0.05 grams of plutonium were seized. And on December 20, 1994, the Czech police reportedly seized some 4 kilograms of enriched uranium believed to have come from Russia.[5] The report did not specify to what degree the material was enriched and thus whether it was weapons-grade.[6]

While all the materials seized in these cases were either of very small quantities or of questionable quality and thus largely irrelevant to bomb making, the smuggled "sample" quantities indicated that leaks in the nuclear complex of the Commonwealth of Independent States (CIS) Union may have already developed. Indeed, German intelligence officers estimated that Russian government officials may have been involved in such smuggling,[7] raising the possibility that much larger quantities of plutonium or enriched uranium could be smuggled out of Russia in the future.[8] Indeed, by August 1994 Russian officials conceded that the nuclear material seized earlier that month in Germany "could have originated in Russia" and that "systems to prevent theft of nuclear materials needed improvements."[9] Thus, the fact that almost all the reported confiscations have occurred in Germany may merely reflect the efficiency of the German police forces; if so, it is quite possible that similar or much larger quantities of fissile material have been and continue to be smuggled through other countries with less efficient law enforcement agencies.

Despite the initial apparent consensus that Russia was the source of all seized materials, it is possible that leaks have also developed in the nuclear fuel cycles of Eastern or Western European states. Some alarm about this possibility was expressed by late 1994.[10] None of the reports of intercepted nuclear smuggling contained credible information about the intended customers. However, the Middle East would likely generate considerable demand for plutonium or enriched uranium regardless of the cost. Should one of the region's states obtain fissile material through smuggling — and Iraq and Iran are not the only potential clients — this could shorten its path to a primitive deliverable nuclear capability to a matter of months. But given the difficulties entailed in ascertaining the likelihood that the smuggling of fissile material might prove fruitful, this chapter is largely confined to an analysis of efforts to develop indigenous nuclear capabilities in the Middle East.

Before turning to these indigenous programs, the possible implications of Pakistan's advanced nuclear program for Middle East countries should be addressed. By the early 1990s, Pakistan was almost universally regarded as possessing nuclear weapons or the capacity to assemble them at very short notice. Final confirmation was provided in mid-1994 by Pakistan's former prime minister, Nawaz Sharif.[11]

In the late 1970s, there was some concern that Pakistan might place its nuclear capacity at the disposal of one or more of the Arab states, either by supplying them with nuclear weapons or fissile material, or by providing a "nuclear umbrella" — a commitment to retaliate with nuclear weapons if a client was attacked first. This concern was fueled primarily by a statement made by Pakistan's Former Prime Minister Zulfikar 'Ali Bhutto that he was determined that his country would develop "an Islamic bomb." The statement was widely interpreted as implying that Pakistan's nuclear capacity was designed to serve other Islamic countries as well. This interpretation was also supported by rumors that Libya and Saudi Arabia had helped finance Pakistan's nuclear program; by the close relations between Pakistan and a number of Arab states, including the stationing of Pakistani military personnel on the territory of Jordan and Saudi Arabia; by the possibility that Pakistan's enduring economic problems might expose it to offers of economic assistance in exchange for nuclear technology; and by a number of agreements for "peaceful" nuclear cooperation signed between Pakistan and a number of Arab states.

Yet open sources provide no evidence that Pakistan has ever supplied nuclear weapons, fissile material, or sensitive nuclear technology to any Arab state. Nor is Pakistan likely to engage in such transfers in the future. Indeed, fears of illicit Pakistani nuclear transfers to Arab states were never based on sound logic. First, Bhutto's statement was probably intended to indicate that a nuclear capability would give Pakistan more clout in the competition for leadership in the Islamic world. This would require that Pakistan also retain a nuclear monopoly among the Islamic states. From this perspective, any significant nuclear transfer by Pakistan to an Arab state would be self-defeating.

Second, from a strategic standpoint, Pakistan's pursuit of nuclear weapons seems to have been intended solely to equip it with an existential deterrent against India's advanced nuclear capability and to provide it with a response to India's preponderance in conventional forces and weapons, which are perceived by Pakistan as posing an existential threat. In this context, it would have been illogical for Pakistan to do anything that might make Israel its adversary, especially since Pakistan believes that Israel possesses robust conventional and unconventional military capabilities, including the capacity to project military power at great distances. Thus, Pakistan is particularly unlikely to do anything that might encourage Israel to engage India in strategic cooperation. In the aftermath of the break-through in Indian-Israeli relations achieved in the early 1990s, there have been indications that Pakistan might follow other Islamic states and establish diplomatic and economic relations with Israel. This further diminishes the likelihood that Pakistan might pursue nuclear transfers to Arab states.

Finally and possibly most important, the transfer of sensitive nuclear technology — let alone the export of nuclear weapons or fissile material — would violate the tacit understanding reached between Pakistan and the United States on nuclear matters. This understanding seems to stipulate that the United States will tolerate Pakistan's nuclear program as long as Pakistan refrains from making any official declaration of its possession of nuclear weapons, avoids any testing of its nuclear devices, and does not make any transfers that might contribute to further nuclear proliferation. Given the important U.S. interests in the Middle East and U.S. sensitivity to developments in the region, Pakistan may have estimated — and Washington may have conveyed clear messages to this effect — that nuclear transfers to Arab states would result in a swift and painful U.S. response.

For all of these reasons, Pakistan is likely to continue to refrain from sharing its nuclear capabilities with any other state, particularly in the Middle East, leaving the region fairly unaffected by the nuclear arms race on the Indian subcontinent.

Israel

In a 1993 survey of global nuclear capabilities, the *New York Times* wrote that Israel possessed the world's fifth largest nuclear arsenal. It estimated that Israel had acquired some 50–200 nuclear warheads and sophisticated delivery means, including a 1,400-km range Jericho-2 missile.[12] Similarly, a 1993 report issued by the KGB's successor — the Russian Foreign Intelligence Service — estimated that Israel might have produced as many as 200 nuclear weapons and has sufficient uranium to last 200 years.[13] An international commission nominated by the UN Secretary General to explore ways of facilitating the establishment of a nuclear weapons free zone (NWFZ) in the Middle East referred to "the 'Israeli deterrent' or 'weapon of last resort'."[14]

Any assessment of the evolution and state of Israel's nuclear program must rely entirely on non-Israeli sources. Israel has never exposed the dimensions of its activities in this realm, although the degree of indirect discourse on the subject increased substantially during the late 1980s and early 1990s.[15] While foreign estimates of Israel's nuclear capability differ, they all share a view that Israel possesses the most advanced nuclear capability in the Middle East.

As early as 1968, the U.S. Central Intelligence Agency (CIA) reportedly concluded that Israel had become a nuclear state.[16] In 1978, the CIA made public a memorandum dated September 4, 1974, which asserted that "we believe that Israel already has produced nuclear weapons." The report stated that this conclusion was "based on Israeli acquisition of large quantities of uranium, partly by clandestine means; the ambiguous nature of Israeli efforts in the field of uranium enrichment; and Israel's large investment in a costly missile system designed to accommodate nuclear warheads."[17]

In 1989, a U.S. Defense Intelligence Agency (DIA) report obtained and released by the Natural Resources Defense Council claimed that Israel possessed nuclear weapons and had acquired nuclear warheads for its Jericho-1 ballistic missiles.[18] In mid-1991, the U.S. intelligence community reportedly estimated that Israel possessed 60–80 nuclear bombs, as well as aircraft and Jericho ballistic missiles that have been configured especially to carry nuclear bombs and warheads.[19] Other sources claimed that the weapons were developed in the late 1970s, with financial assistance and cooperation from the government of the last Shah of Iran. Within that framework, Israel is said to have developed a ballistic missile capable of carrying a 750 kg conventional or nuclear payload.[20] A 1996 Jane's *Yearbook* revealed that Israel possesses a wing (three squadrons) of Jericho missiles.[21] An Israeli journalist later referred to the Micha fields — the air force base where these missiles are reportedly located — as "the nuclear missiles base."[22]

The 1986 "revelations" of Mordechai Va'anunu, a former technician at the Dimona nuclear reactor, were reported by London's *Sunday Times* and have fueled the international discourse regarding Israel's nuclear potential.[23] Following the publication of Va'anunu's account, European papers and journals published varying estimates by nuclear experts that Israel might have "at least 100" and as many as 200 nuclear warheads. Some ventured that Israel might have the capacity to manufacture 20-megaton (Mt) hydrogen bombs.[24] A U.S. analyst reacted to the Va'anunu affair:

If the reports surfacing last month are correct, what they reveal is an Israeli nuclear arsenal that is not only 5–10 times larger than was generally supposed but also one that may contain sophisticated city-busting warheads, not the smaller, though still devastating, Nagasaki-type bombs. No matter how you play with these numbers, its far different from the assumed 20–25 bombs in the basement. Now we're talking about a sizable nuclear arsenal.[25]

Va'anunu claimed that Israel had been separating some 40 kg of plutonium annually at Dimona, and that it also produced tritium, which is used in the production of thermonuclear weapons. Va'anunu's reports led to additional speculations in the foreign press to the effect that Israel was also producing highly enriched uranium through laser as well as centrifuge technologies.[26] Based on Va'anunu's report, experts engaged by the *Sunday Times* concluded that Dimona's original 26-megawatt capacity might have been boosted to 150 megawatts.[27] Francis Perrin, France's former high commissioner for atomic energy, wrote that during the late 1950s and early 1960s, France had supplied Israel with an underground plutonium separation plant.[28]

There have also been many references in the international media to possible Israeli–South African cooperation in the nuclear realm, particularly in testing nuclear explosives.[29] One report also indicated that in exchange for missile boats, South Africa supplied Israel with uranium mined in Namibia.[30] However, the reliability of these reports is questionable and in 1989 Israel's Defense Minister, Itzhak Rabin, categorically denied the existence of such cooperation.[31] Other international press reports also expressed doubt that Israeli–South African cooperation in weapons testing was necessary, pointing to Israel's alleged capability to use advanced computer technologies to simulate weapons' performance.[32] It thus seems that while Israel and South Africa cooperated in a number of sensitive ventures, they have probably not cooperated in the nuclear realm.[33]

A Soviet source reported that in late 1968, Israel diverted a shipment of 200 tons of natural uranium en route from Antwerp to Milan. According to the report, the irradiated uranium was utilized in an Israeli plutonium production plant which became operational in 1969.[34]

In 1985, a U.S. company reportedly sold Israel 800 krytrons, which can be used as a nuclear triggering device.[35] This sale violated U.S. export controls, and following the indictment of the company and the individuals involved, Israel reportedly returned all unused krytrons to the United States, but refused to allow a U.S. inspection of the devices already used.[36] During the early 1980s, Israel reportedly also purchased Swedish equipment permitting laboratory tests of nuclear devices. Pakistan and India have purchased similar equipment.[37]

In 1959, Norway reportedly sold Israel some 21 tons of heavy water (deuterium oxide), which is used to control atomic reactions.[38] In 1988, Israel offered to return to Norway 20 tons of the heavy water, and an Israeli-Norwegian agreement guiding the future use of the heavy water was signed in mid-1988.[39] The agreement was rejected by the Norwegian parliament in October 1988, and further negotiations took place in 1989 and early 1990.[40] In mid-1990, the two governments reached an agreement allowing the return of the heavy water to Norway;[41] the agreement was implemented in December 1991.[42] Meanwhile, foreign press reports also alleged that Israel purchased some 12 tons of Norwegian-made heavy water from Romania and France.[43]

Israel has not purchased a nuclear power reactor, largely because Western suppliers have refused to sell a reactor as long as Israel does not sign and ratify the NPT. An effort to persuade France to provide Israel with such a reactor in the mid-1980s failed, as did a similar approach to Russia.[44] Yet Israel's interest in nuclear power reactors was also limited by the estimate that the energy they produce is likely to be much more expensive than that produced by conventional means. In addition, after the nuclear catastrophe in Chernobyl, the prospect of the purchase of a nuclear reactor met strong opposition on ecological and environmental grounds.[45]

Thus, the following portrait of Israel's nuclear capability emerges from open foreign sources: in addition to its small nuclear reactor at Soreq, Israel has been operating a 26-megawatt natural uranium-fueled, heavy water–moderated nuclear research reactor in Dimona since the early 1960s.[46] Subsequently, according to foreign sources, Dimona's capacity may have been upgraded to 70–150 megawatts. Israel has also reprocessed the fuel of the Dimona reactor to extract weapons-grade plutonium. Israel has manufactured a large number of nuclear weapons; it may be storing some 100–200 warheads; and it may possess nuclear warheads for Jericho-2 ballistic missiles, which have a range of over 1,000 km.

Iran

In 1992–93, U.S. and Israeli officials estimated that Iran might be able to produce nuclear weapons within eight to ten years.[47] By early 1995, however, Israeli Prime Minister Itzhak Rabin and U.S. Secretary of Defense William Perry agreed "that 7 to 15 years was 'a reasonable estimate' of how long it would take Iran [to obtain nuclear weapons] at its present pace."[48] These estimates were based on evidence that Iran's nuclear program was revived in the mid-1980s, and that following the Gulf War, it launched a program to develop an advanced nuclear infrastructure, including the development of nuclear power, research, and potential military applications.[49]

NUCLEAR POWER

Iran has been making efforts to complete the construction of two 1,300-megawatt power reactors at Bushehr, built by the German firms Siemens and Kraftwerk Union in the mid-1970s for the Shah of Iran.[50] Construction of these reactors, which were 80 and 65–70 percent complete, was frozen by Ayatollah Khomeyni immediately after the 1979 revolution. The reactors were damaged by Iraqi bombardments in March 1984, February 1985, November 1987, and July 1988; the extent of damage is unclear.[51] The prerevolutionary Iranian government had also contracted the French firm Framatome to construct a 935-megawatt reactor at Ahvaz; construction had just begun when the 1979 revolution took place.[52] In 1991, Iranian President Hashemi Rafsanjani said that Iran was determined to complete the construction of the nuclear center at Bushehr.[53] After German firms refused to resume work on the reactors, Iranian and Chinese officials discussed the possibility that China would carry out the reconstruction.[54] Subsequently, Iran also attempted to gain access to Brazilian nuclear . technology that was originally part of Iran's agreement with Kraftwerk Union, but Germany refused to allow any transfer of nuclear technology by Brazil.[55] During the early 1990s, Iran also attempted to hire the Czech company Skoda Energy, which is partly owned by Siemens, to complete the reactors. But in December 1993, Czech Foreign Minister Joseph Jlenik reported to Israeli Prime Minister Rabin that the deal would not be implemented.[56]

Finally, in early January 1995, Iran signed an $800 million deal with Russia to complete the first of the two units at Bushehr by 2001.[57] After the signing of the agreement, the head of Iran's Organization for Atomic Energy, Reza Amrollahi, said that the deal was part of Teheran's plan to build ten nuclear reactors for electricity generation.[58] In response to U.S. pressures, Russia later negotiated with Iran a separate agreement stipulating that all spent fuel from the Bushehr reactors would be shipped to Russia.[59] In 1984, nuclear industry sources had estimated that the proliferation risk posed by the reactors at Bushehr was negligible, since it would be "practically impossible" to use the plants, which are pressurized water reactors, to produce enough plutonium to make nuclear weapons.[60] Not surprisingly, ten years later Russian officials made the same argument; on August 24, 1995, Deputy Atomic Energy Minister Yevgeni Reshetnikov said, "only people who are absolutely incompetent in the field of atomic energy are assessing that the station can be used to create an atomic bomb.... [It will be] practically impossible for Iran to use the complex in a military capacity."[61]

The potential contributions of the Russian-Iranian reactors deal to Iran's quest for a military nuclear capability are likely to be largely indirect. Primarily, Iran may benefit from the presence of some 1500 to 3000 Soviet nuclear scientists, engineers, and technicians who are expected to take part in the project.[62] More worrisome, large-scale nuclear purchases for the reactors' completion will make it more difficult for Western intelligence agencies to ascertain that Iran is not also obtaining material needed for its military nuclear designs.

In 1993, China agreed to build a 300-megawatt nuclear power reactor at Darkhovin, near the Iraqi border, as part of a framework agreement calling for the eventual construction of two such Chinese reactors in Iran.[63] The reactor was to be subject to International Atomic Energy Agency (IAEA) safeguards.[64] The construction of the reactors seems to have been delayed for some two years by financial considerations. In September 1995 China informed the Clinton administration that it was backing away from supplying the reactor to Iran, but China's Foreign Minister, Quan Qichen, later said that the deal was "suspended for the time being," indicating that the withdrawal reported in September was tentative.[65]

In addition, Iran signed an agreement with Russia for the supply of two 440-megawatt nuclear power reactors, also under IAEA safeguards.[66] These reactors are to be located at Gorgan, on the Caspian Sea.[67] By May 1993, Russian experts had reportedly arrived in Iran to begin planning the construction of the reactors' infrastructure, though earlier reports had indicated that financial constraints had forced delays.[68] By mid-1995, U.S. officials were increasingly doubtful that Iran would be able to pay the $4 billion needed to complete the two reactors at Bushehr and construct two more at Gorgan.[69]

During the mid-1970s, Iran acquired a 20 percent share in Eurodif, a French company specializing in the production of low-enriched uranium reactor fuel rods. Following the 1979 Khomeyni revolution, France froze all transfers from Eurodif to Iran. After the Gulf War, Iran sought to reactivate its agreement with the French firm.[70] Negotiations between Iran and France from 1991 to 1993 resolved the financial aspects of the dispute, but it is not clear whether Iran has been able to obtain Eurodif access to products.[71] Clearly, as Iran lacks operating nuclear power reactors, its interest in obtaining fuel rods was highly suspicious.[72] An early 1992 sale by Argentina to Iran of a $12 million nuclear fuel fabrication plant — which might have allowed Iran to produce low-enriched uranium — was canceled by Argentina under U.S. pressure.[73]

NUCLEAR RESEARCH

Since the late 1960s, Iran has been operating a 5-megawatt U.S.-built nuclear reactor located at the Teheran University Nuclear Center. It is a pool-type light water reactor, fueled by highly enriched uranium.[74] Subsequently, Iran reportedly consented to downgrade the level of the enriched fuel from 93 to 20 percent "as a sign of its good intentions and as a signatory of the Nuclear Nonproliferation Treaty."[75] At the time, the United States was also said to have supplied Iran with a large number of "hot cells" for separating plutonium from irradiated fuel.[76] Another report indicated that Iran might also have purchased hot cells from Argentina.[77]

Iran's planned purchase of a 20-megawatt nuclear research reactor from China was canceled in 1992 following U.S. pressure on Beijing.[78] A similar fate characterizes Iranian-Indian nuclear relations. In February 1991, Iran and India discussed the possible purchase by Iran of a 5–10 megawatt nuclear research reactor, as well as the possible purchase of a 220-megawatt power reactor.[79] India withdrew the offer following U.S. pressure to forgo the reactor sale.[80]

On November 6, 1985, the Iranian newspaper *Qthan* published an announcement urging Iranian nuclear scientists residing abroad to return to Iran to participate in a conference on nuclear power in Bushehr.[81] A large number of Iranian scientists have since returned to Iran, some of them reportedly interested in working on uranium enrichment or plutonium production through the chemical reprocessing of irradiated nuclear fuel.[82] The same year, a Ph.D. program in nuclear science and technology was inaugurated at Iran's Amir Kabir Technological University.[83]

In 1993, an agreement was concluded between Iran and Russia on cooperation in basic research and applications in nuclear energy, nuclear reactor safety, and the production and use of isotopes.[84] According to Reza Amrollahi, Iran's vice president and head of its Atomic Energy Organization, research on the artificial production of radio-isotopes is conducted at the Agricultural and Medical Research Center near Karaj.[85] Amrollahi also stated that Iran intends to build a cyclotron there.[86] One report indicated that the cyclotron was ordered from the Dutch company Ion Beam Applications, while another mentioned Belgium as the supplier.[87] At any rate, it is clear that some nuclear research equipment was supplied to Iran by Belgium.[88]

Another nuclear research center was constructed in Isfahan.[89] The construction of a subcritical reactor there was noted in 1984 by the head of the Nuclear Technology Center at Isfahan, and in November 1991 Chinese officials confirmed the construction of a 27-kilowatt miniature neutron-source reactor.[90] The Chinese confirmation most likely refers to the same reactor mentioned in the 1984 report.

More recently, Iran is also said to have purchased a single "desktop-sized" calutron.[91] According to David Albright and Mark Hibbs, "a small working calutron could be useful in the development of larger machines."[92] Another report argued that Iran might "modify the [calutron] design and produce from its own resources more, and bigger, calutrons to turn out bomb fuel."[93] Yet Albright and Hibbs point out that "making large calutrons would require either a sophisticated infrastructure — which Iran apparently lacks — or an intensive procurement effort." Such procurement, however, has been made much more difficult following the exposure of Iraq's nuclear program: "Bonn and other western governments have warned their industries not to sell enrichment and other nuclear-related equipment to Iran."[94]

It remains unclear whether a nuclear warhead design center was being established in Qazvin.[95] Other sites suspected of being centers of nuclear weapons-related research are at Saghand and Mo'allem Kalayeh, a $300 million industrial park northwest of Teheran.[96] Karaj and Mo'allem Kalayeh are also suspected as possible sites for the secret development of gas centrifuges for uranium enrichment.[97] One report describes Iran as experimenting with highly sophisticated laser enrichment technology.[98]

Some of Iran's nuclear research focuses on the ability to detect uranium ore, and in 1993 Iranian officials have acknowledged the existence of a dozen different exploration projects.[99] Large reserves of uranium ore have been found in the Yazd province; in late November 1992, the uranium mines developed there merited a visit by Iran's President Hashemi Rafsanjani.[100] Iranian opposition sources claim that a secret nuclear research center is also located at Yazd.[101] A mid-1993 announcement noted that cooperation between the Iranian Atomic Energy Organization and the Amir Kabir Technological University has yielded the development of an X-ray tube using cobalt-57 as a radioactive source. The tube would reportedly be used for the accurate detection of uranium ore.[102]

ASSESSING IRAN'S NUCLEAR CAPABILITY

From February 7 to 12, 1992, a team of IAEA inspectors toured Iran for a "familiarization visit." They were hosted at the nuclear centers in Teheran, Bushehr, Isfahan, Karaj, Saghand, and Mo'allem Kalayeh. Following the visit, IAEA Deputy Director Jon Jennekens told a press conference: "We visited without any restrictions everything we had asked to see. All nuclear activities in Iran are solely for peaceful purposes." Similarly, IAEA spokesman David Kyd denied allegations that Iran has misled the inspectors: "None of our member states ever suggested that we were taken to a wrong location."[103] However, U.S. officials questioned the validity of the IAEA findings, noting that the trip was a "courtesy visit" — touring only sites arranged in advance with the government of Iran — rather than a short-notice "special inspection."[104]

From November 15 to 21, 1993, a second IAEA delegation visited nuclear facilities in Teheran, Isfahan, and Karaj. Due to "bad weather conditions," IAEA inspectors did not visit other Iranian nuclear facilities. The team had been provided with information regarding suspected nuclear facilities by western intelligence services before it left for Teheran. After the visit, an IAEA spokesman told *Nucleonics Week* that the delegation did not find any evidence that was inconsistent with Iran's statements that all its nuclear activities are for peaceful purposes — a more tentative statement than that issued after the 1992 IAEA visit.[105]

Clearly, all calculations that it would take some ten years for Iran to obtain nuclear weapons are based on assessments of the elaborate nuclear infrastructure it is establishing; however, Iran could shorten this period considerably if it were to obtain smuggled nuclear weapons, fissile material, or sensitive expertise from the former Soviet Union. Indeed, there has been a steady flow of rumors that Iran has already exploited the possibilities of nuclear leakage from the CIS. For example, Mas'ud Naragi, a senior Iranian nuclear scientist who defected to the United States, claimed that Iran had obtained at least two nuclear warheads.[106] A second report claimed that Iran purchased, with assistance from Russian criminals, three nuclear warheads from Kazakhastan, and that its agreement with the Russian "Mafia" includes the purchase of plutonium and enriched uranium.[107] These rumors were denied by Kazakhastan and the report was never corroborated by other independent sources.[108] In a U.S. public television report, "Iran and the Bomb," senior officials of the Alma Ata nuclear research center in Kazakhastan claimed that Iran had purchased "hundreds of tons of enriched uranium and beryllium."[109] However, most reports regarding the possible smuggling of enriched uranium from the CIS to Iran have been refuted.[110]

There have been many more unconfirmed reports of Iranian efforts to import nuclear expertise. One report is that Iran has signed an agreement with North Korea to cooperate in the development of nuclear weapons.[111] Russian intelligence and other sources have noted Iranian efforts to recruit nuclear scientists in the former Soviet Union.[112] A separate report indicated that Iran may have recruited six Russian nuclear experts, and that Turkmenistan agreed to provide

Iran with several heavy-water laboratories and uranium enrichment equipment.[113] In mid-1992, the Director General of Israel's Defense Ministry reported that Israel possesses credible intelligence indicating that some tens of nuclear scientists from the former Soviet Union were employed in Iran's nuclear program.[114] Spokesmen for the opposition movement, People's Mujahedeen of Iran, have made similar claims.[115]

Iraq

When it invaded Kuwait, Iraq was only a few years away from possessing atomic weapons.[116] It had assembled a complex nuclear establishment dedicated to producing fissile material and operational warheads at an estimated cost of $8–11 billion. Some 15,000 to 20,000 scientists and engineers took part in an enterprise that was exemplary not only for its technical ingenuity but also for its successful concealment. Iraq had misled the U.S., Israeli, and all other interested intelligence communities.[117]

Since the end of the Gulf War and the application of UN Security Council Resolutions 687 and 715, Iraq's nuclear threat has consisted of four factors: Saddam Hussein's determination and proven leadership in orchestrating a complex nuclear program; the fact that Iraq's expert manpower in the nuclear realm has remained intact; the possibility that not all of Iraq's nuclear facilities have been uncovered and destroyed by the UN inspectors; and finally, the possession of financial and other resources by Saddam's regime.

In January 1993, former IAEA Inspector David Kay assessed that it would not take Iraq more than two years to produce nuclear weapons if the UN inspection and monitoring regime were terminated.[118] Similarly, CIA Director Robert Gates warned that Iraq may be hiding enough equipment and supplies to produce "fissile material for a nuclear weapon in five to seven years" if UN inspections cease and sanctions are lifted.[119]

Iraq's massive effort to build nuclear weapons could not have been undertaken and implemented without the initiation, push, guidance, and leadership of Saddam Hussein, the country's sole leader. Indeed, given the unique combination of skill and determination that such success requires, the fact that Saddam Hussein remains in power is an important determinant of Iraq's potential to revive its nuclear program. This is so despite the mid-1995 defection and subsequent murder of a number of his principals, especially Hussein Kamal Hassan Majeed, a central figure in Iraq's weapons of mass destruction programs.

The second determinant of Iraq's ability to rebuild its nuclear capacity is that its expert workforce in the nuclear realm has remained largely intact.[120] Of the many thousands of scientists and engineers who took part in the effort, very few — if any — were hurt during the Gulf War, and Iraq continues to employ this labor pool in permitted research activities.[121] With time, this capability may deteriorate; experimental scientists and engineers cannot maintain their knowledge and expertise without periodic experimentation. Thus, if the UN continues to monitor the ban on Iraqi nuclear activities and prevents it from reconstructing its nuclear facilities, the level of expertise acquired by its nuclear scientists and engineers will gradually decay.

It should also be noted that of the two captains of Iraq's nuclear project, only one remains in Iraq: J'afar Diah J'afar, a graduate of Birmingham University and London University's Imperial College.[122] Hussein Sharastani escaped to Iran during the Gulf War.[123]

EFFORTS TO OBTAIN FISSILE MATERIAL

The sophisticated Iraqi nuclear project pursued a number of routes to obtaining fissile material. Iraq evaded IAEA safeguards with its two small functioning research reactors, the 5-megawatt Soviet-made IRT-5000 and the French-made Tamuz-2, and separated a small amount of plutonium — six grams — from its spent fuel.[124] While this amount was hardly the required quantity of fissile material, it indicates an effective exercise in the art of circumventing IAEA safeguards and the use of the $51 million "hot-cell" laboratories supplied by Italy. Indeed, Iraq has admitted that such separation took place in a facility visited twice yearly by IAEA inspectors.[125]

Lacking reactors that produce plutonium, Iraq sought to obtain fissile material through uranium enrichment. It pursued two avenues: gas centrifuge and electromagnetic isotope separation. The nuclear complex at Al-Tuwaytha was reportedly the center of research and development for both efforts.[126] Industrial-scale production through the electromagnetic separation was to be conducted at Tarmiya near Baghdad and at Al-Sharqat, near Mosul.[127] Components for the process were manufactured at Radwan, Al-Amir, Dijjila, and Daura.[128]

A second center for the development of gas centrifuge enrichment was Rashidiya, on the northern outskirts of Baghdad. Until the fifteenth IAEA inspection visit in November 1992, Iraq refused to admit that enrichment efforts were conducted there.[129] Industrial-scale enrichment by gas centrifuge was also planned at Al-Furat in Baghdad and at Al-Jesira, near Mosul.[130] All of the maraging steel that was acquired by Iraq in order to construct the gas centrifuges was located by IAEA inspectors, and destroyed in late 1992 by the fifteenth inspection team.[131]

A plant at Za'afaraniya had also been part of Iraq's program for electromagnetic isotope separation. A portion of the industrial complex was used to manufacture calutrons, and other machinery there was suitable for producing centrifuges for uranium enrichment.[132] The plant had been converted to civilian use after the war, but UN experts estimated that the equipment could quickly be put to use in a nuclear program again.[133] In January 1993, the United States bombed the plant.[134]

In addition to these facilities, Iraq has acquired considerable quantities of uranium for enrichment: 313 tons of natural uranium from Niger and Portugal, and 27 tons of UO-2 from Brazil.[135] There is also some suspicion that Portugal sold Iraq an additional quantity of natural uranium without reporting the transfer to the IAEA.[136]

By the mid-1980s, Iraq had begun to accumulate the products of its own uranium mining. The main Iraqi uranium mine was located at Akashat, and an exploratory mine was located near Najar. Uranium extraction and purification, producing "yellowcake," took place at Al-Qa'im.[137] One report indicated that some 164 tons of yellowcake were produced from 1984 to 1990. Production facilities for uranium tetrachloride were located at Al-Jesira.[138]

By the early 1980s, Iraq obtained from Italy 1763 kg of low-enriched uranium (enriched to 2.6 percent). The purchase of this material was reported to IAEA, and the material was subject to IAEA safeguards. One report indicated that had Iraq succeeded in enriching this stock of low-enriched uranium through the use of calutrons to a level of 90–93 percent without detection by IAEA inspectors, it would have been able to obtain nuclear weapons within two years.[139]

By the time Iraq invaded Kuwait, it also possessed some 40 kg of highly enriched uranium. Most of this material was used to fuel the small Soviet-made IRT-5000 and the French-made Tamuz-2 research reactors, but some was originally supplied by France to fuel the 70-megawatt Tamuz-1 (Osiraq) reactor that Israel destroyed in June 1981. Most but not all of this highly-enriched uranium fuel was irradiated. Only in mid-1993 were arrangements made to remove this material from Iraq. The $20 million bid for the transfer of the irradiated fuel was won by MINATOM, the Russian Ministry of Atomic Energy,[140] and in February 1994, the last 7 kg of enriched uranium was transported from Iraq to Russia.[141]

WEAPONIZATION PROGRAM

Iraq's weaponization program seems to have been centered in Al-Atheer and the adjacent Al-Hateen high-explosives test establishment, where several bomb designs — implosion and gun assemblies — were explored.[142] By 1990 Iraq reportedly had not yet overcome some important design problems — particularly in the development of a firing system for the device and a workable neutron initiator to start the chain reaction.[143] Facilities to produce lithium-6 also existed in Iraq, indicating efforts to construct an advanced implosion weapon.[144] All relevant structures at Al-Atheer were demolished under the supervision of IAEA inspectors in April, May, and June 1992.[145]

ASSESSING IRAQ'S NUCLEAR POTENTIAL

Iraq's ability to revive its nuclear program depends on whether all of its nuclear facilities have been uncovered and destroyed by the inspections conducted in the framework of UN Resolution 687. In the judgment of IAEA inspectors, the danger is, at worst, remote. For example, Bob Kelley, who participated in an IAEA inspection of Iraq in July 1993, said that its nuclear program had "been pounded into the ground by bombs, by inspections, and by disruptions."[146] Maurizio Zefferero, who led the fourteenth IAEA inspection, described Iraq's nuclear program as "harmless" and as having been reversed to "point zero."[147] He has also characterized the Iraqi program as "totally dormant," but cautioned: "If this is going to be true in the future, I don't know."[148]

Another IAEA inspector, Richard Hooper, was less certain. During an inspection in May 1993, Hooper said that Iraq could still have a few centrifuges to enrich uranium, but that its current capabilities to enrich uranium were dramatically reduced: "It just allows them to maintain part of their capability."[149] Rolf Ekeus, chairman of the UN Special Commission (UNSCOM), was also more careful: "Although his commission had destroyed Iraq's large nuclear weapons design installations, it may have missed some clandestine laboratories."[150] Ekeus has also said that "he cannot exclude the possibility that Iraq may still possess a secret plutonium factory, as well as clandestine stocks of enriched uranium explosive, or that it might be experimenting with previously undisclosed enrichment methods."[151]

In March 1993, there remained some evidence that Iraq was not yet in full compliance with UN Resolution 687. IAEA inspector Demetrius Perricos reported that his team found dual-use machines that Iraq should have declared because they could be used for nuclear weapons production.[152] In April 1993, IAEA inspectors were reported to have discovered another cache of nuclear-related equipment that had not been reported earlier by Iraq.[153] Members of the 12th IAEA inspection team had discovered 60 kg of natural uranium which the Iraqis had failed to disclose.[154]

The most important aspect of Iraq's noncompliance was its two-year refusal to provide IAEA inspectors with a full list of its nuclear suppliers.[155] This was the clearest indication of Saddam's continued interest in maintaining the option of rebuilding Iraq's nuclear program.[156] The complex and sophisticated procurement network established by Iraq was most important to its success, and any part of the network that might remain undisclosed could be revived in the future.[157] Thus, Perricos noted that obtaining the suppliers' list is "an absolutely essential part of breaking the backbone of the program."[158] In March 1993, following substantial UN pressure, Iraq finally agreed to submit the requested suppliers list; it continued to delay, and submitted the list only in September 1993.[159] Even then, Ekeus noted that there is no certainty that the list was complete.

Ekeus's suspicions were confirmed in mid-1995, when Hussein Kamal defected. In an attempt to minimize the damage that he could do by providing information, the Iraqi government released some half-million pages of documents related to its WMD programs. A preliminary examination of the documents has led Ekeus to testify that Iraq's programs were "larger and more advanced in every dimension than previously declared," and the IAEA to conclude that "Iraq has not disclosed all its nuclear activities and is withholding relevant information."[160]

Finally, any assessment of Iraq's future capacity to revive its nuclear ambitions must take into account the possibility that Iraq may gain access to some of the nuclear assets of the former Soviet Union. One report indicated the possibility that some 50 nuclear scientists from the CIS were recruited by Saddam Hussein.[161] Another report claimed that an Iraqi delegation traveled to the former Soviet Union in early 1992 for the purpose of purchasing nuclear waste.[162] These reports have not been confirmed.

Iraq continues to possess the most advanced nuclear workforce in the Arab world. Hundreds of its scientists and engineers have experience in the actual production of fissile material, even if only at laboratory scale. Iraq has developed an advanced weaponization program, so should it obtain fissile material smuggled from the CIS, it would be able to convert it rapidly into nuclear weapons. But barring this development, the key to Iraq's ability to obtain fissile material is its capacity to rebuild its nuclear facilities, particularly in the realm of uranium enrichment. As long as UN monitoring of Iraq continues, reconstruction will be very difficult. Thus, Iraq's potential to become a nuclear state rests almost entirely on the extent to which the UN Security Council adheres to the intrusive verification and monitoring system imposed on Iraq after the 1990–91 Gulf War.

Egypt

Egypt possesses a large cadre of nuclear scientists and engineers. However, its nuclear power program is dormant and only recently has Egypt reinvigorated its nuclear research efforts by purchasing a 22-megawatt reactor from Argentina. To date, there is no evidence of an Egyptian attempt to acquire fissile material nor are there any other indications that Cairo has launched a program to obtain nuclear weapons.

Egypt's nuclear activities were launched in the early 1950s; its Atomic Energy Commission was established in 1955. In 1957 the Center for Nuclear Research at Inshass was opened, conducting research regarding the use of isotopes in medicine, agriculture, and industry. By 1961 Egypt obtained a 2-megawatt nuclear reactor from the Soviet Union, and began training a cadre of nuclear physicists. For many years, the reactor remained the centerpiece of Egypt's nuclear program. By 1989, the aging reactor was renovated and upgraded, but was still operating at its original 2-megawatt capacity. [163]

Egypt launched a nuclear weapons program in 1960, but a variety of undetermined forces brought about the cancellation of the program in 1967. [164] Egypt has also failed to buy nuclear power reactors. Efforts to purchase a 130-megawatt power reactor from Britain in 1963, and a later attempt to construct a dual-purpose power and water desalination reactor, never came to fruition. Nevertheless, uranium mine explorations were conducted, some with Yugoslav assistance. In the early 1970s, Egypt showed interest in the use of nuclear explosives for a variety of civilian projects, including the possible use of atomic blasts in digging the Al-Quatarah Depression canal.

In 1974 U.S. President Richard Nixon offered to sell Egypt two 600-megawatt nuclear power reactors, and an agreement was initialed when President Anwar Sadat later visited Washington. But the actual purchase of the reactors was stalled for a number of years by prolonged negotiations over safeguards. In 1977, the Carter administration made the implementation of the sale conditional upon Egypt's ratification of the 1968 Nuclear Non-Proliferation Treaty. [165]

On February 16, 1981, Egypt's People's Assembly ratified the NPT. Subsequently, framework agreements were signed for the purchase of two 1,000 megawatt reactors from the United States, two power reactors from France, and two from the Federal Republic of Germany. [166] A separate framework agreement was signed with Canada for the supply of two 600-megawatt CANDU-type nuclear power reactors. [167] The Egyptian nuclear power program called for a total output of 8,000 megawatts by the year 2000. [168] The first two reactors were to be constructed at Al-Daba, 170 kilometers west of Alexandria. [169] The site was chosen after two locations on the shores of the Red Sea, at Al-Za'frana and Al-Ghardaka, were rejected on seismic grounds, and a third site — at Sidi Kharir — was rejected because it was too close to the urban center of Alexandria. [170]

Implementation of the agreements was delayed by lengthy negotiations regarding the financing of these purchases, a critical issue given Egypt's economic constraints. On August 5, 1983, the U.S.

Export-Import Bank (ExIm) announced that it would not provide financing for the project. The bank questioned Egypt's capacity to repay the required loans as well as the safety of the site at Al-Daba.[171]

In mid-December 1984, however, the U.S. government informed Egypt that ExIm would participate in financing the purchase of the two U.S.-made power reactors, and in late January 1985, the Reagan administration authorized a $250 million loan to Egypt for the construction of the first reactor.[172] The government of Belgium also authorized an additional sum of $180 million for the same purpose.[173] By mid-1985, French, West German, Italian, and U.S. firms competed for the first order of reactors from Egypt.[174] In September, German-Egyptian negotiations were held regarding the possible purchase of the two reactors offered by the Federal Republic of Germany.[175]

Meanwhile, Egypt increased its efforts to build a professional infrastructure in the nuclear realm. In late 1984, a course on nuclear energy was conducted in cooperation with the IAEA.[176] In early 1985, a conference brought to Cairo numerous Egyptian nuclear scientists and engineers who had emigrated to the United States and Europe.[177] Reportedly, some 500 Egyptian scientists had been trained in nuclear physics and engineering by 1986.[178] One mid-1986 report indicated that some 1,000 nuclear engineers and technicians were registered with the Egyptian authorities, but that about half of them were working abroad.[179] By 1987, Egyptian universities had reportedly granted some 700 Master's degrees and 450 doctorates to graduates in the nuclear sciences.[180] In addition, a large number of seminars and courses on nuclear safety methods were conducted.[181]

In 1984, a complete German-made nuclear fuel production laboratory was established at the Center for Nuclear Research at Inshass.[182] Egypt also conducted surveys searching for uranium and thorium, and discovered large quantities in the Nile Valley, the Sinai, and the Red Sea area.[183] The Egyptian government also signed agreements to purchase natural uranium from Australia, Niger, the United States, Canada, France, the FRG, and Britain.[184]

Following the 1986 nuclear catastrophe at Chernobyl, the momentum to develop nuclear power in Egypt came to a complete halt.[185] The accident led to widespread public demand that the environmental implications of nuclear power reactors be studied carefully. Particular concern was raised about Egypt's ability to deal with radioactive materials safely, its capacity to detect radiation leaks, and the lack of facilities for the storage of nuclear waste produced by power reactors.[186] In particular, officials of the Alexandria district, where the first two reactors were to be erected, expressed strong opposition on environmental grounds.[187]

In early 1987, Dr. Muhammad 'Abd al-Maksud al-Nadi, one of the founders of Egypt's nuclear program, surprisingly argued that since all nuclear power reactors available for purchase are somewhat defective, the plans to construct such reactors in Egypt should be delayed by about 10 years.[188] This criticism led President Husni Mubarak to order a reexamination of Egypt's plans to construct nuclear power reactors.[189] In late 1989, Egypt's Minister of Electricity and Energy said that in light of the experience at Chernobyl, the construction of the nuclear power stations would be delayed until all safety issues were completely resolved.[190]

Though the pro-nuclear forces in Egypt have made a strong case in favor of nuclear power, throughout the past thirty years they have complained of insufficient standing, resources, and government attention.[191] They argue that Egypt's nuclear program is chronically stalled by bureaucratic inertia, the absence of a national science policy, and the lack of a national plan that would allocate land and resources for nuclear energy. They also point to the lack of sufficient public understanding and support for the pursuit of nuclear power as well as excessive fears of Chernobyl-type nuclear disasters and related concerns that Egyptian labor would not be able to operate and maintain nuclear reactors safely.[192] By late 1989, the pro-nuclear lobby concluded that even in 2000, Egypt would still lack a single operating nuclear power reactor.[193]

Nevertheless, preparatory work for the construction of the first nuclear power reactor at Al-Daba, employing 50 engineers, technicians, and workers, began in early 1987.[194] In 1988, safety measures taken in preparation for the construction of the power station were approved by IAEA.[195] By that time, Egypt's preparations for launching its nuclear energy program were described as having been completed.[196] Land needed for the construction of the nuclear reactors was expropriated by government authorities in late 1989.[197] Uranium explorations, designed to assure that Egypt would enjoy an endogenous supply of nuclear fuel, produced positive results.[198] In a debate at the Shura Council in mid-1987, support for Egypt's continued nuclear program was expressed, and Egyptian nuclear scientists abroad were urged to return home to assist the country's nuclear efforts.[199] By then, initial progress had also been made toward the indigenous production of nuclear fuel rods and heavy water.[200]

However, in mid-1990, Dr. 'Ali al-Sayidi, chairman of Egypt's Nuclear Power Stations Authority, explained why Egypt's nuclear power program was delayed. He pointed out that Egypt's energy strategy, which had been tailored in the early 1980s, assumed very high economic growth rates; the fall in the price of oil, acts of terror that damaged tourism, and the declining income of Egyptians abroad had reduced economic growth and energy demand. Consequently, Egypt's electricity planning was revised and large projects such as nuclear power stations were avoided, shifting the focus of activities back to low-investment, low-risk conventional power stations operating on oil and gas.[201] In November 1992, Egypt's Minister of Electricity and Energy, Mahir Abazah, affirmed that Egypt was reconsidering its plans to build nuclear power stations because of their exorbitant costs, and was focusing instead on sources of energy within its means, primarily conventional power stations.[202]

Activity in nuclear research, however, has continued into the 1990s. By 1990, Egypt finally invited international tenders for the construction of a 20–22 megawatt research reactor to operate at Inshass alongside the aging 2-megawatt reactor.[203] Canada and Argentina competed for the contract, and by March 1992 funds were appropriated for the purchase.[204] In September 1992, Egypt signed an agreement with Argentina for the construction of the reactor within 60 months, but work began only a year later.[205] A new station for the treatment of nuclear waste was also to be inaugurated at Inshass.[206]

While Egypt has made considerable efforts to construct an infrastructure in the nuclear realm and has recently taken measures to revamp its nuclear research programs, there are no signs that its efforts to develop a nuclear power program will soon bear fruit. It is unlikely that Egypt will possess a power reactor or any other source of significant amounts of plutonium by 2005. Nor is there any evidence that Egypt is attempting to enrich uranium or to obtain fissile material by other means. Its nuclear facilities are subject to full-scope IAEA safeguards and there are no indications that Egypt has violated any of the obligations it has undertaken as a signatory of the NPT.

Libya

Libya formed an Atomic Energy Commission in 1973 under the direct supervision of Mu'ammar Qadhafi. Between 1973 and 1976, it signed nuclear cooperation agreements with France, the FRG, Argentina, and Sweden. In 1974 it also reportedly signed an agreement with a West German firm for the construction of a heavy-water production plant.[207] Libya sent hundreds of its most talented youth to study nuclear physics and engineering abroad, and conducted research and teaching programs in this field at the faculty of Nuclear and Electronic Engineering of the Al-Fateh University.[208]

All of Libya's efforts to import a military nuclear capability during the 1970s failed. It did not succeed in obtaining sensitive nuclear technology despite providing financial assistance to Pakistan's nuclear program, nor did it obtain access to Indian nuclear technology in exchange for supplying inexpensive oil or for paying India's external debt.[209] In 1992, India's Ambassador in Washington revealed that in the 1970s, his country declined a Libyan offer of $15 billion in exchange for nuclear technology.[210] In the late 1970s, following the launching of the Israel-Egypt peace process, Qadhafi is said to have approached the Soviet Union with the request that it provide Libya with nuclear weapons. Libya's leader reportedly justified the request by the need to create strategic parity with Israel following Egypt's departure from the Arab war coalition; Moscow rejected his request.[211] Later, he approached China with a similar suggestion and Beijing's response was equally negative.[212]

Libya has also attempted to obtain the Soviet Union's assistance in constructing an infrastructure in the nuclear realm. In 1975, the Soviet Union agreed to supply Libya with a 10-megawatt nuclear research reactor as part of a new nuclear physics research center at Tajura. The Tajura Nuclear Research Center was reportedly completed in 1982 and was maintained by the Soviets until at least 1985.[213] The research center was placed under strict Soviet supervision and IAEA safeguards.[214]

In the mid-1970s, France opted out of an agreement to supply Libya with a 600-megawatt nuclear power reactor. In December 1976,

Libya and the Soviet Union signed a framework agreement for the supply of a 440-megawatt Loviisa-type dual purpose nuclear reactor for power and water desalination, but the Soviet Union later refused to supply the promised reactor.[215] The reactor complex would have cost nearly $4 billion; since the Soviet Union was unsure that Libya would be able to meet its payments, the Soviet Union reportedly asked that another partner to the project be found. To meet this requirement, in 1984 Libya attempted to involve the Belgian firm Belgonucleaire.[216] However, the United States urged Brussels to reject the deal and Israel also made its displeasure with the proposed contract known.[217] Belgium seems to have yielded to these concerns.[218] Libyan-Soviet negotiations continued in late 1984, focusing on the proposed construction of the first of two 440-megawatt units.[219] However, the Soviets refrained from supplying the reactor to Libya.[220] In late 1985, East German nuclear engineers visited Libya to examine possible participation in the project.[221] The outcome of the visit is not known but there is no evidence that the project has materialized.

In mid-1985, Libya's Atomic Energy Secretary, 'Abd al-Majid Qu'ud, said that enough uranium has been discovered in the country to meet the requirements of Libya's nuclear program. He reported that uranium was found in the western desert, in the area south of Ghadamis, in the Ghat region, and near the village of Al 'Uwaynat Al Gharbiyah.[222] Other reports indicated that Libya also found uranium in areas it annexed from Chad and that it obtained stocks of uranium from Niger.[223]

In January 1992, Libya attempted to purchase U.S.-made dual-use technologies with applications for nuclear bomb-making. The delivery of the equipment was intercepted at Frankfurt airport by German authorities.[224] Following the breakup of the Soviet Union, Libya reportedly offered large sums of money in an effort to recruit CIS nuclear scientists, but there is no evidence that any significant brain drain from Russia to Libya has occurred.[225] A September 1992 report that China was in the process of selling a nuclear reactor to Libya also remains unconfirmed.[226] A much more questionable report indicated that China might have supplied a quantity of weapons-grade enriched uranium to Libya.[227]

In February 1992, Libya invited IAEA officials to conduct inspections in order "to prove that Libya was not engaged in weapons research."[228] The results of the inspection cannot be ascertained from open sources, but it would not be surprising if the IAEA team found no evidence of a military nuclear program.

Libya has been characterized as having embarked on a "slow-moving nuclear program."[229] One source described the state of Libya's efforts as follows: "Although Libya is a signatory of the NPT, reportedly it has attempted to purchase nuclear weapons and the equipment needed to develop them. However, despite its past nuclear trade ties with a number of countries, including Argentina, Belgium, Brazil, India, Pakistan, and the former Soviet Union, there is no publicly available evidence to indicate that Libya has made any headway toward a nuclear weapons capability."[230]

Algeria

In early 1992, French Intelligence officials estimated that Algeria might be able to manufacture nuclear weapons within three to five years.[231] Later, Brig. General Doron Tamir, commander of the IDF's Intelligence Corps, estimated that Algeria does not lag far behind Iran in its development of a nuclear capability.[232] In contrast, François Heisbourg, a leading French defense expert and a past director of the International Institute for Strategic Studies in London, has argued that Algeria's nuclear capability was extremely limited. He noted that its program was being monitored and that it was not likely that a country so close to Europe would be able to develop nuclear weapons clandestinely.[233]

The existence of Essalam — an emerging Algerian nuclear complex near 'Ain Oussersa, some 125 km south of Algiers — first became known in April 1991. In January 1992, CIA Director Robert Gates estimated that the construction of the reactor was nearly complete.[234] Following much media attention, China identified itself as the reactor's manufacturer and stated that the contract for its sale was signed in early 1983. Construction of the reactor reportedly began in 1986.[235] The U.S. intelligence community is said to have discovered the pending reactor transfer in 1988 and had obtained a copy of the sale contract.[236] Algeria and China reported that the capacity of the heavy-water reactor was 15 megawatts and that it was being subjected to IAEA safeguards, although Algeria had not signed the NPT.[237] Concern about the reactor centered on its estimated capacity to produce 2–4 kg of plutonium annually, and the fact that Algeria did everything possible to keep the project secret.[238]

In February 1992, Algeria signed a safeguards agreement with the IAEA, permitting inspections of the reactor and its nuclear fuel and heavy water, and also indicated its intention to sign the NPT.[239] Two IAEA visits to the complex were subsequently carried out.[240] According to an IAEA official, the inspections did not yield information that contradicted Algeria's claims regarding the reactor's capacity and purpose.[241]

In the late 1980s, Algeria awarded a contract to Argentina to build a second nuclear research complex that includes a 1-megawatt natural uranium reactor. Construction of the reactor began in 1987, and it was placed under IAEA safeguards. When the reactor was inaugurated in December 1993, Algeria's Foreign Minister Salah Dembri renewed his government's pledge to sign the NPT.[242] Earlier, Algeria had also negotiated with Argentina the possible purchase of a 10–25 megawatt research reactor.[243]

By early 1992, there were reports that nuclear scientists from Iraq and the former Soviet Union were working in Algeria, and that Iraq may have transferred to Algeria some 10 tons of natural uranium for safekeeping.[244] These reports are unconfirmed and were denied by Algeria's prime minister and Foreign Ministry.[245] Algeria's activities manifest a clear interest in developing an advanced nuclear research capability. Its initial efforts to conceal these activities provided reason for concern that its intentions were not entirely benign. Particularly worrisome was the possibility that Algeria's government might be toppled and that its nuclear facilities would fall into the hands of an Islamist-fundamentalist regime. Indeed, the odds that this might occur may have led the Algerian government to slow its nuclear efforts in 1994. These projects may also have suffered from the growing violence against foreigners by Islamists, leading to the departure of most non-Algerian nationals.

By early 1995, Algeria signed the NPT and subjected its nuclear facilities to full-scope IAEA safeguards.[246] While this development renders Algeria's nuclear efforts more benign, the future direction of its nuclear program seems increasingly tied to the stability of its political regime.

Syria

Syria's nuclear program was launched late and kept dormant for almost twenty years. Only in 1976 was an Atomic Energy Commission established in Damascus. Feasibility studies for Syrian acquisition of nuclear power reactors were contracted, and negotiations with France over the possible transfer of French nuclear technology to Syria were conducted. By early 1980, discussions were held regarding the possible launching of a nuclear power program comprising six 600-megawatt reactors, and Syria's Minister of Electricity, Oman Yussuf, promised that the first reactor would be completed by 1991.[247]

In 1983 and 1984, there were a number of indications that the Soviet Union had agreed to assist Syria in constructing a nuclear power reactor.[248] In 1985, Syria reportedly expressed interest in purchasing a reactor from France.[249] By mid-1991, Syria also expressed interest in purchasing a 5-megawatt research reactor from India.[250] To date, none of these projects has materialized.[251]

In 1990, Syria's nuclear authorities obtained an offer to purchase a 10-megawatt research reactor from an Argentine firm, but the government of Argentina blocked the sale, possibly under U.S. pressure. The reactor was to be fueled by uranium enriched to only 20 percent, far lower than weapons-grade. In late 1994, Syria demanded that the reactor be supplied, and threatened to sue the Argentine firm for compensations.[252]

Only in late 1991 did Syria make a first small step toward establishing a nuclear infrastructure: it purchased a 30-kilowatt neutron source mini-reactor from China. Such sub-critical reactors are commonly used for the production of isotopes and the analysis of neutron behavior, and they have no military applications.[253] After the Chinese legislature authorized its government to sign the NPT and after Syria signed a safeguards agreement with the IAEA, the agency approved the sale.[254]

In mid-1995 there were indications that Syria's plans to purchase a nuclear reactor from Argentina might be revived. The reactor involved was said to be of small scale, "for medical research purposes." But Argentine officials quickly ruled out the possibility that such a sale would take place before peace and stability in the Middle East are achieved.[255]

Thus, Syria's nuclear program remains embryonic and limited in scope. There are no indications that Syria is attempting to construct facilities to allow it to produce fissile material. Hence, it does not seem that Syria should be a serious focus of proliferation concerns.

Conclusions

Concern about further nuclear proliferation in the Middle East currently focuses on Iran and Iraq. Despite its deteriorating economy, Iran seems to enjoy the financial resources and the political motivation and determination required for a crash nuclear program. There is much evidence that it has launched a multi-level effort to construct an advanced nuclear infrastructure. The various nuclear facilities it is purchasing and the magnitude of the nuclear research conducted indicate a considerable financial commitment. Although Iran's energy requirements are growing, its considerable oil reserves make it unlikely that its nuclear program is solely energy-related. Although IAEA inspections of declared and suspected Iranian nuclear facilities have not yielded evidence of a military program, the dimensions of Iran's nuclear activities indicate a strong interest in obtaining a nuclear potential. However, it remains unclear how quickly Iran could translate its expanding nuclear infrastructure to a weapons capability.

Similarly, it is uncertain whether, when, and how rapidly Iraq could reconstruct its nuclear program. All its known nuclear facilities have been destroyed, and most of its acquisition channels have become inoperative. However, Iraq's motivation to rebuild its nuclear potential seems to have remained intact, as has the professional expertise it has developed in the nuclear realm. Clearly, the most important factor determining the future of Iraq's nuclear program is the extent to which the UN Security Council will continue to enforce the post–Gulf War sanctions, inspections, and monitoring regime. As long as UN sanctions continue to deny Iraq the funds for and access to sources of sensitive nuclear material and technology, and as long as the UNSCOM/IAEA monitoring regime continues to be applied — backed by U.S. determination to act forcefully in case of Iraqi violations or efforts to circumvent the regime — Iraq's ability to rebuild its nuclear program will remain limited.

It is far easier to evaluate the nuclear potential of Egypt and Israel.

By all non-Israeli accounts, Israel already possesses a robust nuclear capability and the means to deliver its weapons. Egypt is currently expanding its impressive scientific infrastructure by purchasing a 22-megawatt nuclear research reactor from Argentina. However, its nuclear power program remains dormant, largely due to financial and environmental considerations. More important, there are no signs that Egypt has altered its strategic decision to refrain from developing a military nuclear capability; that is, there is no evidence that it has launched plutonium reprocessing or uranium enrichment programs.

The nuclear efforts of Libya, Syria, and Algeria remain embryonic. During the past few years, all three countries have been engaged in developing nuclear scientific and engineering infrastructure, but the reactors they have purchased are too small and their current infrastructures are too thin to create immediate proliferation concerns. In addition, IAEA safeguards are applied to all reactors purchased by these countries.

Syria's nuclear program will remain benign as long as it remains within its present parameters, a likely scenario given Syria's financial and strategic constraints. The long-term threats posed by the Algerian and Libyan nuclear programs are less certain, but at present seem limited. The efficacy of the safeguards applied to Libya's 10-megawatt reactor cannot be ascertained with precision but Libya is not likely to gain much by circumventing these safeguards: there is no evidence that it possesses or is developing the capacity to reprocess spent fuel. Algeria's two nuclear reactors are also safeguarded, and there is no open-source evidence that it is developing plutonium-reprocessing or uranium-enrichment programs. But the efforts it has made to hide its nuclear activities breed alarm and suspicion that Algeria may be seeking to develop a nuclear device.

While Middle East states show considerable interest in developing nuclear infrastructures, and while Iraq and Iran are eager to obtain nuclear weapons, none of the region's Arab or Muslim states are close to producing nuclear arms indigenously. Thus, unless fissile material is soon smuggled into the Middle East, there is still time to reverse the pursuit of nuclear arms in the region; however, given the current poor security of weapons-grade plutonium and enriched uranium in the former Soviet Union, it is impossible to rule out scenarios of "instant proliferation" in Iran and Iraq. Since efforts to avoid nuclear anarchy in the CIS may fail, and since the effectiveness of export controls and other efforts to prevent Iraq and Iran from obtaining nuclear arms is not assured, the possible adoption of regional arms control measures that might help avert such proliferation should at least be explored.

NOTES

1. As is customary, the Israeli censor reviewed the draft manuscript of this book to insure that its contents do not compromise Israel's national security; this review should not be construed as concurrence with the text.

2. See Yehiel Limor, "At least four Russian atomic scientists working in Libya," *Ma'ariv*, January 30, 1992; and "German newspaper reports: 'Saddam recruited 50 nuclear scientists from the former Soviet Union'," *Ha'aretz*, June 8, 1992. But see "Russian Nuclear Official Says Nuclear Scientists Remain Under Control," *International Herald Tribune*, February 1–2, 1992.

3. Most media reports of the smuggling of nuclear material from Russia immediately after the deterioration of the Soviet Union have been proven either unreliable or have involved materials that were not weapons-grade. For a summary of these reports, see Miriam Fuchs, "First indications of the existence of a black market for weapons-grade materials in Russia," *Davar*, November 22, 1991. See also Stephen M. Meyer, "The Post-Soviet Nuclear Menace Is Being Hyped," *International Herald Tribune*, December 16, 1991; Yehiel Limor, "Russian uranium confiscated in Switzerland; Suspicion: Its destination was an Arab country," *Ma'ariv*, December 31, 1991; "German Police Seize Smuggled Uranium," *International Herald Tribune*, October 17–18, 1992; "Bonn Says Seized Uranium Wasn't Suitable for Bombs," *International Herald Tribune*, October 20, 1992; Steve Coll, "European Regulators Alarmed by Rise in Nuclear Smuggling," *International Herald Tribune*, November 30, 1992; and "16 Held in Ukraine Plutonium Ring," *International Herald Tribune*, December 6, 1992.

4. William J. Broad, "Estimate Rises on Russian Uranium," *International Herald Tribune*, September 12–13, 1992.

5. "Czechs Seize Uranium Believed from Russia," *Washington Post*, December 20, 1994.

6. For an excellent account and assessment of the 1994 reports, see *Trust and Verify*, No. 50 (September 1994), p. 1. For more detailed reports see R. Jeffrey Smith and Steve Vogel, "European Authorities Seek a Rumored Plutonium Cache," *International Herald Tribune*, July 26, 1994; Craig R. Whitney, "Germans Find Clues To Big Nuclear Plot," *International Herald Tribune*, August 16, 1994; Craig R. Whitney, "Fear of 'Nuclear Mafia' Widens in Germany," *International Herald Tribune*, August 17, 1994; Yehudit Vinkler, "Fourth attempt to smuggle plutonium is aborted in Bremen, north Germany," *Ha'aretz*, August 17, 1994; Steve Coll, "Tests of Matter Seized in May Point to Russia," *International Herald Tribune*, August 19, 1994; and "Bonn Wants Held To Stop Plutonium," *International Herald Tribune*, August 19, 1994.

7. Yehudit Vinkler, "Russian government officials involved in smuggling pure plutonium from Russia to Germany," *Ha'aretz*, July 18, 1994.

8. See Steve Vogel, "Illicit Nuclear Cache Called a 'Harbinger'," *International Herald Tribune*, July 21, 1994. However, the involvement of Russian government officials in such smuggling, when coupled with the very small "sample" quantities involved, raises the possibility that there are no real leaks in the Russian nuclear complex and that the seized quantities were planted by Russian intelligence agents to keep Western governments continuously alarmed about the safety of Russian nuclear facilities, possibly to encourage the U.S. and Western European governments to continue to provide financial support to Russia as part of their "counter-proliferation" policies.

9. See "Nuclear Thefts Do Happen, Russian Says," *International Herald Tribune*, August 20–21, 1994; and "Weak Points Exist in Nuclear Security, Russians Concede," *International Herald Tribune*, August 24, 1994. Other Russians, notably Serge Stepashin, chief of Russia's Federal Counterintelligence Service, doubted that Russia's nuclear complex was vulnerable to "terrorists and criminal groups." See Lee Hockstader, "Moscow Insists Criminals Can't Get at Nuclear Weapons," *International Herald Tribune*, July 1, 1994.

10. See David E. Sanger, "Fears About Allies' Atom Programs," *International Herald Tribune*, August 22, 1994.

11. "Pakistan Has Bomb, Ex-Leader Declares," *International Herald Tribune*, August 24, 1994.

12. "Israel's nuclear arsenal: 50–200 warheads," *Ma'ariv*, January 11, 1993 (based on a *New York Times* report).

13. See "Russian Federation: Foreign Intelligence Service Report — A New Challenge After the Cold War: Proliferation of Mass Destruction Weapons," Joint Publications Research Service (JPRS), Report JPRS-TND-93-007, March 5, 1993, p. 25. See also "Russia Says Israel Hides a Large Nuclear Stock," *International Herald Tribune*, February 25, 1993; and Alex Doron, *Deadly weapons*, *Ma'ariv*, June 29, 1993. This assessment was repeated in a Russian intelligence April 1995 report. See Alut Ben, "The Russian intelligence service assesses: Israel possesses 100–200 nuclear warheads," *Ha'aretz*, April 19, 1995.

14. James Leonard, Jan Prawitz, and Benjamin Sanders, *Study on Effective and Verifiable Measures Which Would Facilitate the Establishment of a Nuclear-Weapon-Free Zone in the Middle East*, Report of the UN Secretary General, October 1990, Para. 115.

15. For example, a debate in early 1993 regarding possible negative effects of the Dimona reactor on its immediate environment led to the first publicized visit to the reactor by the Minister of Environment Affairs, Yossi Sarid. See "Sarid: Dimona reactor one of safest in the world," *Jerusalem Post*, January 27, 1994.

16. Ran Dagoni, "Already in 1968 the U.S. concluded that Israel had become a nuclear state," *Ma'ariv*, December 16, 1986 (citing the *Boston Globe*).

17. David K. Shipler, "A-Arms Capacity of Israelis: Topic Rich With Speculations," *New York Times*, October 29, 1986.

18. "NRDC says Jericho IRBM is nuclear, chemical armed," *Jane's Defense Weekly*, November 25, 1989; Yoav Karny, "An official American document states for the first time: nuclear and chemical warheads for the Jericho-1 missile," *Ha'aretz*, November 15, 1989.

19. Rami Tal, "Israel possesses at least 60 nuclear bombs," *Yediot Ahronot*, June 21, 1991. In a television interview in early 1993, former CIA Director Robert Gates said he believes that Israel has nuclear weapons; see Ori Nir, "Former CIA director: Israel has nuclear weapons," *Ha'aretz*, March 28, 1993.

20. J. Finkelstone, "Israel and Iran agreed: Oil in exchange for nuclear missiles," *Ma'ariv*, February 2, 1986; and Ran Dagoni, "Israel and Iran cooperated in producing nuclear missiles," *Ma'ariv*, April 2, 1986 (citing the *New York Times*).

21. A British publication located wing 2 of Israel's air force, comprising three squadrons of Jericho missiles (150, 199, and 248), in the Micha fields. See Alex Fishman, "All the bases, all the squadrons, all the airfields," *Yediot Aharonot*, July 30, 1996; and Yossi Melman and Aluf Ben, "Jane's publication exposes the air force structure, including bases, squadrons and aircraft," *Ha'aretz*, July 31, 1996.

22. Ben, "The secrecy belt," *Ha'aretz*, August 1, 1996.

23. "Inside Dimona, Israel's nuclear bomb factory," *Sunday Times* (London), October 5, 1986.

24. Ibid.; and Vernon A. Guidry, Jr., "Press reports say Israel has vast nuclear arsenal," *Baltimore Sun*, November 4, 1986.

25. Guidry, "Press reports."

26. Aluf Ben, "Annual production of plutonium at Dimona: 40 kg," *Ha'aretz*, September 29, 1993 (based on a *Sunday Times* report); see also *The Defense Monitor*, Vol. 21, No. 3, 1992, p. 3.

27. "Inside Dimona."

28. Guidry, "Press reports." See also Perrin's interview in "France admits it gave Israel A-bomb," *Sunday Times*, October 12, 1986; and Yohanan Lahav, "France helped Israel develop a nuclear bomb during the 1950s," *Yediot Ahronot*, October 12, 1986.

29. Ran Dagoni, "Israel and South Africa launched nuclear missile," *Ma'ariv*, October 26, 1989; Dan Sagir, "Israel supplied South Africa with aircraft and missile boats in exchange for uranium," *Ha'aretz*, October 27, 1989; and Yoav Karny, "Anger in U.S. following reports that Israel and South Africa are developing nuclear missile," *Ha'aretz*, October 27, 1989. Former CIA Director Robert Gates said there is reason to doubt South Africa's claims that Israel was not involved in its nuclear program; see Ori Nir, "Former CIA director: Israel has nuclear weapons," *Ha'aretz*, March 28, 1993. See also Arik Bachar, "South Africa emerges out of the closet," *Ma'ariv*, March 28, 1993; and Fred Bridgland, "Space programme grounded in S. African scorched earth," *Sunday Telegraph* (London), April 4, 1993.

30. Shaul Zadka, "Israel supplied South Africa with missile boats in exchange for uranium," *Ha'aretz*, July 7, 1986 (based on a British television report).

31. Amos Ben David, "Rabin: There is not a grain of truth in the reports about nuclear cooperation with South Africa," *Ha'aretz*, October 31, 1989.

32. A recent report argued that "Israel is believed to have developed a boosted weapon with some characteristics of a hydrogen bomb. A fully-fledged H-bomb could not be produced without testing, so Israel appears to have used a simplified design and relied on computer modelling to ensure that it would work." Nigel Hawkes, "Asia leads quickening race for nuclear status," *Times* (London), March 27, 1993.

33. Aluf Ben, "Pretoria emerging from the closet," *Ha'aretz*, October 22, 1993.

34. *Novoye Vremya*, December 20, 1985. The London *Sunday Times* has referred to this operation as the Plumbat Affair. "Inside Dimona," *Sunday Times* (London).

35. Zvi Bar'el, "The seller of krytrons to Israel who escaped in August was caught and arrested in Britain," *Ha'aretz*, March 26, 1986.

36. Guidry, "Press reports."

37. Eliahu Zehavi, "A Swedish company sold equipment for testing nuclear weapons to Israel and Pakistan," *Ha'aretz*, May 7, 1986.

38. "Norway sold heavy water to Israel," *Jerusalem Post*, October 9, 1986, based on a report by Sverre Lodgaard, a Norwegian researcher. The sale was confirmed in 1989 by Norway. See Simon Haidon, "Norway: we may ask to inspect the heavy water we sold to Israel," *Ma'ariv*, October 9, 1986. See also Charles R. Babcock, "Norway Eyes Israel's Use of Nuclear Ingredient," *Washington Post*, November 10, 1986; and Michael R. Gordon, "Norway Questions Israeli Use of Nuclear Material," *New York Times*, February 17, 1987.

39. "Agreement: Norway will supervise the remaining heavy water supplied to Israel," *Ha'aretz*, June 20, 1988; "Israel and Norway updated the heavy water agreement," *Ma'ariv*, June 10, 1988; and "Norway and Israel Resolve Dispute Over Heavy Water," *International Herald Tribune*, June 11–12, 1988.

40. See John J. Fialka, "Norway Rejects a Proposed Agreement With Israel on Nuclear Plant Coolant," *Wall Street Journal*, October 11, 1988; "Norway may want its heavy water back," *Jerusalem Post*, January 26, 1989; "Norway: Israel agreed to renew discussion of the uses of heavy water," *Ha'aretz*, October 2, 1989; and Akiva Eldar, "Effort to reach agreement with Norway on heavy water," *Ha'aretz*, January 9, 1990.

41. Akiva Eldar, "Israel will return 10 tons of heavy water to Norway," *Ha'aretz*, April 27, 1990; "Israel to Send Heavy Water to Oslo," *International Herald Tribune*, April 28–29, 1990.

42. Eliahu Zehavi, "Israel returned 10.5 tons of heavy water to Norway," *Ha'aretz*, December 4, 1991; and "Israel returned the heavy water it received 32 years ago to Norway," *Ma'ariv*, December 4, 1991.

43. Eliahu Zehavi, "New complication: Romania sold Israel unused heavy water purchased from Norway," *Ha'aretz*, April 24, 1988; Eli Cohen, "20 tons of heavy water reached Israel during the 1960s through France," *Davar*, May 23, 1988; Eliahu Zehavi, "Suspicion that Romania sold Norwegian heavy water to Israel," *Ha'aretz*, May 7, 1991.

44. Yoav Toker, "France will re-evaluate the sale of nuclear reactors to Israel," *Ha'aretz*, April 4, 1986; and Yehoshua Bitzur, "France suspended the negotiations for the sale of a nuclear reactor to Israel," *Ma'ariv*, May 29, 1986.

45. The purchase of such reactors was opposed on economic grounds by the Israeli government's General Accounting Office. See Yehuda Sharoni, "Knesset committees will consider the purchase of nuclear reactors," *Ha'aretz*, May 20, 1986; and Yair Tsaban, "Nuclearization is wasteful and dangerous," *Ha'aretz*, May 22, 1986.

46. See Joel Ullom, "Enriched Uranium versus Plutonium: Proliferant Preferences in the Choice of Fissile Material," *Nonproliferation Review*, Vol. 2, No. 1 (Fall 1994), p. 5.

47. See testimony by CIA Director Robert M. Gates in March 1992, reported in R. Jeffrey Smith, "Iran Rearms in Bid For Power in Gulf," *International Herald Tribune*, March 28–29, 1992; and Ori Nir, "Despite denials, a continued Iranian nuclear effort," *Ha'aretz*, December 1, 1992. Gates repeated this assessment in mid-December 1992; see George Lardner, Jr., and R. Jeffrey Smith, "Gates Warns of Iraqi Nuclear Aspirations," *Washington Post*, December 16, 1992. His assessment was adopted in early 1993 by the CIA's new director, James Woolsey. In his testimony of February 24, 1993, Woolsey noted that Iran's nuclear program is at an early stage, but that some Iranian purchases in connection with this program are inconsistent with purely civilian purposes; see Ori Nir, "Iran can develop nuclear weapons endogenously within 8–10 years," *Ha'aretz*, February 25, 1993. A somewhat more reserved Israeli estimate is provided by the IDF's Director of Military Intelligence, Maj. General Uri Saguy; see Eitan Rabin, "Worries in the intelligence," *Ha'aretz*, June 17, 1992; and Aharon Klein and Aharon Barnea, "Iran substituting Iraq and developing a nuclear capability," *Hadashot*, June 9, 1992. See also an earlier interview with Saguy in *Yediot Ahronot*, April 17, 1992.

48. At that time, Secretary Perry added that Iran was still "many, many years" from developing an atomic bomb. See Clyde Haberman, "U.S. and Israel See Iranians 'Many Years' from A-Bomb," *New York Times*, January 10, 1995; Perry's statement was intended to correct earlier reports indicating that the United States and Israel believed that Iran was much closer to obtaining nuclear weapons than had been thought, and that it might be able to possess such weapons within five years. See Chris Hedges, "Iran May Be Able to Build an Atomic Bomb in 5 Years, U.S. and Israeli Officials Fear," *New York Times*, January 5, 1995.

49. Assessments in 1984 that Iran would obtain a nuclear bomb production capability within two years seem to have been extremely premature. For reports on one assessment provided by *Jane's Defense Weekly* see "Iran Said to Near A-Bomb Production," *International Herald Tribune*, April 25, 1984; and "Iran seen developing atom bomb," *Washington Times*, April 25, 1984. See also "Khomeyni atomic bomb entering final production stages with German assistance," *Ma'ariv*, April 25, 1984. U.S. government sources and European experts rejected the report as implausible; see "American administration: Iran far from developing atomic bomb," *Yediot Ahronot*, April 26, 1984; Warren Getler, "Iran Is Unlikely to Have Atom Bomb in 2 Years, Nuclear Experts Assert," *International Herald Tribune*, May 7, 1984; and "Iran: The Nuclear Weapon Story," *Defense & Foreign Affairs Daily*, Vol. 13, No. 84 (May 1, 1984).

50. By 1984, Iran had reportedly concluded an agreement with Kraftwerk Union to complete the Bushehr nuclear power plant. The head of the plants, Mr. Mon'em, said that the two plants were 50 percent and 80 percent complete. See Iran News Agency (IRNA), January 28, 1984 (BBC, February 7, 1984). Kraftwerk Union refused to resume work on the reactors while the Iraq-Iran War continued. "West German manufacturer: The reactor in Iran will not be completed as long as the war continues," *Ha'aretz*, April 24, 1984. For a statement by Mr. Amrollahi, Iran's vice president and head of its Atomic Energy Organization, regarding efforts to persuade the Germans to complete the construction of the reactors, see Voice of the Islamic Republic of Iran, November 6, 1991; IRNA in English, November 6, 1991 (BBC, ME/1224, November 8, 1991 p. A/12; FBIS-NES-91-215, November 6, 1991, p. 70; FBIS-NES-91-216, November 7, 1991, p. 43); "Iran Puts Emphasis on Atomic Power," *International Herald Tribune*, August 3, 1992.

51. Getler, "Iran Is Unlikely." See also "Iranian Nuclear Site Is Attacked by the Iraqis," *New York Times*, February 14, 1985; "Iraq bombed nuclear power station in Iran," *Ma'ariv*, February 14, 1985; and "The Islamic Bomb: Iranian Nuclear Aspirations," Royal United Services Institute (RUSI), *Newsbrief*, Vol. 12, No. 9 (September 1992), p. 69.

52. Jalil Roshandel and Sa'ideh Lotfian, "Horizontal Nuclear Proliferation: Is Iran a Nuclear Capable State?" *Teheran Times*, April 10, 1993 (FBIS-NES-93-075, April 21, 1993, p. 44).

53. "Rafsanjani: Iran will complete the nuclear center at Bushehr," *Davar*, July 8, 1991.

54. Teheran IRNA in English, citing *Kayhan International* (an Iranian English-language newspaper), November 3, 1991 (FBIS-NES-91-214, November 5, 1991, p. 76).

55. Berlin *Allgemeiner Deutcher Nachrichtendienst* (in German), December 3, 1991, citing the Dusseldorf-based newspaper *Handelblatt* (FBIS-NES-91-232, December 3, 1991, p. 41). In 1991, the Chief of the German intelligence bureau, Konrad Prezens, said: "If Iran continues its current military activity, it will attain the capability of making its own nuclear reactor by the year 2000." This led to a strong attack on Germany in Iran's media. See Teheran ABRAR in Persian, December 5, 1991 (FBIS-NES-91-241, December 16, 1991, p. 87). See also Guy Bechor, "Brazilian government conducting negotiations for the sale of a nuclear reactor to Iran," *Ha'aretz*, December 24, 1991.

56. See "Iran will purchase nuclear reactors from a Czech firm," *Ha'aretz*, December 8, 1993; and "Rabin to the Czechs: Do not sell nuclear technology to Iran," *Ma'ariv*, December 14, 1993.

57. "Iran, Russia Agree on $800 Million Nuclear Plant Deal," *Washington Post*, January 9, 1995; and "Russia-Iran Nuclear Cooperation Confirmed," *Nuclear Proliferation News*, No. 32 (September 8, 1995), p. 19.

58. Cited by the Kuwaiti daily newspaper *Al-Watan*. See *Mideast Mirror*, January 10, 1995, p. 9.

59. See "Russia-Iran Nuclear Cooperation Confirmed."

60. "German Firm to Finish Iran N-plants," *International Herald Tribune*, April 29, 1984.

61. "Russia-Iran Nuclear Cooperation Confirmed."

62. Ibid., p. 19.

63. "China will supply a nuclear reactor to Iran," *Ha'aretz*, July 5, 1993. See also Teheran ABRAR in Persian, April 14, 1993 (FBIS-NES-93-080, April 28, 1993, p. 72), citing an interview with Iran's Deputy Foreign Minister, Ala'eddin Berujerdi. According to a report from China, the reactors are to be constructed south of Ahwaz, in the southwestern province of Khuzestan. See Agence France Presse (AFP), November 25, 1992 (BBC, ME/1549 p. A/8, November 27, 1992). See also Xinhua (China Press Agency) in Chinese, February 22, 1993 (BBC, ME/1621 p. A/4, February 24, 1993).

64. Voice of the Islamic Republic of Iran, July 4, 1993 (BBC, ME/1733, pp. i and A/7, July 6, 1993). See also Dan Izenberg, Jon Immanuel, and Bill Hutman, "Quan: Reactor for Iran is not a nuclear weapon," *Jerusalem Post*, September 17, 1992; David Watts, "Teheran Denies Nuclear Charges," *TMS*, March 15, 1993; Eitan Rabin, "Rafsanjani purchased nuclear power station in China," *Ha'aretz*, September 11, 1992; "China helps Iran build nuclear plant," *Jerusalem Post*, September 11, 1992.

65. John M. Goshko, "China Drops Reactor Deal With Iran," *Washington Post*, September 28, 1995; and "China Softens Stance Against Iranian Reactors," *Washington Post*, September 30, 1995.

66. Guy Bechor, "Fear in the West: An Iranian Hiroshima-type nuclear bomb is expected by the end of the 1990s," *Ha'aretz*, January 10, 1992.

67. David Watts, "Teheran Denies Nuclear Charges," *Times* (London), March 15, 1993.

68. Ben Kaspit, "Russians and Chinese begin construction of nuclear infrastructure in Iran," *Ma'ariv*, May 12, 1993 (citing report in the *Wall Street Journal*); and *Al-Sharq al-Awsat*, March 3, 1993 (FBIS-NES-93-042, March 5, 1993, p. 64).

69. Bill Gertz, "Fear destroys U.S.-Russia cooperation," *Washington Times*, September 27, 1995.

70. David Albright and Mark Hibbs, "Spotlight shifts to Iran," *Bulletin of the Atomic Scientists*, Vol. 48, No. 2 (March 1992), pp. 9–11.

71. See France Inter (radio station in Paris) October 25, 1991 (BBC ME/1213 October 26, 1991, p. i[a]); and Teheran IRNA in English, December 11, 1992 (FBIS-NES-92-240, December 14, 1992, p. 40). See also "Saudi Newspaper: France will supply enriched uranium to Iran," *Ha'aretz*, January 9, 1992.

72. "The Islamic Bomb: Iranian Nuclear Aspirations," *RUSI Newsbrief*, Vol 12, No. 9 (September 1992), p. 69.

73. Steve Coll, "How the U.S. Blocked Nuclear Sales to Iran," *International Herald Tribune*, November 17, 1992. See also report by Iranian television, "Vision of the Islamic Republic of Iran," February 5, 1992 (BBC, ME/1298, p. A/5, February 7, 1992). For an Argentine report on this matter see *Noticias Argentinas*, February 7, 1992 (BBC, ME/1300, p. D/10, February 10, 1992). See also Paul Lewis, "Pakistan Tells of its A-Bomb Capacity," *New York Times*, February 8, 1992.

74. Roshandel and Lotfian, "Horizontal Nuclear Proliferation." For an earlier report, see Max Holland and Kai Bird, "Khomeini takes up nuclear push where the Shah left off," *Des Moines Register*, October 12, 1984, p. 12.

75. William Drozdiak, "U.S. Move to Halt Nuclear Technology Sales Angers Iranians," *Washington Post*, November 22, 1991.

76. Albright and Hibbs, "Spotlight shifts to Iran."

77. George C. Church, "Who Else Will Have the Bomb?" *Time*, December 16, 1991, p. 15.

78. Coll, "How the U.S. Blocked Nuclear Sales to Iran."

79. Steve Coll, "Iran Reported Trying to Buy Indian Reactor," *Washington Post*, November 15, 1991. See also AFP Hong Kong office, in English, November 9, 1991, citing *The Independent* (Bombay) (FBIS-NES-91-220 November 14, 1991, p. 51); and Hong Kong AFP in English, November 21, 1991, citing report in *Press Trust of India* (PTI) (FBIS-NES-91-226, November 22, 1991, p. 45).

80. "India withdraws offer to Iranians of N-reactor," *Financial Times*, November 21, 1991. See also Drozdiak, "U.S. Move to Halt Nuclear Technology Sales Angers Iranians"; and Edward A. Gargan, "U.S. Officials in India to Discuss Limiting Spread of Nuclear Arms," *New York Times*, November 22, 1991.

81. See "The Islamic Bomb: Iranian Nuclear Aspirations," *RUSI Newsbrief*, Vol. 12, No. 9 (September 1992), p. 69.

82. Albright and Hibbs, "Spotlight shifts to Iran."

83. According to Teheran home service, September 18, 1985 (BBC, October 1, 1985).

84. See Teheran HAMSHAHRI in Persian, April 14, 1993 (FBIS-NES-93-077, April 23, 1993), p. 57.

85. "Iran Hosts IAEA Mission," *Arms Control Today*, Vol. 22, No. 2 (March 1992), p. 28.

86. See Teheran HAMSHAHRI in Persian, April 14, 1993 (FBIS-NES-93-077, April 23, 1993), p. 57. A cyclotron is a type of particle accelerator in which charged particles are accelerated along a spiral path between the faces of two large magnets by the application of an alternating voltage. The invention of the cyclotron by Ernest Lawrence in the 1930s produced an essential tool of nuclear physics, making it possible to generate in a controlled fashion particles energetic enough to induce nuclear reactions in target materials.

87. Report by Het Belang Van Limburg, February 12, 1992 (FBIS-NES-92-035 February 21, 1992, p. 66); John G. Roos, "Group Unveils Iran's Nuke Weapon Plan, Plots 'Equal Opportunity' Overthrow," *Armed Forces Journal*, March 1992, p. 26.

88. "Israel worried by the supply of equipment by Belgium to Iran," *Davar*, March 17, 1992.

89. Claus Van England, "Iran Defends Its Pursuit of Nuclear Technology," *Christian Science Monitor*, February 18, 1993; Bechor, "Fear in the West." For an earlier reference to the center at Isfahan, see Holland and Bird, "Khomeini takes up nuclear push."

90. Statement by the head of the Nuclear Technology Center at Isfahan, cited by IRNA in English, October 10, 1984 (BBC, October 23, 1984). The 1991 Chinese statement pointed out that the IAEA had been informed of the sale prior to delivery, and had been requested to enforce safeguards. See David Holley, "China: Iran nuclear sale 'peaceful'," *Philadelphia Inquirer*, November 5, 1991. See also "China Offers A-Plants To Egypt and Others,"

International Herald Tribune, July 31, 1992; "Iran Hosts IAEA Mission," *Arms Control Today*, Vol. 22, No. 2 (March 1992), p. 28; and Albright and Hibbs, "Spotlight shifts to Iran." For an earlier report see "CIA fears hi-tech arms sales," *Jane's Defense Weekly*, February 1, 1992.

91. A report on the IAEA inspection of Iran's nuclear facilities in February 1992 noted that the inspectors were shown a "desktop-sized, Chinese-supplied mass spectrometer, or calutron." See "Iran Hosts IAEA Mission." See also Albright and Hibbs, "Spotlight Shifts to Iran." Another report regarding a Chinese sale of a calutron to Iran appeared in the *Economist*, March 14, 1992. For earlier references to Iran's purchase of calutron equipment, see R. Jeffrey Smith, "Officials Say Iran Is Seeking Nuclear Weapons Capability," *Washington Post*, October 30, 1991; and Elaine Sciolino, "Report Says Iran Seeks Atomic Arms," *New York Times*, October 31, 1991. A calutron is a device for separating isotopes of an element by injecting ions of a given energy into a magnetic field. The force exerted by the magnetic field on the ions causes them to travel along a circular arc until they strike a collector placed in their path. Different isotopes, having different masses, follow slightly different trajectories, and can thus be separated by collection at dfferent points. Calutrons were used to enrich uranium for the Manhattan Project, but were later abandoned as an enrichment method by the United States due to high power consumption. They remain a viable low-technology option for uranium enrichment.

92. Albright and Hibbs, "Spotlight shifts to Iran."

93. Church, "Who Else Will Have the Bomb?"

94. Albright and Hibbs, "Spotlight Shifts to Iran."

95. A report mentioning nuclear warhead research in Iran was published in *Jane's Intelligence Review*, Vol. 4, No. 5 (May 1992), p. 212.

96. See "Iran Hosts IAEA Mission"; and Jack Anderson and Michael Binstein, "An Iranian Bomb," *Washington Post*, January 12, 1992.

97. Albright and Hibbs, "Spotlight Shifts to Iran."

98. Church, "Who Else Will Have the Bomb?"

99. See the interview with Reza Amrollahi, Iran's vice president and head of its Atomic Energy Organization, cited by the Voice of the Islamic Republic of Iran, March 13, 1993 (BBC, ME/1637, p. A/6, March 15, 1993).

100. Roshandel and Lotfian, "Horizontal Nuclear Proliferation." For an earlier report on activities at Yazd see Bechor, "Fear in the West." The existence of uranium ore at Yazd was first mentioned in *Kayhan Hava'i* (Teheran, London edition), December 12, 1984 (BBC, ME/W1317 January 1, 1985, p. A 1/4). See also *Akhir Sa'a* (Egypt), December 12, 1984 (translated by HATZAV, December 31, 1984). (HATZAV is the agency of the Israeli intelligence community that translates foreign news media into Hebrew; translations from HATZAV into

English are the author's). Regarding Rafsanjani's visit to Yazd, see Voice of the Islamic Republic of Iran, November 29, 1993 (BBC, ME/W0260, p. A1/2, December 8, 1992).

101. Moscow ITAR-TASS in English, November 28, 1992 (FBIS-NES-92-230, November 30, 1992).

102. Voice of the Islamic Republic of Iran, June 16, 1993 (BBC, ME/1718, p. A/4, June 18, 1993).

103. Voice of the Islamic Republic of Iran, July 8, 1992 (FBIS-NES-92-132, July 9, 1992, p. 49); and Van England, "Iran defends its pursuit of nuclear technology."

104. Jim Mann, "U.S. Suspects China Aids Iran on Arms," *International Herald Tribune*, March 18, 1993.

105. Aluf Ben, "Representatives of IAEA did not find evidence for the development of nuclear weapons in Iran," *Ha'aretz*, January 18, 1994. Indeed, a reliable report pointed out that the U.S. government has so far failed to identify any clandestine facilities that might be part of a secret Iranian nuclear weapons program. See Albright and Hibbs, "Spotlight shifts to Iran."

106. Gad Shomron and Shefi Gabai, "Scientist who defected: Iran had two nuclear bombs," *Ma'ariv*, May 4, 1993. For an earlier report see Amos Regev, "Iran has four nuclear weapons; two are already operational," *Yediot Ahronot*, September 4, 1992 (citing a report from Washington, D.C., published by the *Guardian*).

107. "Iran buying nuclear arms from Kazakhastan," *Jerusalem Post*, October 13, 1992 (citing column by Rowland Evans and Robert Novak published in the *Washington Post*). See also a report from *Al-Watan al-'Arabi* cited in "Iranians purchasing nuclear weapons with help from Russian mafia," *Ha'aretz*, April 18, 1993. For an earlier report citing the German weekly *Stern*, see Daniel Dagan, "Stern: Kazakhastan delivered two nuclear weapons and delivery systems to Iran," *Ha'aretz*, March 16, 1992. For a later report in *The European*, see Amos Ben-David, "European: Iran possesses at least two nuclear weapons," *Ha'aretz*, May 1, 1992. A similar report cited the German weekly *Der Spiegel*; see Yigal Avidan, "Iran purchased two nuclear warheads in the CIS," *Davar*, May 26, 1992.

108. "Kazakhastan: We did not sell nuclear weapons to Iran," *Ma'ariv*, October 14, 1993; and "U.S.: No proof Iran bought nuclear arms," *Jerusalem Post*, October 14, 1992.

109. Oded Shorer, "Iran investing billions in producing nuclear bomb," *Ma'ariv*, April 15, 1993.

110. "Bonn Says Seized Uranium Wasn't Suitable for Bombs"; see also Peter Hounam, "Red Mercury: Hoax or Nuclear Nightmare?" *Sunday Times* (London), October 18, 1992.

111. *Ha'aretz*, March 22, 1993 (citing *U.S. News and World Report*).

112. Jack Kelley, "Russian nuke experts wooed," *USA Today*, January 8, 1992. See also "Campaign to recruit Soviet nuclear scientists," *Sunday Times* (London), January 26, 1992.

113. RUSI, "The Islamic Bomb: Iranian Nuclear Aspirations."

114. "David Ivri: Soviet nuclear scientists — at Iran's service," *Yediot Ahronot*, June 23, 1992.

115. Roos, "Group Unveils Iran's Nuke Weapon Plan, Plots 'Equal Opportunity' Overthrow."

116. In an interview with a Swedish newspaper, Rolf Ekeus, head of UN Special Commission, estimated that Iraq was only two years away from possessing an atomic bomb at the time of the war. Eliahu Zehavi, "If it were not for the war, Iraq would have possessed a nuclear bomb by now," *Ha'aretz*, March 30, 1993. Yet a panel of nuclear weapon designers who were convened in Vienna in May 1992 to inspect all available material on the Iraqi program concluded that Iraq was at least three years away from developing nuclear weapons. The panel noted that the Iraqi program had encountered difficult obstacles in a number of realms: uranium enrichment, constructing a device to squeeze the nuclear charge until it explodes, and understanding how materials react under very high pressures. In addition, Dutch centrifuge-enrichment experts who reviewed the data concluded that the Iraqi centrifuge design was fundamentally flawed. See Paul Lewis, "UN Bomb Experts Put Back Estimate of Iraq's Progress," *International Herald Tribune*, May 21, 1992; Ben Kaspit, "New assessment: Iraq was far from developing atomic bomb," *Ma'ariv*, May 21, 1992. Former Israeli Prime Minister Itzhak Rabin claimed that if Iraq had not invaded Kuwait, it would have obtained nuclear weapons by 1994. See *Davar*, April 17, 1992.

117. See Daniel Schwammenthal, "How the IAEA Assists Iraq," *Defense Media Review*, March 1993.

118. See Yehiel Limor, "Saddam can manufacture an atomic bomb," *Ma'ariv*, January 22, 1993.

119. George Lardner, Jr., and R. Jeffrey Smith, "CIA Chief, Disputing UN, Warns of Iraqi Nuclear Cache," *International Herald Tribune*, December 17, 1992.

120. See the interview with former IAEA Inspector David Kay in Limor, "Saddam can manufacture an atomic bomb."

121. Shefi Gabai, "Twenty thousand Iraqi scientists working on the nuclear bomb," *Ma'ariv*, April 20, 1992. See also Zehavi, "If it were not for the war, Iraq would have possessed a nuclear bomb by now"; and Norman Kempster, "Oil Sales Could Refuel Iraq Nuclear Force, UN Aide Warns," *International Herald Tribune*, March 26, 1993.

122. Tim Barlass and Alan George, "Defecting envoy helped set up Iraqi nuclear project," *Evening Standard* (London), August 25, 1993.

123. In an interview with the Kuwaiti newspaper *Saut al-Kuwait*, Sharastani provided a comprehensive map of Iraq's nuclear program. See "Scientist who defected: Iraq continues to operate nuclear centers," *Ha'aretz*, May 31, 1992. Sharastani was co-director of Iraq's nuclear program with J'afar Diah J'afar.

124. See Tim Ripley, "Iraq's Nuclear Weapons Programme," *Jane's Intelligence Review*, Vol. 4, No. 12 (December 1992), p. 555.

125. Stephanie Cooke, "Nuclear Inspections: Time for Hardball," *International Herald Tribune*, July 30, 1992.

126. See Ripley, "Iraq's Nuclear Weapons Programme," p. 554. On p. 557 Ripley reports that one mystery about the activities conducted at al-Tuwaytha remains: IAEA inspectors discovered uranium enriched to 93 percent, which is isotopically distinct from the fuel supplied by the French and was not considered by the IAEA to be a product of the indigenous Iraqi enrichment program. According to IAEA inspector Richard Hooper, nuclear material requiring IAEA oversight remained at the al-Tuwaytha complex in mid-1993. AFP from Baghdad, May 1, 1993 (FBIS-NES-93-083, May 3, 1993).

127. The existence of the facilities at Tarmiya and Al-Sharqat was revealed by a young Iraqi nuclear engineer who defected to the West after the Gulf War. See Shlomo Nakdimon, "The defector confirmed: this is an advanced atomic installation," *Yediot Ahronot*, October 18, 1992. The facilities in these two locations were destroyed by the 12th and 13th IAEA inspection teams in June and July 1992. See "UN team supervises destruction of structures at Iraq's nuclear sites," *Ha'aretz*, June 1, 1992; and "UN experts left for Iraq to complete the destruction of nuclear facilities," *Davar*, July 14, 1992. One report indicated that at the time of the Gulf War, Iraq's calutron program, was at least a year behind schedule. See David Albright and Mark Hibbs, "It's All Over at Al-Atheer," *Bulletin of the Atomic Scientists*, Vol. 48, No. 5 (June 1992), pp. 8–10.

128. See Ripley, "Iraq's Nuclear Weapons Programme," p. 555.

129. This illustrates that even in the aftermath of the Gulf War the IAEA inspection system remains flawed: "The Rashidiya design center has been extensively modified by Iraq since the war, complicating inspectors' efforts to gain more data on its pre-war use. Ironically, Rashidiya was visited during the fourth inspection in the summer of 1991, when it was first discovered. But that visit was conducted so quickly that it failed to reveal Rashidiya's centrifuge activities." David Albright and Mark Hibbs, "New discoveries in Iraq," *Bulletin of the Atomic Scientists*, Vol. 49, No. 1 (January–February, 1993), p. 8.

130. See Ripley, "Iraq's Nuclear Weapons Programme," p. 555.

131. "Security Council Extends Iraqi Sanctions; Inspections Continue," *Arms Control Today*, Vol. 22, No. 9 (November 1992), p. 28. Maraging steel is a class of high-strength steels that are easily worked and can be hardened by moderate heat treatment with only slight dimensional changes. Maraging steels are important for proliferation because they are useful

for manufacturing high-speed gas centrifuge rotors for centrifuge enrichment plants.

132. "UN Aide Says Plant Wasn't Key Site," *International Herald Tribune*, January 19, 1993; and Stephen Bryen, "Hidden Dangers in Iraq Inspections," *Washington Times*, February 16, 1993.

133. "Iraqis Rebuild Plant, UN Aide Says," *International Herald Tribune*, March 12, 1993.

134. Statement by the General Command of Iraq's Armed Forces on Baghdad Radio, January 13, 1993 (FBIS-NES-92009, January 14, 1993).

135. "UO-2 (uranium dioxide) is the form in which uranium is most commonly used as a reactor fuel for light water, heavy-water, and fast-breeder reactors. It is a stable ceramic that can be heated almost to its melting point, around 2760 degrees C, without serious mechanical deterioration. It does not react with water, so that it is not affected by leakage of cladding in water-cooled reactors." See Manson Benedict, et al., *Nuclear Chemical Engineering* (New York: McGraw-Hill, 1981), p. 223.

136. "Suspicion: Portugal secretly sold uranium to Iraq," *Ma'ariv*, April 7, 1992.

137. Ripley, "Iraq's Nuclear Weapons Programme," p. 557. "Yellowcake" is a general term for uranium ore concentrates containing high concentrations of UO. Such ore concentrates are generally produced by chemical leaching from raw ores, and are later purified by solvent extraction, then converted to UF or other compounds for enrichment.

138. IAEA Inspector Demetrius Perricos reported that some 200 tons of material containing uranium were found at Al-Jesira. See "UN inspectors in Iraq find 200 tons of material containing uranium," *Ha'aretz*, November 11, 1992.

139. Albright and Hibbs, "It's All Over at Al-Atheer."

140. "Iraq's Nuclear Fuel to Go to Russia." One unconfirmed report claimed that during the Gulf War, Iraq smuggled an unspecified quantity of enriched uranium to Sudan. See "Iraq smuggled enriched uranium to Sudan," *Ha'aretz*, June 2, 1992.

141. See Paris AFP in English, February 12, 1994 (FBIS-NES-94-030, February 14, 1994).

142. Albright and Hibbs, "It's All Over at Al-Atheer."

143. See Ripley, "Iraq's Nuclear Weapons Programme," p. 554.

144. Ibid., p. 557.

145. "Baghdad Agrees to Destroy Sites For Atom Arms," *International Herald Tribune*, April 8, 1992; and "UN Dismantles 90% of Iraqi Plant," *International Herald Tribune*, April 10, 1992. See also AFP, April 8, 1992 (FBIS-NES-92-069 April 9, 1992, p. 13); AFP, April 9, 1992 (FBIS-NES-92-070 April 10, 1992, p. 15); "UN team describes destruction of Iraqi nuclear facilities," *Jerusalem Post*, April 16, 1992; Albright and Hibbs, "It's All Over at Al-Atheer"; and "Iraq smuggled enriched uranium to Sudan."

146. "UN Nuclear Expert Sees No Purpose Now to Iraq Sanctions," *International Herald Tribune*, July 1, 1993.

147. "The Iraqi nuclear program has been eliminated," *Davar*, September 3, 1992.

148. AFP, September 7, 1992 (BBC, ME/1481, September 9, 1992, p. A/4).

149. AFP, from Baghdad, May 1, 1993 (FBIS-NES-93-083, May 3, 1993).

150. Kempster, "Oil Sales Could Refuel Iraq Nuclear Force."

151. Schwammenthal, "How the IAEA Assists Iraq."

152. AFP, from Baghdad, March 11, 1993 (FBIS-NES-93-046 March 11, 1993, p. 27).

153. Diana Edensword and Gary Milhollin, "Iraq's Bomb — An Update," *New York Times*, April 26, 1993. It is possible, however, that this report refers to the same inspection and findings described by Perricos.

154. See "Iraq concealed 60 kg of uranium from IAEA," *Ha'aretz*, June 21, 1992.

155. "Security Council Extends Iraqi Sanctions; Inspections Continue," *Arms Control Today*, Vol 22. No. 9 (November 1992), p. 28. See also "Iraq won't reveal nuclear suppliers," *Jerusalem Post*, May 29, 1992.

156. Ripley, "Iraq's Nuclear Weapons Programme," p. 554.

157. This assessment was issued by Rolf Ekeus, head of the UN Special Commission. See Kempster, "Oil Sales Could Refuel Iraq Nuclear Force." Testimony to the same effect by IAEA inspector Perricos is cited in AFP, from Baghdad, March 11, 1993 (BBC, ME/1635, March 12, 1993, p. A/16). IAEA Deputy Director Maurizio Zefferero reported that Iraq claimed that it has already submitted the names of 90 percent of its nuclear suppliers to IAEA inspectors. See "Iraq turns over list of nuclear suppliers," *Jerusalem Post*, January 26, 1993.

158. "Security Council Extends Iraqi Sanctions; Inspections Continue." Elsewhere, Perricos described the importance of securing the list of Iraq's nuclear suppliers: "The brains are there. They have good engineers and they have the machine tools to be able to start things again. This is why we're trying to find enough information so that we can base our long-term

monitoring, because without it anything can happen. The people who have supplied the information and sensitive equipment ... are still in place. You can bet there will be some who are going to sell their things. And definitely, there will be people here who will be tempted to buy.... The only guarantee is the full list of suppliers and long term monitoring." AFP from Baghdad, March 7, 1993 (FBIS-NES-93-043, March 8, 1993).

159. Paris AFP, March 11, 1993 (FBIS-NES-93-046, March 11, 1993 p. 27).

160. R. Jeffrey Smith, "Two Monitoring Groups Accuse Iraq Of Withholding Data on Weapons," *Washington Post*, October 12, 1995.

161. "German newspaper reports: Saddam recruited 50 scientists from the former Soviet Union," *Ha'aretz*, June 6, 1992.

162. "Libya, Iraq, and Iran attempting to purchase nuclear waste in Russia," *Davar*, April 30, 1992.

163. For a description of a visit to the reactor see *Al-Mansur* (Egypt), March 3, 1989 (translated by HATZAV, April 12, 1989); see also a statement by Hamid Rushdi, head of Egypt's Atomic Energy Authority, cited by Middle East News Agency (MENA), January 10, 1990 (BBC, ME/W0112, p. A1/1, January 23, 1990).

164. Assam al-Din Jalal, Chairman of the UN Consultative Committee for Science and Technology and a member of the board of Pugwash, in a seminar conducted and reported by *Al-Sha'b* (Egypt), December 1, 1987 (translated by HATZAV, January 31, 1988).

165. For further details regarding the history of Egypt's nuclear activities during the 1950s, 1960s, and 1970s, see Shai Feldman, *Israeli Nuclear Deterrence: A Strategy for the 1980s* (New York: Columbia University Press, 1983), pp. 71–72.

166. Feldman, *Israeli Nuclear Deterrence*, pp. 71–72; see also "Sale of French Nuclear Plants to Egypt Hangs on Political Decision," *Al-Nahar Arab Report and Memo*, January 10, 1983, p. 7.

167. See joint statements made at a conference held at Al-Daba by Egypt's Nuclear Power Stations Authority and the Al-Ahram Center for Political and Strategic Studies, as reported in *Al-Siyasa al-Duwaliya* (Egypt), January 1989 (translated by HATZAV, February 23, 1989). For earlier indications of the Egyptian-Canadian agreement, see *Al-Difa' al-'Arabi* (Lebanon), May 9, 1984 (translated by HATZAV, July 8, 1984); and *Mayo* (Egypt), August 26, 1985 (translated by HATZAV, September 10, 1985).

168. See statement by Mahir Abazah, Egypt's Minister of Power and Energy, cited by MENA in English, May 19, 1984 (BBC, May 29, 1984).

169. See "Egypt Receives Bids for Nuclear Plants," *New York Times*, November 27, 1983; and "Egypt: All set to go nuclear," *The Middle East*, (March 1985), pp. 35–36.

170. See joint statements made in a conference held at El-Daba by Egypt's Nuclear Power Stations Authority and the Al-Ahram Center for Political and Strategic Studies; see also interview with Dr. 'Ali al-Sayidi, chairman of Egypt's Nuclear Power Stations Authority, in *Al-Mansur* (Egypt), April 13, 1990 (translated by HATZAV, May 8, 1990).

171. See *Al-Jumhuriyya* (Egypt), November 8, 1984 (translated by HATZAV, December 23, 1983).

172. *October* (Egypt), December 16, 1984 (translated by HATZAV, December 30, 1984). See also the statement by Egypt's Prime Minister Kamal Hassan Ali, reported by MENA, January 5, 1985 (BBC, January 7, 1985). The issue had already been discussed in November 1984, during the farewell meeting between the departing Egyptian Ambassador in Washington, Ashraf Ghorbal, and President Ronald Reagan. See *Al-Ahram*, November 27, 1984 (translated by HATZAV, December 3, 1984). See also Zvi Barel, "U.S. authorizes $250 million loan for constructing a nuclear reactor in Egypt," *Ha'aretz*, January 30, 1985; and "Egypt Wins Loan for Nuclear Plant," *International Herald Tribune*, January 30, 1985.

173. *Al-Akhbar* (Egypt), June 10, 1985 (translated by HATZAV, August 8, 1985).

174. "France and U.S. press Egypt to purchase nuclear reactors from them," *Ha'aretz*, June 13, 1985. See also *Al-Sharq al-Awsat* (Saudi Arabia), February 5, 1986 (translated by HATZAV, April 9, 1986).

175. *Al-sharq Al-Awsat*, September 7, 1985 (translated by HATZAV, September 26, 1985).

176. *Al-Akhbar*, October 31, 1984 (translated by HATZAV, November 23, 1984).

177. *Al-Ahram* (Egypt), February 6, 1985 (translated by HATZAV, February 14, 1985).

178. See the debate on this issue held by the Egyptian Shura Council as reported by *Al-Ahram*, *Al-Akhbar*, and *Al-Jumhuriyya* (Egypt), December 21–22, 1986 (translated by HATZAV, December 29, 1986).

179. *Al-Ahram*, May 26, 1986 (translated by HATZAV, June 24, 1986).

180. Sawt al-'Arab Radio (Egypt), January 25, 1987 (translated by HATZAV, February 26, 1987).

181. See the interview with Fauzi Hammad, chairman of the nuclear safety organization, in *Akhir Sa'a* (Egypt), March 9, 1987 (translated by HATZAV, March 23, 1987). See also *Al-Ahram*, February 28, 1987 (translated by HATZAV, March 31, 1987); and *Al-Ahram*, March 3, 1987 (translated by HATZAV, May 8, 1987). A U.S.-Egyptian seminar on nuclear safety was

conducted in November 1987. See *Al-Ahram* (international edition), November 20, 1987 (translated by HATZAV, December 28, 1987).

182. MENA, May 19, 1984 (BBC, May 29, 1984); see also *Al-Akhbar*, June 20, 1985 (translated by HATZAV, July 16, 1985).

183. See Feldman, *Israeli Nuclear Deterrence*, pp. 71–72. See also *Al-Yawm* (Saudi Arabia), January 23, 1984 (translated by HATZAV, March 25, 1984); *Al-Ahram*, October 30, 1984 (translated by HATZAV, December 5, 1984); and *Watani* (Egypt), November 3, 1985 (translated by HATZAV, November 19, 1985). The report that uranium was found in the Abu-Znaima region of the Sinai was first published in *Al-Ittihad* (Abu Dhabi), and is cited in *Yediot Ahronot*, November 22, 1987.

184. See the statement by Mahir Abazah, Egypt's Minister of Electricity and Energy, cited by MENA, December 14, 1984 (BBC, January 1, 1985); and *Akhir Sa'a* (Egypt), February 13, 1985 (translated by HATZAV, April 4, 1985).

185. Mustafa Sharedi, editor of the opposition newspaper *Al-Wafd*, wrote: "The explosion at Chernobyl also exploded the dangerous trend to construct nuclear reactors in Egypt, which might bring about the death of thousands." *Al-Wafd* (Egypt), May 1, 1986 (translated by HATZAV, May 28, 1986). See also the statement by Gamal Al-Adin Hamed Musa in *Al-Jumhuriyya*, May 6, 1986 (translated by HATZAV, May 15, 1986). A debate on this issue in the People's Assembly is reported in *Al-Ahram*, May 19, 1986 (translated by HATZAV, May 19, 1986); see also the extended report in *Al-Sharq al-Awsat*, May 10, 1986 (translated by HATZAV, June 9, 1986). See also a comparison of the advantages and disadvantages of nuclear power in *Al-Ahram Al-Iqtisadi* (Egypt), June 2, 1986, pp. 32–33 (translated by HATZAV, July 7, 1986).

186. See *Al-Akhbar*, January 27, 1986 (translated by HATZAV, March 16, 1986). A facility for destroying low and medium radiation waste was built in Egypt in 1987 with the assistance of the IAEA. See *Al-Ahram*, December 30, 1986 (translated by HATZAV, February 25, 1987); *Al-Mansur*, August 21, 1987 (translated by HATZAV, September 29, 1987); and *Al-Wafd* (Egypt), November 14, 1987 (translated by HATZAV, December 12, 1987).

187. See the debate on this issue held by the Egyptian Shura Council as reported by *Al Ahram*, *Al-Akhbar*, and *Al-Jumhuriyya*, December 21–22, 1986 (translated by HATZAV, December 29, 1986). See also reflections of this debate in an interview given by Salah Hashish, chairman of Egypt's Nuclear Authority, to the Kuwaiti newspaper *Al-Ray al-'Am*, October 8, 1986 (translated by HATZAV, November 19, 1986).

188. *Al-Jumhuriyya*, February 1, 1987 (translated by HATZAV, March 2, 1987).

189. *Al-Ahram*, May 19, 1986 (translated by HATZAV, May 19, 1986).

190. See interview in *Ruz al-Yusuf* (Egypt), November 6, 1989 (translated by HATZAV, November 29, 1989).

191. See interview with 'Azat 'Abd al-'Aziz, chairman of Egypt's Atomic Energy Authority, in *Al-Jumhuriyya*, December 3, 1986 (translated by HATZAV, December 26, 1986). For the strong case made in Egypt in favor of nuclear power, see statements made by Ali al-Sayadi, chairman of Egypt's Nuclear Power Stations Authority, and Mustafa Kamal Sabri, former Minister of Electricity, in *Al-Sha'b* (Egypt), February 26, 1993 (translated by HATZAV, April 22, 1993). For earlier references, see the detailed analysis provided by Egypt's Minister of Electricity, reported in *Al-Sha'b*, January 26, 1986 (translated by HATZAV, March 10, 1986); and the statement by Mustafa Al-Dibi, deputy director of the Nuclear Power Authority in the Ministry of Electricity, in *Al-Jumhuriyya*, May 8, 1986 (translated by HATZAV, May 25, 1986).

192. See statements made by participants at a seminar on "Egypt and Atomic Energy" conducted at Ein Shams University, reported by *Al-Sha'b*, December 1, 1987, and *Sawt al-'Arab*, December 13, 1987 (translated by HATZAV, January 31, 1988). See also the interview with Muhammad El-Kassas in *Al-Mansur*, February 12, 1988 (translated by HATZAV, March 25, 1988); and statements made at a conference held at Al-Diba by Egypt's Nuclear Power Stations Authority and the Al-Ahram Center for Political and Strategic Studies, as reported in *Al-Siyasa Al-Duwaliya*, January 1989 (translated by HATZAV, February 23, 1989).

193. See statements made by officials of Egypt's Nuclear Power Authority, cited in *Al-Sha'b*, November 28, 1989 (translated by HATZAV, December 14, 1989).

194. *Akhir Sa'a*, January 7, 1987 (translated by HATZAV, January 29, 1987). Egypt's nuclear activities were then being conducted at four centers: the nuclear center at Inshass; the National Center for Radiation Research and Technology; a "hot laboratory" for the treatment of radioactive material; and the Organization for Nuclear Safety. See interview with Dr. Azat 'Abd al-Aziz, chairman of Egypt's Nuclear Energy Authority, in *Al-Ittihad* (United Arab Emirates) March 29, 1987 (translated by HATZAV, May 28, 1987). Nuclear activities were being conducted by three authorities: the Atomic Energy Authority; the Nuclear Power Stations Authority; and the Nuclear Materials Authority. See *Mayo* (Egypt), July 6, 1987 (translated by HATZAV, August 8, 1987).

195. *Al-Ahram*, November 22, 1988 (translated by HATZAV, January 13, 1989).

196. See interview with Egypt's Minister of Energy in *Al-Ittihad*, June 16, 1987 (translated by HATZAV, July 23, 1987).

197. *Al-Akhbar*, November 27, 1989 (translated by HATZAV, December 26, 1989).

198. According to various reports, uranium was found in three areas of the Eastern Desert: the Gebtar, 65 km north of Hurghada; Al-Mosaykat and Ardia, between Safaga and Qena; and Am Ara, southwest of Aswan and Abu Znaima in east Sinai. Other findings have been made in the Bahariya oasis and Qatrani in the Western Desert. See Mahmoud Bakr, "Moving towards nuclear power," *Al-Ahram Weekly* (in English), May 13–19, 1993. For earlier reports on uranium findings in Egypt see *Mayo* (Egypt), July 6, 1987 (translated by HATZAV, August 8, 1987).

199. *Al-Akhbar*, June 29, 1987 (translated by HATZAV, July 7, 1987).

200. See statement made by Hammad Rashdi, chairman of Egypt's Nuclear Power Stations Authority, reported by MENA, December 1, 1988 (translated by HATZAV, December 6, 1988).

201. See interview with *Al-Mansur*, April 13, 1990 (translated by HATZAV, May 8, 1990).

202. MENA, November 29, 1992 (FBIS-NES-92-231, December 1, 1992; and BBC, ME/W0260, December 8, 1992 p. A1/1).

203. See statement by Fawzi Hammad, chairman of the Atomic Energy Authority, in MENA, April 1, 1990 (BBC, ME/W0123 P. A1/2 April 10, 1990).

204. See "Canada will supply a research reactor to Egypt," *Davar*, January 1, 1992; and *Al-Ahram*, cited by Cairo Arab Republic of Egypt Radio, March 19, 1992 (FBIS-NES-92-055, March 20, 1992 p. 13; and BBC, ME/W0224, March 31, 1992, p. A1/1).

205. Fergus Nicoll, "Egyptian reactor deal for Argentina," *Financial Times*, September 23, 1992; "Egypt purchasing a nuclear reactor from Argentina for $60 million," *Ha'aretz*, September 20, 1992; "Egypt, Argentina sign nuclear reactor contract," *Jerusalem Post*, September 21, 1992; and MENA, September 28, 1993 (FBIS-NES-93-187, September 29, 1993, p. 16).

206. "On the threshold of a 'new nuclear era'." *Al-Ahram Weekly*, June 3–9, 1993.

207. For further details, see Feldman, *Israeli Nuclear Deterrence*, pp. 79–82.

208. *Middle East Magazine*, September 1984 (translated by HATZAV, October 19, 1984).

209. See Feldman, *Israeli Nuclear Deterrence*, pp. 79–82, See also testimony by India's ambassador to the United States, in Keith Bradsher, "India Says Libya Tried to Buy Bomb," *International Herald Tribune*, October 11, 1991.

210. Lee Michael Katz, "Nuke knowledge coveted," *USA Today*, January 8, 1992.

211. *Bemachane* (Israel), June 10, 1992 (citing the Arab weekly *Al-Duwaliya*).

212. Details regarding the Libyan approach were conveyed by China's prime minister to Egypt's President Mubarak who, in turn, conveyed them to Israel's then–Prime Minister Shimon Peres. See "Qadhafi asked the Chinese for an atomic bomb," *Yediot Ahronot*, September 15, 1986.

213. Jack Kelley, "Russian nuke experts wooed," *USA Today*, January 8, 1992.

214. For further details, see Feldman, *Israeli Nuclear Deterrence*, pp. 79–82.

215. 'Aqat (Saudi Arabia), November 3, 1991 (translated by HATZAV).

216. "Belgians May Build Libya Atom Plant," International Herald Tribune, May 19, 1984. See also Middle East Magazine, September 1984 (translated by HATZAV, October 19, 1984).

217. Fred Hiatt, "Belgium Urged To Reject Pact With Libyans," Washington Post, October 9, 1984; Shaul Zadka, "Israel pressing Belgium to cancel nuclear assistance to Libya," Ha'aretz, October 15, 1984; and Daniel Dagan, "U.S. offers Belgium compensation if it cancels nuclear reactor sale to Libya," Ha'aretz, October 28, 1984.

218. Steven J. Dryden, "Belgian-Libyan Deal Called Unlikely," Washington Post, October 20, 1984; and Paul Lewis, "U.S. Said to Stop Libya Nuclear Deal," New York Times, November 21, 1984.

219. "Libya bids to go nuclear with Soviet aid," Jerusalem Post, October 22, 1984 citing an AP report from Libya; Tripoli home service, October 20, 1984, (BBC, October 30, 1984). See also Nigel Wade, "Khadafy may visit Moscow with N-power on his mind," San Francisco Chronicle, July 14, 1985.

220. General Al-Din Salim, "Arab nuclear capabilities," 'Aqat, November 3, 1991 (translated by HATZAV).

221. Jeune Afrique, January 8, 1986 (translated by HATZAV, January 17, 1986).

222. "Libyan Uranium Deposits," Financial Times, June 10, 1985.

223. See Feldman, Israeli Nuclear Deterrence, p. 79; and Dalia Sharon, "The President of Chad claims: Libya will soon have a nuclear bomb," Ha'aretz, October 18, 1985.

224. Steve Vogel, "Libya-Bound U.S. Gear Seized in Germany," Washington Post, January 23, 1992; and Steve Vogel, "Germany to Allow Taps in Arms-Related Exports," Washington Post, January 24, 1992.

225. Tyrus W. Cobb, "Look After Ex-Soviet Nuclear Brains," International Herald Tribune, January 7, 1992; Jack Kelley, "Russian nuke experts wooed," USA Today, January 8, 1992; "Libya Wants Russians," International Herald Tribune, January 9, 1992; Yehiel Limor, "At least 4 Russian nuclear scientists said to be operating in Libya," Ma'ariv, January 20, 1992; and "The Devil's Work," Newsweek, February 17, 1992.

226. Dan Izenberg, Jon Immanuel, and Bill Hutman, "Quan: Reactor for Iran is not a nuclear weapon," Jerusalem Post, September 17, 1992.

227. Richard Lacayo, "Atom Bomb? What Atom Bomb?" Time, February 3, 1992.

228. Mednews (Paris), February 17, 1992.

229. "Saddam helps Algeria make Islamic nuclear bomb," *Sunday Times*, January 5, 1992.

230. *The Defense Monitor*, Vol. 21, No. 3 (1992), p. 5.

231. Shefi Gabai, "Algeria would be able to produce nuclear weapons in less than five years," *Ma'ariv*, January 21, 1992 (quoting the French newspaper *Liberation*). Algeria's nuclear efforts reportedly also became a subject of intense interest to British intelligence branch MI-6. See "British intelligence fears Algeria preparing to produce nuclear weapons," *Ha'aretz*, January 8, 1992.

232. Interview with Brig. General Doron Tamir, *Bemachane*, June 17, 1992, p. 6.

233. Shlomo Pepirblat, "China selling nuclear know-how obtained with Israel's assistance," *Yediot Ahronot*, January 17, 1992 (quoting *Le Monde*).

234. Testimony by CIA Director Robert M. Gates to the Senate Committee on Government Affairs, January 26, 1992.

235. "Fear that Algeria is developing nuclear weapons," *Ha'aretz*, September 11, 1991 (citing *Nucleonics Week*).

236. Elaine Sciolino and Eric Schmitt, "Algerian Reactor: A Chinese Export," *New York Times*, November 15, 1991; and Church, "Who Else Will Have the Bomb?" p. 16.

237. "Dimona et al.," *Economist*, March 14, 1992. At the time, there were speculations that Algeria might be able to expand the reactor's capacity to 50–60 megawatts. See Church, "Who Else Will Have the Bomb?" p. 16; Algeria announced its intentions to enter into a safeguards agreement with the IAEA on Algerian TV (Algiers, in Arabic), September 26, 1991 (BBC, ME/W0200, October 8, 1991, p. A1/1).

238. "Fear that Algeria is developing nuclear weapons."

239. "Algeria and the bomb," *Economist*, January 11, 1992, p. 38; Radiodiffusion-Television Algerienne, Algiers, February 27, 1992 (BBC, ME/1318 March 2, 1992, p. A/20); Algiers ENTV Television Network, February 27, 1992 (FBIS-NES-92-040 February 28, 1992); and "Algeria to Sign Nuclear Pact, Aide Says," *International Herald Tribune*, January 8, 1992.

240. Vipin Gupta, "Algeria's nuclear ambitions," *International Defense Review*, April 1992, p. 329. See also "IAEA inspectors toured Algerian reactor, *Ha'aretz*, January 21, 1992; Algiers Radio, January 19, 1992 (FBIS-NES-92-014 January 22, 1992, p. 15); and Algerian Press Service (APS) from Algiers, March 11, 1992 (FBIS-NES-92-049, March 12, 1992, p. 8).

241. Republic of Algeria Radiia, Algiers, March 11, 1992 (BBC, ME/1327, March 12, 1992, p. A/6). See also *The Defense Monitor*, Vol. 21, No. 3 (1992), p. 4.

242. "Algeria gives nuclear pledge," *Financial Times*, December 22, 1993.

243. Gupta, "Algeria's nuclear ambitions." See also *'Aqat*, November 3, 1991 (translated by HATZAV).

244. David Leppard, Nock Rufford, and Ian Burrel, "Saddam helps Algeria make Islamic nuclear bomb," *Sunday Times*, January 5, 1992; David Watts, "Concerns grow at signs of nuclear links with Algeria," *Times* (London), January 6, 1992; "Algeria Offers Atom Arms Vow," *New York Times*, January 8, 1992; "Algeria and the bomb," p. 38; Lacayo, "Atom Bomb? What Atom Bomb?" p. 16; and Gupta, "Algeria's nuclear ambitions," p. 329. In Congressional testimony, CIA Director Robert M. Gates suggested Algeria as a possible destination for a "brain drain" of scientists from the former Soviet Union. See "CIA fears hi-tech arms sales," *Jane's Defense Weekly*, February 1, 1992, p. 153. See also "When the average salary is 15 dollars," *Ha'aretz*, February 27, 1992 (translated from *Newsweek*).

245. See BBC, ME/1270, p. i, January 6, 1992; and Radiodiffusion-Television Algerienne (BBC, ME/1272 i, January 8, 1992, p. A/16). See also *Defense Monitor*, Vol. 21, No. 3, (1992), p. 4.

246. Nicholas Doughty, "Algeria renounces nuclear arms, joins NPT," Reuters, January 12, 1995.

247. For further details see Feldman, *Israeli Nuclear Deterrence*, p. 78.

248. "Syria will construct a nuclear reactor with Soviet assistance," *Ma'ariv*, May 24, 1983; and Shefi Gabai, "Syria and the Soviet Union agreed on nuclear cooperation," *Ma'ariv*, March 28, 1984. In 1986, Israel's Minister of Energy, Moshe Shachal, was still convinced that Syria was constructing a Chernobyl-type nuclear power reactor. See Gabi Kessler, "Syria constructing a nuclear reactor of the type damaged at Chernobyl," *Ma'ariv*, May 22, 1986.

249. Edwin Eitan, "Syria and Lebanon seek to purchase a nuclear reactor jointly from France," *Yediot Ahronot*, March 4, 1985.

250. Delhi All-India Radio, August 26, 1991, citing Dr. P.K. Iyenger, chairman of the Indian Atomic Energy Commission (FBIS-NES-91-165, August 26, 1991, p. 47). See also "India will sell nuclear reactors to the Third World," *Ha'aretz*, August 13, 1991.

251. See interview with General Al-Din Salim, *'Aqat*, November 3, 1991.

252. Aluf Ben, "Syria demanding that Argentina materialize the sales agreement for nuclear reactor," *Ha'aretz*, December 11, 1994.

253. Eitan Rabin, "Concern in the security establishment about information regarding China's intention to supply a nuclear reactor to Syria," *Ha'aretz*, November 29, 1991. See also "Reactor Sale," *USA Today*, December 3, 1991.

254. Michael Z. Wise, "UN Agency Blocks Sale of Reactor to Syria," *Washington Post*, December 7, 1991; and "China Acts on Nonproliferation Pact," *International Herald Tribune*, December 30, 1991.

255. "Argentina Alleged Conditional Planned Sale of Reactor to Syria," *Nuclear Proliferation News*, No. 30, (August 7, 1995), pp. 8–9.

Chapter 3

Nuclear Weapons in Israel's Security Policy

This chapter and the next focus on how the region's states view nuclear weapons and their likely impact in the Middle East. This chapter examines the origins of Israel's nuclear policy and the strategic imperatives that led it to develop a nuclear option. It traces the evolution of Israel's nuclear ambiguity and analyzes Israel's nuclear threat perceptions, that is, what Israelis find most worrisome about the possibility that the Arab states and Iran might acquire nuclear weapons.

Together, Chapters 3 and 4 show that the different strategic imperatives of Israel and the region's Arab and Muslim states have resulted in different approaches to the possible acquisition of nuclear arms. At the same time, most of these states express alarm regarding the perceived existence or the possible spread of nuclear capabilities in the Middle East. These fears may provide a basis for exploring the prospects for applying some nuclear arms control measures in the region.

Israel's Nuclear Policy

Israel's approach to nuclear arms control in the Middle East is affected by the same considerations that led it to develop a nuclear potential and to surround its potential with maximum ambiguity.

David Ben Gurion — Israel's founding father and first prime minister — seems to have urged the development of a nuclear potential as part of the state's efforts to acquire a qualitative edge over its quantitatively superior Arab adversaries. Ben Gurion was impressed that a nuclear option could serve as a "great equalizer," providing the Jewish state with some capacity to face the threat presented by the Arabs' larger numbers. The nuclear potential also became an important part of Ben Gurion's concept of "cumulative deterrence": that an evolving Israeli track record of defeating the efforts of Arab states to destroy the Jewish state would eventually lead them to understand that Israel cannot be defeated militarily and must be accommodated politically.[1] Implicitly, the development of Israel's nuclear potential was intended to contribute to such a track record and thus to become part of its peace policy.[2]

From the outset, Israel surrounded its nuclear policy with a high degree of ambiguity. To date, it is not clear how far Ben Gurion intended for Israel to advance along the path of developing its potential, or when (and if) critical junctions along the road were crossed. Similar if not greater ambiguity continues to surround the evolution of Israeli thinking in the nuclear realm. Hence, it is not clear whether Israeli decision makers ever considered such a nuclear potential as relevant beyond its contribution to the state's general ("existential") and cumulative deterrence. It is therefore impossible to ascertain whether such a capability was ever considered as potentially providing specific deterrence, namely, the capacity to affect specific strategic or battlefield contexts.

Publicly, Israel adhered to a policy of avoiding any reference to the precise state of its nuclear capacity. Its declarations were limited to repeated statements to the effect that Israel "would not be the first to introduce nuclear weapons to the Middle East."[3] Senior Israeli officials sometimes added that Israel would "not be the second, either." For example, on December 12, 1974, Prime Minister Itzhak Rabin said that Israel "would not be the first to introduce nuclear weapons in the region," but when asked how fast Israel would be able to be the second to do so, he responded: "This is difficult to say. I hope the other side would not be tempted to introduce nuclear weapons. I believe that we cannot afford to be the second country to do so. But we will have to be neither the first nor the second to introduce such weapons."[4] This supplement was probably designed to dispel any illusion among Arab states that they might ever enjoy a nuclear monopoly in the Middle East. Indeed, the utility of Israel's nuclear potential as a hedge against Arab acquisition of nuclear weapons was elaborated again by Prime Minister Rabin in 1994: "We [are keeping] our commitment not to be the first to introduce [nuclear weapons in the Middle East], but we still look ahead to the dangers that others will do it and we have to be prepared for it."[5]

The objective of denying an Arab nuclear monopoly was explained by Yuval Ne'eman, who was involved in tailoring Israel's nuclear policy, and has served as a senior military intelligence officer, Israel's science attaché in Paris, the Chairman of Israel's Atomic Energy Commission, and Minister of Science.

During the 1950s and 1960s, I was a partner to the creation of a security concept, the essence of which was that Israel would build a nuclear infrastructure — largely in research — which could be materialized in time of need. The infrastructure consists mainly of professional manpower. If some of the Arab countries were to acquire nuclear weapons, this [potential] would enable us to develop a nuclear capability quickly, without having to beg the U.S. or the UN to save us. Israel said explicitly that it has no interest in crossing the nuclear threshold because it does not want to force the Arabs to arm themselves with nuclear weapons.... Thus Israel is ambiguous about its nuclear capability. It follows two principles: first, it would not be the first to "nuclearize" in the Middle East; second, should it be required, it would not take Israel very long to materialize its nuclear potential.[6]

Shalheveth Freier, former Chairman of Israel's Atomic Energy Commission, provided a wider external and internal context to Israel's nuclear ambiguity:

As I understand it, the purpose of such a statement is to give a sense of reassurance to Israelis in time of gloom, to serve as possible caution to states which contemplate harming Israel by dint of their preponderance in men and material, and to relieve states that do not wish to take up definite positions in this matter from doing so.[7]

Israel's nuclear ambiguity thus served a number of strategic, international, regional, and domestic imperatives. As a strategic tool, it seems to have been designed to produce effective "deterrence through uncertainty." The Arab states' inability to rule out the possibility that Israel might possess an operational nuclear capability and might use it in retaliation was expected to deter them from posing threats to Israel's existence and survival. In the international arena, Israel's implicit policy helped avoid a clash with the United States. After making a brief but significant contribution to global nuclear proliferation in the framework of the Eisenhower administration's

"Atoms for Peace" program, Washington later attempted to prevent the further spread of nuclear arms. While a number of U.S. administrations have raised the nuclear issue with successive Israeli governments, Israel's ambiguous policy has helped to avert far greater tension and to prevent an explicit clash with Washington.[8] Indeed, in 1994 Prime Minister Rabin explained Israel's ambiguous nuclear policy primarily in the context of the assurances that Israel provided to the United States: "We are committed to the United States for many years, not to be the first to introduce nuclear weapons or weapons within the context of the Arab-Israeli conflict."[9]

More generally, Israel's nuclear ambiguity served to avoid a clash with international nonproliferation norms. Israel has never challenged the efficacy and legitimacy of the global nuclear nonproliferation regime, but has merely reasoned that its security imperatives and the strategic circumstances prevailing in the Middle East prevent it from joining the NPT. In contrast, India, another NPT non-signatory, continues to attack the "discriminatory" character of international nonproliferation efforts. Far more than its continued ambiguous posture, the adoption of overt nuclear deterrence would have placed Israel in a direct collision course with global nonproliferation norms — a situation it was eager to avoid.

Regionally, as Ne'eman pointed out, Israel's ambiguous policy was designed to avoid encouraging neighboring Arab states to seek a countervailing nuclear capability. The argument here seems to have been that if Israel adopted an explicit nuclear deterrence policy, some Arab leaders might face heavy domestic pressures to do the same, even if they considered such efforts to be too costly and technically uncertain, and even if they regarded such a capability to be largely irrelevant to their own strategic objectives. Thus, as long as Arab leaders could confess uncertainty regarding Israel's nuclear potential, they would be able to continue resisting domestic pressures to produce an adequate response.

Internally, Israel's ambiguous nuclear policy seems to have served the need to maintain domestic consensus and support for its general defense policy. Among Israel's policy elite, the ambiguous posture was originally a compromise between advocates of greater reliance on nuclear deterrence, and those who claimed that such deterrence was irrelevant in the Middle East or counterproductive for Israel. Moshe

Dayan, then IDF Chief of Staff, and Shimon Peres, then Deputy Minister of Defense, seem to have been the most determined and outspoken among the former, while Yigal Allon, a distinguished IDF General during the 1948 War and later leader of the Ahdut Ha'avoda (United Labor) party, seems to have been the most explicit among the latter. The compromise seems to have been that a nuclear potential would be developed, but that reliance upon it for specific deterrence would be limited by keeping its precise nature ambiguous.[10]

Moreover, the ambiguous posture helped arrest the development of a public debate regarding Israel's nuclear policy. This not only maintained domestic consensus, but also provided those involved in directing the development of Israel's nuclear potential with a high degree of policy autonomy. In the absence of reliable information about Israel's nuclear activities and designs, no debate about its nuclear policy could be conducted; in the absence of public debate, the individuals navigating Israel's nuclear potential could remain largely immune to public checks and controls.

Finally, by refraining from adopting an overt nuclear posture, the Israeli Defense Forces were prevented from relying excessively on deterrence. This was probably deemed important in order to maintain the IDF's "fighting spirit" — a prerequisite to its capacity to face less than existential threats. Moreover, the pretense that Israel's nuclear potential does not exist created a mental separation between the nuclear and the conventional realms, and encouraged the IDF to think that there are no "fallbacks" and hence that there is no alternative to making its conventional forces as robust as possible.

Indeed, the ambiguity surrounding Israel's nuclear potential was maintained despite some clear costs. First, the credibility of its general nuclear deterrence was somewhat limited as long as Israel's neighbors remained uncertain about its capability. Second, the development of a balanced nuclear doctrine may have been hindered by the absence of open debate. Third, the ability to conduct a direct or indirect strategic dialogue on nuclear matters with Israel's neighbors — or to communicate specific threats or threat perceptions — remained limited by secrecy. Finally, the process of convincing the Arab publics of Israel's permanence in the region was delayed by the limited capacity to project Israel's nuclear potential as contributing to such permanence.[11]

Yet Israel's nuclear policy continues to enjoy a high degree of domestic consensus. For example, public opinion surveys conducted as part of the Project on Public Opinion and National Security of Tel Aviv University's Jaffee Center for Strategic Studies demonstrated wide and growing public support for "the development of a nuclear capability." While 78 percent of the respondents approved of such efforts in 1987, the number increased to 91 percent in 1991. Equally impressive was the increase in public support for the use of nuclear weapons "under some circumstances": from 36 percent in 1986, to 53 percent in 1987, and to 88 percent in 1991.[12] The figure for 1991 probably reflected Israeli public reaction to the use of Iraqi ballistic missiles and the threat that Iraq might use chemical weapons against Israel during the Gulf War; by 1993 the figure dropped to 67 percent.[13]

It is hardly surprising that of the 67 percent of respondents to the 1993 survey who said they would support using nuclear weapons under some circumstances, some 90 percent said that the employment of nuclear weapons by Israel in response to an Arab nuclear attack was either "justified" or "very justified." More surprising is that a relatively large number of these respondents — 73 percent — said that such use would also be either "justified" or "very justified" in the case of an Arab attack using chemical or biological weapons. Equally interesting is that only 47 percent thought that the use of nuclear weapons would be either "justified" or "very justified" in order to prevent defeat in a conventional war.

Finally, the January 1993 survey also showed a high degree of support for keeping Israel's nuclear posture "ambiguous" — some 71 percent of the respondents supported maintaining Israel's nuclear capabilities "secret." Only 29 percent of the respondents preferred the adoption of overt nuclear deterrence, a small increase in the percent supporting overt deterrence compared to 1987, when 76 percent of the respondents supported keeping Israel's nuclear capabilities "secret."[14]

The Evolution of Israel's Nuclear Ambiguity

Twenty years ago, Israel's nuclear potential was surrounded by a high degree of ambiguity; today, Israel is almost universally regarded as possessing an advanced nuclear capability. The change was caused primarily by the large number of international media reports regarding

Israel's nuclear capability, especially during the past ten years. Many of these reports (which are documented at length in Chapter 2) have featured leaks by U.S. and European government sources of various intelligence assessments and reports regarding Israel's nuclear capability. They also included confirmed and unconfirmed foreign reports that Israel was testing surface-to-surface missiles and rocket launch vehicles, which were widely interpreted as indicating an intention to deliver nuclear payloads. Mordechai Va'anunu's descriptions of the activities taking place at Dimona seem to have been particularly important in confirming to many in the Arab world and beyond that Israel has developed a deliverable nuclear force.[15]

Israel's nuclear ambiguity has also been reduced by the gradually increasing clarity of references to Israel's nuclear potential by acting or former Israeli statesmen and officials during the past twenty years. Thus, on December 1, 1974, Israel's President Efraim Katzir stated that "Israel has a nuclear potential." He refused to say when its potential might be materialized.[16] On February 28, 1976, Moshe Dayan, former minister of defense and then a member of the Knesset, said in Paris: "In the future, Israel must have a nuclear option and the ability to possess nuclear weapons without outside control. I think we are capable of producing the bomb now. I also think that if the Arabs introduce nuclear weapons into the Middle East sometime in the future, we should have the bomb before them. But clearly not in order to use the bomb first."[17]

Five months later, Dayan stated in Canada: "Israel possesses the scientific and technological capacity to produce the atomic bomb — in case the Arabs threaten to use such a bomb — but Israel would never be the first to open nuclear warfare in the Middle East."[18] In February 1978, as Foreign Minister, Dayan told a delegation of the U.S. House Armed Services Committee: "We will not be the first to use nuclear weapons — but we do not wish to be the third party to do so."[19] In July 1980, Dayan — by that time no longer in office — said that "the Arabs will not have the only nuclear option [in the region]. To the best of my knowledge, should the state of Israel face a threat of extermination it would be able to tell the Arabs: 'if you wish to destroy us, you should know that we can also destroy you'."[20] In 1981 Dayan characterized Israel's nuclear state: "We don't have any nuclear bombs now. But we have the capacity, we can do that in a short time. We are not going to be the first ones to introduce nuclear weapons into the Middle East, but we do have the capacity to produce nuclear weapons, and if the Arabs are willing to introduce nuclear weapons into the Middle East, then Israel should not be too late in having nuclear weapons, too."[21]

Over the years, Itzhak Rabin's statements also became slightly less ambiguous. As mentioned earlier, in 1974 he merely stated that Israel would not be the first to introduce weapons into the Middle East. Twelve years later, during a visit to Sweden, he reportedly stated that "Israel does not belong to the 'nuclear club'."[22] But in 1992 Rabin said that Israel has a "significant deterrent" to Iranian and Iraqi nuclear threats. He added that the deterrent was developed "many years ago, before the Likud [came to power in 1977]."[23]

Finally, a number of statements made by Israeli and U.S. officials, intentionally and unintentionally, before and during the Gulf War, could have been interpreted as implying that Israel already enjoyed an effective nuclear deterrent.[24] When Saddam Hussein threatened on April 2, 1990, that if Iraq were attacked he would make use of binary chemical weapons that would "consume half of Israel," Israel's Defense Minister Rabin acknowledged that "we have the means for a devastating response, many times greater than [the magnitude of] Saddam Hussein's threats."[25]

In mid-February 1991 Rabin seemed to confirm that Israel relied heavily on the deterrent effect of its capacity to wipe out Arab population centers. In a discussion among Labor Party members of Knesset during the Gulf War, he reportedly said: "How do you think we deterred the Syrians? What did we tell them? We told them: 'If you strike Tel Aviv with surface-to-surface missiles — Damascus will be destroyed. If you attack Haifa with such missiles, Damascus and Haleb would not remain — they would be destroyed. We will not deal with the missile launchers, we will destroy Damascus instead'."[26] Yet Rabin refrained from specifying with what means such devastation was contemplated, leaving open the possibility that he intended to achieve this with conventional payloads.

On December 29, 1990, IDF Chief of Staff Lt. General Dan Shomron deviated from Israel's standard policy statement that it "would not be the first to *introduce* nuclear weapons in the Middle East."[27] In a speech to the Chamber of Commerce and Industry in Tel

Aviv, Shomron stated that "Israel would not be the first to *use* nuclear weapons in the Middle East."[28] As far as could be ascertained, Shomron simply misspoke on that occasion; his deviation was not intentional. Unaware of this, however, Israel's Ambassador to the United States, Zalman Shoval, took Shomron's words as a signal that Israel's declaratory policy regarding its nuclear potential had changed, and publicly repeated the Chief of Staff's statement.[29] Three days later, the statement was repeated again, this time by Israel's Ambassador to Belgium.[30] It would not be surprising if these statements were interpreted by some of the region's leaders as suggesting that Israel had already introduced nuclear weapons to the region.

During the Gulf War, Israel's nuclear ambiguity was further eroded by U.S. Secretary of Defense Richard Cheney. When asked in a CNN interview whether he believed that Israel might respond with tactical nuclear weapons to an Iraqi nuclear attack, Cheney responded: "That decision the Israelis would have to make — but I would think that [Saddam Hussein] has to be cautious in terms of how he proceeds in his attacks against Israel."[31] The Secretary of Defense refrained from any comment regarding the premise that informed the question: that Israel had a nuclear arsenal that would be useful for such a retaliation.

On June 6, 1993, Israel's Deputy Defense Minister, Mordechai (Motta) Gur stated publicly:

Any Arab leader of a country hostile to Israel must carefully weigh what he stands to win or lose if he decides to drop a nuclear bomb on Israel. Each and every Arab leader knows full well that we will not sit idly by, that [Israel] has an active defense, and that it will not be worth his while to expose his country to the risk of an Israeli retaliation. As far as Israel is concerned, we are capable of turning the situation around in such a way as to make it too costly for anybody to wage a nuclear war against us here in the Middle East. The damage Israel will inflict on the nuclear aggressor will far outweigh the so-called profits they may be able to reap. They will never catch us in a moment of weakness, because Israel is capable of dealing a devastating blow which will make a nuclear war not worth their while.[32]

Gur's message registered in at least some quarters of the Arab world; for example, his speech was quoted extensively in a June 14, 1993, letter by Iraq's minister of foreign affairs to the president of the

UN Security Council.[33]

Israel's diminished nuclear ambiguity has increased the credibility of its deterrence. Arabs have become convinced that Israel possesses a nuclear capability, thus contributing to an evolving Arab perception regarding Israel's permanence.[34] Similarly, although Israel has yet to experience a significant public debate regarding its nuclear policy, the foundations for such a debate have been established by the proliferation of references to this issue in the Israeli media during the past ten years. Finally, a strategic dialogue on nuclear issues has begun; indeed, as Cheney's words illustrate, nuclear threats have been indirectly communicated to an Arab state, at least during the Gulf War.

As the reduction in ambiguity surrounding Israel's nuclear potential provides more robust deterrence, the costs associated with its present posture have also diminished, thereby reducing the incentives to change it. But at the same time, the effects of reduced ambiguity have also diminished some of the potential costs of adopting a more explicit nuclear posture. Primarily, it is becoming increasingly difficult to argue that a more explicit Israeli nuclear posture might encourage further proliferation in the region by producing domestic pressures among Israel's neighbors to create an Arab nuclear response. Since almost all Arab leaders and most of the Arab media already refer to Israel publicly as an advanced nuclear state, such pressures — if they were ever to arise — should already have developed.

Israeli Nuclear Threat Perceptions

All Israelis view the possible acquisition of nuclear weapons by an Arab or a non-Arab Muslim state in the Middle East with considerable apprehension, though they differ on the extent to which they view it as threatening. Many Israelis believe that the possible proliferation of nuclear weapons in the Middle East presents their state with an existential threat.[35] A small minority seems to go so far as to see such possession as risking a Third World War.[36]

Israel's concern about nuclear proliferation in the region comprises seven main considerations. First, Israelis are terrified about the sheer dimensions of the damage that they might have to endure if attacked by nuclear weapons. For example, on June 5, 1981 — the day Israel bombed Iraq's Osiraq reactor — Prime Minister Menachem Begin recounted:

Our experts tell us that with one 20-kiloton bomb the Iraqis would be able to immediately kill 50,000 Israeli citizens and to cause the death of 150,000 additional citizens. Those damaged by radioactivity would either die, lose the capacity to give birth, or would give birth to children damaged in their body and soul. With three atomic bombs the enemy would be able to destroy Jerusalem and its vicinity, Tel Aviv and its suburbs, and Haifa and its neighboring [towns]. Twenty percent of Israel's population would be exterminated or damaged. In American terms this implies some 46 million casualties. This is why Iraqi atomic bombs would comprise an existential threat to Israel.[37]

In a letter to U.S. President Ronald Reagan written after the bombing, Begin drew a parallel between the effects of nuclear weapons and the Holocaust inflicted upon Jews by Nazi Germany during the Second World War:

A million and a half children were poisoned with Zyklon gas during the holocaust. Now Israel's children were about to be poisoned by radioactivity. For the past two years, we have been living under the nightmare of the danger confronting us by the Iraqi nuclear reactor. When I see children and talk to them, I fear their fate: what will happen to them within a few years? In the generation in which a third of our people were exterminated, the Israeli people were exposed to a new war of extermination: Jerusalem, Tel Aviv, Haifa and their vicinities could have been hit by an Iraqi atomic bomb. Some 600,000 would have been damaged by an Iraqi nuclear attack. In American terms, this would have amounted to some 46 million casualties. This would have been a new holocaust.[38]

More generally, Israelis fear the unwillingness of some of their neighbors to accept the permanent existence of a Jewish state in the region. The ideological prism through which their state is seen as a foreign, "imperialistic," and heretic force, and the resulting commitment to its destruction, might lead an Arab or Muslim leader to launch a nuclear attack on the Jewish state. Consequently, they fear that such leaders may find the option of destroying the Jewish state too tempting to ignore.

By the early 1990s, Iran seems to have become the focus of such concerns. Iran's mix of Muslim religious fanaticism and its possession of unconventional weapons is viewed by Israelis as creating the danger of a nuclear attack on Israel regardless of the costs to the attacker. For example, in mid-1993 Foreign Minister Shimon Peres said: "We must clarify to the world the real nature of Rafsanjani's Iran. [They] regard Israel as a 'collective Salman Rushdie' and would like to do to us what they would like to do to him."[39]

Second, Israelis tend to regard some of the region's leaders as prone to irresponsible and irrational behavior and choices, and as insensitive to costs and as extremely prone to misassessments and risk-taking, and some are also seen as allowing their emotions to overrule their reason.[40] For example, Iraq's President Saddam Hussein is often characterized as a reckless, dangerous, and adventurous leader, prone to repeated strategic miscalculations and willing to have his citizens suffer the painful consequences of his misjudgments.[41] In 1980, Prime Minister Begin reportedly told U.S. Ambassador Samuel Lewis: "Saddam Hussein is the same type of leader as Libya's Mu'ammar Qadhafi. Both lead governments that are irresponsible in the extreme. They may try to obtain nuclear weapons in order to exterminate Israel's civilian population."[42] Similarly, a 1981 Israeli government statement noted that had Saddam Hussein acquired nuclear weapons "he would not have hesitated to drop them on Israel's cities and population centers."[43] The statement reflected the views expressed clearly by Prime Minister Begin in a Defense Cabinet meeting convened in October 1980 to debate the possible bombing of the Osiraq reactor. In the meeting, Begin is reported to have said that "if Saddam Hussein obtained a nuclear bomb, he would not hesitate to drop it on Tel Aviv, resulting in 300,000 casualties."[44] Likewise, Moshe Arens, then chairman of the Knesset Committee for Foreign and Defense Affairs, warned that Iraq's possession of nuclear weapons might lead to a global conflagration. He said that Iraq was among the most adventurous of the Arab states and that Iraqi use of nuclear weapons could soon transcend the boundaries of the Middle East. He added that it was frightening to think that nuclear weapons would be provided to Iraq's unstable leaders.[45]

Ten years later, Israel's view of Saddam Hussein was only reinforced. In mid-1990, Defense Minister Moshe Arens said: "I believe that the entire world will take measures to make sure that Saddam

Hussein does not have weapons of mass destruction because people understand that such weapons in his hands are dangerous, not only for Israel, but for the entire world."[46] A milder assessment was made by an Israeli expert: "Against the backdrop of Saddam Hussein's conduct and activities, nuclear power in his hands could become a supreme means of extortion that could lead to a total upsetting of the rules of the game between Israel and the Arab world."[47]

Third, Israelis fear that the vulnerability of their small state may lead an Arab leader to attempt a decapitating strike, destroying Israel's retaliatory means in a first strike and ridding the Muslim region of the Jewish state. Some Israelis also consider that the demographic gap between Israel and the Arab states — reflected both in the sizes of populations and the sizes of families — makes Arab leaders less sensitive to costs. For example, in 1990 Prime Minister Itzhak Shamir said that in the Middle East "human life is held cheap."[48] Similarly, Defense Minister Arens said in early 1991: "Saddam Hussein does not view human life in the same manner that we do. He has a different system of values than ours and this is why it is so difficult for us to understand his behavior."[49]

Fourth, Israelis who may be less prone to attribute irrationality and genocidal commitment to leaders in the region nevertheless fear that in the absence of advanced technologies in the region, deployed nuclear weapons would be inadequately controlled. As a consequence, nuclear weapons might be launched accidentally, resulting in regional catastrophe.

Fifth and more generally, most Israelis reject the notion that a stable nuclear "balance of terror" could be established in the Middle East.[50] There is much concern that it would be difficult to manage a multi-nuclear Middle East even under the best of circumstances. Such concern centers on the basic difference between the orderly Cold War bipolar strategic relationship and a more anarchic multipolar nuclear Middle East. The requirements of managing nuclear relations with a number of states simultaneously is regarded as too taxing for the region's leaders. These concerns are voiced by Israel's former minister of science, Yuval Ne'eman:

In the Arab world there are governments similar to those of Qadhafi and [Saddam] Hussein. Is it possible to be sure that the judgment of these leaders, for whom human life does not count, will be as rational as the judgment of the leaders of the great powers? Moreover, the "balance of terror" existed between the superpowers — the United States and the Soviet Union. What Saddam aspires to is a "balance of terror" between Israel and 21 Arab states which are not unified and which compete with each other without inhibitions, and more than once have actually fought one another.[51]

Sixth, some Israelis are concerned that the proliferation of nuclear weapons in the Middle East could lead to their acquisition by terrorist groups. This could happen if a sovereign state transfers nuclear weapons to terrorists, a danger sometimes referred to as "state-sponsored nuclear terrorism." Alternatively, inadequate control of nuclear weapons may simply lead terrorists in the region to steal or otherwise to assume control over such weapons. The acquisition of nuclear weapons by terrorists might allow them either to explode a nuclear device or to exercise nuclear blackmail, thus confronting the Israeli government with impossible choices.

Seventh, a particularly salient theme in much Israeli discussion of the possible nuclearization of the Middle East is the dangers involved in nuclear proliferation in a region that has experienced recurrent warfare and continues to be characterized by active conflict. It is claimed that nuclear stability in Europe, by contrast, resulted largely from the absence of heated conflict and the fact that NATO and Warsaw Pact forces never met in battle. Hence, it is argued that everything should be done to postpone the region's nuclearization until Arab-Israeli peace is achieved, and that the peace process should be accelerated so that peace prevails before nuclearization.[52]

Some Israelis doubt that successful Arab-Israeli peacemaking would mitigate the threat posed by nuclear proliferation because the states that are presently the main focus of proliferation concerns — Iraq, Iran, and Libya — remain outside the peace process. Yet advocates of such a linkage insist that once peace is achieved between Israel and the surrounding Arab states, the threat posed by the nuclearization of Israel's remaining adversaries would be lessened; peace would transform the political context of such threats. Some observers argue that Iraq and Iran would not exercise nuclear intervention unless invited to do so by one of Israel's immediate neighbors, a scenario that could only materialize as long as the Arab-

Israeli conflict remains unresolved.

The combination of all these fears has led the Israeli government to determine that it would take extreme measures to ensure that Arab countries do not acquire nuclear weapons. Thus, Prime Minister Menachem Begin issued a directive in November 1977 to the effect that his government would not permit any neighboring country that remains in "a state of war" with Israel to construct a nuclear reactor that could manufacture mass destruction weapons that might be used against Israel. From 1978 to 1981, Israel took a series of measures to delay the process of Iraq's nuclearization, ultimately resulting in the June 1981 bombing of the Osiraq reactor in al-Tuwaytha. The bombing was accompanied by a public statement by the Israeli government that "under no circumstances would we allow the enemy to develop weapons of mass destruction against our nation; we will defend Israel's citizens, in time, with all the means at our disposal."[53] After Begin made a similar statement at a post-operation news conference, Israel's commitment to prevention was termed by the media "the Begin doctrine."[54]

Israeli leaders repeated this doctrine on many occasions.[55] For example, in a major policy address, then–Defense Minister Ariel Sharon stated in December 1981: "The third element in our defense policy for the 1980s is our determination to prevent confrontation states from gaining access to nuclear weapons. Israel cannot afford the introduction of the nuclear weapon. For us it is not a question of a balance of terror but a question of survival. We shall therefore have to prevent such a threat at its inception."[56]

The spirit of the "Begin doctrine" was somewhat tamed as early as 1984: in an official letter submitted by its representative to the IAEA, the Israeli government committed itself not to attack "nuclear facilities dedicated to peaceful purposes."[57] Still, some members of Israel's defense community continue to advocate the 1981 doctrine. For example, then–IDF Deputy Chief of Staff, Maj. Gen. Amnon Shahak, said in April 1992: "I think Israel should invest all its energy and efforts in preventing the development of a nuclear capability in an Arab state. In my opinion, all means are legitimate to obtain this objective."[58] Later that year, the Commander of the Israeli Air Force, Maj. Gen. Herzel Bodinger, said that "Israel must do whatever it can to prevent the introduction of nuclear weapons to the region."[59] In late

1994, the commander of the IDF's Planning Division, Maj. Gen. Uzi Dayan, hinted that Israel might be forced to take preemptive action against Iraq's and Iran's nuclear facilities as soon as 1995.[60]

Israeli leaders are not unanimous in their support for the so-called Begin doctrine. Asked about his deputy's earlier support for preventive action, then–IDF Chief of Staff, Lt. Gen. Ehud Barak, said in 1992:

We must be ready to make extensive efforts in various spheres to reduce and postpone the attainment of nuclear capability by an Arab country. The political aspect is the main tool of this effort: international cooperation in the sphere of intelligence and in political spheres, with the objective of stopping these developments. Then there is the intelligence aspect. Marginally, there can also be an operational aspect. We must remember, however, that after all, we have no way of knowing today what the situation will be like in 10 years, and I do not think that we should make advance decisions or speculative assumptions on what we will do in certain contingencies 10 years from now.[61]

Indeed, even at the time of the 1981 Osiraq bombing not all members of Israel's policy elite were highly anxious about the prospect that the region's states might acquire an advanced nuclear capability. Among those who expressed reservations regarding the bombing of Osiraq were Deputy Minister of Defense Brig. Gen. (Res.) Mordechai Zipori; the Head of the Mossad, Maj. Gen. (Res.) Itzhak Hofi; Director of Military Intelligence Maj. Gen. Yehoshua Saguy; Director of the National Security Planning Unit of the Ministry of Defense, Maj. Gen. Avraham ("Abrasha") Tamir; the Commander of the IDF's Planning Branch, Maj. Gen. Nati Sharoni; Likud leader and former Defense Minister Ezer Weizmann; Deputy Prime Minister Yigal Yadin; and opposition leader Shimon Peres.[62]

The chief objection seems to have been the raid's timing; they feared that the operation would derail the fragile Israeli-Egyptian peace process, fuel Arab anxieties about Israel's profile in the region, and damage Israeli-French relations (because France was heavily involved in Iraq's nuclear program). They also estimated that the Osiraq reactor was not likely to become operational soon, so that Israel could keep the option of destroying it later with little risk of radioactive contamination if other means to halt its construction failed. Opponents of the raid also seemed to have a somewhat more sober view of the likelihood that a nuclear capability might be acquired by an Arab state. Deputy Minister of Defense Zipori, for example, said that "an Arab nuclear option is only a matter of time. Israel would not be lost even if they acquire a nuclear bomb."[63]

In the early 1990s, similar differences of opinion were reflected in the debate regarding Israel's approach to Iran's nuclear program. While the statement made by General Bodinger manifests an approach similar to that espoused more than a decade earlier by the Begin government, other Israeli defense leaders urge that Israel avoid making Iran's nuclear program "an Israeli issue."[64] For example, the Commander of its Intelligence Corps, Brig. Gen. Doron Tamir, said: "We argue that it is possible to delay and even stop the process of Iran's nuclearization. But this is a function of the intensity with which we will deal with the issue. At any rate, it would be difficult for Israel to arrest this process on its own."[65]

The perception that the implications of nuclear proliferation in the Middle East might be less than catastrophic is reflected in official calls for Israel to adjust to the prospect of the possible nuclearization of the region. For example, in late 1991, Defense Minister Moshe Arens told the Knesset Committee on Foreign and Defense Affairs that the region is "marching toward the nuclear era" and that Israel "would have to adjust itself to life in this new reality."[66] The fact that he used the word "life" rather than "death" indicates that Arens did not view such a "new reality" solely in catastrophic terms. Elsewhere, Arens justified Israel's development of the Arrow anti-tactical ballistic missile system at least partly in terms of the need to thwart a possible nuclear attack.

Thus, a multi-nuclear Middle East was mentioned in the context of the debate on the Arrow in terms similar to those used in the past debates on the requirements of nuclear stability in the U.S.-Soviet context. At the very least, this suggests a less-than-apocalyptic view of the consequences of nuclear proliferation in the region. Had Israeli decision makers ruled out the possibility that some degree of nuclear stability could be achieved, they would more likely have ignored all "active defense" and "second strike" options, and would instead have devoted all assets to prevention, even by the most violent means. Indeed, even if discussions of these options merely reflect an assessment that the nuclearization of the Middle East — however dangerous — is inevitable, their tone did not reflect panic. Obviously, this rather dispassionate attitude might change rapidly were one of the region's states to acquire a nuclear capability, just as the general reaction to weapons of mass destruction was much shriller during the Gulf War.

Statements that Israel "would not be the second" to introduce nuclear weapons in the region may also reflect a perception that the acquisition of nuclear weapons by Arabs is highly undesirable for Israel, but would not necessarily result in disaster. Indeed, the argument that developing a nuclear option was necessary to ensure a nuclear equilibrium reflects an underlying premise that such an equilibrium, resulting in some measure of stability, could evolve. For example, the Head of the IDF Rear Command, Maj. Gen. Ze'ev Livne, noted in 1992: "I don't know if we will be able to prevent [the development of] an Arab nuclear bomb forever.... [But] even if someone would have the bomb, this does not mean that the following day he would use it. The U.S. and the Soviet Union lived for decades under the [shadow of the] balance of terror and the Cold War."[67]

Underlying this more sober view of the potential danger entailed in the proliferation of nuclear weapons in the Middle East is a rejection of the notion that Arab leaders are irrational. That is, some Israelis regard these leaders as sufficiently sensitive to costs to make deterrence work.[68] For example, in late 1991 a leading Israeli commentator wrote:

Crazy, crazy, but the fact is that [Saddam Hussein] did not launch a single chemical warhead against Israel despite the fact that he possessed [them]. He knew that in dealing with Israel there was a red line that one does not cross. Israel was spared damage to its [civilian] rear [areas] and the use of mass destruction weapons in most of its wars not only due to its military doctrine but mostly due to nuclear deterrence. The balance of terror and the red line which we created without excessive words and show-off are understood clearly even by the craziest of our adversaries.[69]

This more sober view of the dangers of nuclear proliferation is, however, rejected by Israel's public at large. In a public opinion survey conducted in January–February 1994 as part of the Project on Public Opinion and National Security, some 92 percent of the respondents noted that they felt "threatened" or "very threatened" (25 percent and 67 percent) by Arab possession of unconventional weapons. This reflected a slight lessening of Israeli fears since immediately after the

Gulf War; in a survey conducted in March 1991, 76 percent of the respondents had said they felt "very threatened" by Arab possession of unconventional weapons.[70]

Conclusions

Israel's decision to develop a nuclear option was driven by its unique strategic imperative: the need of a small state, rejected by its numerically preponderant neighbors, to deter threats to its existence and to hedge against the possible acquisition of nuclear weapons by its numerically preponderant adversaries. While seeking effective "deterrence through uncertainty," Israel adopted an ambiguous nuclear posture to avoid clashing with U.S. nuclear nonproliferation policy and with international nonproliferation norms, and to refrain from encouraging the Arab states to acquire nuclear capabilities. This ambiguous posture also served as a compromise between advocates and opponents of nuclear deterrence, and it shielded Israel's nuclear bureaucracy from public scrutiny. The ambiguity surrounding Israel's nuclear option has gradually eroded. This is evident not only in the more revealing references to Israel's nuclear potential made by the country's leaders but also in the manner in which their neighbors' perceptions of this capability has evolved, as Chapter 4 shows.

At the same time, Israelis seem deeply concerned about the possibility that some of their neighbors might obtain nuclear weapons. While the extent of the threat is a subject of considerable debate, most Israelis are doubtful that a multi-nuclear Middle East can be stable; many are uncertain that Arab leaders can be trusted to pursue rational nuclear choices; a number of them are concerned that an Arab leader might attempt a 'decapitating' nuclear strike; and many fear the acquisition of nuclear weapons or materials by terrorist groups. Consequently, many Israelis are determined to make every effort to avoid nuclear anarchy in the Middle East.

NOTES

1. Although he did not use the term, Ben Gurion developed the concept of "cumulative deterrence" more than ten years before Israel's independence was established. In 1936 he stressed: "Only with the increase of our strength will the Arabs understand that this destructive and futile war against the forces building this country must be brought to an end.

Only if we become a large force which cannot be shaken or silenced will the Arab leaders understand the inevitability of reconciliation with the presence of the Jewish people in this country." And elsewhere that year he said: "[Arab peace with us] is possible only if we are able to prove to them ... that the Jewish factor [in this country] is not hopeless or temporary, but is rather potent and permanent, and is a historical fact that cannot be canceled or weakened or ignored." See David Ben Gurion, *Bama'aracha*, Vol. 1 (Tel Aviv: Am Oved Publishers, 1957), pp. 16, 62.

2. For writings by Ben Gurion on the nuclear factor, dating as early as 1948, see G. Rivlin and E. Oren, eds., *The War of Independence: Ben Gurion's Diary*, Vol. 1 (Tel Aviv: Ministry of Defense Publishing House, 1982), p. 245; ibid., pp. 827, 889; and David Ben Gurion, *The Eternity of Israel* (Tel Aviv: Ayanot Publishers, 1963), pp. 191, 196–198, 329.

3. See Shalheveth Freier, "A Nuclear-Weapon-Free-Zone (NWFZ) in the Middle East and its Ambience," unpublished paper, July 14, 1993, p. 2.

4. Gil Kaisari, "Dayan: 'If the Arabs introduce nuclear weapons in our region, we should have the bomb before them'," *Ma'ariv* (Israel), November 12, 1986.

5. Prime Minister Rabin responding to a question by a Jordanian journalist during a press conference in Washington, D.C., July 26, 1994.

6. Yuval Ne'eman, "I oppose the concept favoring explicit nuclear deterrence," *D'var Hashavua* (Friday supplement of *Davar*), August 13, 1993, p. 17. In a later interview, Ne'eman elaborated: "The human infrastructure we created and the facilities we created were meant to create a potential and to provide us with an option to arm ourselves one day with nuclear weapons, if this will become necessary — if such weapons will be obtained by our enemies." Yuval Ne'eman, "1993: the balance of nuclear threats," *Ma'ariv*, January 4, 1993.

7. Freier, "A Nuclear-Weapon-Free-Zone (NWFZ) in the Middle East and its Ambience," p. 2.

8. See Shai Feldman, *Israeli Nuclear Deterrence: A Strategy for the 1980s* (New York: Columbia University Press, 1982), pp. 211–233.

9. Response to a question by a Jordanian journalist during a press conference in Washington, D.C., July 26, 1994.

10. Yair Evron, *Hadilemma Hagarinit Shel Israel* (Israel's nuclear dilemma) (Tel Aviv: Yad Tabenkin, 1987), p. 18.

11. For an elaboration of these points, see Feldman, *Israeli Nuclear Deterrence*, pp. 7–24.

12. Asher Arian, Ilan Talmud and Tamar Hermann, *National Security and Public Opinion in Israel*, JCSS Study No. 9 (Tel Aviv: Jaffee Center for Strategic Studies [JCSS], Tel Aviv University, 1988); and Asher Arian, "Security and Political Attitudes: The Gulf War," in Joseph

Alpher, ed., *War in the Gulf: Implications for Israel* (Tel Aviv: JCSS, Tel Aviv University, 1992), pp. 305, 316–318.

13. Asher Arian, *Security Threatened: Surveying Israeli Opinion on Peace and War* (Cambridge: Cambridge University Press, 1995).

14. Arian, *Security Threatened.*

15. For example, an Arab expert who examined Israel's nuclear capability reacted to the 1986 Va'anunu revelations and the interview given by Jean-François Perrin: "The Arab states will study the implications of the revelations for the future balance of forces in the region. This will have an enormous impact for any future conflict in the region. Until now there was much speculation but no documentation. The data on laboratory-2 and the plutonium reprocessing plant is entirely new." Yohanan Lahav, "France helped Israel during the 1950s to develop a nuclear bomb," *Yediot Ahronot* (Israel), October 12, 1986.

16. Kaisari, "Dayan: 'If the Arabs'."

17. Ibid.

18. Ibid.

19. Ibid.

20. Shlomo Nakdimon, *Tamuz on Fire*, 2d ed. (Tel Aviv: Idanim Publishing, [in Hebrew], 1993), p. 134.

21. David Shipler, "A-Arms Capacity of Israelis: Topic Rich With Speculations," *New York Times*, October 29, 1986.

22. Eliahu Zehavi, "Rabin in Sweden: Israel does not belong to the 'nuclear club'," *Ha'aretz* (Israel), November 10, 1986.

23. Rabin interview in *Ma'ariv* on June 18, 1992 (AP from Jerusalem, June 18, 1992).

24. Notably, the Va'anunu affair did not alter Israel's official policy. Israel's then prime minister, Shimon Peres, reacted to the 1986 *Sunday Times* (London) report by restating that "Israel will not be the first to introduce nuclear weapons into the region." Peres characterized the report as "sensationalist" and added that Israel has become "used to sensational reports on the nuclear research center in Dimona, and does not make a practice of commenting on them." See Akiva Eldar, "Peres: Israel will not be the first to introduce nuclear weapons in the Middle East," *Ha'aretz*, October 7, 1986; and "Peres terms A-bomb story 'sensationalist'," *Jerusalem Post*, October 7, 1986.

25. For Saddam Hussein's statement, see Jill Smolowe, "Turning Up the Heat," *Time*, April 16, 1990. For Rabin's response see Eldar, "Saddam Hussein: 'If attacked — we'll destroy half of Israel'"; "Rabin: 'Let him not provoke us'," *Ha'aretz*, April 3, 1990; and "Rabin: 'Iraq is not beyond our range'," *Ma'ariv*, April 3, 1990.

26. Dan Margalit, "Rabin: 'For Israel, this is a deluxe war; the next ones will be more painful'," *Ha'aretz*, February 19, 1991; and Reuven Pedatzur, "Beginning to emerge from the basement," *Ha'aretz*, April 3, 1991.

27. See Evron, *Hadilemma Hagarinit Shel Yisrael*, p. 20 (emphasis added).

28. "Israel's retaliatory capacity is sharp and painful," *Ma'ariv*, December 30, 1990 (emphasis added).

29. Ran Dagoni, "Ambassador Shoval: 'The Iraqi chemical and biological threat must be eliminated'," *Ma'ariv*, December 30, 1990.

30. "Israel's Ambassador to Belgium: 'Israel will not respond with nuclear weapons to an Iraqi chemical attack'," *Ha'aretz*, January 1, 1991.

31. Transcript of interview of U.S. Secretary of Defense Richard Cheney by CNN Pentagon Correspondent Wolf Blitzer on CNN Cable Network, "Evans and Novak" program, February 2, 1991.

32. This remark was made at a seminar examining Israel's 1981 bombing of the Osiraq nuclear reactor held by Tel Aviv University's Jaffee Center for Strategic Studies. See Voice of Israel, June 6, 1993 (BBC, ME/1709 June 8, 1993, p. A/5).

33. See "Letter dated 14 June 1993 from the permanent representative of Iraq to the United Nations addressed to the President of the Security Council" (No. S/25950, June 14, 1993).

34. Israel's deterrent profile has been affected by the extent to which statements such as those cited earlier have registered in Arab states. In fact, such statements have been amplified by the Arab media. For example, a mid-1991 commentary in Egypt cites a "statement by former Israeli Defense Minister Yitzhak Rabin [made at] Haifa University last week that Israel possesses nuclear weapons, as well as other weapons of mass destruction, capable of obliterating any state." See "Columnist derides Cheney on Israeli nuclear arms," *Akhir Sa'a* (Egypt), June 12, 1991 (FBIS-NES-91-121, June 24, 1991).

35. For example, Director of Military Intelligence Maj. Gen. Uri Sagi said in mid-1992: "Iran is engaged in a nuclear program in a scale that would worry us — to the point of presenting a real threat to Israel's existence when and if this process becomes irreversible." "Worries in the Intelligence," *Ha'aretz*, June 17, 1992. More generally, U.S. newspaper columnists who met with Prime Minister Itzhak Rabin were told by senior Israeli officials that "Israel faces an existential threat which may materialize within 7–10 years ... in light of Arab efforts to obtain nuclear weapons." "A meaningful move towards peace will please me even without the Nobel

Prize," *Ma'ariv*, August 13, 1992.

36. For example, Commander of the Israeli Air Force Maj. Gen. Herzel Bodinger warned in mid-1992 that, "preventing the introduction of nuclear weapons into the Middle East is also in the interest of the world at large.... Once the Arabs obtain nuclear weapons, a conflagration in the region might escalate, possibly to the dimensions of a new World War." See "The commander of the air force: Nuclearization must be disturbed by political or military means," *Bemachane* (Israel), June 17, 1992; "Within 10 years Syria Will Have a Nuclear Capability," *Yediot Ahronot*, June 15, 1992.

37. Nakdimon, *Tamuz on Fire*, p. 246.

38. Ibid., pp. 275–276.

39. "It is important to reveal Iran's real face," *Ma'ariv*, July 1, 1993.

40. For example, in 1976 Israel's Foreign Minister Yigal Allon warned the French Ambassador to Israel that "the supply of a nuclear capability to irresponsible states in the Middle East was dangerous." See Nakdimon, *Tamuz on Fire*, p. 60.

41. For example, in 1980 Moshe Arens, then chairman of the Knesset Committee for Foreign and Defense Affairs and later minister of defense, said that Iraq's possession of nuclear weapons could result in a global conflagration. He noted that Iraq is among the most adventurous of the Arab states and that Iraqi use of nuclear weapons — or even the mere threat to do so — would soon transcend the borders of the Middle East. Arens added that "it was frightening to think that nuclear weapons would be possessed by the unstable leaders of Iraq who are willing to complicate the region and the entire world in their aggressive adventures." See Nakdimon, *Tamuz on Fire*, p. 136.

42. Ibid., p. 137. On another occasion, Begin said: "With the murderer in Iraq [Saddam] and the crazy man in Libya [Qadhafi] there is no telling what might happen in the region if they obtained a nuclear force." Ibid., p. 223. After the bombing of Osiraq, Begin said: "Libya's Leader Mu'ammar Qadhafi wants an atomic bomb.... Qadhafi is crazy and has no inhibitions." Ibid., p. 317.

43. *Ha'aretz*, June 9, 1981.

44. Nakdimon, *Tamuz on Fire*, p. 169. Separately, IDF Chief of Staff Eitan provided an estimate of 200,000 casualties if Iraq used a nuclear weapon against Israel: 50,000 dead and 150,000 wounded. Ibid., p. 227. In a later meeting of the Cabinet Defense Committee, Begin said: "We must ask ourselves what are the implications of the production of nuclear weapons in a country like Iraq. The implication is: placing in danger the life of every man, woman and child in Israel. In five years, maybe in only three, the Iraqis will have one or two atomic bombs with an explosive power similar to the bombs dropped on Hiroshima and Nagasaki. Saddam is a cruel tyrant who would not hesitate to use mass destruction weapons against us.... The use of this weapon against our population concentration will lead to bloodshed at a scale not

experienced since those days, in the 1940s." Ibid., p. 176. On another occasion Begin said that Iraqi use of nuclear weapons would have created "damage to [Israel's] infrastructure from which we would not have been able to recuperate." Ibid., p. 227.

45. Nakdimon, *Tamuz on Fire*, p. 136.

46. "Arens on Palestinian problem, U.S. arms sales," *Ha'aretz*, August 24, 1990 (FBIS-NES-90-165, August 24, 1990, p. A1).

47. See "Alleged Iraqi nuclear capability viewed," *Ha'aretz*, August 26, 1990 (FBIS-NES-90-166, August 27, 1990, p.4A).

48. "Shamir addresses Knesset on Iraqi threat" (BBC, ME/0897, October 17, 1990, p. i [a]).

49. "Arens: The low profile will be abandoned if Saddam Hussein attacks Israel," *Ma'ariv*, January 3, 1991. Israelis viewed the order given to Syria's security forces by President Hafez al-Asad in 1982 that they level the city of Hamma, which resulted in the death of 5000–20,000 Syrian citizens, as indicating a valuation of human life very different than their own. Thus, they are concerned that Arab leaders would be less attentive and fearful of the costs of nuclear retaliation.

50. Former Defense Minister Ariel Sharon was most vocal in rejecting this notion; see, for example, his October 1980 statement to the Committee of Ministers for Defense Affairs. In the same meeting, then–IDF Chief of Staff Lt. General Raphael ("Raful") Eitan said that "the size of Israel's territory and population precludes the possibility [of establishing] a balance of terror." For both statements, see Nakdimon, *Tamuz on Fire*, pp. 169, 171. Eitan has also said: "In my opinion, a nuclear balance meant accepting that Israel would not continue to exist. The Arabs are able to pay a much higher price than we can. Other Arab states will survive so it would be impossible to deter them. The threat of a second strike after we absorb a nuclear attack would have meant suicide." Ibid., p. 171.

51. Ibid., p. 350.

52. For example, in 1991, Shimon Peres, then leader of Israel's Labor Party, said: "In 1948 we built a state that could withstand the hostilities in this region. Today we must build a region in which no state would have to face hostility bordering on the nuclear danger." See "Changing the Defense Doctrine," *Bemachane*, October 30, 1991.

53. *Ha'aretz*, June 9, 1981.

54. William Claiborne, "Begin Threatens to Destroy Any Reactor Menacing Israel," *Washington Post*, June 10, 1981. At the press conference, Begin was careful to point out that the preventive imperative would not apply to any Arab state that is at peace with Israel, thus excluding Egypt from the stipulations and consequences of his doctrine.

55. For additional references to Israeli statements to the same effect, see Shai Feldman, "The Bombing of Osiraq — Revisited," *International Security*, Vol. 7, No. 2 (Fall 1981), p. 122, fn. 21.

56. Jerusalem, Government Press Office, December 15, 1981 (FBIS, December 18, 1981, p. I–17). "Confrontation states" refers to Arab states that have not entered into peace treaties with Israel. Thus it excluded Egypt and would now exclude Jordan as well.

57. James Leonard, Jan Prawitz, and Benjamin Sanders, *Study on Effective and Verifiable Measures Which Would Facilitate the Establishment of a Nuclear-Weapon-Free Zone in the Middle East*, Report of the UN Secretary General (October 1990), Paragraph 129.

58. Ya'acov Erez and Emanuel Rosen, "All means are legitimate in preventing an Arab state from obtaining a nuclear capability," *Ma'ariv*, April 17, 1992. Shahak currently serves as IDF Chief of Staff with a rank of Lieutenant General.

59. "The Nuclear Danger," *Jerusalem Post*, June 16, 1992. Elsewhere Bodinger is cited as having said: "Every effort should be made — by political and other means — to prevent the enemy from obtaining a nuclear capability. The more the introduction of such capability is postponed, the greater are the chances that developments in the region would meanwhile have a relaxing impact, with the hope that peace agreements might be concluded. [These agreements] ultimately comprise the best prevention against undesired escalation." See "The commander of the air force: Nuclearization must be disturbed by political or military means," *Bemachane*, June 17, 1992.

60. See Zvi Gilat, "General Dayan: Israel may decide on an action against Iran and Iraq already in 1995," *Yediot Ahronot*, December 30, 1994; and Nicolas B. Tatro, "Iran gains ground in drive for nukes," *Washington Times*, January 1, 1995.

61. IDF Radio, Tel Aviv, September 27, 1992 (BBC, ME/1498, September 29, 1992, p. A/6).

62. See Nakdimon, *Tamuz on Fire*, pp. 90, 169, 170, 172, 175.

63. Ibid., p. 173. In a late October 1980 meeting of the Defense Cabinet, Zipori said: "The state of Israel would not be able to prevent the development of nuclear weapons in Arab states. While Iraq is within our [operational range], it is doubtful whether we would be able to damage a reactor built in a more distant Arab state. The reactor's bombing would merely delay its construction and might accelerate the development of nuclear weapons in geographic [areas] that are beyond our [operational] range." Ibid., p. 175.

64. For example, in mid-1993 Israel's Foreign Minister, Shimon Peres, told the Knesset that Israel should let the United States lead the campaign against Iran (and Iraq): "I admit, in all modesty, that it is better to let the U.S., rather than us, stand at the head of this campaign." See "Peres: Israel should let the U.S. lead campaign against Iran," *Jerusalem Post*, July 1, 1993.

65. "Chief Intelligence Officer, Brig. Gen. Doron Tamir: 'Iraq's chances of recovery should not be underestimated'," *Bemachane*, June 17, 1992.

66. "Minister Arens at the Knesset Committee for Foreign and Defense Affairs: The Middle East is marching toward the nuclear era," *Ha'aretz*, October 23, 1991. Arens's statement made the government vulnerable to criticism that its new civil defense policy did not give proper weight to the nuclear threat, particularly in avoiding investment in building nuclear shelters. See Aluf Ben, "Ignoring the nuclear threat," *Ha'aretz*, December 23, 1991.

67. "A protected rear cannot win a war," *Bemachane*, January 15, 1992.

68. For such an analysis of Arab leaders as a general proposition and as an explanation of Saddam Hussein's decision to avoid attacking Israel with chemical warheads during the 1991 Gulf War, see Feldman, *Israeli Nuclear Deterrence*, pp. 143–147; and Feldman, "Israeli Deterrence During the Gulf War," in Alpher, *The Gulf War: Implications for Israel*, pp. 184–208.

69. Joel Marcus, "Is there a need for gas masks?" *Ha'aretz*, December 24, 1991.

70. Arian, "Security and Political Attitudes," pp. 305, 316–318.

Chapter 4

Arab Approaches to Nuclear Weapons

While the nuclear policies of the Arab states and Iran have often been propelled primarily by developments in one another's capabilities, their publicly stated nuclear threat perceptions have focused on Israel. Their fears and concerns have focused on the destructive capacity of nuclear weapons; on the possibility that Israel's possession of nuclear weapons would allow it to coerce the Arab states into accepting Israel's terms; on the possibility that a future Israeli leader might not control the country's nuclear option responsibly; on the cultural-technological challenge that Israel's nuclear capability poses for the less advanced Arab states; Israel's determination to maintain its regional monopoly by denying the Arab states access to nuclear technology; and the possibility that Israel might have developed tactical nuclear weapons and might use them in war-fighting.

In response to these perceived challenges, as well as their concerns about one another's nuclear developments, the Arab states and Iran have each adopted measures that reflect their geostrategic standings. Some lack the ability to match Israel's potential and have relied on a Soviet or U.S. nuclear umbrella. Egypt considered waging a preventive war, but later opted to join the global nonproliferation regime while reassuring Israel by launching a peace process, thus minimizing "existential" threats to Israel. Two states decided to develop their own nuclear capabilities — a weapons arsenal in the case of Iraq and an advanced infrastructure in the case of Iran. A number of the region's states are pursuing chemical and biological weapons as well as ballistic missiles for deterrence and war-fighting.

Arab Perceptions of Israel's Nuclear Capability

The gradual erosion of the ambiguity surrounding Israel's nuclear option has resulted in an increasingly certain Arab assessment that Israel possesses a deliverable nuclear force or the capacity to assemble nuclear weapons at very short notice. For example, after Israel's bombing of the Osiraq reactor in June 1981, Saddam Hussein said that "all experts and all concerned with atomic weapons and the affairs of the Middle East admit that Israel possesses several nuclear bombs."[1] Similarly, in a September 1992 speech to the UN General Assembly, Egypt's Foreign Minister 'Amru Musa, said that "Israel possesses nuclear weapons that are not safeguarded."[2]

With the destruction of Iraq's nuclear program after the Gulf War, Arabs feel that their lack of a countervailing capability has become all the more pronounced. For example, an April 1991 commentary in the Egyptian newspaper *Al-Ahram* noted that as a consequence of Iraq's disarmament, "Israel will be the only country in the region to preserve its missiles and anti-missile missiles, in addition to the Patriot missiles it received during the war and the sophisticated chemical and nuclear weapons it possesses."[3]

In Arab eyes, the Middle East is characterized by an Israeli nuclear monopoly, which they regard with varying degrees of alarm.[4] For example, Egypt's former Minister of War, 'Abd al-Ghany Gamasy, noted in late 1991: "Now that the UN Security Council decided to destroy Iraq's nuclear and chemical weapons and to establish close supervision on any production of such weapons — it can be said that in the coming years Israel would be the only state in the region to possess nuclear weapons."[5] Similarly, a commentary in the Egyptian newspaper *Akhir Sa'a* reads: "Israel was the first state to introduce nuclear weapons in the Middle East and it remains the only nuclear power in the region."[6]

Arabs believe that one reason Israel has developed nuclear weapons is for deterrence. For example, an Iraqi commentary estimated in mid-1991 that "Israel has gone a long way in the pursuit of mass destruction weapons on the premise that this type of weapon is likely to deter the Arabs from thinking about attacking Israel."[7] There are indications of Arab perceptions that a smaller state can successfully deter threats posed by larger states if it manifests greater resolve.[8] For example, Hamed Rabia, an Egyptian writing in *Al-Wafd*, referred to the first stage of Israel's nuclear strategy — which in his view extended up to the 1973 war — as "the strategy of deterrence." He writes that until 1973 nuclear weapons were instruments of "strategic psychological warfare." He also argued that between 1973 and the 1982 War in Lebanon, the original strategy was replaced by "the strategy of suicide," in which nuclear weapons may have become "weapons of last resort — when the only thing Israel would be interested in would be the extermination of its enemy, even at the price of suicide."[9] This view was seconded by Egypt's former Minister of War, Muhammad Fauzi, who stressed that if the Arab states succeeded in uniting their forces, Israel would feel that its existence was threatened "and would use nuclear weapons to avoid its military defeat and to save itself from destruction."[10]

Other Arab commentators fear that Israel's nuclear potential might be designed primarily for compellence. One Syrian commentary argued that "Israel's nuclear strategy stipulates that since Israel alone possesses nuclear weapons in the region, a nuclear peace has been formed which will compel the Arabs [to accept] a peaceful solution [to the Arab-Israeli dispute,] the terms of which will be dictated by Israel."[11] Similarly, Dr. Naffa al-Hassan argues that "the purpose of Israeli nuclear deterrence is to rule the area militarily or to compel the Arabs to sign a peace agreement with Israel."[12]

Israel's nuclear option seems to present the Arabs with a cultural-technological challenge. Arabs believe that Israel's nuclear capability and its stated intention to prevent the acquisition of nuclear weapons by the region's states together indicate a commitment to maintain its nuclear monopoly indefinitely.[13] Indeed, Arabs perceive Israel as having succeeded in maintaining its technological edge despite their own successful efforts to erode it, primarily through the acquisition of ballistic missiles and chemical weapons. In this context, an Egyptian commentary noted in mid-1990:

Israel has between 100 and 200 nuclear warheads. Iraq did not abandon its nuclear program although its reactor was bombed in 1981. Iraq is engaged in the large-scale production of chemical weapons. Syria, Iraq, Libya, Yemen, Egypt and Saudi Arabia possess ballistic missiles. The region's states are developing an option for independent satellite intelligence. These and other developments point to the fact that a new strategic chapter has been opened and Israel's monopoly over nuclear deterrence has been replaced by mutual deterrence (nuclear, chemical, biological, missiles and advanced aircraft) which weakens Israel's qualitative edge. Yet Israel continues to enjoy strategic superiority as a consequence of its technological edge, its superiority in nuclear weapons and the relative weakness of chemical weapons.[14]

Some Arabs believe that the strategic and the cultural-technological facets of Israel's nuclear policy combine to present the Arabs with an existential threat. Indeed, there is a tendency to view these two features in the context of the "humiliation" that Arabs see themselves suffering by the very existence of a Jewish state in the Middle East. To many Arabs, Israel's presence in the region is a permanent reminder of the inability of 120 million Arabs to overcome four million Jews. Israel's nuclear monopoly — possibly the ultimate guarantor of such permanence — is viewed by some as one of the more potent reflections of this humiliation. Israel is also viewed as threatened by any sign that Arab states might be closing the technological gap, and determined to make every effort to ensure that the Arab world should remain technologically backward.[15] In a December 1992 speech delivered to the Faculty of Economics and Political Science of Cairo University, Egypt's Minister of Defense, Hussein Tantawi, said that "only Israel possesses a nuclear capability and chemical and biological weapons and it maintains its superiority in nuclear and chemical weapons over all the Arab states."

Iraqi President Saddam Hussein voiced stronger sentiments after Israel's June 1981 bombing of the Osiraq nuclear reactor. Saddam argued that given the chance, Israel would compel "the Arabs to eliminate chemistry, physics, mathematics, and astronomy in the curricula of their colleges and high schools because they would give the Arabs knowledge in the military sphere, thus threatening Israel's security."[16] Saddam even argued that Israel would not have been bothered by Iraq's nuclear program if it were not for wider cultural-technological implications:

I am certain that had the Israeli officials discovered that Iraq had 20 atomic bombs while being afflicted by a decrepit political system, a backward economic system and individuals who neither have self-confidence nor look forward to the future and who neither trust nor soundly deal with their regime, Begin would not have given any importance to these atomic bombs. However, what terrified Begin was our scientific, cultural, human, political, economic, social and educational development and our sound concern with knowledge since we consider this to be one of the basic assets for building a new society and for achieving development and impregnability both for warding off dangers and achieving the happiness of the individual. This is what made Begin spend sleepless nights.[17]

Such perceptions might explain why Iraq's efforts to challenge Israel's qualitative edge and redress the technological imbalance were applauded in some quarters of the Arab world, even in Egypt — a country that joined the coalition confronting Iraq during the Gulf War and may have felt challenged by Iraq's nuclear program. For example, General 'Abd al-Ghany Gamasy, who negotiated with Israel the first disengagement-of-forces agreement after the 1973 war, said in late 1991 that he was sorry that Saddam Hussein did not succeed in manufacturing a nuclear bomb. He argued that had Saddam succeeded, "the overall military and political balance in the region would have changed in the Arabs' favor."[18] Similarly, Muhammad Hasanin Haykal, a prominent Egyptian journalist, wrote:

The fact that Iraq's nuclear program turned out to be larger and more advanced than what has been anticipated in the past did not alter the Arab attitude. In Arab eyes these comprised Arab weapons which were pointed at Israel, not Iraqi weapons which were aimed against other Arabs. The Arab state was entitled to try to catch up with Israel's military technology. Saddam Hussein's mistake was not in attempting to develop these weapons but in his statements that he was prepared to challenge Israel before he was actually ready to do so.[19]

By contrast, some Egyptians who are not interested in Arab nuclearization perceive Israel's nuclear option primarily as a source of regional instability. For example, Egypt's Ambassador to the United Kingdom, Muhammad Shaker, argued that as long as Israel retains its nuclear capacity, "different Arab states will attempt to acquire their own nuclear capabilities. This was the case with Iraq; in the past, this was the case with Libya, and [now] this is the case with Algeria. The main problem is Israel's secret nuclear program. As long as Israel adheres to its secret program, other states in the region will also continue to attempt to obtain a nuclear capability."[20]

The Arab sense of humiliation is also fueled by the perceived discriminatory approach of the advanced industrial world to Israeli and Arab nuclearization.[21] While the West is seen as tolerating Israel's nuclear capability despite the many signs of its advanced nature, every indication of Arab nuclear development is seen as viewed by the West — particularly the United States — with enormous alarm.[22] For example, a commentary in Egypt's *Akhir Sa'a* complained in mid-1991 that "Washington maintains silence and professes ignorance over Israel's nuclear arsenal at the same time that it raises a hue and cry over any Arab effort — mere effort, mind you — to acquire advanced technology."[23] Two years later, this U.S. approach was characterized by Egypt's prominent commentator, Muhammad Sayyid Ahmad, as "nuclear apartheid."[24]

To Arabs, such discrimination reflects a strategic reality: the alliance between Israel and the United States. Many Arabs view the United States as entirely identified with Israel's nuclear policy, including its determination to prevent the Arabs from acquiring a nuclear capability. Thus, in defending Iraq's nuclear program before the break in Egyptian-Iraqi relations, Egypt's President Mubarak complained in 1990: "Why then does not the spotlight fall on Israel's acquisition of the atom bomb instead of the media focusing on facilities used for known purposes?.... Isn't it purely a question of self-defense to seek to respond to those who attempt aggression against us...? It is as if Iraq is the only target. It seems that the Arabs are to be denied any kind of access to technology."[25]

Some Arabs believe that the perceived discrimination reflects a cultural judgment — a predisposition to see Arabs as people who cannot be trusted with potentially very dangerous technologies, while Israelis are regarded as responsible, trustworthy, and quite capable of handling such weapons. Iraq's President Saddam Hussein best articulated this notion in a November 1990 interview: "U.S. newspapers, media and politicians in power are talking about Iraq's chemical weapons but fail to discuss the chemical, bacteriological and nuclear weapons in Israel's possession. Consider the disdain in which Arabs and Muslims are held by certain Western politicians who regard them as inferiors, but look upon others differently."[26]

Some radical Arabs tend to see such perceived discrimination in the framework of an alleged Christian-Jewish struggle against Islam. In response to a statement by Britain's defense minister that the United Kingdom "was studying the development of its own defense system," because it regarded certain countries, including Libya, as a nuclear threat to Britain, a mid-1994 Libyan statement reads: "The British official statement is further proof that the Christians are attacking the Muslims within the framework of the Christian-Jewish alliance against Islam. The nuclear weapons which exist now include 200 nuclear warheads owned by the Jews who occupy Palestine; they admit to owning them in spite of their refusal to sign the nonproliferation treaty. No one has talked about these nuclear warheads. No one mentioned them or asked for their removal."[27]

The sense of humiliation is heightened by the tendency of some Arabs to view themselves as incapable of handling nuclear facilities safely. For example, in Egypt's late-1980s debate regarding the environmental ramifications of constructing and operating nuclear power reactors, a senior Egyptian official pointed to the lack of professional expertise and dependable technicians and workers as a main reason for the repeated delays in the implementation of Egypt's nuclear power program.[28]

Related to the theme of cultural humiliation, as well as to the Arabs' sense of strategic inferiority, is the concern that no single Arab state has been able to produce a nuclear capability equivalent to Israel's perceived advantage. Consequently, numerous voices have called upon the Arab governments to pool their human and financial resources in order to balance Israel's nuclear option.[29] These commentators and former officials warned repeatedly that without such pooling, it will be impossible to end Israel's nuclear monopoly.

At a less abstract level, Arabs are concerned about the destructive capacity of the weapons they believe Israel possesses.[30] Arab officials explain that "just by being there," nuclear weapons pose an existential threat. Informally, some Egyptians argue that they would be even more worried had some of the Arab states acquired such weapons. Since 1992, they have stressed that while they are quite satisfied that Israel's Labor-led government would handle its nuclear capacity responsibly, less responsible and possibly even irrational Israeli leaders might be elected in the future. Specifically, some fear that a nuclear-armed Israel might be led by a personality similar to that of former Minister of Defense Ariel Sharon, who is widely perceived in the Arab world as the architect of Israel's 1982 invasion of Lebanon.

Some Arab strategists are particularly concerned about the ambiguous nature of Israel's nuclear policy. Their worry is not so much that Arabs have been unable to ascertain the size and composition of Israel's perceived nuclear capability, but that they have been unable to ascertain under which circumstances Israel might consider employing its potential, and unable to confirm Israel's nuclear doctrine and the broader manner in which Israelis think about their capability. Unofficial Israeli and foreign references to Israel's nuclear option as weapons of last resort do not diminish Arab anxiety; such references have never been made official, and the term "last resort" has never been authoritatively defined.

Moreover, some Arab strategists argue that their concern about Israel's nuclear ambiguity have been sharpened dramatically as a consequence of the "Va'anunu affair." They argue that until Va'anunu's account was published in 1986, they assumed that Israel possessed an existential strategic nuclear deterrent: they believed that if Israel's survival were challenged, it would threaten to annihilate the Arabs' population centers and central strategic assets such as water dams and oil fields. Among strategic assets, they counted no more than a dozen potential targets in the Arab world, and they assumed that the size of Israel's nuclear capacity corresponded to this count. They add that the surrounding Arab states could tolerate such a capability and doctrine, since by the end of the 1956 war — and certainly after the 1967 war — no Arab leader regarded challenging Israel's survival within its 1949 boundaries as a realistic option.

By contrast, later publications, which attribute to Israel a nuclear force of up to 200 warheads, have reportedly shocked Arab strategists. In their eyes, such figures are totally inconsistent with the requirements of strategic deterrence and imply that Israel had developed a tactical capability for nuclear war-fighting as well.[31] This possibility constitutes another source of Arab fears and has further exacerbated the Arabs' perceived need to ascertain Israeli thinking about the possible utility of nuclear weapons. Arabs argue that if Israel considers the use of nuclear weapons under less than existential threats, neighboring states must know the nature of such possible scenarios so that they might be avoided. Hence, in Arab eyes, Israel's nuclear ambiguity may become more threatening as undetermined tactical scenarios are added to the imprecisely defined situations of last resort, as contexts in which Israel might use nuclear weapons.

Yet other Arabs seem no less alarmed by the prospect of transparency that would make Israel's nuclear capability explicit. This is particularly pronounced among Arab officials who oppose the nuclearization of the Middle East. These officials argue that if Israel's nuclear posture becomes overt, their governments would no longer be able to resist domestic pressures to produce a countervailing capability. A related fear, expressed especially by Egyptian officials and experts, is that an explicit Israeli nuclear posture could legitimize the nuclear programs of Iraq and Iran, resulting in the acceleration of these programs. Under such circumstances, the governments of Syria and Egypt would be pressed to launch crash nuclear programs of their own.

Finally, some Arab observers and officials have expressed alarm about the environmental effects of Israel's nuclear program.[32] For example, mid-1993 news reports about possible contamination of water and land in the vicinity of Israel's Dimona reactor were followed "with great interest" by Egypt.[33] Egyptians regarded these reports as indicating that Israel might be "dumping nuclear waste ... near the Egyptian border." An Egyptian official "said that the state authorities received confirmed reports that the Israeli government is dumping nuclear waste near the Dimona reactor, thus posing a threat to human, plant, and animal life."[34]

It thus appears that Arab officials, strategists, and commentators feel threatened both by Israel's nuclear ambiguity and by the prospect that Israel's nuclear option might become explicit. Common to much Arab commentary is the concern that Israel's nuclear option is dangerous simply by being there. Also common is the resulting conclusion that from an Arab standpoint, Israel's perceived nuclear monopoly in the Middle East is intolerable.[35]

Nuclear Policies of the Arab States and Iran

Open-source data on the nuclear policies adopted by the Arab states and Iran, and on the rationales for such policies, are extremely scarce.

Arab leaders offer few public statements regarding their policies, possibly as a hedge against domestic criticism. Hence, the policies must be inferred largely from Arab leaders' behavior.

JORDAN, SAUDI ARABIA, AND SYRIA

Jordan and Saudi Arabia, and possibly Syria as well, seem to have decided to stay out of the nuclear realm. This decision may have been motivated by a number of considerations. First, the limited financial resources of Syria and Jordan made it impossible for them to assume the considerable burden of constructing a significant nuclear infrastructure. Second, their contiguity to Israel probably makes them feel vulnerable to Israeli preventive action. Leaders in both countries might have reasoned that if in 1981 Israel could act effectively to demolish a nuclear facility in faraway Iraq, it would certainly do so even more effectively in Syria or Jordan.

Third, until the breakup of the Soviet Union, Syria may have seen itself as enjoying a nuclear counter-deterrent umbrella: Syrian spokesmen have hinted that a secret clause to the 1980 Syrian-Soviet Treaty of Friendship promised Moscow's aid if Israel threatened Damascus with nuclear weapons. Similarly, Saudi Arabia probably calculates that its close relations with the United States provide the most effective guarantee of its security. Indeed, it may also figure that given Israel's dependence on the United States and the U.S. commitment to Gulf security, Israel would never dare to threaten Saudi Arabia with nuclear punishment. Since the Gulf War, Saudi Arabia may also view the U.S. determination to contain Iran and Iraq as a guarantee against any other possible nuclear threats.

EGYPT

Egypt's nuclear policy evolved largely in response to Israel's efforts in the nuclear realm. During the early 1960s, the Nasser regime undertook two efforts: first, it created a nuclear infrastructure. Second, it attempted to buy a nuclear capability by recruiting German scientists who played a role in Nazi Germany's nuclear program during the Second World War. This effort was soon aborted by sabotage operations carried out by Israel's security services, and because of the political storm that the scientists' activities created in Germany and Egypt's disappointment at their failure to produce quick results.

At the same time, prominent Egyptians, such as President Nasser's confidante Hasanin Haykal, called for the launching of a preventive war against Israel before its nuclear option could become operational. Egypt's defeat in the 1967 War ended all discussions of adopting this course.

By the 1970s, President Anwar Sadat had made a strategic decision that Egypt would not seek to obtain nuclear weapons. While the factors motivating Sadat's decision remain unclear, he may well have concluded that Egypt lacked the technical expertise to develop a military nuclear capability, and that the financial costs would be prohibitive, particularly given the magnitude of Egypt's economic problems. Based on Egypt's experience during the 1973 War, Sadat may also have reasoned that if Egypt did not threaten Israel's existence within the pre-1967 international borders, Israel's nuclear option would not pose a threat to Egypt's security and survival. He may have also been persuaded that within these boundaries, Israel's existential deterrence could not be neutralized, even by a countervailing Egyptian nuclear capability. In addition, following the experience of the 1970 War of Attrition and the 1973 War, it is unlikely that Egypt feared any Israeli conventional attack that might justify the development of an Egyptian existential deterrent.

Additionally, Sadat may have been persuaded that rather than build a nuclear capability, Egypt would be wiser to reduce the likelihood that Israel might feel so threatened as to consider using its reported arsenal. If Israel's nuclear potential was indeed designed only to deter threats to its existence, Egypt's best avenue for diminishing the risks of nuclear war was to reassure Israel through political accommodation. Thus, Egypt's decision to pursue a negotiated solution to the Arab-Israeli problem — manifested in Sadat's peace initiative — may have been propelled partly by a need to address Israel's nuclear potential. Hints to this effect were provided by senior Egyptian officials who accompanied President Sadat on his historic trip to Jerusalem in November 1977.

In 1980, Egypt ratified the NPT. This decision seems to have evolved largely from Sadat's prior decision to dissociate Egypt from the Soviet Union and to base his country's future on an alliance with the United States. In light of the emphasis placed by the Ford and Carter administrations on efforts to arrest nuclear proliferation, Sadat may have judged that efforts to develop a nuclear capability would hinder improvement in U.S.-Egyptian relations.

Yet Sadat's decision to ratify the NPT resulted in considerable domestic criticism. Primarily, it was argued that by signing the treaty without preconditions, Egypt had closed its own nuclear option while Israel had not been similarly constrained. Opponents of the decision later also claimed that Egypt's failure to obtain nuclear power reactors is evidence that its NPT signature brought no benefits in the realm of nuclear energy.

To date, there are no signs that Egypt is about to withdraw from its commitment not to develop nuclear weapons. However, with the purchase of a new research reactor from Argentina, Egypt is accelerating its efforts to develop a nuclear infrastructure. This may be tied not only to Israel's nuclear potential but also to the post–Gulf War revelations regarding the extent of Iraq's nuclear efforts. As the leading Arab power, Egypt seems to be particularly sensitive to the possibility that Israel might enjoy a nuclear monopoly indefinitely. While some Egyptians refer to such a monopoly as tolerable in the short range, most regard an indefinite Israeli nuclear monopoly as unacceptable.[36]

By contrast, Iraq's nuclear efforts presented Egypt with a more immediate political and strategic challenge. Not surprisingly, Egypt seemed shocked and alarmed at the revelations of how close Iraq was to obtaining a nuclear bomb. In the context of their traditional competition for leadership in the Arab world — reflected, for example, in President Nasser's 1950s efforts to torpedo the Baghdad Pact — Egypt could not remain indifferent to the prospect that Iraq would become the first Arab country to possess nuclear weapons. Egypt was probably also concerned that Iraq's acquisition of nuclear weapons would expose its weaker but wealthy neighbors in the Gulf to repeated Iraqi aggression, thus challenging Egyptian interests and threatening to transform the nature of international politics in the Middle East.

The fact that some Arabs, including Egyptians, applauded Saddam Hussein for presenting the first serious Arab challenge to Israel's technological edge — for his 1990 threat to burn "half of Israel" with binary chemical weapons, for his ballistic missile attacks against Israel during the Gulf war, and for the advanced nuclear infrastructure he constructed — was not a source of amusement to Egypt's government.

More recently, Egypt seems equally alarmed about the prospect that Iran might obtain nuclear armaments. While the rise of fundamentalism in Egypt, Sudan, Algeria, Lebanon, and elsewhere in the Arab world is caused primarily by factors indigenous to these countries, some Egyptian observers believe that Iran's inspiration has been important in all these cases. To some extent, the acquisition of nuclear weapons by Iran is bound to increase its regime's standing in the Muslim world. Concern about such a development was reflected in a mid-1993 statement by President Mubarak that "if Iran succeeds in acquiring the bomb, it will be a great danger for the world. The UN imposed sanctions on Iraq because it was willing to build nuclear weapons. The Iraqis were punished for this ambition, and the UN should not allow Iran to search for the means to obtain nuclear weapons."[37] More recently, Mubarak stated that "by the year 2000, Iran will have a nuclear arsenal that would threaten not only the Middle East but the U.S. as well."[38]

Yet Egypt cannot afford to appear to make distinctions between Iraq and Iran on the one hand, and Israel on the other, in the latter's favor. Thus, its concern regarding Iraqi and Iranian nuclear armament seems to lead Cairo to express ever more vocally its demand that Israel also subject its nuclear facilities to the instruments of the international nuclear nonproliferation regime.

In addition, some Egyptians are calling for a review of Egypt's decision to sign the NPT and to refrain from developing a military nuclear program. They point out that their country's decision was based on the assumption that Israel would soon follow Egypt's lead, and argue that in the absence of any evidence that Israel intends to roll back its nuclear program, Egypt should develop a countervailing capability.[39]

Egyptians calling for the development of nuclear weapons often place their demand in a wide context. For example, at a 1987 conference at Ein Shams University it was asserted that "nuclear weapons have become an imperative not just against Israeli aspirations to destroy Egypt but also because the regional and international environment will not be stable if the Arab nation does not obtain nuclear weapons. The weak invite aggression and he who desires peace requires strength."[40] A mid-1990 article in *Al-Jumhuriyya* elaborated further:

A nuclear balance between neighbors is necessary as long as the states possessing nuclear devices do not accept nuclear disarmament. Hence, as long as Israel opposes nuclear disarmament or the transformation of the Middle East to a zone free of such weapons, there is no alternative to the manufacturing of an Arab atomic bomb.... Peace between the Arabs and Israel will materialize only through the establishment of a balance of power, either by Arab acquisition of the same weapons possessed by Israel or by internationally verified disarmament, so that neither Israel nor the Arabs possess such weapons.[41]

Similarly, Egyptian strategist Major-General Ahmed Nabil Ibrahim urged the Arab states to cooperate in building a nuclear deterrent: "Israel certainly possesses nuclear weapons and, since it remains the Arabs' arch enemy, in the foreseeable future we have no choice but to obtain a nuclear deterrent. It is extremely important for the Arabs to start a nuclear industry which cannot be bought or sold."[42]

Yet stronger voices in Egypt continue to stress that their government should continue to prefer economic well-being over nuclear ambitions. For example, the prominent Egyptian commentator Anis Mansur wrote in mid-1990 that "U.S. academics are asking Egyptians what they were prepared [to do] in order to withstand the nuclear weapons deployed by Israel or the chemical weapons used by Iraq. These are very important questions but they are not more important than our daily food allowance or what should be our daily food allowance."[43]

LIBYA

Libya's Mu'ammar Qadhafi made a number of efforts to obtain nuclear weapons in the 1970s. But after discovering the difficulties of acquiring a quick-fix nuclear capability, Libya opted instead for a more modest attempt to build a scientific infrastructure in the nuclear realm. With time, Qadhafi became increasingly aware not only of the financial costs of constructing a nuclear force, but also of the constraints facing Arabs when considering the use of nuclear threats against Israel. Thus, in mid-May 1992, he told the Popular Committees:

I wish we had the capacity to produce nuclear weapons. But these weapons cost billions of dollars which we do not have. The budget is in front of you. Thousands of experts are needed to produce a bomb and we do not have such sums. But even if we obtain such a bomb or produce it, we would not be able to drop it on Palestine, because if we bomb Palestine it would be as if we had bombed Syria, Lebanon, Egypt and Jordan. Namely, all Arabs will be lost. No one is thinking of using an Atomic bomb on Palestine. It is impossible to use weapons of mass destruction in this area. The entire world remembers Hiroshima and Nagasaki.[44]

IRAQ

Iraq's nuclear policy was originally designed to counter the ambitious nuclear program of the Shah of Iran. Iran's program was launched in the mid-1970s; it included the construction of ten nuclear power reactors, threatening to transform Iran into the region's first truly nuclear power. Iraq's first significant nuclear acquisition — its 1976 contract with France for the purchase of the 70-megawatt Osiraq research reactor — was clearly spurred by Iran's rapidly expanding nuclear program. By contrast, there are no known changes in Israel's nuclear policy or capabilities in the mid-1970s that could have prompted Iraq's decision. Indeed, since Iraq's nuclear disarmament through the application of UN Resolution 687, Iran's nuclear program has again become a major source of Iraqi concern. For example, Baghdad Radio publicized an Iraqi newspaper commentary that warned that "the world has a responsibility to quickly and immediately thwart Iran's efforts to produce a nuclear bomb.... Iranian nuclear weapons, which are first and foremost aimed at threatening the Arab nation and disturbing stability and security in the Gulf, constitute a threat to world peace." The commentary also argued that if Iran were to become a regional nuclear power it could "frighten neighboring Arab states ... as a deterrent, which would give it freedom of action and movement of its conventional arms arsenal in the Arab region."[45]

Given the close relations between Israel and Iran during the 1970s, it is quite possible that Saddam Hussein never viewed the Israeli threat entirely separately from that posed by Iran. This is particularly likely in the nuclear realm, since Israel identified the Iraqi program as a threat very soon after its inception and is believed to have initiated a number of activities to halt the Iraqi program. After the Shah fell in 1979 and Iran's new leader, the Ayatollah Khomeyni, froze Iran's nuclear program, Israel seems to have become a prime focus of Iraq's nuclear efforts, and the desire to balance Israel's nuclear capability became a central component of Saddam Hussein's quest for leadership in the Arab world. However, the war with Iran preoccupied Iraq throughout most of the 1980s; particularly during the second half of the decade, Saddam Hussein may have seen nuclear weapons as a way to balance Iran's three-to-one quantitative superiority.

Thus, Iraq's quest for nuclear weapons in the early 1980s may be seen as an attempt to establish mutual deterrence in the Middle East. This was clearly reflected in Saddam Hussein's speech to his Cabinet two weeks after Israel's June 1981 bombing of Osiraq:

I believe that anyone or any state in the world which really wants peace and security and which really respects peoples and does not want them to be subjugated to foreign forces should help the Arabs in one way or another to acquire atomic bombs to confront the actual Israeli atomic bombs, not to champion the Arabs and not to fuel war, but to safeguard and achieve peace. Irrespective of the Arabs' intentions and capabilities and even if the Arabs do not want them and are unable to use them, I believe that any state in the world that is internationally and positively responsible to humanity and peace must tell the Arabs: Here, take these weapons in order to face the Zionist threat with atomic bombs and prevent the Zionist entity from using atomic bombs against the Arabs, thus saving the world from the dangers of using atomic bombs in wars. This logic is applied by the United States in its dealing with the Soviet Union and by the Soviet Union in dealing with the United States. Others also apply this logic toward each other. I do not believe that the Soviet Union now wants to use the atomic bomb against the United States or that the United States wants to use it against the Soviet Union. This is due to the advanced state reached by humanity in its thinking, conscience and attitudes, including public opinion in the United States, the Soviet Union and the world at large. I do not believe that either the Americans or the Soviets will use the atomic bomb against each other. However both of them and others like them are always endeavoring to develop their weapons to prevent the eruption of war.[46]

After the Osiraq bombing and Begin's statement that Israel would prevent its adversaries from developing nuclear weapons, Saddam seems to have become even more determined to end Israel's perceived nuclear monopoly and to erase the humiliation felt by Arabs due to Israel's perceived commitment to use every means to maintain its monopoly. While the fierce conventional war against Iran delayed the restoration and expansion of Iraq's nuclear program for four or five years, Saddam vowed to rebuild a more diversified and less exposed nuclear program that could not be preempted by Israeli action.

IRAN

A number of statements made by Iranian leaders since the mid-1980s indicate their intention to develop an advanced nuclear capability. As early as mid-1984, Hashemi Rafsanjani, then Iran's parliament speaker and currently its president, reacted to a report about Iran's nuclear program as follows: "We have an English newspaper carrying a false report to the effect that within two years we would manufacture an atomic bomb. Needless to say, they are lying, for it is not clear whether we shall have atomic bombs that soon."[47]

Most Iranian statements indicating interest in developing a nuclear capability identify Israel as a motivation and justification for the acquisition of this potential. In November 1991, Iran's deputy president, Ayatollah Mohajerani, told the *Teheran Times* that "if the Zionist regime has the right to possess nuclear weapons, then all Moslem countries have this right as well." In another interview he said that "all Muslims must reach a high level [of expertise] in the nuclear realm, so they can face the Israeli nuclear challenge. The Muslims must act to obtain a nuclear capability that would strengthen them."[48] Elsewhere he added: "Regardless of the United Nations effort to prevent nuclear proliferation, Muslims must continue to cooperate among themselves and produce their own nuclear bomb, because the enemy has nuclear facilities."[49] It is noteworthy that these statements do not set out imperatives particular to Iran; instead, Mohajerani restricts himself to a discussion of what Muslims should do.[50]

Other Iranians have addressed Iran's requirements more directly but have remained vague regarding the focus of its nuclear efforts. In 1988, Rafsanjani, then speaker of the Iranian Parliament, told a group of followers: "We must fully equip ourselves with defensive and offensive chemical, biological, and radioactive weapons. From now on, you must use every opportunity to accomplish this task."[51] By contrast, Homayun Vahdati, a senior official presumed to be in charge of Iran's nuclear program, said: "We just want to revive a branch of scientific research that no country that wants to be taken seriously can afford to neglect. We should like to acquire the technical know-how and the industrial facilities required to manufacture nuclear weapons, just in case we need them. This does not mean that we currently want to build them or that we have changed our defense strategy to include a nuclear program."[52]

Verbal acrobatics were also used in late 1991 by the Ayatollah 'Ali Akbar Meshkini, Speaker of the Assembly of Experts:

Islam ... does not allow anyone to initiate the making of something which will be used for killing people, but if others do such a thing, if others disobey God and make such instruments, then God allows Muslims to make comparable things in response for the sake of defense. There are also [Koranic] verses in this respect.... Iran is not making an atomic weapon; maybe it has never done so, but if it were to do so, it has the right to do so because you have it. The East has it and the West has it. We do not want atomic weapons to be deployed, but no one should have it. If some have it, then everyone should have it. Why should you have it and not others?[53]

While Israel became the focus of Iran's stated justification to develop a nuclear potential, Iran's true motivation may be more connected to Iraq's nuclear efforts. For example, Khomeyni's decision that Iran should abort the Shah's nuclear efforts remained effective until the late 1980s, when information about the extent of Iraq's nuclear efforts began to accumulate. Like the United States, Egypt, and Israel, Iran was probably shocked by the post–Gulf War revelations of how close Iraq had come to obtaining nuclear weapons. Moreover, in light of the certainty that Iraq's human resources in this field have remained intact, the probability that not all of Iraq's nuclear suppliers have been identified and thus some might be reactivated, and the possibility that not all of Iraq's installations, facilities, and fissile materials have been discovered, it would have been illogical for Iran to refrain from launching an effort to develop a countervailing nuclear option.

POOR MAN'S NUCLEAR BOMBS

Lacking the ability to produce a nuclear response to Israel's perceived nuclear capability, some Arab states and Iran have sought a countervailing capability in the non-nuclear realm. In particular, chemical weapons have been called the "poor man's atomic bomb" by Iran's President Rafsanjani, who has said that Iran "should at least consider [such weapons] ... for our defense."[54]

Similarly, in April 1990, Saddam Hussein declared that Iraq possessed binary chemical weapons, and he warned that if Israel attacked Iraq with nuclear weapons, he would employ these weapons to burn "half of Israel." A few days later, in response to the strong international reaction to his statement, Saddam attempted to clarify his position:

We made a statement that we meant. We meant to say that we have such a weapon, but we also said that Israel has the nuclear bomb. We say that any weapon that we possess, whether as Iraqis or as Arabs, we will use only for self-defense and to defend rights. When anyone threatens us with aggression ... then it would be natural for the Arabs to say to him: "if you try to attack us, we will retaliate to your aggression with the weapons we have."[55]

Two months later, Saddam Hussein elaborated further:

When talking to the Americans about the speech I made, on April 2, I believe the Zionists quoted sentences out of context. They said Saddam Hussein wanted to burn half of Israel. Fine, but continue the sentence. Say: If we attack Iraq and the Arabs, Iraq this time will reply powerfully. Yes we will strike at them with all the arms in our possession if they attack Iraq or the Arabs.[56]

After the August 1990 invasion of Kuwait and the launching of Operation Desert Shield, the Iraqi media made another attempt to specify the counter-deterrent context of Saddam's April statement:

Iraq has warned that it would retaliate against Israel only if the latter attacked Iraq with nuclear weapons. Iraq has also said that it would hit Israel if it [Iraq] were attacked by imperialist forces stationed in Saudi Arabia and the Gulf region. Iraq has deployed binary chemical weapons to be used as a deterrent against any aggression by enemies of the Arab nation like the USA and Israel.[57]

Together, these statements suggest three different roles for Iraq's chemical weapons capability, two of which are nuclear-related: to deter a possible Israeli nuclear attack on Iraq; to provide extended deterrence against a possible Israeli nuclear weapons strike against other Arab states; and to deter a U.S. attack on Iraq by threatening an Iraqi chemical strike against Israel in retaliation.

At least one prominent Egyptian, former Minister of War 'Abd al-Ghany Gamasy, suggested that even ballistic missiles may provide non-nuclear counter-deterrence. In a 1991 interview, he urged "the Arab states that possess long- and medium-range surface-to-surface missiles to agree upon a unified strategy in the framework of a joint defense pact, for the purpose of large-scale and effective employment of these missiles against Israel, so that the latter would have to think twice before daring to use nuclear weapons against an Arab state."[58]

Conclusions

Chapters 3 and 4 suggest that nuclear weapons play different roles in Israeli and Arab security thinking. In Israel, a nuclear option was sought as an existential deterrent: a hedge primarily against the Arabs' capacity to threaten the survival of the Jewish state either by employing their preponderant conventional capabilities or by obtaining nuclear weapons first. Nuclear weapons could also help Israel establish cumulative deterrence: a track record that might persuade the Arab states that Israel cannot be defeated militarily and that it should instead be accommodated politically. Israel preferred that these roles remain implicit. Its ambiguous nuclear posture discourages excessive reliance on nuclear deterrence, attempting to minimize the degree to which Arab states would view the pursuit of a countervailing nuclear capability as an absolute imperative, and relieves the United States and other interested parties from the need to take a position with respect to Israel's nuclear potential. While the degree of ambiguity surrounding Israel's nuclear option has diminished considerably over the years, just enough ambiguity has been retained to allow the continued attainment of these three objectives.

Most Israelis regard the possibility that a state in the region might obtain nuclear weapons with considerable alarm. Primarily, these weapons are viewed as potentially exposing Israel to a second Holocaust, even complete extinction. Some of the region's leaders are considered too irrational to handle nuclear weapons safely. More widely, it is feared that proliferation of nuclear weapons in a region that has experienced recurrent warfare is a dangerous proposition. Although not all Israelis share these fears, there is domestic support for Israel's propensity to adopt preventive measures against further proliferation.

For the Arabs, Israel's perceived nuclear monopoly presents an enormous strategic and cultural challenge. The destructive capacity of these perceived weapons, their contribution to Israel's overall robust capabilities, uncertainty regarding the circumstances that might lead Israel to use these weapons, and fear that these weapons might expose the Arab states to nuclear blackmail combine to forge the Arabs' nuclear threat perceptions. Equally important is the role of Israel's nuclear potential in its qualitative edge and its perceived determination to prevent the Arab states from gaining access to similar capabilities; these are seen by many Arabs as part of a humiliating scheme aimed at ensuring that they remain "in the Middle Ages." These feelings are reinforced by the perception that the United States and other Western powers have adopted a double standard with respect to the pursuit of nuclear technology by Israel and the Muslim countries.

The different nuclear policies pursued by the region's Arab states and Iran reflect not only their responses to Israel's perceived nuclear threat, but also their particular political, economic, and strategic circumstances. Jordan, Saudi Arabia, and possibly Syria have refrained from joining the nuclear club. Libya, after attempting to buy an "off-the-shelf" nuclear capability, has also remained outside the nuclear realm. During the 1960s, Egypt briefly considered its options for waging a preventive war and made some efforts to gain a quick-fix nuclear capability, but decided in 1980 to join the global nonproliferation regime by ratifying the NPT. Although Cairo seems increasingly focused on persuading Israel to roll back its nuclear potential, it is interested in arresting the nuclear programs of Iran and Iraq as well.

Iraq has attempted to construct a strategic rationale for its nuclear efforts that seem to have been borrowed directly from classic deterrence literature. While its declared nuclear policy focused on the imperative of countering Israel's capabilities, its pursuit of nuclear technology seems to have been designed originally to withstand Iran's growing capabilities.

Similarly, Iran's nuclear rhetoric focuses on Israel, but its recent interest in nuclear weapons seems to be largely propelled by its post–Gulf War discovery that Saddam Hussein was very close to obtaining a nuclear bomb. As a result, by the early 1990s Iran had launched the most rapidly expanding nuclear program in the Middle East. At the same time, like a number of Arab states, Iran is seeking a non-nuclear counter-deterrent by building an arsenal of ballistic missiles and chemical weapons.

NOTES

1. See text of Saddam Hussein's June 23 Cabinet statement, Baghdad Domestic Service (in Arabic), June 23, 1981 (FBIS, June 24, 1981, p. E-3). In August 1990 Saddam wrote Egypt's President Husni Mubarak that "Israel is a country that has 200 nuclear warheads and forty-seven atomic bombs." See "Open letter from President Saddam Hussein to President Husni Mubarak" (FBIS-NES-90-165, August 24, 1990). Later, Saddam said that "according to western testimony, Israel possesses nuclear weapons." "Saddam Hussein: Iraq aspires to a nuclear balance with Israel," *Davar* (Israel), December 9, 1990. When asked in a November 1990 interview with Peter Jennings why Iraq feels it necessary to develop chemical and biological weapons, Saddam responded: "Because Israel is in the possession of chemical, biological, and nuclear weapons." See "Saddam Hussein's Interview for ABC," Iraq News Agency (in Arabic), November 17, 1990 (BBC, ME/0925, November 19, 1990, p. A/1). Similarly, Iraq's Deputy Prime Minister Taha Yassin Ramadan said in April 1990 that Israel has more than 100 nuclear bombs and warheads. "Iraq: 'We will react with all our strength to an attack on an Arab state'," *Ha'aretz* (Israel), April 19, 1990. This was repeated in another Iraqi commentary: "Israel is believed to have a stockpile of more than 100 atomic bombs." "Iraqi commentary on Western view of Israeli and Iraqi weapons"; INA in English, October 8, 1990, BBC, ME/0892, October 11, 1990, p. E/3.

2. See speech by Foreign Minister 'Amru Musa to the Forty-seventh Session of the UN General Assembly, September 25, 1992. The Libyan media seems to share this assessment. For example, Libyan newspaper editors stressed in early 1994 that "the nuclear weapons that now exist include 200 nuclear warheads owned by the Jews who occupy Palestine." "Jana's editor criticizes British statement on nuclear weapons," Great SPLAJ Radio (Tripoli) in Arabic, February 19, 1994 (BBC, ME/1927, February 21, 1994, p. MED/20). Syria's Minister of Foreign Affairs, Faruq A-Sha'r, referred in 1990 to "Israel's nuclear weapons." Other Syrian commentators said that "Syria will not remain idle in the face of the possession of nuclear weapons by Israel"; "'Israel's borders will not be immune to missiles,' warned a Syrian commentator," *Davar*, February 5, 1990.

3. See "U.S. conditions on Iraq strengthen Israel," *Al-Ahram* (in Arabic), March 25, 1991 (FBIS-NES-91-062, April 1, 1991).

4. For example, General Hassan al-Din Suliam of Egypt noted that weapons of mass destruction "entered the Middle East because Israel obtained nuclear weapons, regarded it as its monopoly, and prevented any other state in the region from obtaining similar weapons. This forced other states in the region to obtain other weapons such as chemical and biological arms." *Mayo* (Egypt), April 8, 1990 (translated by HATZAV).

5. Interview in *Al-Fursan* (Paris, in Arabic), cited in *Bemachane* (Israel), December 11, 1991, pp. 7, 12, 17. Earlier, a Lebanese newspaper referred in 1990 to "the existing gap in nuclear weapons" and noted that "no one doubts that Israel has acquired a large nuclear arsenal and that this gap is more significant than the gap existing in the realm of conventional weapons.... Israel also possesses the means of delivering these weapons to any Arab capital, such as Jericho missiles, F-15, F-4 and Kfir aircraft — means that can deliver these weapons to a

distance of 1250 miles." *Al-K'fah al-'Arabi* (Lebanon), May 14, 1990 (translated by HATZAV).

6. See "Columnist derides Cheney on Israeli nuclear arms," *Akhir Sa'a* (Egypt), June 12, 1991 (FBIS-NES-91-121, June 24, 1991). An Egyptian nuclear arms control expert, Ambassador Muhammad Shaker, said that "the Arab world acknowledges Israel's nuclear potential and views it as a source of instability in the Middle East." Reuven Pedatzur, "The lesson of Brazil," *Ha'aretz*, May 20, 1991. Hamed Rabia, writing in *Al-Wafd*, argued that "Israel is determined not to permit any Arab state to obtain progress in [the nuclear] realm," *Al-Wafd* (Egypt), September 29, 1989 (translated by HATZAV). The spokesman of Egypt's Foreign Ministry, Naj al-Tarifi, has referred to Israel as "considered to be the only country in the region that possessed a nuclear capability." *Al-Ahram*, August 1, 1992 (translated by HATZAV).

7. *Al-Qadisiyya* (Iraq), May 27, 1991 (translated by HATZAV).

8. Interview with General Zakaria Hussein Ahmed in *Al-Sharq al-Awsat* (Saudi Arabian newspaper published in London), December 16, 1992 (translated by HATZAV).

9. *Al-Wafd* (Egypt), September 29, 1989 (translated by HATZAV).

10. Interview with Muhammad Fauzi in *Al-Dustur* (Jordan), March 31, 1990 (translated by HATZAV).

11. *Al-Sha'b* (Syrian newspaper published in London and Paris), July 5, 1990 (translated by HATZAV).

12. From the conclusion of al-Hassan's book (published in Cairo), *The Credibility of Israeli Nuclear Deterrence*, cited in *Shira'* (Lebanon), January 9, 1989 (translated by HATZAV). Another Egyptian writer, 'Abd al-Samia, argued that the purpose of Israeli nuclear weapons was "to impose [Israel's] concepts on Arab realities and international relations." *Al-Atsam* (Egypt), December 1, 1989 (translated by HATZAV).

13. For statements defining Israel's preventive doctrine, see Shai Feldman, "The Bombing of Osiraq — Revisited," *International Security*, Vol. 7, No. 2 (Fall 1982), p. 122.

14. *Al-Sayas* (Egypt), June 30, 1990 (translated by HATZAV).

15. An Egyptian journalist called for protecting Egypt's nuclear facilities "against the Zionist betrayal which for quite some time has targeted the Arab scientists in an effort to ensure that Arabs would remain far behind in the scientific realm." See *Al-Akhbar*, May 25, 1990 (translated by HATZAV). Similarly, Iraq's President Saddam Hussein complained that Israelis "raised a hue and cry when they learned that Iraq had mastered some science and technology." Excerpts from recording of speech by President Saddam Hussein at the International Popular Islamic Conference for Solidarity with Iraq in Baghdad on June 18, 1990 (BBC, ME/0749, June 18, 1990, p. A/2).

16. Text of Saddam Hussein's June 23 Cabinet statement, Baghdad Domestic Service in Arabic, June 23, 1981 (FBIS, June 24, 1981, p. E-4).

17. Baghdad Domestic Service in Arabic, June 23, 1981 (FBIS, June 24, 1981, p. E-2). Saddam later added: "We believe that by centering on this issue, Begin has terrorized the Zionist entity instead of giving it security. If this has not been demonstrated now it will be demonstrated in the future. Begin and others must clearly realize that so-called preventive strikes to prevent the Arab nation from achieving progress, scientific development and technology is not a method that will prevent the nation from forging ahead toward its objectives. This method will not provide the protection which the Jews are talking about whether they are in or outside Palestine." Ibid., p. E-5.

18. Interview in *Al-Fursan* (Paris weekly in Arabic), cited in *Bemachane*, December 11, 1991, pp. 7, 12, 17.

19. "During the 1980s Egypt transferred to Iraq nuclear and chemical know-how" (excerpts from a book by Muhammad Hasanin Haykal), *Yediot Ahronot* (Israel), March 27, 1992.

20. "Egypt's ambassador to the UK: 'Israel should close down the nuclear reactor in Dimona as a sign of good-will'," *Ha'aretz*, May 8, 1991.

21. For example, Izzat Ibrahim, vice president of Iraq's Revolutionary Command Council, complained: "Iraq sees countries that claim to be interested in preventing the spread of nuclear weapons turn a blind eye to the Israeli entity's possession of such weapons." "Iraqi Atomic Energy Conference Opens," INA in Arabic, November 21, 1989 (BBC, ME/0621, November 23, 1989). Similarly, the Egyptian journalist Muhammad Hasanin Haykal wrote in 1992: "Washington's double standard with respect to Israeli and Arab armament programs are a source of great danger. The United States, which forgave Israel the possession of 100–300 nuclear warheads, or at least did not do anything to prevent Israel from such acquisition, destroyed Iraq's nuclear research facilities, using for this purpose bombs and missiles with a combined destructive capacity equivalent to a small nuclear bomb." See "During the 1980s Egypt transferred to Iraq nuclear and chemical know-how."

22. For example, an editorial in *Al-Akhbar* complained: "At a time when some pro-Israel members of the U.S. Congress vie with each other in casting suspicion on the way certain Arab countries are using the traditional weapons they bought from the U.S. with their own money to defend themselves, we do not see one single Congressman or U.S. Defense Department official raising the issue of Israel's exclusive possession of a nuclear arsenal in this region." "UN 'silence' on Israeli nuclear arms viewed," Cairo MENA in Arabic, April 21, 1992 (FBIS-NES-92-078, April 22, 1992). Similarly, an Iraqi commentary complained that "Mr. Bush [is] careful not to annoy his Israeli friends who have defied international norms when they refused to open their nuclear facilities at Dimona for inspection by specialized bodies. Israel is believed to have a stockpile of more than 100 atomic bombs. However, the U.S. and other western powers have not called upon the Israeli aggressor to destroy its nuclear weapons that have heightened tension in the Middle East region." "Iraqi commentary on western view of Israeli and Iraqi weapons," INA in English, October 8, 1990 (BBC, ME/0892, October 11, 1990, p. E/3).

23. "Columnist derides Cheney on Israeli nuclear arms."

24. *Al-Ahali* (Egypt), November 17, 1993, p. 2 (FBIS-NES-93-225, November 25, 1993, p. 12). A month later, a similar comment appeared in *Al-Akhbar*: "Often U.S. officials shy away from answering questions on Israeli nuclear power and its effect on stability in the region. A few days ago State Department Spokesman Michael McCurry said he needs preparation to answer such a question.... The atmosphere of peace into which the region is moving badly needs this nuclear contradiction or policy of double standards applied in one area and forgotten in another to end." *Al-Akhbar*, December 6, 1993 (FBIS-NES-93-238, December 14, 1993).

25. "Saddam Hussein and Husni Mubarak hold news conference following Baghdad talks," INA in Arabic, April 8, 1990 (BBC, ME/0745, April 10, 1990, p. A/1). Egypt's opposition was more blunt. In a statement published in *Al-Sha'b* the opposition leaders said: "We are following with great amazement the concern focused on Iraq's nuclear energy projects while the U.S. ignores the dangerous Israeli projects and plans in this realm." INA, July 30, 1991 (translated by HATZAV). An earlier article in *Al-Sha'b* claimed that Israel was responsible for the delay in Egypt's nuclear program: "The American and western conspiracy, under the influence of the Zionist lobby, are pressuring Egypt in order to prevent it from developing its nuclear potential, and indeed, so far not a single nuclear reactor has been constructed in Egypt." *Al-Sha'b*, April 30, 1991 (translated by HATZAV). A Syrian commentary went so far as to argue that "Israel's military planning for the next war is tied to [the efforts] to solve the threat entailed in the development of nuclear weapons by the Arabs. The Americans are cooperating with Israel in this realm through the 'Star Wars' program." See *Al-Sha'b*, July 5, 1990 (translated by HATZAV). Similarly, in Iraqi eyes, a principal U.S. objective during the Gulf War was to "defend Israel by destroying all the means at the Arabs' disposal that might have contained Israeli power in the region." See "Iraqi Minister said missiles have obliterated Israel's concept of security," *Ha'aretz*, April 30, 1991.

26. "Saddam Hussein's interview with ABC," INA in Arabic, November 17, 1990 (BBC, ME/0925, November 19, 1990, p. A/1). On another occasion, Saddam contested the assumption prevalent in the West that the Arab character precludes the possibility of establishing a stable balance of mutual deterrence in the Middle East: "Why are the Arabs and Muslims not permitted what is permitted to others? The U.S. and the Soviet Union have reached peace thanks to a balance of power and the entire Western world is adhering to this logic in order to reach peace. Why is the West not excited by, and why does it not protest, the destruction capabilities that Israel possesses?" See "Saddam Hussein: 'Iraq aspiring to a nuclear balance with Israel'," *Davar*, December 3, 1990. Elsewhere Saddam argued: "It should no longer be thought that if the Arabs have a certain weapon they will use it while others will not." "Saddam Hussein and Husni Mubarak hold news conference following Baghdad talks," INA in Arabic, April 8, 1990. (BBC, ME/0745, April 10, 1990, p. A/1).

27. "Jana's editor criticizes British statement on nuclear weapons."

28. At a conference conducted at Ein-Shams University, 'Abd al-Juad Amara said that the focus on the technological and financial aspects of constructing nuclear reactors is misplaced. He warned that the technology involved is completely new and very complex for

a society suffering deep-rooted backwardness, so that even if funding will be found, Egypt would still have to cope with many problems such as the education level of the simple Egyptian citizen, his work capacity, and his capability to operate and control nuclear power reactors. See *Al-Sha'b*, December 1, 1987 (translated by HATZAV). On another occasion, the chairman of Egypt's Power Stations Authority noted that some of the fears regarding the possible production of nuclear energy are based on the notion that nuclear technology does not accord with the nature of the Egyptian society. Such fears became even more pronounced following the nuclear accident at Chernobyl. See *Al-Mansur* (Egypt), April 13, 1990.

29. For example, at a conference conducted at Ein-Shams University, Halmi Murad pointed out that nuclear research is an expensive matter that does not bear fruit in the short range. He argued that it would require international cooperation among all the Arab states in order to obtain the necessary funding, and that a joint Arab authority is needed for the peaceful and scientific as well as the security dimensions of the project. See *Al-Sha'b*, December 1, 1987 (translated by HATZAV). Similarly, an Egyptian scientist, Ahmed al-Khasa'ad, called upon the Arabs "to unite in order to enter the nuclear era.... This is important because when separate, the Arab states will not be able to obtain anything from the rich and advanced members of the European Community.... The Arab states must enter the nuclear era through joint action, because the matter involves many details, funding and scientific resources which require coordination and cooperation." See *Al-Mansur*, February 12, 1988 (translated by HATZAV). In late 1988, General Ahmed Nabil Ibrahim of Egypt also called upon the Arab states to cooperate in obtaining a nuclear capability. See "An Egyptian general: The Arabs must obtain a preventive nuclear force against Israel," *Ha'aretz*, October 4, 1988. In his book *The Credibility of Israeli Nuclear Deterrence*, Naffa al-Hassan reached the same conclusion. He argues that "all the Arab states must act as one body in order to obtain a countervailing nuclear deterrent that would eliminate Israel's monopoly in this realm." Quoted in *Shira'* (Lebanon), January 9, 1989 (translated by HATZAV).

30. For example, Ahmed al-Khasa'ad explained that "if Israel used a medium-size nuclear bomb, this would have both a direct and a residual effect. The death of a large number of people would be the direct effect of the bomb and the dispersal of fallout would be its residual effect." He also pointed out that Israel would also suffer the effects of such use: "A bomb dropped on Syria, Lebanon, Jordan, or Egypt will affect Israel directly. Israel would suffer nuclear fallout even if it dropped a bomb on the more distant areas of Egypt." *Al-Mansur*, February 12, 1988.

31. This tactical capability was called by Hamed Rabia the third stage of the development of Israel's nuclear capability. He claimed that tactical nuclear weapons "became a tool of [Israel's] offensive strategy enabling the conquest of land and the uprooting of its [Palestinian] people." He also wrote that Israel developed "small nuclear bombs" because "this enables it to hit a large number of targets in a large area." Rabia argues that the purpose of tactical weapons "is to hit sensitive targets in the Arab [world], enabling [Israel] to distance the Middle East from its external environment. Thus nuclear weapons can both cause chaos and create a siege without causing nuclear radiation in areas which Israel intends to enter. Later we shall see Israel using chemical and biological weapons against most of the bordering states while using nuclear weapons" in more distant areas. Rabia suggests four specific targets for Israel's tactical nuclear weapons: the High Dam in Upper Egypt; the Tripoli area in Libya; the

Mosul area in northern Iraq; and the Straits of Hormuz near Oman. See *Al-Wafd*, September 29, 1989 (translated by HATZAV).

32. In the 1980s, Arabs expressed concern about the possibility that Israel might utilize nuclear waste for military purposes. For example, in 1986 an interesting note by the Syrian commentator Abdullah al-Ahmed appeared in the Syrian government newspaper *Tishrin*: "The British government decided to transfer to Israel a quantity of nuclear waste.... What would Israel do with this quantity of nuclear waste given the fact that it already possesses nuclear weapons?.... Yet Israeli military officers are likely to respond that this is important material which can be rained on any enemy — particularly its cities — in order to create massive panic among its civilians, to paralyze its government operations for a considerable length of time, and then to visit it with additional blows.... This, in light of the fact that direct nuclear bombing would not be possible without the Israelis themselves suffering the resulting nuclear radiation. This implies that Israeli nuclear weapons are effective only in very special circumstances and for bombing very distant Arab states since only in such cases would the Zionist enemy not be damaged himself by the bombing." *Tishrin* (Syria), June 5, 1986 (translated by HATZAV).

33. "Israel contacted on reports of nuclear reactor leak," Cairo MENA in Arabic, April 17, 1993 (FBIS-NES-93-703, April 19, 1993).

34. "IAEA asked to investigate Israeli dumping," *Al-Ahali* (Egypt), March 17, 1993 (FBIS-NES-93-055, March 24, 1993).

35. For example, Ambassador Muhammad Shaker stressed that "there is no possibility that Egypt could accept any arrangement that would leave Israel the only nuclear power in the region." See "Egypt's ambassador to the UK: Israel should close down the Dimona reactor as a sign of good will," *Ha'aretz*, May 8, 1991.

36. "Egypt's Reply to the Report of the Secretary General on 'Establishment of a Nuclear Free Zone in the Region of the Middle East'." (Item A/46/150, June, 1991, p. 13).

37. MENA (Cairo) in Arabic, April 10, 1993 (FBIS-NES-93-068, April 12, 1993).

38. Aluf Ben, "One of the journalists who met Mubarak: We have a tape of the meeting," *Ha'aretz*, June 1, 1994.

39. For example, in 1990 an Egyptian journalist argued that Israel could not have hinted that it might use nuclear weapons against Iraq if the Arabs been able to manufacture such weapons as well, much less if the Arabs actually possessed such weapons. He suggested the establishment of an Arab university for nuclear studies, and that all Egyptian nuclear scientists abroad be asked to return home to help achieve "Egypt's integration in the nuclear world after half a century of neglect." See *Al-Akhbar*, May 25, 1990 (translated by HATZAV).

40. *Al-Sha'b*, December 1, 1987 (translated by HATZAV).

41. *Al-Jumhuriyya*, May 6, 1990 (translated by HATZAV). The Egyptian journal *Al-Manar* carried in mid-1990 a similar recommendation: "Arab planning and determination to acquire weapons of mass destruction are the only means of obtaining deterrence against Israeli deterrence and preventing Israeli expansion at the Arabs' expense." *Al-Manar* (Egypt), May 1990 (translated by HATZAV).

42. "Egypt close to achieving a nuclear capability," *Times* (London), April 5, 1990. For Ibrahim's earlier calls for the Arab states to cooperate in obtaining a nuclear capability, see "An Egyptian General: the Arabs must obtain a preventive nuclear force against Israel," *Ha'aretz*, October 4, 1988. In chapter 4 of his book *The Credibility of Israeli Nuclear Deterrence*, Naffa al-Hassan reaches the same conclusion. He argues that "all the Arab states must act as one body in order to obtain a countervailing nuclear deterrent that would eliminate Israel's monopoly in this realm." In the conclusion to his book, the author calls upon the Arabs to obtain nuclear weapons at all costs. See *Shira'* (Lebanon), January 9, 1989 (translated by HATZAV).

43. *Al-Ahram* (Egypt), June 21, 1990 (translated by HATZAV).

44. "Qadhafi: Libya does not have a nuclear bomb; we do not have the money needed," *Ha'aretz*, May 10, 1992.

45. "Newspaper says world should thwart Iran's efforts to build a nuclear bomb," Baghdad Radio, December 27, 1992 (BBC, ME/1573, December 29, 1992, p. A/19).

46. Text of Saddam Hussein's June 23 Cabinet statement, Baghdad Domestic Service in Arabic, June 23, 1981 (FBIS, June 24, 1981, p. E-3). Indeed, Arabs in other states also seem to have attributed a deterrent role to Iraq's nuclear capacity. For example, in early 1991 Syria's Minister of Information said that "strategic experts emphasize that the Iraqi force destroyed [by coalition bombing] could have provided strategic deterrence in the main confrontation arena [i.e., the Arab-Israeli conflict], [provided that] it were pointed in the correct direction — against the enemy of the Arab nation [namely, Israel]." See interview with Syria's Minister of Information in *Akhir Sa'a* (Egypt), February 13, 1991.

47. Warren Getler, "Iran Is Unlikely to Have Atom Bomb in 2 Years, Nuclear Experts Assert," *International Herald Tribune*, May 7, 1984.

48. See Steve Coll, "Teheran Ambiguous on its A-Arms Plans," *Washington Post*, November 17, 1992. See also Guy Bechor, "Fear in the West: An Iranian Hiroshima-type nuclear bomb is expected by the end of the 1990s," *Ha'aretz*, January 10, 1992.

49. Jack Anderson and Michael Binstein, "An Iranian Bomb," *Washington Post*, January 12, 1992.

50. Mohajerani emphasized that he was not necessarily referring to Iran's role in balancing Israel's nuclear capability. For example, he said: "Israel has attained a nuclear capability. No Islamic country should consider this an issue of secondary importance; in other words, in

view of the enemy's nuclear capabilities, the Islamic countries should also have nuclear facilities." When asked "Don't you think that if we gained access to nuclear capabilities similar to Israel, they would be prone to Western attack?" he responded: "I did not mean one particular country. The Islamic countries should collectively utilize their resources to achieve nuclear strength. We can defend this by saying that Israel should not be allowed to have a nuclear capability; that is, what was done to Iraq should also be done to Israel.... In other words, the question is not one of any one particular country. It is possible that just as we organized this [international] conference [to support the Islamic revolution of the Palestinian people], the Islamic countries should collectively pool their material, technical and technological resources to reach this objective." See interview of Ayatollah Mohajerani, Deputy President for Legal and Parliamentary Affairs, Teheran ABRAR in Persian October 23, 1991 (FBIS-NES-91-214, November 5, 1991, p. 5). Also quoted in Elaine Sciolino, "Report Says Iran Seeks Atomic Arms," *New York Times*, October 31, 1991. Nevertheless, Mohajerani's interview was interpreted abroad as referring to Iran's intentions in the nuclear realm, causing much concern in the U.S. intelligence community. See R. Jeffrey Smith, "Officials Say Iran Is Seeking Nuclear Weapons Capability," *Washington Post*, October 30, 1991. Mohajerani later "refuted remarks attributed to him that Iran was trying to gain access to unconventional weapons, describing it as a 'propaganda ploy and a psychological warfare waged by the U.S. and the West against Iran'." IRNA in English, November 13, 1991 (BBC, ME/1230, November 15, 1991, p. A/10).

51. Sciolino, "Report Says Iran Seeks Atomic Arms"; and Anderson and Binstein, "An Iranian Bomb."

52. "Reports of nuclear weapons program denied," *Die Welt*, January 27, 1992. Other Iranian spokesmen explicitly denied any activity to develop or produce mass destruction weapons. See denial issued by Iran's delegation to the UN following testimony by CIA Director James Woolsey to the effect that Iran was seeking to acquire nuclear weapons, in broadcast by IRNA in English, February 26, 1993 (FBIS-NES-93-037, February 26, 1993, p. 39). See also a statement made by Mahmud Mohammadi of the Iranian Foreign Ministry broadcast by IRNA in English on May 12, 1993 (BBC, ME/1687, May 13, 1993, p. A/10). Other spokesmen emphasized that Iran's pursuit of a nuclear capability is limited to peaceful purposes. See statement made by Majlis Speaker Hojjat ol-Eslam Ali Akbar Nateq-Nuri, broadcast by IRNA in English, July 8, 1993 (BBC, ME/1711, July 10, 1993, p. A/9). Yet another spokesman, Hassan Ruhani, Secretary of the Supreme Council for National Security, also denied any intention to develop nuclear weapons but possibly reflected the disagreement among Iranian policymakers on this issue; he argued that the acquisition of nuclear weapons could be a threat to Teheran's own security. See David Watts, "Teheran Denies Nuclear Charges," *Times* (London), March 15, 1993. Another possible indication of such a policy disagreement can be found in an interview given by Akhbar Torkan, Iran's Minister of Defense and Armed Forces Logistics: "Access and the use of nuclear weapons is not included in the defense strategy of Iran. We are also trying to maintain and preserve the existing weapons in the country, and we don't need to purchase new ones." IRNA in English, March 2, 1993 (BBC, ME/1628, March 4, 1993, p. A/2). Earlier denials were issued by Foreign Minister Ali Akbar Velayati; see Voice of the Islamic Republic of Iran, August 1, 1992 (FBIS-NES-92-150, August 4, 1992, p. 4); and November 27, 1992 (FBIS-NES-92-230, November 30, 1992, p. 77). An earlier denial was issued by Deputy Foreign Minister Ali Muhammed Besharati, who described

reports that Iran was planning to acquire nuclear weapons as "a lie and a plot." See Elaine Sciolino, "CIA Draft Says Iran Nears Nuclear Status," *International Herald Tribune*, December 1, 1992. See also Voice of the Islamic Republic of Iran, November 27, 1992 (FBIS-NES-92-230, November 30, 1992, p. 73). Similarly, Iran's Ambassador to the UN, Kamal Kharrazi, denied any Iranian intention to develop nuclear weapons. Voice of the Islamic Republic of Iran, November 24, 1992 (BBC, ME/1547 p. A/6, November 25, 1992). Also, a Majlis Deputy, Sa'id Raja'i-Khorasani, challenged the CIA to supply to the IAEA any information it might have on prohibited Iranian nuclear activities so that the IAEA might inspect the suspected sites and verify the credibility of such information. Teheran RESALAT in Persian, December 5, 1992 (FBIS-NES-92-240, December 14, 1992, p. 39).

53. Voice of the Islamic Republic of Iran, December 6, 1991 (BBC, ME/1250, December 9, 1991, p. A/10).

54. IRNA, October 18, 1988 (FBIS-NES, October 19, 1988, pp. 55–56), cited by Peter Herby, *The Chemical Weapons Convention and Arms Control in the Middle East* (Oslo: International Peace Research Institute [PRIO], 1992), p. 42.

55. "Saddam Hussein and Husni Mubarak hold news conference after Baghdad talks," INA in Arabic, April 8, 1990 (BBC, ME/0735, April 10, 1990, p. A/1). Iraq's deputy prime minister, Taha Yassin Ramadan, further elaborated: "Iraq has obtained equilibrium in deterrent power by producing chemical weapons in order to be able to withstand the Israeli nuclear threat. We say this openly: Iraq will not surrender to blackmail." See "Iraq: We will react with all our power to any attack on an Arab state," *Ha'aretz*, April 19, 1990.

56. Excerpts from recording of speech by President Saddam Hussein at the International Popular Islamic Conference for Solidarity with Iraq in Baghdad on June 18, 1990 (BBC, ME/0749, June 18, 1990, p. A/2); and Republic of Iraq Radio, Baghdad, June 18, 1990 (BBC, ME/0795, pp. A/1–3).

57. Indeed, the Iraqi commentary complained that it was the discriminatory approach of the Western media that led it to ignore the context of Saddam Hussein's April 1990 threat to use unconventional weapons against Israel: "The western media deliberately deleted from their reports that Iraq has warned that it would retaliate against Israel only if the latter attacked Iraq with nuclear weapons." See "Iraqi Commentary on Western View of Israeli and Iraqi weapons." INA in English, October 8, 1990 (BBC, ME/0892, October 11, 1990, p. E/3).

58. Interview in *Al-Fursan*, cited in *Bemachane*, December 11, 1991, pp. 7, 12, 17.

Chapter 5

The Global Agenda for Nuclear Arms Control

This chapter outlines the global nuclear nonproliferation agenda to which Middle East states must respond, focusing on existing and proposed global and regional arms control treaties that have been addressed or would need to be addressed by the region's states.

The nuclear nonproliferation regime comprises a complex of unilateral and multilateral efforts, measures, initiatives, and incentives, and constraints that are designed to discourage and prevent states from obtaining nuclear weapons or the capacity to produce them. The centerpiece of the global regime is the 1968 Nuclear Non-Proliferation Treaty (NPT) — a global "grand deal" that joins nuclear-weapon states and non-nuclear weapon states in a commitment to avoid contributing to the spread of nuclear weapons. The Comprehensive Test Ban Treaty (CTBT), and the proposed international convention to ban the production of fissile material (plutonium and enriched uranium) are similar grand deals.

A number of agreements aim to prevent proliferation of nuclear weapons at the regional level: the Tlatelolco Treaty establishes Latin America as a nuclear-weapon-free zone (NWFZ); the Raratonga Treaty creates an NWFZ in the Pacific; and African and South East Asian NWFZs have recently been negotiated. Proposals to transform the Middle East into such a zone have also been presented (see Appendix 5).

Third, actual or potential suppliers of nuclear technology attempt to limit nuclear exports by adhering to common guidelines on nuclear trade. Such efforts were undertaken by the Nuclear Suppliers Group (NSG) as well as by the five permanent members of the UN Security Council. While the latter's guidelines were originally defined in broad terms, the NSG's common limitations have become increasingly specific, particularly since the 1991 Gulf War.

A fourth aspect of the nonproliferation regime is state controls on the export of nuclear and nuclear-related technologies. These controls are applied by states whose scientific and industrial infrastructure enables them to become suppliers or potential suppliers of such technologies. Since these states are quite interested in the benefits of exporting power-related and research-related nuclear technology, their diligence in applying export constraints depends upon the extent to which they are also committed to helping prevent the further spread of nuclear weapons.

Unilateral incentives and penalties designed to dissuade states from developing nuclear weapons are the fifth facet of the nuclear nonproliferation regime. U.S. legislation such as the 1978 Nuclear Non-Proliferation Act and the Symington-Glenn and Pressler amendments to the International Security Assistance Act are examples of such measures. These laws threaten to deny economic and military assistance as well as the benefits of U.S. nuclear technology to countries that produce fissile material or develop nuclear weapons.

Complementing these legal instruments are policies to dissuade specific states from developing nuclear weapons. For example, during the 1970s, U.S. pressures led South Korea and Taiwan to abort their nuclear weapons programs. During the 1990s, similar efforts aimed to ensure the nuclear disarmament of Ukraine and the rollback of North Korea's program.

Under very unusual circumstances, the international regime may also include the forceful disarmament of a state's nuclear capability. So far, such an effort has been applied in only one instance — the nuclear disarmament of Iraq by the United Nations Special Commission (UNSCOM). The particular conditions in which this took place — following Iraq's defeat by the U.S.-led coalition in the Gulf War — are unlikely to materialize very often in other regions.

This chapter focuses on global and regional nuclear nonproliferation efforts. Unilateral and multilateral efforts by nuclear suppliers and other outside powers, which do not involve the participation or policy responses of Middle East states, are not discussed here. (Chapter 6 addresses U.S. nuclear nonproliferation policy and its application in the Middle East.)

The Nuclear Non-Proliferation Treaty

The Nuclear Non-Proliferation Treaty (NPT) which was signed in 1968 remains the centerpiece of the global nuclear nonproliferation regime. The treaty includes an agreement by non-nuclear weapon states to avoid the acquisition of nuclear weapons, and a commitment by nuclear weapon states to avoid the transfer of such weapons (Articles I and II). The Preamble declares the intention of nuclear weapon states "to achieve at the earliest possible date the cessation of the nuclear arms race and to undertake effective measures in the direction of nuclear disarmament." Article VI commits these states to pursue negotiations toward this objective "in good faith." Nuclear weapons states are defined in Article IX of the treaty as states that have "manufactured and exploded a nuclear weapon or other nuclear explosive device prior to 1 January, 1967," thus limiting official membership in the nuclear club to the United States, the Soviet Union (now Russia as its heir), France, Britain, and China.

Article III of the treaty delegates the task of verifying its members' compliance to the International Atomic Energy Agency (IAEA). The treaty allows its signatories to "develop research, production and use of nuclear energy for peaceful purposes" — even to use nuclear explosives for such objectives — but requires them to submit all the facilities, activities, and fissile material involved to full-scope IAEA safeguards (Articles III, IV, and V).

The treaty further stipulates that its members should convene every five years to review the progress made toward implementation (Article VIII) and directs that twenty-five years after becoming effective in 1970, treaty members should meet to determine whether the treaty should be extended indefinitely or for a fixed period or periods (Article X). The NPT allows states to withdraw their membership by submitting a three-month prenotification, which must explain what extraordinary circumstances induce the state to undertake this step (Article X).

To date, 175 countries have become signatories to the treaty. In recent years, its global application was significantly boosted by the decisions of France, China, South Africa, Argentina, and Algeria to sign the treaty. South Africa's decision to join the NPT was accompanied by an even more important decision to liquidate its nuclear weapons program. Argentina seems to have made a similar decision

— at still an earlier stage of its nuclear efforts — when it reached a bilateral agreement with Brazil and joined the Tlatelolco Treaty.

Yet the NPT has come under increasing attack. Most frequent has been criticism of its discriminatory nature: while the non-nuclear weapon states agreed to avoid the acquisition of nuclear weapons, the nuclear powers were merely required "in good faith" to enter negotiations leading to the elimination of their nuclear arsenals. Moreover, a number of Third World countries have argued that throughout the first twenty years after the treaty came into force, the nuclear powers continuously violated its stipulations by engaging in an intense nuclear arms race.

Another focus of criticism is that the treaty is characterized by a constant tension between two inherently contradictory purposes: preventing the proliferation of nuclear weapons, and encouraging the peaceful use of nuclear technology. The main problem is the "dual-use" nature of nuclear technology: peaceful and weapons-related nuclear technologies are closely related and highly convertible. For example, Japan's postwar nuclear program has been strictly peaceful, yet it is now widely considered to be capable of transforming its research and nuclear power capacity into weapons production almost overnight.[1]

A related weakness of the NPT is that within its framework, a country can develop an advanced nuclear capability "for peaceful purposes" and then withdraw from treaty membership by simply providing three months' notice. This can leave the withdrawing state with the facilities and fissile material required to assemble nuclear weapons quickly. In 1993–95, North Korea threatened to exercise this right.

An additional important weakness of the NPT is its reliance on the inadequate verification mechanisms and procedures of the IAEA. Like the NPT, the IAEA is torn between encouraging the use of "peaceful" nuclear technology and discouraging the spread of nuclear weapons. Until recently, the agency limited its inspections and its application of safeguards to nuclear facilities that have been declared as such by the member states. It has given much prior notice before launching inspections, leaving governments ample opportunity to conceal prohibited activities, and has not conducted "short notice" or "challenge" inspections of sites where the conduct of weapons-related nuclear activities was suspected. This limitation contributed to the IAEA's failure to discover the extent of Iraq's nuclear efforts in the late 1980s.[2]

The IAEA is also chronically underfunded and understaffed. While member states have pronounced their commitment to nuclear nonproliferation, they have not been generous in providing the IAEA with the financial resources required to meet its objectives. For its part, the IAEA is accused of having spent too much on safeguarding the large number of nuclear facilities in advanced industrial countries such as Germany and Japan, and spending too little on inspecting countries of more immediate nuclear proliferation concern, such as Iraq, Iran, and North Korea. In addition, the inspected states are able to help determine the national composition of the inspectors; for example, North Korea could ensure that the early 1994 inspection of its facilities did not include inspectors from any of the Western advanced industrial states.

The IAEA's mandate is also limited; it lacks the ability to act independently. It has neither responsibility nor mechanisms for enforcement, and instead refers such matters to the UN Security Council. Yet if the Security Council is paralyzed by a veto by one of its permanent members, little can be done to sanction treaty violations. For example, in 1993–94, China refused to support the application of punitive measures against North Korea in response to repeated violations of its NPT obligations.

The IAEA also lacks an adequate intelligence gathering and analysis capability that might allow it better to prepare for inspections. It is entirely dependent on the intelligence provided by its members, but until the early 1990s it seldom received relevant information from the intelligence agencies of its member states. Intelligence sharing with the IAEA has improved but remains limited by the concern of states that possess relevant classified information that their sources and methods may be compromised. This concern is partly fueled by uneasiness regarding the national composition of the inspection teams — which often include representatives of states with close relationships with the inspected parties.

The cumulative effect of these shortcomings has been to allow an NPT signatory — Iraq — to develop an advanced nuclear weapons program under the nose of IAEA inspection mechanisms. More recently it was also reported that IAEA inspectors were not told until 1986 that Sweden, which signed the NPT in 1968, maintained the capacity to restart its Agesta nuclear reactor at very short notice.[3] Sweden is also said to retain the expertise of more than thirty-five nuclear weapons designers for the purpose of "working on non-proliferation issues." Thus, an advanced nuclear weapons option can be maintained under the NPT framework.

In response to the post-Iraq criticism, the IAEA has attempted to tighten its inspections procedures and to expand its verification mechanisms. After much deliberation and long delays, in late March 1995 its Board of Governors "endorsed the direction" and reached "consensus on the general thrust" of "Program 93-2," which is designed to strengthen verification of declared facilities and to improve the capacity to detect undeclared activities. It includes the use of "no-notice" inspections. However, while a significant attempt has been made to strengthen the monitoring of declared facilities, the task of better detecting undeclared nuclear activities has been set aside for further deliberations. The Board has stated that it lacks the legal basis for implementation, and it has asked the IAEA Secretariat to present "model legal documents through which it would be given the necessary additional authority."[4]

Thus the IAEA remains far from adopting the type of intrusive verification mechanisms envisioned for the Organization for the Prohibition of Chemical Weapons (OPCW). Nevertheless, the fact that Program 93-2 has been proposed illustrates that the IAEA acknowledges that past inspection practices were deficient and that a serious attempt must be made to address the problem.

In accordance with Article X of the NPT, the twenty-five-year NPT Review and Extension Conference took place in April–May 1995. As a consequence of extensive negotiations and considerable U.S. pressures exerted before and during the conference, all 175 signatories consented to the indefinite extension of the treaty.

In approaching the 1995 conference, a number of the NPT's non-nuclear signatories expressed concern that if the treaty were extended indefinitely, they would lose all leverage with which to press the five nuclear weapon states to meet their treaty obligations. While some of the non-nuclear states were primarily concerned with ensuring that the nuclear weapon states would act "in good faith" to disarm their nuclear arsenals, others were more interested in making sure that the transfer of "peaceful nuclear technology" would not be hindered. For example, U.S. efforts to persuade Russia to cancel its contract with Iran for the completion of the 1300-megawatt German-made reactor in Bushehr, were cited as a clear violation of Article IV. In addition, a number of Arab states led by Egypt objected to the indefinite extension of the NPT as long as Israel does not sign and ratify the treaty, or at least until it commits itself to do so within an acceptable timetable (see Chapter 7).

Sufficient support for extending the treaty indefinitely was won once South Africa proposed that these objections and concerns would be addressed through the adoption of a number of conference resolutions. The first of these, called "Strengthening the Review Process for the Treaty," stipulated that NPT Review conferences would continue to be held every five years, and that in each of the three years preceding a conferences, ten-day Preparatory Committee meetings would be held "to consider principles, objectives and ways in order to promote the full implementation of the treaty." The document was intended to prevent non-nuclear states from losing all leverage, giving future NPT Review conferences a greater role in ensuring that the objectives of the treaty are being met.[5]

A second document adopted for the same purpose addressed the "Principles and Objectives for Nuclear Non-Proliferation and Disarmament." It emphasized the importance of concluding negotiations on the CTBT by the end of 1996, and of beginning negotiations on a treaty banning the production of fissile material. It also encouraged the establishment of nuclear-weapon-free zones in additional regions. Finally, the importance of ensuring the parties' right to develop nuclear energy for peaceful purposes was also emphasized.[6]

The NPT's application remains short of universal; important states widely believed to possess nuclear arsenals — notably India, Pakistan, and Israel — remain outside the treaty framework. The common reference to these states as "undeclared nuclear powers" also makes the NPT's definition of nuclear weapon states seem outdated, thus challenging the potency of the regime.

One proposal designed to address this problem was advanced in late 1993 by three distinguished U.S. scholars and former statesmen: McGeorge Bundy, National Security Advisor to Presidents Kennedy and Johnson; Admiral William Crowe, former chairman of the Joint Chiefs of Staff (JCS); and Sidney Drell, a long-time advisor to the U.S. government on technical, national security, and arms control issues. In a joint manifesto, they called for the incorporation of India, Pakistan, and Israel within the NPT framework as new nuclear weapons states in order to constrain them from contributing to further proliferation.[7]

Earlier, a similar suggestion had been made by François Heisbourg, former Director of the International Institute for Strategic Studies (IISS) in London; Heisbourg proposed that Israel sign the NPT as a nuclear weapon state.[8] Independently, a similar idea was communicated to this author in July 1992 by a senior Arab arms control official.

Clearly, granting the undeclared nuclear powers NPT membership as nuclear states would require that Article IX of the treaty — defining nuclear weapons states — be altered. It is highly unlikely that such an amendment would be ever undertaken. The proposals are bound to be opposed on the ground that they would signal a willingness to accommodate and thus legitimize "illegal" nuclear programs — thus encouraging further proliferation. It is also feared that any change in the treaty text would expose the treaty to numerous other demands for amendments. Hence, the issues related to the status of nuclear-capable NPT holdouts is unlikely to be resolved in the near future.

Nuclear-Weapon-Free Zones

Nuclear-weapon-free zones (NWFZs) are a regional approach to nuclear nonproliferation.[9] An NWFZ is an undertaking by a region's states to avoid the acquisition of nuclear weapons. In principle, the task of verifying compliance can be delegated to an international organization such as the IAEA, to a regional organization specifically established for this purpose, or to any other mechanism agreed upon by the parties. For example, the treaty can stipulate that IAEA full-scope safeguards be supplemented by additional verification procedures implemented by the IAEA, procedures adopted by a regional organization created for this purpose, the agreed exercise of national technical means (NTM), reciprocal and cooperative verification mechanisms and procedures such as on-site inspections, or any combination of these.

To date, the most successful application of the NWFZ concept has been the Latin American zone established by the Treaty of Tlatelolco in 1967. In recent years, the treaty has become more robust following the decisions of Brazil and Argentina to roll back their nuclear programs and to ratify the treaty unconditionally.[10] Also important has been Chile's early-1994 decision to make itself subject to the treaty.[11] Two additional protocols of the treaty incorporate within the regime's framework states outside the region that have responsibility for territories within the region, and nuclear-weapon states "present and future." "Additional Protocol 2" commits the nuclear weapon states to respect the "statute of denuclearization of Latin America for warlike purposes," and contains their negative security assurance "not to use or threaten to use nuclear weapons against the parties to the treaty."[12] The Tlatelolco Treaty established a supervisory organ — the Agency for the Prohibition of Nuclear Weapons in Latin America (OPANAL) — to verify treaty compliance, and stipulated a system of inspections to deal with alleged violations. It also incorporated the full application of IAEA safeguards. Like the NPT, the Tlatelolco Treaty permits the development of nuclear technology for "peaceful purposes" — including the use of nuclear explosives.[13] Interestingly, the United States and the Soviet Union, both strong advocates of the NPT, have criticized the Tlatelolco Treaty on that score. For example, when signing and ratifying Additional Protocol 2, the U.S. government stated that it "considers that the technology of making nuclear explosive devices for peaceful purposes is indistinguishable from the technology of making nuclear weapons and that nuclear weapons and nuclear explosive devices for peaceful purposes are both capable of releasing nuclear energy in an uncontrolled manner and have the common group of characteristics of large amounts of energy generated instantaneously from a compact source."[14]

A number of factors seem to have facilitated the establishment of the Tlatelolco regime. Primarily, as Mahmoud Karem has pointed out, the treaty was not perceived as "altering any existing security arrangement or tilting the nuclear or military balance." None of the countries in Latin America possessed nuclear weapons at the time, and the nuclear weapon states had no particular reason to deploy nuclear weapons in the subcontinent. Consequently, "no state felt that Tlatelolco would place it in a disadvantageous position or jeopardize its military situation or national interests, no state was threatened by the treaty regime, and accordingly, no state had incentives to oppose the treaty."[15] This, of course, was only partly true. Brazil and Argentina were actively engaged in developing a nuclear capability, and Chile was also determined to keep its options open in this realm; thus, all three failed to become full members of the Tlatelolco regime until the early 1990s. Indeed, an important motivation for all other Latin American states to conclude the treaty may have been their desire to create a forum that might pressure these three countries to arrest their nuclear designs.

Another important motive for the agreement was that South America never became an arena of superpower competition during the Cold War era. Indeed, the area continued to constitute a U.S. security zone, consistent with the Monroe Doctrine. Washington and Moscow had refrained from stationing nuclear weapons in the continent, and the United States could ensure that the region's states would not present one another with existential threats.

Some years after the Tlatelolco Treaty was concluded, a second NWFZ was established in the South Pacific. The Treaty of Raratonga (formally, the South Pacific Nuclear Free Zone Treaty) took effect in 1986 and was signed by Australia, the Cook Islands, Fiji, Kiribati, Nauru, New Zealand, Niue, Papua New Guinea, Western Samoa, the Solomon Islands, and Tuvalu.[16] The treaty is a somewhat less impressive achievement than the Latin American NWFZ, primarily because none of the countries of the South Pacific has ever had an active interest in obtaining nuclear weapons.

In 1993, negotiations were initiated in Harare, Zimbabwe, on a treaty to transform Africa into an NWFZ. On June 2, 1995, after two years of negotiations, the Organization of African Unity approved the treaty text at a meeting in Pelindaba, South Africa. It envisages the creation of an African Commission on Nuclear Energy as an implementing agency.[17] By 1995, considerable interest in establishing an NWFZ was also developing in South East Asia — and for the first time, the United States announced that it might not oppose the creation of the zone, despite earlier concerns that such a zone might limit the free movement of U.S. nuclear vessels in the region.[18]

PROPOSALS FOR A MIDDLE EAST NWFZ

A proposal calling for establishment of an NWFZ in the Middle East was first introduced to the UN General Assembly in 1974 by Iran. In 1980, the resolution was adopted for the first time without a vote. In 1988, the UN Secretary General, following the adoption of General Assembly Resolution 43/65, named a three-member expert group to study all matters concerning the possible establishment of an NWFZ in the Middle East. The members were James Leonard, Jan Prawitz, and Benjamin Sanders. They submitted their study to the UN Secretary General in October 1990.[19] The report was not primarily devoted to defining the modalities of a possible NWFZ in the region, but rather explored the prerequisites to the creation of such a zone.

The UN report noted the potential advantages of an NWFZ over the NPT: "A zone can, for example, involve even more extensive and rigorous verification procedures; it can establish additional constraints on peaceful nuclear activities, and it can provide for an extensive system of positive and negative security guarantees; [finally], it can prescribe even more difficult requirements for withdrawal than the NPT" (Paragraph 109).

Regarding the boundaries of a Middle East NWFZ, the study recommended the adoption of the "IAEA definition" of the Middle East; this would extend the proposed zone from Iran in the east to Libya in the west, and from Syria in the north to Yemen in the south, thus excluding Turkey (a NATO member), Malta, and Cyprus. The report noted that in contrast with the Latin American NWFZ, the Middle East zone would be surrounded by neighbors and would border nuclear-armed NATO and the states of the former Soviet Union (Paragraph 76).

The study argues that IAEA safeguards must be imposed through out the region: "To establish an effective nuclear-weapons-free zone in the Middle East it would be essential to place all nuclear facilities under appropriate international safeguards, either through adherence of the state in question to the NPT or by concluding a full-scope safeguards agreement with the IAEA. For practical purposes this requirement is of relevance to Israel only, since all other prospective participants in the zone with nuclear facilities have placed their facilities under IAEA safeguards" (Paragraph 81).

The study mentions the danger that, having developed an advanced "peaceful" nuclear program, a member state would break out from the safeguards regime.

The report analyzed the difficulty Israel would face in altering its nuclear posture and of attaining Arab confidence that it has in fact done so. Paragraph 95 of the report refers to Israel as a country that "if it has not already crossed that threshold, has the capability to manufacture nuclear weapons within a very short time." Based on its analysis of Israel's security problems, the report assesses that Israel "will not see its way clear to a renunciation of nuclear use — by adherence to any arrangement that would oblige it to submit all its nuclear activities to international safeguards — unless it has credible assurances that no military action is likely" (Paragraph 101). The report proposes that Israel's willingness to submit its reactor in Dimona to safeguards would comprise a halfway point on Israel's road to an NWFZ; it would not affect Israel's deterrent of a "weapon of last resort," which is based on plutonium that has already been processed (Paragraph 115).

The difficulty of meeting the prerequisites to establishment of an NWFZ led the report's authors to conclude that "realistically such a zone can be realized step by step in a process extending over years, a process in which all states would work to create a total environment in which no state feels its security is threatened" (Paragraph 109). The report also suggests a long list of confidence-building measures, in the nuclear realm as well as in other military fields, that might facilitate the establishment of an NWFZ in the Middle East. These include issuing unilateral declarations of activities in the nuclear field; allowing "invitational inspections" of suspected nuclear activities; making public a commitment to refrain from reprocessing reactor fuel; exercising maximum transparency and openness, including the application of an "open skies"–type agreement; agreeing to restrict the right to withdrawal from the NPT; issuing a commitment not to test a nuclear device and not to create a nuclear explosion of any kind, not even for peaceful purposes; making a commitment to refrain from attacking nuclear installations; adherence by all the region's states to the 1972 Biological Weapons Convention (BWC) as well as the then-proposed Chemical Weapons Convention (CWC); freezing the acquisition of ballistic missiles and the conduct of missile test flights; and applying conventional military confidence-building measures similar to those implemented in the framework of the Conference on Security and Cooperation in Europe (CSCE) process (Paragraphs 112–174).

The report also outlines the role of the nuclear powers in the establishment of an NWFZ in the Middle East. It requires these powers to provide negative security assurances: commitments to refrain from threatening or attacking any of the region's states with nuclear weapons and to avoid stationing nuclear weapons anywhere in the zone. The authors found that requiring the nuclear powers to provide positive security assurances is a much more complex issue because the possible content of such assurances cannot be clearly defined (Paragraphs 186–187).

Finally, the annex of the study addresses the importance of making progress toward the establishment of an NWFZ in the Middle East before all the region's states would be willing to join the proposed zone. It suggests that by signing an agreement to establish such a zone, the core countries of the region would commit themselves — for an interim period, until all the region's states become members of the zone — "not to act in a manner that would undermine the basic objectives of the agreement" (Annex, Paragraph 3). (See Appendix 9 for Israel's reply to the study.)

The Comprehensive Test Ban Treaty

In September 1993, President Bill Clinton announced U.S. support for the conclusion of a Comprehensive Test Ban Treaty (CTBT). The treaty is designed to supplement the 1963 Limited Test Ban Treaty (LTBT, officially called the 1963 Treaty Banning Nuclear Weapons Tests in the Atmosphere, in Outer Space and Under Water). According to a treaty draft, a party to the CTBT is to undertake "not to carry out any nuclear weapon test explosion or any other nuclear explosion, and to prohibit and prevent any such nuclear explosion at any place under its jurisdiction or control."[20] Furthermore, each state party undertakes "to refrain from causing, encouraging, or in any way participating in the carrying out of any nuclear weapon test explosion or any other nuclear explosion." The final treaty text is understood to prohibit all test explosions down to a zero yield.[21]

Soon after Clinton's announcement, negotiations of the treaty text were accelerated at the UN Conference on Disarmament (CD) in Geneva. For this purpose, the CD created an Ad Hoc Committee on a

Nuclear Test Ban and elected Mexico's Ambassador Miguel Marin-Bosch as its chairman. Sweden and Australia then submitted alternative treaty drafts for the delegations' consideration.[22] These drafts formed the basis for the "rolling text" of the treaty that has been negotiated since mid-1994. In January 1996, Marin-Bosch was replaced by Ambassador Jaap Ramaker of the Netherlands as chairman of the Ad Hoc Committee.[23]

Work on different provisions of the CTBT was launched simultaneously by a number of CD working groups. The Legal and Institutional Issues working group drafted the text of provisions related to the treaty's scope and entry into force. The Verification working group has made a number of technical presentations to the CD and has appointed "friends of the chair" to head three verification subgroups: India for seismic verification; Britain for non-seismic verification; and Russia for on-site inspections.

Following two years of extensive negotiations, on June 28, 1996, Ambassador Ramaker tabled a draft CTBT. The draft called for the establishment of a Comprehensive Test Ban Treaty Organization (CTBTO) to supervise the implementation of the treaty. The new body is modeled after the Organization for the Prohibition of Chemical Weapons (OPCW), created to verify the Chemical Weapons Convention.[24] The CTBTO is to include the Conference of the State Parties, a fifty-one-member Executive Council, and a Technical Secretariat headed by a Director-General.[25] The organization will be located in Vienna in order to allow maximum cooperation with the IAEA.

By late July 1996, almost all major obstacles to the signing of the treaty were removed. Most important, China dropped its long-standing demand that the treaty permit the conduct of peaceful nuclear explosions (PNEs). In 1994, Clinton administration officials had ruled out suggestions that PNEs would be permitted, referring to such proposals as "non-starters."[26] The June 1996 draft treaty addressed China's priorities by stipulating that the Conference of State Parties will hold a CTBT review conference every ten years. "On the basis of a request by any State Party, the Review Conference shall consider the possibility of permitting the conduct of underground nuclear explosions for peaceful purposes. If the Review Conference decides by consensus that such nuclear explosions may be permitted, it shall commence work without delay, with a view to recommending to State Parties an appropriate amendment to this Treaty that shall preclude any military benefits of such nuclear explosions."[27]

A question resolved earlier was whether the conduct of "periodic safety tests" would be allowed. For some time, the Clinton administration's position on this issue remained unclear. In late 1994 the administration seemed to reject such suggestions while France and, to a lesser extent, Britain insisted that it was important to maintain the right to conduct such tests. By early 1995, negotiations of this critical issue were stalled as Pentagon officials favored keeping open the option for conducting safety tests with a yield of up to 500 tons. This matter was not resolved until September 1995, when President Clinton ruled that there would be no exceptions to the total ban. France and Britain have adopted similar positions, thus allowing the formation of an axis favoring "a truly zero yield" ban.[28]

Compliance with the treaty provisions is to be verified by International Data Center (IDC) that will operate an International Monitoring System (IMS). Data collected by national technical means (i.e., national intelligence assets) may be used to back up a call for an on-site inspection if it has been obtained "in a manner consistent with generally recognized principles of international law." This is understood to exclude human intelligence for espionage purposes.[29]

The IMS is to be based on four monitoring technologies: seismological, radionuclide, hydro-acoustic, and infrasound. It will include 50 primary and some 120 secondary seismic sensor stations, feeding data about vibrations of the earth; 80 radionuclide stations, testing the atmosphere for radioactive debris from nuclear explosions; 11 hydro-acoustic stations, which detect sound waves traveling through the oceans; and 70 infrasound detectors, which detect soundwaves traveling through the atmosphere at frequencies far below those heard by the human ear. These various sensors are to transmit the information collected to the IDC.[30] These technical means would be supplemented by transparency measures and mechanisms for consultation, clarification, and the conduct of on-site inspections.

The July 1996 CTBT draft stipulates that "the decision to approve the on-site inspection shall be made by a majority of all members of the Executive Council" (Article IV, Paragraph 46). The fear that the right to conduct such inspections might be abused was addressed in

Paragraph 57 (c) of the same article, requiring a State Party subject to an inspection "to provide access within the inspection area for the sole purpose of determining facts relevant to the purpose of the inspection, taking into account [national security and confidentiality concerns] and any constitutional obligations it may have with regard to propriety or searches and seizures."[31]

Article IX of the June 1996 draft states that the CTBT is of unlimited duration, allowing any state to withdraw from the treaty by providing six months' notice "if it decides that extraordinary events related to the subject matter of this Treaty have jeopardized its supreme interests." Notice of such withdrawal must include a statement describing such extraordinary event or events. France, Russia, the United Kingdom, and the United States have each stated that loss of confidence in their nuclear arsenals would be such an event.[32]

According to the June draft text, the CTBT will enter into force 180 days after the deposit of instruments of ratification by forty-four states listed in Annex 2 of the treaty.[33]

By mid-August 1996, India's objections to the treaty remained the last obstacles to its conclusion. India demanded that the CTBT contain a much stronger commitment to "a total elimination of nuclear weapons 'within a time-bound framework'."[34] It also objected to making the treaty's entry into force contingent on India's ratification of the treaty as a state listed in the group of forty-four (Annex 2).[35] India was particularly angered by a provision in the final text stipulating that if after three years the eight nuclear nations (the five declared nuclear powers plus Israel, India, and Pakistan) have not all signed, the Conference of State Parties will reconvene and "decide by consensus what measures consistent with international law may be undertaken to accelerate the ratification process."[36] India announced that it would "not accept any language in the treaty text which would affect our sovereign right to decide, in the light of our supreme national interests, whether we should or should not accede to such a treaty."[37]

Since the UN Conference on Disarmament operates on the basis of consensus, India's objections prevented the CD from reporting the CTBT to the UN General Assembly. India's move was supported by Iran. In late August 1996, this prompted Australia to present to the

UN General Assembly the CTBT text accepted by all members of the CD except India and Iran.[38] On September 10, the General Assembly approved the treaty and on September 24 it was opened for signature. During the following two days, more than 70 countries signed the treaty. Yet India's refusal to sign would prevent the treaty from coming into force. Moreover, it is quite evident that Pakistan will not sign the CTBT as long as India refuses to sign.

Banning the Production of Weapons-Grade Material

A proposal to freeze the production of fissile material was first made by President George Bush on May 29, 1991, as part of a comprehensive initiative on arms control in the Middle East (see Appendix 7). The initiative called upon the "regional states to implement a verifiable freeze on the production and acquisition of weapons-usable nuclear material (enriched uranium or separated plutonium)."[39] In July 1992, the Bush administration announced a global arms control initiative that included a call for a ban on the production of fissile material. The initiative specified the Middle East as one of five areas where special efforts should be made to apply the ban. (See Appendix 10.)

On September 27, 1993, President Bill Clinton took the Bush proposals a step further. In a statement defining his administration's approach to arms control, Clinton called for a global treaty banning weapons-grade material production. The initiative committed the United States to "propose a multilateral convention prohibiting the production of highly-enriched uranium or plutonium for nuclear explosive purposes or outside of international safeguards." It contained a separate promise that the United States would "encourage more restrictive regional arrangements to constrain fissile material production in regions of instability and high proliferation risks."[40] Thus, whereas the Bush proposals advocated a complete ban, the Clinton initiative permitted the continued production of fissile materials under safeguards. (See Appendix 12.)

The principal strength of all three U.S. "capping" proposals is their realistic approach. Recognizing that under prevailing political and strategic circumstances some states will continue to avoid rolling back their nuclear programs and signing the NPT as non-nuclear states, the proposed treaty aims to freeze such capabilities at their present levels.

Thus it represents a next-best alternative, instead of ignoring unsafeguarded nuclear programs.

The assumption driving these initiatives is that some states whose strategic circumstances propelled them to develop a nuclear capability clandestinely might be content with the quantities of fissile material they have already acquired, and might accept a ban on further production of such material. Hence, states that have not joined the NPT and have not agreed to the application of full-scope IAEA safeguards to all their nuclear facilities might more readily accept a convention banning the further production of weapons-usable material. Consequently, the proposed ban may be acceptable to the declared nuclear powers, to undeclared nuclear weapon states, and to non-nuclear weapon states alike. The potential universal participation in the proposed treaty adds to its attractiveness.

Yet the Clinton initiative contains a number of complicating qualifications. As already noted, the formulation of the suggested convention implies that the production of plutonium or highly-enriched uranium would be permitted if it is subjected to international safeguards or is unrelated to nuclear explosive purposes. Thus, the convention would suffer the same weakness of the NPT: it would allow a country to produce weapons-grade material under international safeguards and to withdraw from the treaty if it deems it necessary or advantageous to develop a nuclear arsenal. By that time, a country might possess a large quantity of plutonium or highly-enriched uranium with which nuclear warheads could be produced.

Also, the Clinton initiative suggests that the United States will "seek to eliminate where possible the accumulation of stockpiles of highly-enriched uranium or plutonium, and to ensure that where these materials exist they are subject to the highest standards of safety, security, and international accountability." While the words "where possible" illustrate a pragmatic approach, they also further weaken an already weak clause that merely defines an objective without stipulating how it might be achieved. More important, the suggested clause opens a very sensitive issue which the United States has thus far attempted to avoid: its long-standing dilemma whether to pursue nonproliferation measures or a proliferation management approach with respect to ambiguous nuclear programs. If a stockpile of plutonium or highly-enriched uranium were produced by a covert nuclear program, it would be impossible to apply the suggested mechanisms for "safety, security, and international accountability" without transforming the accumulated material from "undeclared" to "declared" stockpiles, thereby granting retroactive legitimacy to the accumulation of such material. Consequently, the clause might encourage proliferation; states could believe that once they develop a covert nuclear program, the United States will act to make it both safe and overt.

A separate clause in the initiative addresses the fissile material stockpile of the United States itself, committing it to "submit U.S. fissile material no longer needed for our deterrent to inspection by the International Atomic Energy Agency." That is, the United States promises to subject to IAEA inspections only that part of its fissile material stockpile "no longer needed for [its] deterrent," but does not make a similar allowance for other nations. Rather, it urges them to subject their entire stockpiles of fissile material to "international accountability" and "international safeguards." Thus, the initiative is vulnerable to long-standing Third World complaints that the United States continues to pursue a highly discriminatory nonproliferation policy.

For many months following Clinton's September 1993 speech, Washington did not initiate negotiations of the proposed treaty text. This may have reflected the priority it gave to negotiating the CTBT as well as its awareness of the problems inherent in negotiating a cut-off treaty. In November 1993 the UN General Assembly finally adopted a resolution authorizing the negotiations of the proposed treaty. Yet it took the Conference on Disarmament (CD) in Geneva another year to agree on a three-paragraph "mandate" necessary for launching these negotiations.[41] The mandate was adopted on March 23, 1995, and stipulated the creation of an Ad Hoc Committee for the purpose of negotiating the treaty. But by late 1995, the CD had not yet decided who would serve on this committee.[42]

The formulation adopted by the UN General Assembly to describe the envisaged treaty was less permissive than Clinton's proposal but more permissive than the complete freeze suggested by President Bush. The resolution called for a treaty "banning the production of fissile material for nuclear weapons or other nuclear explosive devices." This formulation was repeated in the text of the negotiations mandate adopted by the CD.

The delays in negotiating the "fiss-ban" treaty point to the likelihood that agreement on a treaty text will take many years.[43] A central issue requiring resolution is whether the treaty will apply only to present and future activities — in effect freezing the status quo in fissile material production — or whether it would apply to past activities as well. In the latter case the treaty may require — as the Clinton initiative proposes — that stockpiles of fissile material be subjected to international safeguards. For countries currently enjoying an ambiguous nuclear status this would imply the end of ambiguity. And, for declared nuclear powers, international safeguards could lead to new constraints on the use of their fissile material stockpiles. Some countries — notably China, India, and South Africa — have already indicated that they would oppose the treaty's application to the products of past activities.[44]

Terminating the ambiguity of undeclared nuclear powers by requiring that they declare their existing fissile material stockpiles will not prove easy: they are not likely to view such clarification as serving their best interests. Primarily, they might be concerned that an announcement of the results of their past activities would invite immediate and massive pressures to roll back their nuclear programs, not merely to freeze them at existing levels. But the rejection of the treaty by states such as India would defeat one of its original purposes — to bring non-NPT signatories into the nonproliferation regime.

Clearly, then, negotiations for a treaty banning the production of fissile material must address some very serious dilemmas. Nevertheless, now that negotiations of the CTBT are completed, the proposed fissile material production ban treaty may become the next most important new item in the global nuclear nonproliferation agenda. Middle East states will need to address the issues involved and determine their approach toward the proposed treaty.

Conclusions

The effects of the global nuclear nonproliferation regime on the Middle East are considerable and varied. The 1968 Nuclear Non-Proliferation Treaty — signed by all of the region's states except Israel and Oman — seems to have established a norm. This yardstick for measuring states' behavior in nuclear matters was also important in providing the legal basis for international action when one of the region's states — Iraq — broke the norm by violating its NPT obligations.

Similarly, the evolution of nuclear-weapon-free zones in other regions — notably in Latin America — provides a model to be emulated in the Middle East. And the Comprehensive Test Ban Treaty (CTBT) and the proposed convention banning the production of fissile material will add more regional ramifications to the global nuclear nonproliferation regime. The reactions of Israel and the Arab states to these facets of the regime are elaborated in Chapters 7 and 8.

NOTES

1. Shunji Taoka, "Would Japan Build the Bomb?" *Newsweek*, June 13, 1994.

2. See Gary Milhollin, "The Iraqi Bomb," *New Yorker*, February 1, 1993, pp. 47–55.

3. Steve Coll, "Neutral Sweden Quietly Keeps Nuclear Option Open," *Washington Post*, November 25, 1994.

4. *Newsbrief* (published by the Programme for Promoting Nuclear Non-Proliferation), No. 30 (2nd quarter, 1995), p. 9. See also Patricia M. Lewis, "Strengthening Safeguards," *Verification Matters*, Verification Technology Information Center (VERTIC), London, Briefing Paper 95/2, March 1995.

5. See UN Document NPT/CONF.1995/32/DEC.1, May 11, 1995.

6. See UN Document NPT/CONF.1995/32/DEC.2, May 11, 1995.

7. McGeorge Bundy, William J. Crowe, Jr., and Sidney Drell, *Reducing Nuclear Danger: The Road Away from the Brink* (New York: Council on Foreign Relations, 1993), pp. 67–72.

8. Pepirblat, "China selling nuclear know-how," *Yediot Ahronot*, January 17, 1992.

9. See Jon Brook Wolfsthal, "Nuclear-Weapon-Free Zones: Coming of Age?" *Arms Control Today*, Vol. 23, No. 2 (March 1993), pp. 3–9.

10. In 1967, Argentina signed but did not ratify the treaty. Brazil and Chile signed and ratified the treaty but did not satisfy the requirements for the treaty to enter into force laid down in Article 28. See Mahmoud Karem, *A Nuclear-Weapon-Free Zone in the Middle East — Problems and Prospects* (Westport, Conn.: Greenwood Press, 1988), p. 28, fn 6.

11. See "Argentina and Chile Bring the Latin American Nuclear-Weapons-Free Zone into Force," The White House, Office of the Press Secretary, January 21,1994.

12. Karem, *A Nuclear-Weapon-Free Zone in the Middle East*, pp. 21, 24–25.

13. Ibid., pp. 21, 23.

14. Cited in ibid., p. 26.

15. Ibid., p. 25.

16. Zachary S. Davis and Warren Donnelly, "The South Pacific Nuclear Free Zone Treaty [The Treaty of Raratonga]," *CRS Report for Congress*, Congressional Research Service, Library of Congress, 93-610 ENR, June 25, 1993.

17. "Africa Nuclear-Weapon-Free Zone Agreed by OAU," *Nuclear Proliferation News*, No. 27, June 15, 1995, p. 11.

18. "U.S. 'Open Minded' on South East Asian Nuclear-Weapons-Free Zone," *Nuclear Proliferation News*, No. 31, August 21, 1995, p. 17.

19. James Leonard, Jan Prawitz, and Benjamin Sanders, *Study on Effective and Verifiable Measures Which Would Facilitate the Establishment of a Nuclear-Weapon-Free Zone in the Middle East*, Report of the UN Secretary General, October 1990 (United Nations General Assembly, Forty-fifth session, Agenda item 49, Document A/45/435, October 10, 1990).

20. See *Nuclear Proliferation News*, No. 32 (September 8, 1995), p. 4.

21. *Trust and Verify*, Bulletin of the Verification Technology Information Center, London, No. 67 (July 1996), p. 1.

22. See "Conference on Disarmament Sees Progress Toward CTB Treaty," *Arms Control Today*, Vol. 24, No. 4 (May 1994), pp. 17, 23.

23. Rebecca Johnson, "CTB Negotiations—Geneva Update No. 29," *Disarmament Diplomacy*, No. 6 (June 1996), p. 17.

24. *Nuclear Proliferation News*, No. 32 (September 8, 1995), p. 2.

25. *Trust and Verify*, Bulletin of the Verification Technology Information Center, London, No. 67 (July 1996), p. 1.

26. Ibid., p. 23.

27. Ibid., p. 2.

28. See *Nuclear Proliferation News*, No. 32 (September 8, 1995), p. 2. See also *Nuclear Proliferation News*, No. 31 (August 21, 1995), pp. 1, 9; and *Nuclear Proliferation News*, No. 27 (June 15, 1995), p. 1.

29. Johnson, "CTB Negotiations — Geneva Update," p. 21.

30. Ibid., p. 3.

31. Ibid., p. 2.

32. Ibid.

33. Ibid. These forty-four states are: Algeria, Argentina, Australia, Austria, Bangladesh, Belgium, Brazil, Bulgaria, Canada, Chile, China, Colombia, Democratic People's Republic of Korea, Egypt, Finland, France, Germany, Hungary, India, Indonesia, Islamic Republic of Iran, Israel, Italy, Japan, Mexico, Netherlands, Norway, Pakistan, Peru, Poland, Republic of Korea, Romania, Russian Federation, Slovak Republic, South Africa, Spain, Sweden, Switzerland, Turkey, Ukraine, United Kingdom, United States of America, Viet Nam, and Zaire. The criteria for inclusion on the list are that a state should be a member of the CD as of June 18, 1996, and appear in either Table 1 of the April 1996 edition of *Nuclear Power Reactors of the World* or Table 1 of the December 1995 edition of *Nuclear Research Reactors in the World*, both published by the IAEA.

34. Johnson, "CTB Negotiations — Geneva Update," p. 19.

35. Ibid., p. 12. See also "India asks for change in nuclear agreement," *Boston Globe*, August 20, 1996.

36. Barbara Crossette, "India to Block Completion Of Pact to Ban Nuclear Tests," *New York Times*, July 31, 1996. See also Nicholas Doughty, "India, China Oppose Parts Of Nuclear Test Ban Pact," *Washington Post*, July 30, 1996.

37. Johnson, "CTB Negotiations — Geneva Update," p. 23.

38. Barbara Crossette, "Efforts in U.N. To Salvage Test-Ban Pact," *New York Times*, August 23, 1996. See also Reuters, "Geneva negotiators admit defeat on nuclear accord," *Boston Globe*, August 23, 1996.

39. "Fact Sheet on Middle East Arms Control Initiative," release from the White House, Office of the Press Secretary, Kennebunkport, Maine, May 29, 1991; excerpted in Appendix 7.

40. "UN Nonproliferation and Export Control Policy," White House Fact Sheet issued on September 27, on President Clinton's address to the UN General Assembly.

41. Resolution 48/75 was adopted by consensus on December 16, 1993. See also UN General Assembly, Forty-eighth session, First Committee, Agenda item 71 (c), Document A/C.1/48/L.44, November 4, 1993. The mandate for the cut-off negotiations approved by the CD reads: "1. The Conference on Disarmament decides to establish an Ad Hoc Committee on a 'Ban on the production of fissile material for nuclear weapons or other nuclear explosive devices.' 2.The Conference directs the Ad Hoc Committee to negotiate a non-discriminatory, multilateral and internationally and effectively verifiable treaty banning the production of fissile material for nuclear weapons or other explosive devices. 3. The Ad Hoc Committee will report to the Conference on Disarmament on the progress of its work before the conclusion of the 1995 session." See *Trust and Verify*, Bulletin of the Verification Technology Information Center, London, No. 56 (April 1995), p. 1.

42. See *Nuclear Proliferation News*, No. 29 (July 11, 1995), p. 1; and *Nuclear Proliferation News*, No. 31 (August 21, 1995), p. 2.

43. For further discussion of the problems entailed in the proposed fissile production ban treaty, see *Halting the Production of Fissile Materials for Nuclear Weapons*, Research Paper No. 31 (New York and Geneva: United Nations Institute for Disarmament Research, 1994).

44. See *Nuclear Proliferation News*, No. 29 (July 11, 1995), pp. 1, 3–4; and *Nuclear Proliferation News*, No. 31 (August 21, 1995), p. 3.

Chapter 6

U.S. Nuclear Nonproliferation Policies in the Middle East

This chapter outlines U.S. nuclear nonproliferation and counter-proliferation policy and its impact in the Middle East. The United States continues to play a key role in shaping the global nuclear nonproliferation regime, and has exerted ever-greater influence on Middle East politics and security in the post–Cold War era. Many key states in the region — Israel, Jordan, Egypt, Saudi Arabia, and most of the smaller Gulf Cooperation Council states — maintain very close ties with the United States; in determining their approach to the global arms control agenda, they must take Washington's priorities into account.

The first part of the chapter surveys U.S. nonproliferation policy and its implementation worldwide. While the United States has consistently been committed to halting the spread of nuclear weapons, it has often implemented this policy inconsistently, reflecting the weight of competing U.S. national interests.

The second part of the chapter examines the U.S. approach to Israel's nuclear option. Washington's view of Israel as a "special case" in U.S. nonproliferation policy is a clear example of its ambivalent policy. It is propelled by the many factors that account for the generally close ties between the United States and Israel, including their strategic cooperation. Therefore, until a comprehensive peace in the Middle East is achieved and is tested over time, the United States is unlikely to press Israel to take steps that might erode its present nuclear posture.

U.S. Global Nonproliferation Efforts

During most of the 1950s, the United States took a rather relaxed view toward the possible proliferation of nuclear technology.[1] In 1954, the

Eisenhower administration launched the Atoms for Peace program, through which the United States helped install twenty-six nuclear research reactors in other countries. Between 1954 and 1979, some 13,456 foreign researchers from non–Warsaw Pact nations received training in the United States in the nuclear sciences.[2]

At other times, notably from 1945 to 1952, and later during the Johnson and Carter administrations, the United States demonstrated a more restrictive nonproliferation policy. In 1946, the United States proposed the Baruch Plan to create an International Atomic Development Authority under UN supervision, which would control the world's relevant raw materials (primarily uranium), manage all atomic energy activities considered potentially dangerous to world peace, and have the power to inspect all atomic installations.[3] Later, the Johnson administration invested considerable energy in negotiating the Nuclear Non-Proliferation Treaty. Finally, in the late 1970s, the Carter administration placed efforts to halt the proliferation of nuclear weapons at the top of its foreign policy agenda.

The Carter years resulted in far-reaching antiproliferation legislation. The first was the 1978 Nuclear Nonproliferation Act, which prohibited cooperation in nuclear matters and material with any country that did not place all its nuclear installations under full-scope safeguards.[4] The second was the Glenn amendment to the 1977 International Security Assistance Act, which strengthened the Symington amendment adopted during the Ford administration. It stipulated that all economic and military aid would be cut off to any country that detonated a nuclear device or imported or exported a uranium enrichment facility or plutonium reprocessing plant.[5]

The Glenn amendment has been altered several times. In 1985 it was supplemented by the Pressler amendment, which required the administration to certify that "Pakistan does not possess a nuclear explosive device and that the proposed United States Assistance program will reduce significantly the risk that Pakistan will possess a nuclear explosive device." In 1990, this resulted in the cutoff of economic and military assistance to Pakistan. Another amendment adopted in 1985 at the initiative of Congressman Stephen Solarz stipulated that U.S. military and economic aid would be cut off to any country that illegally imported from the United States material that would "contribute significantly to the ability of a country to make a nuclear explosive if the President determines that the items are so used."

Since the late 1960s, U.S. nuclear nonproliferation policy has usually reflected six general concerns: that nuclear proliferation increases the likelihood of nuclear war; that the use of nuclear weapons would lend them legitimacy and might lead to further usage; that a regional nuclear war might be the catalyst for a superpower nuclear exchange; that the higher likelihood of nuclear war would require more frequent U.S. interventions in other regions to prevent local parties from escalating to nuclear war; that nuclear proliferation would decrease the U.S. margin of power and thus curtail its ability to influence developments in other regions; and that proliferation would increase the likelihood of nuclear terrorism.

Yet U.S. efforts to halt proliferation have sometimes been inconsistent and selective for three reasons. First, the United States was reluctant to invest in something that others would enjoy for free. Particularly during the Nixon-Ford-Kissinger years, Europe's unwillingness to invest in a less proliferated world made the United States increasingly reluctant to bear the costs on its own. Washington's pessimism regarding the possibility of stopping proliferation also reduced its incentives to invest in this objective. This pessimism was based on the assessment that other nuclear suppliers were less willing to restrict themselves, and that a highly determined state, propelled by what it regards as supreme national interests, could not be dissuaded from acquiring nuclear weapons.

Finally, competing national interests have limited the extent to which nonproliferation goals can be pursued. For example, as long as the Soviet Union continued its military intervention in Afghanistan, and Pakistan played a key role in supporting those combatting the Soviet and the pro-Soviet forces in Afghanistan, the United States exempted Pakistan from the stipulations of its nuclear nonproliferation policy. Throughout the 1980s, Pakistan was granted presidential waivers from the stipulations of the Symington-Glenn amendment, "in the national interest of the United States." Similarly, in response to the Pressler amendment, the executive branch certified to Congress that it did not have clear and conclusive evidence that Pakistan had developed nuclear weapons, a disingenuous statement. However, in late 1990, following the Soviet withdrawal from Afghanistan, the Bush administration would no longer provide the required certification, thus triggering the implementation of the Pressler amendment.[6] This included a ban on the transfer of some twenty-eight F-16A fighter aircraft that Pakistan had already paid for.

In 1995, the Clinton administration again changed the course of U.S. policy regarding Pakistan's nuclear program. It concluded that Pakistan's Prime Minister, Benazir Bhutto, will not roll back this program, and that U.S. sanctions no longer serve U.S. interests. Consequently, following Bhutto's mid-1995 visit to Washington, the administration decided to reinstate the two countries' military relations. This was to entail compensating Pakistan for the banned F-16s by selling them to a third country, while permitting less salient transfers to the Pakistani armed forces, including three antisubmarine aircraft (P-3-Cs), twenty-eight Harpoon sea-to-sea missiles, and 360 AIM-9L Sidewinder air-to-air missiles.[7]

Similarly, competing U.S. national interests tamed the U.S. reaction to South Africa's nuclear program in the 1980s. While it complied with international sanctions and applied its own sanctions against Pretoria's apartheid regime, Washington took no forceful action against South Africa's nuclear designs, probably because during the Cold War, South Africa was perceived as confronted by Soviet-backed and Cuban-supported regimes in Angola and Mozambique. In fact, Pretoria's former foreign minister, Pik Botha, recently testified that in 1981, President Ronald Reagan helped Pretoria obtain enriched uranium "after receiving an assurance about its nuclear arms program." Botha, who became Minister of Mines and Energy in Nelson Mandela's government, reported that he had assured Reagan at a White House meeting that his country "would not detonate a nuclear weapon without first telling Washington." It was also reported that the United States allowed South Africa to obtain uranium fuel for its Koeberg reactor in return for a commitment to begin negotiations on the independence of Namibia (then known as South West Africa).[8]

The end of the Cold War, the breakup of the Soviet Union, and the 1990–91 Gulf War considerably affected Washington's nuclear non-proliferation agenda. On one hand, the odds of a U.S.-Russian nuclear exchange have diminished — at least temporarily — to nearly zero, thus eliminating the danger that nuclear proliferation might catalyze a superpower nuclear exchange. On the other hand, the breakup of the Soviet Union resulted in three additional independent states possessing considerable nuclear arsenals. The emergence of Ukraine, Belarus, and Kazakhstan presented a serious challenge to the viability of the NPT, which recognizes only five nuclear powers. This problem was particularly difficult with respect to Ukraine, which viewed itself as threatened by Russia, and was therefore reluctant to divest itself of its nuclear assets.

A second issue was the possible loss of control over nuclear weapons, facilities, fissile material, and scientists and engineers in the former Soviet Union, and the danger of a resulting "nuclear leakage" to potential proliferators such as Iran and North Korea. Consequently, at the initiative of Senators Sam Nunn and Richard Lugar, the U.S. Congress appropriated $1.6 billion to support denuclearization measures in the former Soviet Union from 1992 to 1995. Additional smaller programs to meet the same objectives are being implemented by the U.S. Department of Energy.

Some of the problems that worried U.S. policymakers in the immediate aftermath of the Soviet Union's breakup have been mitigated in recent years. The three new republics that inherited nuclear arsenals have joined the NPT as non-nuclear states. Kazakhstan transferred all the nuclear weapons stationed on its territory to Russia, and the process of denuclearizing Ukraine and Belarus continues. So far there is no evidence that nuclear weapons, expert manpower, or significant amounts of fissile material have been smuggled from the former Soviet Union. The combination of foreign assistance that has allowed Russian nuclear scientists to survive, the functioning — even if imperfectly — of the internal security apparatus, and a continued sense of loyalty and patriotism together explain why nuclear leakage seems to have been averted thus far. However, the possibility that weapons-grade material or expert manpower will leak from Russia to potential proliferators cannot be ruled out.

The prospects that the United States and Russia can cooperate to prevent the further spread of nuclear weapons are mixed. On the one hand, Russia can now pursue a more active nonproliferation policy in cooperation with the United States, since it no longer needs to compete. Most countries that have become the focus of proliferation concerns are much nearer to Russia than to the United States, making nonproliferation attractive. On the other hand, Russia's poor economy compels it to emphasize exports — including nuclear exports. Hence Russia could not be persuaded to ignore the potential benefits of nuclear trade with Iran.

The 1990–91 Gulf crisis and war crystallized U.S. concerns about the implications for regional stability and the security of U.S. forces overseas of the possible acquisition of nuclear weapons by a country such as Iraq. Therefore, the focus of U.S. nuclear nonproliferation policy has shifted from the global arena to specific regions where U.S. interests are directly involved: the Persian Gulf, which is affected by the nuclear programs of Iraq and Iran; and the Korean peninsula, where North Korea's nuclear designs affect the security of South Korea and U.S. forces stationed there, as well as the future of Japan's nuclear posture.

Increasingly, U.S. policy emphasizes that the nature of a country's regime is a key determinant of whether it is a proliferation concern. In particular, the Clinton administration distinguishes between democratic and non-democratic governments. This largely explains Washington's more relaxed view of the nuclear capabilities of India — and, to a lesser degree, of Pakistan as well — in contrast to its assessment of the risks entailed in the possible acquisition of nuclear weapons by the dictatorial regimes of Iraq, Iran, and North Korea. The latter three are viewed as "rogue regimes" — governments that have demonstrated a strong propensity to disregard international norms. The implication has been that should they obtain nuclear weapons, they would be far more likely to use them.

The Bush administration was the key to enforcing the nuclear disarmament of Iraq under UN Security Council Resolutions 687 and 715. The United States demonstrated its determination to disarm Iraq in the face of repeated Iraqi efforts to sabotage the implementation of the resolutions. Indeed, U.S. policy was largely successful in ensuring that Iraq's nuclear program would be "pounded into the ground by bombs, by inspections, and by disruptions."[9]

U.S. nuclear nonproliferation policy increasingly recognizes that while in recent years some nuclear programs — notably in Brazil, Argentina, and South Africa — have been rolled back, such reversal will not occur in regions where countries perceive more enduring threats to security and existence. Consequently, the United States has shifted from an absolute approach — requiring universal adherence to the NPT and the application of IAEA safeguards to all nuclear facilities — to the phased approach adopted by the Bush and Clinton administrations, centering on the proposed ban on the production of weapons-grade materials in the Middle East and other regions.

Indeed, the Bush proposals for freezing the production of fissile material also marked a shift in U.S. nonproliferation policy from a largely global approach to greater emphasis on the circumstances of specific regions. As a result, while it is still committed to the NPT as the backbone of the nuclear nonproliferation regime, the United States has demonstrated growing interest in the application of regional nuclear-weapon-free zones (NWFZs). In the past, Washington feared that the establishment of such zones would curtail its ability to disperse its own nuclear retaliatory forces overseas; thus, it was lukewarm toward proposals to establish an NWFZ in the Middle East, fearing that such a zone would affect its nuclear assets in the Mediterranean. The only exception to this reservation was Latin America, where the United States had no interest in stationing nuclear weapons.

Similarly, while the Clinton administration has delayed the start of negotiations on the treaty banning the future production of fissile material, it has made some efforts to obtain the objectives of the suggested treaty in one region: southwest Asia. In exchange for Pakistan's agreement to cap its production of fissile material and to accept a formal freeze of its nuclear program, in 1993 the Clinton administration offered to suspend the application of the Pressler amendment and to permit a one-time delivery of the F-16 combat aircraft purchased and paid for by Pakistan before the amendment was applied. Despite indications that by 1989 Pakistan had already capped its nuclear program, the Clinton administration's initiative failed because Pakistan rejected a formal commitment to a unilateral freeze. In turn, India refused to reciprocate by capping its own nuclear program.[10] The attempt provided a strong indication of the administration's new, more regionally oriented approach.

Nevertheless, the United States remained unequivocally committed to the indefinite extension of the NPT.[11] As the April 1995 NPT Review and Extension neared, the Clinton administration launched a major diplomatic campaign to obtain this objective and announced that it regarded indefinite extension as a top foreign policy priority. To further illustrate this, Vice President Al Gore led the U.S. delegation to the New York conference.

An additional facet of the Clinton administration's stated policy with respect to the challenges posed by nuclear weapons proliferation is its "Defense Counter-proliferation Initiative" announced on December 7, 1993, by U.S. Secretary of Defense Les Aspin.[12] The initiative emphasized that in the post–Cold War era, U.S. defense policy will accord nonproliferation a much higher priority, and that this would be reflected in its armed forces' missions, force structure, doctrine, and modes of intelligence gathering.[13]

The Aspin speech seemed to reflect two conclusions U.S. policymakers reached after the post–Gulf War revelations regarding the magnitude of Iraq's nuclear efforts: first, that it would be easier to deal with clandestine nuclear programs in their infancy, rather than at later stages of their development. Hence the United States attached increasing importance to early detection of such programs. This priority had already led the Bush administration to devote greater intelligence assets to detecting weapons proliferation and to consolidate them into a new Nonproliferation Center. Second, and in contrast to U.S. objections against Israel's 1981 bombing of Iraq's Osiraq nuclear reactor, Washington now adopted the position that the use of force might sometimes be required to combat the spread of nuclear weapons. While preemptive and preventive missions for U.S. armed forces were not mentioned in Aspin's speech, the February 1994 National Security Council memorandum on "Agreed Definitions" for its counter-proliferation policy, nor the Defense Department's May 1994 *Report on Nonproliferation and Counter-proliferation Activities and Programs*,[14] in January 1994 Pentagon officials stressed to NATO countries that the destruction of nuclear sites was one of the pillars of the new counter-proliferation policy.[15] In addition, the Pentagon's 1992 Defense Planning Guidance (DPG) noted that "the U.S. may be faced with the question of whether to take military steps to prevent the development or use of weapons of mass destruction."[16]

U.S. policy statements about North Korea's nuclear program also reveal that preventive missions were not excluded from the new counter-proliferation policy. By early 1994, U.S. officials hinted that if their diplomatic efforts to persuade North Korea to allow IAEA inspections of all its nuclear facilities failed, Washington would consider "other options" for dealing with the emerging nuclear threat. As a result, a public debate on the possible implications of a U.S. military strike against North Korea's nuclear facilities evolved, encompassing U.S., South Korean, and Japanese officials and commentators.

In addition, and despite initial indications otherwise, the Clinton administration proved as determined as President Bush to compel Iraq to comply with UN Security Council resolutions 687 and 715, particularly with respect to Saddam Hussein's nuclear program. During 1993, Iraq tested the U.S. determination to enforce the UN monitoring regime on more than one occasion. Each time, forceful U.S. responses led to Iraqi acquiescence. Under Washington's orchestration, the UN remained adamant that Iraq must comply with all the stipulations of the resolutions before the economic sanctions applied against it could be lifted.[17]

Department of Defense officials argue that the Aspin initiative provides a comprehensive response to the threat posed by the proliferation of ballistic missiles and unconventional weapons. In addition to a greater willingness to consider more assertive preventive measures, it incorporates traditional nonproliferation efforts with active and passive defense measures for U.S. forces and regional allies. Yet the efficacy and standing of the Aspin initiative are far from clear. Critics charged that Aspin's announcement was not coordinated with the State Department and the Arms Control and Disarmament Agency and that it was not cleared by the White House, thus hinting that it does not necessarily reflect administration policy. Some also argue that the initiative merely comprises a mix of repackaged traditional nonproliferation efforts, passive defense measures that became standard practice during the Cold War in the face of the threat that Warsaw Pact forces might use chemical or biological weapons, and active defense measures that were already being funded by the Defense Department's Ballistic Missile Defense Organization. Finally, the only truly novel dimension of the Aspin approach — the increased willingness to consider forceful prevention — continues to be surrounded by ambiguity. Most important, it is not clear whether the administration, Congress, and the U.S. public would be willing to assume the risks and costs associated with the use of force to arrest proliferation.[18]

By early 1994, uncertainty about U.S. determination to prevent proliferation was further increased by apparent inconsistencies in U.S. nonproliferation policies. For example, indications of an assertive approach toward the nuclear programs of Iraq and North Korea were mixed with a willingness to engage North Korea in endless negotiations. The agreement finally reached in late 1994 allowed North Korea to maintain its nuclear potential, as well as the ambiguity surrounding this potential, for a considerable length of time. Yet North Korea did commit to an immediate freeze on its nuclear efforts and to roll back the more dangerous aspects of its program eventually; Washington's willingness to use force, as implied by its counter-proliferation approach, played a key role in extracting North Korea's concessions. In addition, the unwillingness of Japan and South Korea to publicly back a preventive military attack had placed serious limitations on Washington's bargaining power, thus diminishing its capacity to extract a better deal.

In the Middle East, the test of America's counter-proliferation policy may come in Iran. If the United States were to obtain conclusive evidence that Iran was constructing an illicit uranium enrichment plant for the production of fissile material (and had accurate target information), would Washington act preventively? This question cannot be answered in the abstract; much would depend on the political circumstances when any such evidence is uncovered. More generally, the selectivity of past U.S. efforts to arrest proliferation is likely to create resistance among legislators and the public to the use of force for counter-proliferation.

Yet by early 1995 there were indications that the Clinton administration was moving toward implementing some of the more daring dimensions of its the new counter-proliferation approach. For example, the U.S. Strategic Command (STRATCOM) was reported to be revising its targeting plans to include strikes against stockpiles of weapons of mass destruction in various "rogue states" such as Iraq, Iran, Libya, and North Korea.[19]

The United States and Israel's Nuclear Potential

Throughout the past four decades, the selective nature of U.S. nuclear nonproliferation policy was reflected in its approach to Israel, the clearest case of proliferation in the Middle East, and one of the United States' closest allies.

The United States has been particularly concerned about Israel's nuclear capability for three reasons. First is the fear that Israel's nuclear potential would propel the Arab states to emulate it, thus exposing the region and the world to the risks associated with a multi-nuclear Middle East. In particular, there was concern that if Israel made its nuclear capability explicit, a number of other states within and outside the Middle East would quickly follow, resulting in serious damage to the NPT regime.

Second, the intense involvement of both superpowers in the region during the Cold War led the United States to estimate that there was a higher danger in the Middle East than elsewhere that a local nuclear confrontation might escalate to a superpower nuclear exchange. Finally, there was considerable anxiety that Israeli nuclearization could undermine U.S. relations with its other allies in the region, which might view Washington as Israel's nuclear accomplice.

Yet throughout most of the same period, there has also been a strong U.S. tendency to regard Israel's nuclear option as a special case and to exempt Israel from the letter and spirit of U.S. nuclear nonproliferation policy. In 1992, the *Defense Monitor* characterized Washington's approach to Israel's nuclear option: "U.S. officials have adopted a 'see no evil, hear no evil' attitude toward Israel's nuclear weapons activities. Israel pretends not to have nuclear weapons and the U.S. pretends to believe this."[20]

PAST RESPONSES TO ISRAELI NUCLEAR ACTIVITY

In the 1950s, the United States aided Israel's nuclear program through its Atoms for Peace program, providing it with a small 5-megawatt (thermal) "swimming pool" reactor for the Soreq Research Center.[21] The reactor was subject to U.S. and then to IAEA safeguards. Later, however, the Eisenhower, Kennedy, and Johnson administrations strongly opposed Israeli acquisition of nuclear weapons. Nevertheless, efforts by Assistant Secretary of Defense George Ball in 1968 to extract an Israeli commitment not to develop nuclear weapons, as a condition for the supply of F-4 Phantom aircraft, were called off in the face of Congressional support for the arms sale.

The Kennedy and Johnson administrations demanded that U.S.

officials be allowed to inspect the Dimona reactor. Israel yielded, and a number of such visits took place during the 1960s. These visits were terminated in 1969 by Henry Kissinger when he became President Nixon's national security advisor. In 1974, when Israel's President Ephraim Katzir stated that Israel had created a nuclear potential, U.S. Secretary of State Henry Kissinger, after repeated attempts to evade the issue, merely remarked that he would have used a different formulation.[22]

Washington has never expressed a forceful, overt reaction to Israel's nuclear potential despite mounting official assessments, leaks of these assessments, and other media revelations regarding Israel's nuclear activities. Over the years, neither the executive nor the legislative branch of the U.S. government has taken significant overt steps to halt Israel's program.[23] U.S.-Israeli relations have not been affected negatively, and U.S. economic and military assistance to Israel has not been reduced.

For example, the Johnson administration did not pursue a 1968 report issued by the Central Intelligence Agency's Department of Science and Technology stating that Israel had nuclear weapons.[24] On July 7, 1970, the Nixon administration's CIA director, Richard Helms, briefed the Senate Foreign Relations Committee regarding CIA assessment of Israel's nuclear capability.[25] As far as is known, the administration and Congress both avoided taking any measure in response to this assessment. Nor did the Ford administration take any measure in response to a CIA report dated September 4, 1974, which stated clearly its assessment that Israel had acquired nuclear weapons. The report cited Israeli purchases of large quantities of uranium, partly through covert methods, and "the peculiar nature of Israel's efforts in the field of uranium enrichment as well as large investments in the development of a weapons system capable of delivering nuclear warheads."[26] In February 1976, still during the Ford administration, the CIA allegedly provided a report regarding Israel's nuclear capability to an interdepartmental coordinating committee on nuclear affairs.[27] On March 11, 1976, a senior CIA official revealed at a private briefing that Israel was estimated to have ten to twenty nuclear weapons ready for use.[28] None of these reports seems to have elicited U.S. action against Israel.

Similarly, when the existence of these reports was made public in

1978, neither the Carter administration nor Congress took any measures against Israel. On the contrary, the leak regarding the 1974 report elicited the following response from White House Press Secretary Jody Powell: "The Israeli government has declared that Israel is not a nuclear power and will not be the first to introduce nuclear weapons into the area. We accept this as the official position of the government of Israel."[29] Later, President Carter said in a conversation with newspaper editors that the United States accepted Israeli statements about its nuclear capability and added: "I don't have any independent sources of information beyond that."[30] Yet after leaving office, Carter stated in a 1985 interview that Israel "either has nuclear weapons or the capacity of having them at very short notice."[31]

The Carter administration took a lenient approach to Israel's nuclear capability despite its record as the postwar administration most committed to nuclear nonproliferation. In fact, a senior Carter administration official — Undersecretary of State Lucy Benson — even hinted that under specific conditions the administration would tolerate Israeli *use* of nuclear weapons. This occurred during testimony to the Senate Government Affairs subcommittee aimed at persuading the committee "presidential escape clause" to the Glenn amendment, which would permit the president to refrain from implementing the amendment if U.S. national interests required the granting of such a waiver. The subcommittee chairman, Senator John Glenn, himself a strong advocate of nonproliferation, did not take exception to Benson's suggestion — thus associating himself with the view of Israel as a "special case" in U.S. nuclear nonproliferation policy.[32] It is therefore hardly surprising that in June 1977, a distinguished U.S. Senate delegation recommended that the United States should not condition the sale of U.S. nuclear power reactors to Israel on the latter's prior submission of all its nuclear facilities to full-scope safeguards.[33] Similarly, in 1979 the U.S. Senate rejected by a margin of 76 to 7 an amendment proposed by Senator Jesse Helms aimed at making the special aid package to Israel following the Israeli-Egyptian peace treaty conditional on Israel's prior signature and ratification of the NPT.[34]

This pattern continued during Ronald Reagan's presidency. In a 1981 press conference two weeks after Israel bombed the Osiraq reactor in Iraq, Reagan was asked whether Israel should sign the NPT. His answer was evasive but nevertheless indicated his sentiments:

"How many countries do we know that have signed [the NPT] that very possibly are going ahead with [the development of] nuclear weapons? It's, again, something that doesn't lend itself easily to verification. It is difficult for me to envision Israel as being a threat to its neighbors. It is a nation that from the very beginning has lived under the threat of neighbors that did not recognize its right to exist as a nation."[35]

Congress took a similar view of Israel during the Reagan years. For example, no action was taken against Israel after CIA testimony to the House Foreign Affairs Committee in 1981 that Israel "was now believed to possess ten to twenty nuclear weapons that could be delivered either by fighter-bombers or by Israel's domestically designed and built Jericho missile."[36] The administration's approach was made clear a few months later when two members of the House Foreign Affairs Committee, Stephen J. Solarz and Jonathan B. Bingham, planned to introduce an amendment requiring a cutoff of U.S. aid to any country found to be developing a nuclear weapon. They agreed to drop the provision after they were told, at a meeting with Undersecretary of State James L. Buckley, "that such a requirement might well trigger a finding by the administration that Israel has manufactured a bomb."[37] This episode indicates clearly that the Reagan administration regarded Israel as nuclear-capable but made a political decision to avoid public references to its nuclear potential.

However, when the Reagan administration learned in late 1984 of Israel's plans to purchase a nuclear power reactor from France, it moved quickly to press Paris not to make the sale. Prevented from selling such reactors to Israel by the 1978 Nuclear Non-Proliferation Act and by Israel's refusal to sign the NPT and to place all its nuclear facilities under full-scope safeguards, Washington was not about to permit French firms to gain an edge in the Israeli market by pursuing a less restrictive nuclear policy. Even in this case, however, it is far from clear that the Reagan administration's reaction was determined primarily by nonproliferation concerns. More likely, its position was also motivated by Secretary of State George Shultz, who doubted the wisdom of a large financial investment in such a project at a time when Israel's economic stabilization program compelled it to seek emergency aid from the United States.[38]

The Reagan administration also abstained from public action in mid-1985, when it learned that krytrons — high-speed electronic switches that can be used to control the timing of nuclear detonations — might have been shipped to Israel. The United States accepted Israel's explanation that the krytrons were used solely for non-nuclear research. The administration thus avoided making the affair a public issue with the Israeli government, and State Department spokesman Edward Djerejian told reporters that "the government of Israel has been cooperative in our investigation." Administration officials said that the United States had not asked to inspect the sites where the krytrons were in use. Israel did promise to return to the United States all unused krytrons and certified that the remaining krytrons would not be used in nuclear-related projects.[39]

The United States also came to Israel's aid repeatedly at IAEA meetings. For example, in 1985, Washington's response to a draft resolution sanctioning Israel in connection with the 1981 bombing of Iraq's Osiraq reactor was to threaten to terminate its membership in the agency. Washington provides the largest financial contribution to the IAEA; a more moderate resolution was adopted.[40]

By 1986, when London's *Sunday Times* issued a detailed report about Israel's alleged nuclear weapons program based on testimony and photographs by Mordechai Va'anunu (see Chapter 2), acceptance of Israel as a nuclear power was apparently widespread in Washington. The Reagan administration and Congress hardly reacted to the report. The drama of Va'anunu's subsequent abduction and delivery to trial by Israeli agents received far more U.S. media attention.

The closest the U.S. government ever came to actually endorsing Israel's nuclear capability was during the Gulf War. After ten nights of ballistic missile attacks had failed to obtain Iraq's apparent objective of involving Israel in the war by eliciting its forceful response to such attacks, there was much concern that Saddam Hussein might escalate to the use of chemical warheads. It was further feared that Saddam might be encouraged to do so by a misstatement made by White House Chief of Staff John Sununu to the effect that the United States would not respond to Iraqi unconventional attacks by employing its own unconventional arsenal. At this point, U.S. Secretary of Defense Richard Cheney was asked in a CNN interview whether he believed Israel might respond with tactical nuclear weapons to an Iraqi chemical attack. Cheney responded: "That decision the Israelis would have to make — but I would think that [Saddam Hussein] has to be cautious in terms of how he proceeds in his attacks against Israel."[41] Notably, Cheney did not comment on the premise that informed the question — that Israel had a nuclear arsenal that it could utilize for retaliation — nor did he distance the United States from this premise or from a possible Israeli employment of its nuclear capability. Thus, at least indirectly, Cheney's response constituted an endorsement of Israeli nuclear deterrence.[42]

The Clinton administration has continued the U.S. predisposition to avoid pressing Israel to sign the NPT.[43] Indeed, on only a small number of recent occasions have U.S. officials suggested that Israel should sign the treaty.[44] Two such instances were a press briefing given by U.S. Undersecretary of State Robert Gallucci in July 1993 and a statement made in Jerusalem by Assistant Secretary of Defense Frank Wisner in December 1993.[45] On the other hand, a study released in October 1993 by the Office of Technology Assessment (OTA), a research arm of the U.S. Congress, cautioned against pressing Israel "to give up its nuclear weapons," arguing that such pressure might "endanger Israel's survival." The report asked: "Would the U.S. be ready to sacrifice its relations with Israel and even to endanger Israel's survival by pressing it to forgo its nuclear arsenal which it believes is essential to its security?"[46]

More important, on January 16, 1994, in a joint press conference with Syria's President Hafez al-Asad, President Clinton was asked whether Israel's refusal to sign the NPT did not contradict the concept of peace toward which he was striving. Clinton responded that "the best way to arrest the proliferation of mass destruction weapons — which includes not only nuclear weapons but chemical and biological weapons as well — and to slow the conventional arms race in the Middle East, is the successful conclusion of the [peace] process."[47]

The U.S. tendency to exempt Israel from the thrust of U.S. nonproliferation policy seems to have stemmed from four considerations. The first and most important is an unstated belief that Israel's quest for an existential deterrent is justified. For many years, Israel was seen as a small country surrounded by numerous and more populous nations, all unwilling to accept its existence and ready to destroy it. Thus, if ever there were a justification for the few to enjoy an ultimate deterrent against the many, Israel was considered to be such a case.[48] This justification was parallel to that of the "New Look," the Eisenhower administration's nuclear doctrine: to deter the Warsaw Pact's quantitatively superior conventional forces.[49]

Second, the Holocaust may have played a particularly important emotional role in affecting the U.S. approach to Israel's nuclear potential. Indeed, regret that the U.S. government failed to help Jews escape Europe before the Second World War erupted, and to act effectively to demolish the Nazi death machine during the later stages of the war, may have led some people in key U.S. positions to conclude that given the threat to Israel's existence, it was not unreasonable for it to possess an ultimate deterrent.

A third and related consideration was that the U.S. moral commitment to Israel's security and survival would force it to intervene if a threat to Israel's existence ever developed. Thus, successive U.S. administrations and key members of Congress may have believed that Israel's existential deterrent exempts the United States from ever having to exercise such intervention. For example, in a 1992 book, McGeorge Bundy explained that he was no longer so opposed to Israeli nuclearization because Israel's governments have demonstrated "nuclear restraint," and that if the United States were to force Israel to abandon its nuclear arsenal, it would have to provide it with an alternative guarantee.[50]

This concern seems to have been foremost in the mind of Henry Kissinger, national security advisor and secretary of state under Presidents Richard Nixon and Gerald Ford. According to one observer, "Kissinger saw no harm in Israel's possession of nuclear weapons. In his view this exempted the U.S. from having to [intervene] to defend Israel."[51] Similar sentiments seem to have guided congressional attitudes regarding Israel's nuclear option as well.[52]

Finally, a combination of factors—the basic values common to the United States and Israel, the United States' perception of Israel as an advanced industrialized country, Israelis' expressed affinity for Americans and their culture, and Israel's commitment to pluralist democracy— has combined to form a tendency among the U.S. public to regard Israelis as "just like us." In the nuclear realm, this has translated to a willingness to consider Israel and Israeli governments as responsible and capable of handling a nuclear option. With time, Washington's trust in Israel's ability to handle its nuclear option responsibly became based on considerable experience. The fact that very different Israeli governments remained committed to the same nuclear policy, and that no Israeli government has used the nuclear option, gave the United States confidence that Israel would never treat its nuclear potential lightly. Today, this sympathy and trust remains the only valid explanation for Washington's tolerance of Israel's nuclear program.

This tacit understanding between the two governments seems to have evolved during the Kissinger-Nixon era and survived even the antiproliferation administration of President Jimmy Carter:[53] namely, that if Israel refrained from making its nuclear option explicit, and if it avoided contributing to further nuclear proliferation, Washington would exempt Israel from the trials and tribulations of U.S. nuclear nonproliferation policy.[54] In 1994 Prime Minister Rabin provided the first public hint that this commitment comprised a central determinant of Israel's ambiguous nuclear policy: "We are committed to the United States *for many years*, not to be the first to introduce nuclear weapons or weapons within the context of the Arab-Israeli conflict."[55]

U.S. arms control policy in the Middle East represents a grand compromise between Washington's commitment to global and regional nuclear nonproliferation and its sympathy and understanding for Israel's extenuating circumstances. In practice, this means that the United States might urge all Middle East states — including Israel — to sign the NPT and to transform the region into an NWFZ, but that it would not press Israel to adopt these measures as long as the latter is required to maintain a credible existential deterrent. Implicitly, it is understood that Israel would require an effective deterrent at least until a stable and comprehensive Arab-Israeli peace is achieved.

Indeed, according to one report, this understanding was first reached in 1969, when President Richard Nixon promised Prime Minister Golda Meir that the United States would not press Israel to sign the NPT. The report also recounted that during their first meeting in the White House in March 1993, President Clinton and Prime Minister Rabin spent ten minutes in complete privacy, and that it was then that Rabin was assured that the United States would continue to refrain from pressing the issue with Israel, at least as long as the peace process continued.[56] In mid-July, 1996, President Clinton is said to have provided a similar assurance to Israel's new prime minister, Benjamin Netanyahu. During their first White House meeting, Clinton reportedly promised that the United States would contiue to prevent international action that might harm Israel's capacity to maintain and develop its nuclear capability.[57] Thus, during the past thirty years, the United States has largely avoided pressing Israel to sign the NPT, and the Bush administration — and, to date, the Clinton administration as well — refrained from pressuring Israel to accept the U.S. proposal to ban the production of weapons-grade material.

This grand compromise was also reflected in the positions adopted by the United States at the Arms Control and Regional Security (ACRS) multi-lateral talks. Indeed, despite its prerogatives as one of the two co-sponsors of ACRS, the Bush administration did not present its May 1991 Middle East arms control initiative for discussion in these talks. Instead, it urged the parties to be ambitious in defining the ultimate objectives for arms control in the Middle East — which implied support for Egypt's preference that all Middle East states adhere to the NPT and support the establishment of an NWFZ in the region — but shared Israel's opinion that progress toward the realization of these objectives should be slow and based on the gradual growth of mutual confidence, as in the preparatory phases of the U.S.-Soviet arms reduction process. This approach was particularly apparent during the September 1992 ACRS plenary meeting in Moscow, where the United States brokered a compromise along these lines between the Egyptian and Israeli approaches that stressed the early implementation of regional confidence-building measures and requested the parties to indicate their attitude toward a long list of confidence-building measures submitted by the U.S. and Russian cosponsors.[58]

Following the Moscow meeting, the U.S. approach was explained by Dennis Ross, then the State Department's director of policy planning. In a detailed policy statement, Ross stressed that the United States regards the initial stages of the multi-lateral discussions as aimed at laying the foundations for a regional arms control process. It expected the process to move "incrementally, step by step and brick by brick," but that the slow pace should not prevent the parties from elaborating ambitious goals such as the establishment of a secure peace, the implementation of systemic transparency, the transformation of the Middle East to a region free of weapons of mass destruction, and the reduction of conventional arsenals.[59] However, Ross also emphasized that given the complexity of the problem and its connection to the progress made in the bilateral peace process, the realization of these objectives is "not around the corner." He also argued that it would not make sense to attempt to deal with the parties' central strategic systems first. Instead, it would be wise to focus on modest confidence-building measures that would not include limitations on existing force structures, measures that do not change the parties' overall situation and would not put one of the parties at a disadvantage.

The tendency to regard Israel as a "special case" in U.S. nuclear nonproliferation policy was apparent as the Clinton administration became more engaged in attempting to secure the indefinite extension of the NPT at the April 1995 Review and Extension Conference. In early December 1994, Thomas Graham, deputy director of the U.S. Arms Control and Disarmament Agency (ACDA), traveled to the Middle East to meet with officials and experts in a number of the region's states.[60] While expressing a desire that Israel produce some "statement of intent" indicating its eventual willingness to sign the treaty, Graham made it quite clear that the Clinton administration understood Israel's security concerns and did not expect it to sign the NPT — at least not before the Review Conference.[61] Another report cited Graham as having stressed that the United States was not insisting that Israel sign the NPT immediately: "We would like an indication that Israel is ready to discuss this issue at some point in the future. We certainly are sensitive to Israel's concerns now." Graham added that "the prospects for Israel joining the NPT become enhanced by the strength of the NPT regime and its durability. So the U.S. would argue that if the treaty is made permanent, the chances are better for Israel eventually joining the NPT."[62]

Ten days earlier, Assistant Secretary of State for Near East Affairs, Robert Pelletreau, used similar language. In response to a question on whether the United States had asked Israel to sign the NPT, Pelletreau said: "We would like there to be full international compliance with the treaty." Pressed on whether Washington had urged Israel in particular to sign the NPT, Pelletreau ducked again, saying, "We have urged many countries to sign it."[63]

A subsequent visit to Egypt and Israel by Secretary of Defense

William Perry yielded a similar pattern. But while confirming that he was "urging the Arab nations and Israel to sign an extension [of the NPT]," and while conveying to Israeli leaders Egypt's position with regard to the NPT's extension and stressing that "the U.S. wants a nuclear non-proliferation regime applied to the whole area," Perry reportedly "did not specifically ask Israel to join the NPT."[64] At a Tel Aviv news conference, Perry was said to have been "mostly silent when Israeli Prime Minister Itzhak Rabin dismissed the effectiveness of the treaty."[65]

A few days later, the Clinton administration reaffirmed that it was not pressing Israel to sign the NPT. The Director of the Arms Control and Disarmament Agency, John D. Holum, stated: "I wouldn't say there is heavy [U.S.] pressure on Israel.... We believe Israel should be a member [of the NPT ... but] we understand the situation in which Israel finds itself. A number of its neighbors insist on its extermination."[66] At the same time, the Clinton administration expressed publicly its displeasure regarding Egypt's efforts to hold the NPT's indefinite extension hostage to Israel's consent to join the treaty. In mid-February 1995, Secretary of State Warren Christopher said that "from the U.S. standpoint, one most undesirable development would be for groups of states to organize in order to prevent the NPT's indefinite extension — one of our most important interests."[67]

Conclusions

From the outset, U.S. nuclear nonproliferation policy has been a central pillar of the global nuclear nonproliferation regime. As the prime sponsor of the NPT, the United States invested considerable efforts in obtaining nearly universal membership in the treaty. Similarly, it became the key to negotiating a CTBT. Other efforts include unilateral nonproliferation legislation and policy — notably, the Glenn-Symington amendment to the Foreign Assistance Act and the Aspin Counter-proliferation Initiative. U.S. efforts play a key role in stemming the global spread of nuclear weapons.

At the same time, the United States recognizes that sometimes perceived threats to national survival might lead a state to regard the acquisition of a nuclear option providing existential deterrence as an absolute imperative, and that it would be exceedingly difficult to enforce nonproliferation objectives in such a case. Competing U.S. interests have also limited the extent to which nonproliferation objectives could be pursued; this was reflected in the U.S. approach to Pakistan's nuclear efforts until the Soviet Union withdrew its forces from Afghanistan.

Clearly, there are limits to the costs that the United States is willing to expend in order to attain its nonproliferation objectives; this is likely to remain the case in the future. For example, because it was reluctant to assume the expected consequences of applying preventive military action against North Korea's nuclear installations, the United States was compelled to accept the latter's nuclear option, at least temporarily.

The selective application of U.S. nuclear nonproliferation policy has been reflected in the Middle East as well. While seeking universal membership and compliance with the NPT, the United States did not move to arrest Iraq's advanced nuclear program until Iraq directly threatened U.S. national interests, by invading Kuwait. Similarly, it remains unclear whether the United States would be prepared to apply the military-preventive dimensions of its late 1993 counter-proliferation policy to Iran, even if Iran were discovered to be enriching uranium or reprocessing plutonium.

Nowhere is the selective character of U.S. nuclear nonproliferation policy reflected more clearly than in the case of Israel. The United States implicitly accepts the logic and legitimacy of Israel's need for an existential deterrent; is committed to Israel's security but is reluctant to become its sole guarantor; is identified with Israel's pluralist democracy and shares its basic values; and is convinced that Israel's democratically elected governments can be trusted to behave responsibly. Washington seems to apply to Israel the rationale it adopted for its own decision to retain a nuclear deterrent despite the end of the Cold War and the deterioration of the Soviet Union. As long as the United States adheres to its present approach, maintains close ties with Israel, and perceives it as facing some form of existential threat, Israel will remain a special case in U.S. nuclear nonproliferation efforts.

Under these circumstances, Washington will continue to refrain from pressing Israel to sign the NPT. However, Washington can be expected to urge Israel to accept interim nuclear arms control measures such as the CTBT. And, if the UN Conference on Disarmament ever completes the negotiations of a treaty banning the production of fissile material, the United States is most likely to press Israel to sign this treaty as well.

NOTES

1. This section represents the development and updating of ideas first presented in chapter 5 of Shai Feldman, *Israeli Nuclear Deterrence: A Strategy for the 1980s* (New York: Columbia University Press, 1982), pp. 192–236; and in Shai Feldman, "Superpower Nonproliferation Policy: The Case of the Middle East," in Steven L. Spiegel et al., eds., *The Soviet-American Competition in the Middle East* (Lexington, Mass: D.C. Heath, 1988), pp. 95–105.

2. David Hoffman, "Aliens Gain U.S. Atomic Arms Lore," *Philadelphia Inquirer*, May 19, 1979 (citing a report by the U.S. Congress, General Accounting Office).

3. William Bader, *The United States and the Spread of Nuclear Weapons* (New York: Pegasus, 1968), p. 18.

4. Public Law 95-242, *The Nuclear Nonproliferation Act of 1978*.

5. Public Law 95-92, *International Security Assistance Act of 1977*.

6. See R. Jeffrey Smith, "Pakistan Warned on Nuclear Parts," *Washington Post*, January 14, 1992; and Norman Kempster, "Despite Nuclear Effort In Pakistan, U.S. Kept Aid Flowing for 7 Years," *International Herald Tribune*, March 19, 1992.

7. See "Clinton Presses for Arms Sale to Pakistan," *Nuclear Proliferation News* (No. 30), August 7, 1995, p. 7. See also "The Wrong Message to Pakistan," *New York Times*, September 23, 1995; and "The Pakistan Deal," *Washington Post*, September 27, 1995.

8. "Botha confirms Reagan helped nuclear program," *Washington Times*, January 11, 1995.

9. "UN Nuclear Expert Sees No Purpose Now to Iraq Sanctions," *International Herald Tribune*, July 1, 1993.

10. See "Official Says Nuclear Program Frozen at 1989 Level," Karachi DAWN in English, February 11, 1992 (FBIS-NES-92-029, February 12, 1992, p. 59); "U.S. May Lift Pakistan Sanctions," *International Herald Tribune*, November 27–28, 1993; Islamabad PTV Television Network in English, November 26, 1993 (FBIS-NES-93-226, November 26, 1993, p. 67); "U.S. Perceptions of N-Policy," *Nation* (Pakistan, English-language newspaper) (FBIS-NES-93-230, December 2, 1993, p. 53); "General Beg Comments on Nuclear Policy," *The Pakistan Observer*, December 2, 1993 (FBIS-NES-93-230, December 2, 1993, p. 54); "Pressler's Visit and the Nuclear Program," *Nawa-I-Waqt* (Rawalpindi) December 15, 1993 (FBIS-NES-93-240,

December 16, 1993, p. 66); "Pakistan and the U.S. in Nuclear Talks," *International Herald Tribune*, March 18, 1994; "U.S. to Test Pakistan on Nuclear Plan," *International Herald Tribune*, March 23, 1994; John F. Burns, "India Rebuffs New U.S. Move To Cap Nuclear Arms Arsenal," *International Herald Tribune*, March 28, 1994; Vivek Raghuvanshi, "Pakistan Seeks Waiver on F-16 Fighter Restrictions," *Defense News*, March 28–April 3, 1994; Thomas W. Lippman, "Business in Mind, Clinton Team Put India Back on the Map," *International Herald Tribune*, April 4, 1994; "Bhutto Links India to Nuclear Halt," *International Herald Tribune*, April 8, 1994; "Minister Opposes Linking F-16 Sale, Nuclear Program," Islamabad Radio Pakistan Overseas Service in English, April 15, 1994 (FBIS-NES-94-073, p. 42); "Bhutto on Nuclear Program, Kashmir, Foreign Policy," Islamabad PTV Television Network in English, April 16, 1994 (FBIS-NES-94-074, April 18, 1994, p. 69).

11. This was well reflected in Washington's swift and sharp response to a comment by Japan's foreign minister, Kabun Muto, during the July 1993 ASEAN foreign ministers' conference. The comment was widely interpreted as an expression of doubt whether the treaty's extension should be endorsed. See Shunji Taoka, "Would Japan Build the Bomb?" *Newsweek*, June 13, 1994, p. 4.

12. Remarks by Les Aspin, Secretary of Defense, National Academy of Sciences, Committee on International Security and Arms Control, December 7, 1993.

13. For a detailed analysis of the counter-proliferation initiative, see Zachary S. Davis and Mitchell Reiss, "U.S. Counter-proliferation Doctrine: Issues for Congress," CRS Report for Congress 94-734-ENR (Washington, D.C.: Congressional Research Service, Library of Congress, September 21, 1994).

14. Davis and Reiss, "U.S. Counter-proliferation Doctrine," pp. 8–9.

15. These pillars were termed the eight "D's" of U.S. counter-proliferation policy: dissuasion, denial, disarmament and arms control, diplomatic pressure, defusing, destruction, and defense. See "The Rule of the "8 D's," *Intelligence Newsletter*, January 13, 1994, p. 7.

16. *The Defense Monitor*, Vol. 21, No. 3 (1992), p. 5.

17. An excellent example of U.S. determination took place in May–July 1993, when Iraq opposed UN attempts to place cameras in Iraqi missile test-firing installations. Consequently, a UN team attempted to seal the two sites — a move blocked by Iraq as well. See "The inspectors left Baghdad: 'We were not permitted to fulfill our mission'," *Ha'aretz* (Israel), July 12, 1993. Following a U.S. threat to conduct a punitive military strike, and extensive negotiations between Iraq and Rolf Ekeus, the chairman of the UN Special Commission (UNSCOM), agreement was reached on the modes of continued UN monitoring of Iraq. See AFP in English, July 19, 1993 (BBC, ME/1746, July 21, 1993 p. A/5).

18. Davis and Reiss, "U.S. Counter-proliferation Doctrine," pp. 6, 10. See also "The Counter-proliferation Debate," a panel discussion from the conference on "Nuclear Non-Proliferation: The Challenge of a New Era," Carnegie Endowment for International Peace, Washington, D.C.,

November 17–18, 1993.

19. Barbara Starr, "STRATCOM sees new role in WMD targeting," *Jane's Defense Weekly*, January 14, 1995. Earlier, in November 1994, a major operation successfully extracted some 600 kilograms of weapons-grade enriched uranium from Kazakhstan, following intelligence data indicating that the material was stored in a fashion that made it vulnerable to theft. The secret operation, code-named "Project Sapphire," involved flying a team of engineers and U.S. military personnel to Ulba aboard three C-5 transport aircraft, and then flying the material for safe storage at Oak Ridge, Tennessee. R. Jeffrey Smith, "U.S. Takes Nuclear Fuel," *Washington Post*, November 23, 1994; Bill Gertz, "U.S. defuses effort by Iran to get nukes," *Washington Times*, November 24, 1994.

20. *The Defense Monitor*, The Center for Defense Information, Vol. 21, No. 3 (1992), p. 3.

21. John K. Cooley, "Cairo Steers Clear of A-Race," *Christian Science Monitor*, June 9, 1969.

22. For further details see Feldman, *Israeli Nuclear Deterrence*, pp. 210–211.

23. This is the central point made in Seymour M. Hersh, *The Samson Option: Israel's Nuclear Arsenal and American Foreign Policy* (New York: Random House, 1991).

24. *Ma'ariv* (Israel), March 2, 1978.

25. Hedrick Smith, "The U.S. Assumes the Israelis have A-Bomb or Its Parts," *New York Times*, July 18, 1970.

26. *Yediot Aharonot* (Israel), January 27, 1978.

27. *Ma'ariv*, March 2, 1978.

28. Arthur Karnish, "CIA: Israel Has 10–12 A Weapons," *Washington Post*, March 15, 1976.

29. *Ma'ariv*, March 2, 1978.

30. *Ma'ariv*, April 9, 1978.

31. *Jerusalem Post* (Israel), June 2, 1985.

32. Senate Committee on Foreign Relations, *Hearings on S-1160*, April 21–22, 28, and May 2, 1977 (Washington, D.C.: U.S. Government Printing Office [U.S. GPO], 1977), pp. 234–235. The text of the exchange is reprinted in Feldman, "Superpower Nonproliferation Policy," p. 98.

33. U.S. Senate, *Senate Delegation Report on American Foreign Policy and Nonproliferation Interests in the Middle East* (Washington, D.C.: U.S. GPO, 1977).

34. *Congressional Record*, May 14, 1979, pp. S-5748, S-5751.

35. President Ronald Reagan's press conference, June 17, 1981. The full text of the exchange is reprinted in Feldman, "Superpower Nonproliferation Policy," p. 98.

36. Judith Miller, "Three Nations Widening Nuclear Contacts," *New York Times*, June 28, 1981.

37. Judith Miller, "Two in House Withdraw Atom Curb," *New York Times*, December 9, 1981.

38. *Ma'ariv*, December 13, 1984; *Ha'aretz*, December 13, 1984; *Ma'ariv*, January 31, 1985; and *Ha'aretz*, February 10, 1985.

39. Richard Halloran, "Israelis Illegally Got U.S. Devices Used in Making Nuclear Weapons," *New York Times*, May 16, 1985; *Ma'ariv*, May 17, 1985.

40. *Ha'aretz*, September 29, 1985.

41. Transcript of interview with U.S. Secretary of Defense Richard Cheney by CNN Pentagon Correspondent Wolf Blitzer on CNN Cable Network's "Evans and Novak" program, February 2, 1991.

42. Only after the imperatives of the Gulf War were no longer relevant did Cheney revert to Washington's traditional evasiveness. In June 1991 he was reported to have said: "I don't know that Israel has any nuclear capability. They have certainly never announced it." *Defense Monitor*, Vol. 21, No. 3 (1992), p. 3.

43. Aluf Ben, "The understanding with the U.S. is a central pillar of Israel's nuclear policy," *Ha'aretz*, September 29, 1993.

44. Aluf Ben, "U.S. urging Israel to join the Biological Weapons Convention," *Ha'aretz*, August 4, 1993.

45. Aluf Ben, "Christopher's assistant: Israel must join the Nuclear Nonproliferation Treaty," *Ha'aretz*, July 25, 1993. See also "U.S. Official Backs Non-Nuclear Israel," Reuters News Service, July 22, 1993; and Amir Oren, "Bamba in the Sense of Bomba," *Davar* (Israel), December 3, 1993.

46. Aluf Ben, "U.S. pressure on Israel to disarm its nuclear arsenal may endanger its survival," *Ha'aretz*, October 17, 1993.

47. See transcript of the Clinton-Asad joint press conference held following their meeting in Geneva on January 16, 1994, translated and printed in *Yediot Aharonot* (Israel), January 17, 1994, p. 5. Equally instructive was President Clinton's response at an April 1994 press conference to an Indian journalist who inquired why the United States was pressing the

nuclear issue with India while avoiding a similar approach with respect to Israel: "Well, first of all, sir, we are trying to deal with the international nuclear problems. We also believe very strongly that the fewer countries who become nuclear powers the better off we are going to be and if there is a system in which the security of nations who think they may have to develop nuclear weapons to protect themselves can have their security guaranteed in other ways — we think that [it] is our job to try to put that system out there — to put those alternatives out there so that people will see that it is not in their long-term security interests to develop such weapons. That is our position. What we are trying to do is to keep the number of people in the nuclear club as small as possible and then reduce the nuclear arsenals that they have, including their own. As you know — we have worked hard to reduce our own with the Russians. So — that is our position. But our position further is that no one should be asked to put their own security at risk to achieve that. So any dialogue that we have with India on this will be in the context of what is pivotal for India's security. How can we enhance your security — not diminish it. It would be wrong for the United States to tell your great nation or the smallest nation on the face of the earth that we recommend a course of action for them that would reduce security. But we believe that you can increase your security and avoid becoming a nuclear power. Japan did it — Germany did — a lot of other countries have done it, we can do it together." See transcript of President Bill Clinton's press conference with India's Prime Minister Rao, Washington, D.C., May 19, 1994.

48. In a hearing conducted by the House Foreign Affairs Committee on March 2, 1993, Geoffery Kemp of the Carnegie Endowment for International Peace characterized Israel as "the one [country] that can make the best case for having nuclear weapons." Kemp warned that it "would be counter-productive at this point in time for the United States Congress — or anyone else — to lean on Israel with respect to its nuclear program if, by leaning, we're talking about somehow rolling it back." See M.C. Jaspersen, "Experts Discuss Nuclear, Chemical Weapons Proliferation Policy," *The Wireless File*, U.S. Information Agency, March 8, 1993.

49. Sympathy for this view could be found even in the liberal U.S. media. For example, a 1989 *New York Times* editorial noted that despite its concern about nuclear proliferation, the United States manifested an understanding for Israel's desire to obtain missiles and nuclear weapons. It stressed that while Israel's borders now seem immune to conventional attacks, the Israelis are worried about the possibility of chemical attacks and assume that the Israeli Air Force would not be able to operate after the first missile strike. See Ran Dagoni and Yosef Harif, "New York Times: Do not sell supercomputers to Israel," *Ma'ariv*, November 16, 1989. It should also be noted that the willingness to consider Israel a "special case" in the nuclear nonproliferation realm is also supported by non-U.S. western media. For example, in reaction to the urging of Russia's then–Foreign Minister, Edward Shevardnadze, that the Middle East be transformed to a nuclear-weapon-free zone, an *Economist* editorial read: "One day, perhaps, peace will reign forever. Until then, however, Israel is unlikely to be tempted Mr. Shevardnadze's way. It keeps its nuclear weapons for the same reason NATO needs short-range missiles on European soil: as a deterrent against enemies whose potential advantage in conventional warfare is simply too great to match any other way"; *Economist*, April 8, 1989, p. 13.

50. Amir Oren, "Sweet heavy water," *Dvar Hashavua* (Friday supplement to *Davar*), November 17, 1989.

51. Ben, "Even after the Va'anunu story," *Ha'aretz*, November 29, 1991.

52. In early 1992, Lise Hartman, then legislative assistant to Representative Howard Berman, noted that Israel's possession of nuclear weapons enjoys considerable support in the U.S. Congress. Hartman, an active participant in drafting nonproliferation legislation in the U.S. House of Representatives during the late 1980s, argued that most members of the House were content that Israel's existential deterrence releases the United States from responsibility for Israel's survival. Proceedings of the First Ginosar Conference on Security and Arms Control in the Middle East, January 1992. Likewise, in a seminar held at the Massachusetts Institute of Technology in February 1993, Brad Gordon, a former deputy director of the Arms Control and Disarmament Agency and former staff director of the Senate Foreign Relations Subcommittee on the Middle East, reportedly said that it was inconceivable that the United States would press Israel to disarm its strategic assets. He added that any mention of the term "disarmament" ignores the depth of the tacit U.S. understanding of Israel's need to maintain strategic deterrence, regarding which there would be no difference between the Bush and Clinton administrations. He emphasized that the United States would not press Israel on such a politically — and, even more so, psychologically — sensitive issue. See Avner Cohen, "Hawks, Doves, and Ostriches," *Davar*, February 26, 1993.

53. See Ben, "Even after the Va'anunu story"; Ben, "The Understanding with the U.S. is a Central Foundation of Israel's Nuclear Policy"; and Aluf Ben, "Diminishing the Risks of Peace," *Ha'aretz*, February 11, 1994.

54. William Quandt, who served as Middle East advisor to President Jimmy Carter, reported that the basis of this understanding was the acceptance in 1970 by Israel's Prime Minister Golda Meir of the demands of U.S. President Richard Nixon to the effect that Israel would refrain from conducting a nuclear test or use nuclear weapons, with the tacit understanding that the latter commitment would become invalid if Israel were ever to face an immediate threat of destruction. Quandt notes that the exchange took place during a private meeting between the two leaders, without the presence of any other officials. Reportedly, Meir and Nixon later dictated summaries of the discussion; she to Ambassador Itzhak Rabin, and he to National Security Advisor Henry Kissinger. See Amir Oren, "Nuclear card," *Davar*, June 18, 1993; Ben, "Minimizing the Risks of Peace"; and Aluf Ben, "U.S. expects Israel to take measure to insure Egypt's support of nuclear treaty," *Ha'aretz*, December 7, 1994.

55. Prime Minister Rabin's response to a question by a Jordanian journalist during a press conference in Washington, D.C., July 26, 1994 (emphasis added).

56. Aluf Ben, "The Last Mountain," *Ha'aretz*, November 11, 1994.

57. Shimon Shiffer, "Clinton did not ambush [Netanyahu]," *Yediot Aharonot*, July 12, 1996.

58. Aluf Ben, "Arms control talks: Discussion of operating joint communication center in Gulf of Eilat," *Ha'aretz*, September 14, 1992; "Multi-lateral arms control committee talks in Moscow ended," *Ha'aretz*, September 18, 1992; Aluf Ben, "Summary of arms control talks: Compromise between Israel and Egypt," *Ha'aretz*, September 20, 1992; and Aluf Ben,

"Cornerstone for building trust," *Ha'aretz*, January 26, 1993.

59. Ross also suggested that the first stage of the talks would be a process of mutual education and a discussion of the possible implementation of confidence-building measures. Within this context, he recommended that a menu of CBMs applied in the U.S.-Soviet context be created and that the possible applications of these measures in the Middle East be examined. Ross also suggested that an effort be made to define and elaborate basic concepts, since the history of U.S.-Soviet arms control negotiations reveals numerous misunderstandings resulting from the absence of common definitions for such concepts.

60. "U.S. sends arms control negotiator to Middle East," Reuters, December 1, 1994.

61. Ben, "U.S. expects Israel to take measure to insure Egypt's support of nuclear treaty." In February 1995, the United States had again asked Israel to provide the Arab states with some assurances regarding its future nuclear intentions. A senior U.S. official said that Israel has been asked "to take some steps — public steps or private steps — to reassure that their longer term goals are the same as our longer term goals, including their joining the Non-proliferation Treaty." See Carol Giacomo, "Israel urged to satisfy nuclear concerns," Reuters from Washington D.C., February 2, 1995.

62. See *Mideast Mirror*, December 15, 1994, p. 4.

63. See *Mideast Mirror*, December 5, 1994, p. 15.

64. "Perry issues nuclear arms warning," *Baltimore Sun*, January 9, 1995; Arieh O'sullivan, "Perry warns Mideast to curb spread of nuclear weapons," *Washington Times*, January 9, 1995. See also *Mideast Mirror*, January 9, 1995, p. 9.

65. Doug Struck, "Israel continues to refuse to sign anti-nuclear treaty," *Baltimore Sun*, January 12, 1995.

66. Martin Sieff, "Nuclear treaty's ratification may not come easily," *Washington Times*, January 25, 1995.

67. Akiva Eldar, Aluf Ben, and Gideon Alon, "Musa: Egypt does not expect Israel to give up its nuclear program, merely to accept controls," *Ha'aretz*, February 16, 1995.

Chapter 7

Nuclear Arms Control: Arab Policies

This chapter and the next one elaborate the approaches adopted by the Arab states and by Israel to the prospects of nuclear arms control in the Middle East. This chapter outlines Arab approaches to nuclear arms control within the context of the Arms Control and Regional Security (ACRS) talks and the elements of the global arms control regime. Among the Arab countries, particular emphasis is given to Egypt's approach to the nuclear issue, because of Egypt's centrality in the Arab world as the largest and most populous of the Arab states, and also because for many years Egypt has been the spearhead of Arab diplomatic activity in the arms control realm. Chapter 8 portrays Israel's views.

Clearly, there is no single Arab approach to arms control. Many Arabs express general apprehension about the subject matter, believing that arms control proposals are usually largely initiated by the United States and are primarily designed to guarantee Israel's qualitative edge and ensure the permanence of Arab weakness. For example, an Egyptian commentary claimed that President Bush's May 1991 Middle East arms control initiative exposes "America's desire to weaken the Arabs relative to Israel and to solidify Israel's superiority over all the Arab states, since the initiative ignores the nuclear, chemical, biological and micro-biological weapons that Israel possesses."[1]

Conversely, however, other Arab commentaries suggest that arms control can redress these perceived Israeli advantages. While a vast majority of Arab policy elites would like Israel to eliminate its perceived nuclear capability, they differ on a number of issues: how urgent the objective is; what priority should be attached to it relative to other national interests of the Arab states; the merits of alternative strategies for obtaining this objective; and the likelihood that Israel could be persuaded to meet Arab sensibilities on this issue.

The ACRS Talks

Judgments on nuclear arms control issues vary among the Arab states. Generally, Syria is probably the most skeptical about the desirability of arms control in the Middle East. President Hafez al-Asad reportedly rejected the 1991 Bush initiative, arguing that the initiative would merely institutionalize Israel's perceived advantage.[2] Similarly, a Syrian commentary predicted that "in light of the regional balance of power which tilts in Israel's favor, Israel will insist on disarming Syria."[3] On another occasion the 1993 Chemical Weapons Convention (CWC) was described as an effort "to enforce unilateral disarmament in the Middle East by disarming the Arabs and depriving them of any deterrent means for self-defense."[4] Among the Arab states, Egypt seems to attach the highest priority to obtaining Israeli concessions in the nuclear realm. For example, Foreign Minister 'Amru Musa reportedly told the *New York Post* that the 1991 Bush initiative "was not realistic because it ignored the nuclear weapons possessed by Israel."[5]

From 1992 to 1994, Egypt's emphasis on the nuclear issue was reflected most clearly in the positions pronounced by its representatives to the ACRS talks. These representatives repeatedly called for an early consensus regarding the goals of a Middle East arms control process, and pressed Israel, directly and indirectly, to commit itself to eventual denuclearization.[6] Egyptian spokesmen — including Foreign Minister Musa in a March 1993 interview — urged Israel to adopt a long list of declaratory, political, and legally binding measures that would express a willingness to transform the Middle East into a nuclear-weapon-free zone (NWFZ) and to sign the NPT.[7]

Explaining their approach in formal and informal settings, Egyptian officials and scholars stressed that the ACRS process should deal first with nuclear arms, because these are the most destructive and most destabilizing weapons. They also emphasized that Egypt cannot voice its opposition effectively against the nuclear ambitions of Iran and Iraq as long as Israel's nuclear program is ignored.[8] Hence, they argued that Egypt is simply not able to tolerate Israeli possession of nuclear weapons indefinitely. Thus in late 1993 Foreign Minister

Musa explained that "Egypt's stand on the elimination of nuclear weapons in the Middle East is based on the premise that no exceptions or preferential treatment be given to any country in the region." He stressed that "if there are any exceptions or preferential treatment as far as nuclear weapons are concerned this will create 'a major problem' in the Middle East."[9]

It is not clear that Egypt's approach to the ACRS talks represents a wide Arab consensus. Jordan — a very active participant in ACRS — shares the objective of achieving Israeli nuclear disarmament but does not approach the issue with the same sense of priority and urgency as Egypt. Jordan, like Israel, seems to believe in the step-by-step approach. Jordanian representatives to the talks seemed more willing to consider this matter in the context of the wider Middle East arms control agenda. Hence, they were reluctant to make the nuclear issue the prime focus of ACRS, or to judge the talks' progress solely by the yardstick of the gains made toward nuclear disarmament.

This more comprehensive Jordanian approach was also reflected in the joint agenda for negotiating the resolution of the Israeli-Jordanian dispute, signed in Washington in September 1993. The agenda includes the two parties' "mutual commitment, as a matter of priority and as soon as possible, to work towards a Middle East free from weapons of mass destruction — conventional and unconventional weapons." It also states that "this goal is to be achieved in the context of a comprehensive, lasting and stable peace characterized by the renunciation of the use of force, reconciliation and openness." This formulation represents both Jordan's understanding of Israeli concerns and its own belief that from a regional perspective, conventional weapons should be viewed as weapons of mass destruction. Indeed, in contrast to Egyptian negotiators who argue that the task of nuclear disarmament is too important and urgent to await the transformation of political relations in the region, Jordan's representatives expressed the belief that disarmament cannot take place outside an environment of political reconciliation. For example, in a late 1992 television interview, the head of Jordan's delegation to the ACRS talks, Abdullah Toukan, said that plans for nuclear arms reductions are not merely a technical issue and that "arms control is actually a political dialogue between adversaries who moved from military and political confrontation to an atmosphere of cooperation that did not exist in the past.... [Therefore,] arms control cannot be placed before the political process — this is a fundamental issue."[10]

During 1992–94, Syria's President Hafez al-Asad also linked disarmament efforts and the attempts to resolve the political-territorial dimensions of the Arab-Israeli dispute. In a March 1992 speech, Asad said that "Syria favors disarmament in the region on condition that peace which will allow the return of the conquered territories would first be obtained."[11]

For Syria, the perceived linkage between peacemaking and arms control resulted in a decision to boycott the ACRS talks altogether. In early 1996 Syria remained resistant to joining any of the Middle East multi-lateral working groups, insisting that greater progress in Israeli-Syrian bilateral talks must first be achieved.[12] The Syrian position seems to be that arms control cannot be implemented as long as the use of force is possible, and that such use cannot be ruled out until the Arab-Israeli conflict is resolved. In Asad's view, any discussion of disarmament prior to a resolution of the Arab-Israeli conflict would be premature, out of context, and hence pointless. Thus, while Jordan and Syria disagree on tactics — Jordan has taken an active part in the ACRS talks while Syria opted not to join — the two countries implicitly share with Israel the view that the resolution of the conflict must precede arms reductions.

At least initially, some of Egypt's negotiators were also sensitive to the linkage between the progress made in the various Arab-Israeli bilateral peacemaking efforts and the regional arms control process. For example, in 1992 Nabil Fahmy, the Head of Egypt's delegation to the ACRS talks, acknowledged that "while [the ACRS process] may commence and achieve some progress, it cannot be expected to flourish to its full potential if the bilateral negotiations remain stagnant or lacking in direction. Progress in the bilateral negotiations is imperative for the multilateral process to succeed."[13] During the early stages of the ACRS talks, Foreign Minister Musa also seemed to indicate that the arms race could only be arrested if there was progress toward peace. He noted that under such conditions "Israel's excuse for increasing its amount of weapons under the pretext of security would be refuted."[14] Similarly, Egypt's Ambassador to the United Kingdom Muhammad Shaker said that "the concept of nuclear weapons as weapons of last resort would lose its validity once Israel reached peace agreements. In this case, there would no longer be reason for Israel to retain its nuclear capability. The first step on the road to reaching such agreements would be a resolution of the Palestinian problem."[15]

At first, Egypt also seemed to accept the U.S. definition of Middle East arms control as "a determined step-by-step process which sets ambitious goals and proceeds towards them in a realistic way."[16] Fahmy has emphasized that it is necessary to "set ambitious goals, and then chart our path realistically and gradually."[17]

The representatives of Egypt and Jordan to the ACRS talks seem to differ in their assessment of the likelihood that Israel might consider nuclear disarmament without prior resolution of the Arab-Israeli dispute. They also attach different priorities to nuclear disarmament relative to other objectives, a disagreement that reflects the very different strategic circumstances of the two countries. Thus, while Egypt views itself as the strongest country in the Arab world, enjoying a clear national identity forged over millennia of rich history, Jordan is keenly aware of its vulnerability as a weak country pressed between three powerful neighbors — Syria, Iraq, and Israel — and that its large territory and small heterogeneous population must be defended by relatively small armed forces. More than once, Jordan has found itself the victim of wars it did not initiate or even participate in, such as the Gulf War. For the Hashemite Kingdom, the task of Arab-Israeli peacemaking, including more modest efforts to build mutual confidence and minimize the likelihood of inadvertent war, is clearly of higher priority. In this wider context, Israeli nuclear disarmament is important but less urgent.

To further complicate matters, it is far from certain that the urgency attached to the nuclear issue by Egypt's negotiators at the ACRS talks during 1992–94 reflects the priority given to this issue in the context of Egypt's overall foreign and defense policy. While President Mubarak remained committed to the objective of transforming the Middle East to a region free of weapons of mass destruction and there was little doubt that he approved the objectives pursued by his representatives to the ACRS talks, there were indications that Mubarak's principal national security and foreign policy advisor, Osama al-Baz, would have been content with achieving more modest operational objectives in the realm of nuclear arms control. Publicly, al-Baz adhered to Egypt's insistence that Israel's perceived nuclear monopoly could not be tolerated and must be addressed by the arms control process. For example, he noted that "the ban on the weapons of mass destruction should extend to all chemical, biological, and nuclear weapons and should be binding on all sides, Israel included." He argued that it is "inconceivable that Egypt or anyone else would accept any arrangement that granted Israel a special privilege of possessing nuclear weapons it could use to confront the Arab side."[18] Al-Baz further suggested that "certain arrangements banning the possession of mass destruction weapons and later even conventional force reductions" might result in peace and security agreements, and that once Arabs become accustomed to contacts with Israel and to the functioning of border security arrangements, such arrangements could be applied beyond these border areas.[19]

Yet, on more than one informal occasion, al-Baz has expressed understanding that Israel cannot be expected to alter its nuclear policy in the absence of Arab-Israeli peace and at a time when it is called upon to make difficult decisions and painful concessions in the various bilateral negotiations. At the same time, al-Baz stressed that even in these taxing circumstances Israel should agree to engage Egypt in a discussion of the issues involved in its nuclear posture.

There are two possible interpretations of the apparent discrepancy in Egyptian policy. The first is that differences among Egyptian officials about the urgency of nuclear disarmament reflect their different professional backgrounds and the positions they hold. The foreign ministry, which is entrusted with the task of leading the multi-lateral negotiations, is bound to perceive an institutional imperative to achieve Egypt's goals in the ACRS talks as rapidly as possible. Since Egypt's bilateral dispute with Israel was resolved by the 1979 Egypt-Israel peace agreement, Egypt found itself in the early 1990s without a direct role in the Madrid bilateral process. This gave the foreign ministry all the more incentive to be very active in the multi-lateral tracks. The professional and institutional backgrounds of the Egyptian officials involved in these talks may have also played a role in determining their tone, if not their approach to the process. The foreign ministry team headed by 'Amru Musa and his senior advisor, Nabil Fahmy, reflected their previous service at the UN, and particularly their experience with the deliberations of the UN General

Assembly's First Committee, Musa as Egypt's Ambassador to the UN and Fahmy as his principal associate. Conversely, the president and his advisors may have been more sensitive to Egypt's overall national interests and to the relative importance of the nuclear issue within this wider framework; this might have led the president's office to emphasize the importance of advancing the bilateral dimensions of Arab-Israeli peacemaking.

It is also possible that the different priorities expressed by al-Baz and Fahmy merely reflected a division of labor, with the Foreign Ministry making every effort to push the arms control agenda forward, while the presidency, informally, attempted to minimize Israel's anxieties regarding this very sensitive issue at a delicate stage of Arab-Israeli peacemaking. These explanations are not mutually exclusive, and both dynamics may have played a role.

While some members of Egypt's policy elite have argued that Egypt should withdraw its NPT signature unless Israel also signs the treaty, other members question the wisdom of pressing Israel to sign the NPT immediately. Specifically, they doubt that Israeli signature can be expected prior to the establishment and stabilization of Arab-Israeli peace and in the absence of the Arab states' willingness to cut their large conventional forces, a step that Egypt opposes, partly because this would entail the release of thousands of officers and soldiers to a troubled civilian economy that is already unable to keep up with Egypt's rapid population growth. Given the strengthening of radical Islamists in recent years, a restructuring of Egypt's armed forces that created thousands of discontented unemployed soldiers with extensive military experience might present additional challenges to the country's stability.

Yet it is not Egypt alone that demands Israel's nuclear disarmament. Referring to the Chemical Weapons Convention, Syria's Minister of Foreign Affairs, Faruq al-Shar', stated in a 1989 interview with *Le Monde* that "scrapping one category of weapons of mass destruction while leaving the other unscrapped is tantamount to unilateral disarmament."[20] He expressed the same view in February 1992, insisting that "in the framework of any arms control initiative, Israel must first eliminate its nuclear weapons."[21] Similarly, President Asad said that "arms control in the region means first of all the closing of all Israeli factories manufacturing nuclear weapons, missiles and tanks."[22] Asad also told *Time* magazine that Syria was "willing to help obtain a breakthrough with regard to weapons in the region, provided that a balance be achieved. We demand the elimination of the mass destruction weapons that we and Israel possess. To achieve greater security, they should destroy their weapons and we shall destroy ours."[23]

By late 1994, the rapid approach of the April 1995 NPT Review Conference had crystallized the debate over the prospects for nuclear arms control in the Middle East. First, Egypt increased its efforts to press Israel to sign the NPT by intensifying its diplomatic activity and escalating its rhetoric. Second, President Mubarak and his political advisor al-Baz began to assume a much more visible role in Egypt's NPT-oriented public diplomacy efforts. Finally, Cairo forcefully urged other Arab states to close ranks with Egypt. Thus, at least temporarily, some distinctions among the positions adopted on this issue within Egypt and among various Arab states were becoming less clear. Therefore, Egypt's evolving position about the urgency of nuclear arms control in the Middle East reveals the different manner in which Israel and Arab states react to the salient elements of the global nuclear arms control agenda. By the mid-1990s, Egypt's position increasingly became the key to the Arabs' approach to nuclear arms control in the Middle East.

The Nuclear Non-Proliferation Treaty

Since the NPT's inception, Egypt's declaratory arms control policy has called upon all Middle East states to sign the treaty.[24] Generally, Egypt's demands in this realm have expressed a wide Arab consensus. For example, in September 1992 the Head of Jordan's delegation to the ACRS plenary meeting in Moscow, Abdullah Toukan, was cited to the effect that Jordan would insist that Israel sign the NPT and open its nuclear facilities to international inspections.[25] Shaykh Hamed Ben Jabir al-Thani, foreign minister of Qatar, expressed a similar demand when opening the ACRS May 1994 plenary meeting at Doha.[26]

In 1979, during negotiations on the Egypt-Israel peace agreement in Washington, Egypt's minister of state, Boutros Boutros Ghali, proposed that Israel commit itself to signing the NPT. Israeli negotiators rejected the suggestion, and the matter was dropped. Having made the strategic decision not to develop a military nuclear option and instead to base Egypt's well-being on economic development and close ties with the United States, President Sadat decided in 1979–80 to ratify Egypt's signature of the NPT.

Throughout the 1980s, Egypt rarely approached Israel directly regarding the nuclear issue, but continued to voice the demand that Israel sign the NPT in various public forums. For example, in his speech to the UN General Assembly in June 1988 (Appendix 3), Egypt's foreign minister called upon Israel "to accede to the non-proliferation treaty and to place all its nuclear facilities under the system of inspection and verification of the International Atomic Energy Agency."[27] Elsewhere, Egypt clarified the purpose of these inspections by suggesting that once Israel signs the NPT, "further measures will also be necessary to ascertain that no secret, unde-clared nuclear stockpile remained in Israel's possession."[28]

In November 1990, Egypt argued that Israel's acceptance of the NPT must precede other measures for arresting the spread of nuclear weapons in the Middle East.[29] Moreover, it stressed that while the resolution of the political disputes would facilitate efforts to address the dangers of a nuclear arms race in the region, "the world commu-nity cannot afford to await the successful conclusion of either before addressing the other.... Simply put, the situation in the Middle East does not provide for the luxury of time. The ominous implications posed by the introduction of the nuclear dimension into the turmoil of the region must be addressed promptly."[30]

In the context of its demand that Israel sign the NPT and that a nuclear-weapon-free zone be established in the Middle East (see below), Egypt also emphasized the importance of nuclear transpar-ency. It emphasized that "suggestions regarding the transparency of nuclear programs, past, present and future through declarations made by states of the region, as well as extra-regional states which have participated in the development of such programs, would be useful in developing the necessary confidence in the present status and peaceful nature of such programs. Full disclosure and accountability of the nuclear programs in the region is of fundamental importance."[31]

As noted earlier, Egypt's demand that Israel sign the NPT was also made clear in the framework of the ACRS talks. For example, the head of its delegation to the talks, Nabil Fahmy, called upon the region's states to "declare their commitment to adhere to the treaty on the non-proliferation of nuclear weapons" and "to accept the international atomic energy safeguards regime whereby all their nuclear facilities become subject to international inspections." In this context, Fahmy added that "the arms-producing states and the parties to the treaty on the non-proliferation of nuclear weapons should step up their efforts to ensure that all Middle East nations which have not yet done so adhere to the treaty in recognition of the fact that this is a step of the utmost importance and urgency."[32]

Fahmy's paper describes the suggested statements of commitment to sign the NPT as "declaratory political confidence-building measures" but argues that they alone would not suffice and that they ought to be complemented by "concrete legally binding disarmament commitments":

A. States in the region, that have not already done so, should immediately and unilaterally submit all their nuclear facilities to International Atomic Energy Agency safeguards system, and conclude a fullscope safeguards agreement with the agency.

B. States in the region that have not yet joined the NPT should urgently become a party and conclude the relevant safeguards agreement.[33]

Fahmy did not say what should happen politically to warrant progress from the declaratory phase to actual implementation. On the contrary, the proposal requires states to sign the NPT "immediately," implying that there should be no break between the "declaratory" measures and the implementation of "legally binding" commitments, and that Egypt's position did not require that a transformation of political relations in the region take place before Israel could be expected to sign and ratify the NPT. Parallel to its efforts to obtain Israel's signature of the NPT in the framework of the ACRS talks, Egypt also attempted to organize a united Arab effort to press Israel to sign the NPT by threatening not to sign the Chemical Weapons Convention (CWC) if Israel did not sign the NPT. This position was presented at the 1989 Paris Convention on Chemical Weapons and did not change despite Egypt's active role in subsequent CWC treaty negotiations at the Conference on Disarmament (CD) in Geneva.[34]

When these negotiations were successfully concluded in 1992, Egypt orchestrated a decision by the Arab League that all its members would boycott the CWC until Israel joined the NPT or at least committed itself to signing.[35] In presenting Egypt's position to the UN General Assembly, Foreign Minister 'Amru Musa said: "From a regional standpoint, we do not think that the [CWC] should be considered separately from other efforts relating to mass destruction weapons, notably the NPT."[36] Egypt's position was supported by Syria, whose representative to the CD, Ahmed Fathi al-Sabri, said on September 3, 1992: "While we concurred regarding the importance of the agreement.... we believe that its objectives cannot be obtained if it is not tied to a similar ban on nuclear weapons and [other] weapons of mass destruction."

Cairo adhered to its position despite clear signs of Washington's displeasure with its approach. Indeed, given the priority attributed by President Bush to completing the CWC treaty negotiations and to having the treaty signed before he left office, it was not unexpected when Assistant Secretary of State Robert Gallucci was dispatched to Cairo in an attempt to "soften" Egypt's position. Yet Egypt refused to yield on this issue, despite its clear interest in continued close ties with the United States.[37] This illustrated the intensity with which Egypt had pursued its objectives with respect to the NPT.

However, most Arab states did not share the priority attached by Egypt to the NPT, and most members of the Arab League have abandoned the boycott. A number of the Maghreb states became original signatories of the CWC in January 1993, and by mid-1993 the treaty had been signed by Saudi Arabia, Algeria, Morocco, Tunisia, Mauritania, Qatar, Kuwait, the United Arab Emirates, Oman, and Yemen. Iran also joined the CWC; since it suffered a number of Iraqi chemical attacks during the later stages of the Iran-Iraq war, Iran publicly welcomed the conclusion of the treaty.[38]

In March 1993, Egypt added an environmental dimension to its NPT campaign by asking the IAEA to investigate reports that Israel was dumping nuclear waste in the Negev desert, "near the Egyptian border." An Egyptian official reportedly said that his government "had received confirmed reports that the Israeli government is dumping nuclear wastes near the Dimona reactor, thus posing a threat to human, plant, and animal life. Egypt asked the IAEA to strictly monitor Israel's dumping of nuclear wastes."[39] Later, an Egyptian

Foreign Ministry source said that "reports about the leakage [of nuclear waste] prove the wisdom and soundness of Egypt's constant demand that Israel join the Nuclear Non-Proliferation Treaty and subject all its nuclear facilities and programs to the International Atomic Energy Agency's comprehensive safeguards system, not only to ensure their peaceful use, but also to make sure they meet the international standards for nuclear safety and do not threaten people with radiation."[40]

Egypt also raised its environmental concerns at a meeting of the working group on environmental affairs. Egypt's representatives asked that the issue of nuclear waste be placed on the agenda as an urgent matter. Later, during the December 1993 Tokyo meeting of the multi-lateral negotiations Steering Committee, Egypt insisted that the report of the multi-lateral working group on environmental affairs be altered to reflect Egypt's emphasis on the need to discuss the issue of nuclear waste. The delegation also hinted that it would not allow a discussion of other issues if the subject of nuclear waste was excluded from the working group's agenda. While this position was rejected in Tokyo, the episode illustrates the intensity with which Egypt has pursued its NPT-related objectives.

The approach of the 1995 NPT Review and Extension Conference presented Egypt with a difficult dilemma — whether to support the indefinite extension of the NPT despite Israel's continued refusal to sign the treaty. Given the linkage that Egypt had earlier established between Arab states' signature of the CWC and Israel's NPT membership, it would have been surprising had Egypt not attempted to link its support for the NPT's indefinite extension to Israel's signature of the treaty. Yet Cairo was clearly free to decide how intently it would pursue its NPT-related objectives before and during the 1995 Conference.

By late 1994, in reaction to the initial U.S. efforts to obtain universal support for extending the NPT indefinitely, and with the April 1995 conference fast approaching, Egypt's position on this issue evolved dramatically. As expected, it refrained from supporting indefinite extension as long as Israel did not sign the treaty. Indeed, Egypt initially went so far as to warn that if a majority of the NPT signatories voted to extend the treaty indefinitely, Egypt might withdraw its signature.

Egypt also decided to confront Israel directly. In almost every meeting with Israeli leaders in late 1994 and early 1995, Foreign Minister Musa reiterated Egypt's demand that Israel sign the NPT. More important, for the first time President Mubarak became personally identified with these efforts, stressing his unwillingness "to sign the treaty" as long as Israel did not join the NPT. In a late December 1994 interview with the Israeli daily *Ha'aretz*, Mubarak said: "We understand your concerns and we cannot compel you to sign the treaty. But if you will not sign, Egypt will also refrain from signing. Egypt's government will not be able to face public opinion that is aware that Israel did not sign a treaty that we will sign. The fact that you do not sign and that the U.S. accepts this raises suspicions. What does it mean — that the U.S. wishes that Israel would control the entire area?"[41]

Mubarak's involvement was also reflected in the sharper words used by his political advisor Osama al-Baz. In a December 1994 speech at Cairo University, al-Baz said that "it is inconceivable for Egypt and the Arab states to sign treaties for the nonproliferation of weapons of mass destruction when Israel continues to refuse to sign the NPT, subject its nuclear installations to international inspection and get rid of its nuclear stockpile."[42]

Egypt also launched a major effort to win wide Arab support for its position. For example, during their December 1994 meeting in Alexandria, President Mubarak and Syria's President Asad pressed King Fahd of Saudi Arabia to join Egypt in refusing to support the indefinite extension of the NPT if Israel would not sign the treaty. Sensitive to Washington's priorities, Fahd resisted the adoption of language stipulating such a linkage in the meeting's summary statement. Instead, the statement merely urged the transformation of the Middle East to a nuclear-weapon-free zone.[43]

Earlier, however, Syria had adopted a position identical to Egypt's regarding the NPT's extension. At an Arab League meeting in mid-September 1994, Foreign Minister al-Shar' attempted to persuade the League's twenty-one other members to pledge that they would not renew their NPT signature unless Israel also signed the treaty. But al-Shar''s efforts failed and the meeting adopted a more benign statement stating that the League would "put pressure on Israel to make it adhere to the nuclear non-proliferation treaty and to open its installations to inspection by the International Atomic Energy Agency (IAEA)."[44] In February 1995 al-Shar' again identified Syria with Egypt's efforts, stating that if Israel refused to sign the NPT, "this means [that] it will open up the region to a race for nuclear armament."[45]

Egypt further intensified its efforts, for the first time including the resolution of the nuclear issue in its definition of "comprehensive peace." During an August 1994 visit to Jerusalem and on subsequent occasions, Foreign Minister Musa argued that peace in the Middle East could not be considered "comprehensive" as long as Israel refused to place its nuclear installations under international safeguards.[46] In a late December 1994 interview, Musa further stressed that Israel's signature of the NPT is "a precondition to peace" and constitutes one of the three steps Israel must take "to achieve peace." He argued that "the question of weapons of mass destruction must be dealt with immediately and linked to the peace process and the general view of the future of the region."[47]

Such statements represented a serious escalation in the means employed by Egypt in conducting its NPT campaign: since Egyptian spokesmen have often made the full normalization of relations with Israel conditional on the establishment of a comprehensive peace, normalization now became hostage to a complete rollback of Israel's nuclear potential. In mid-December 1994, this linkage was also made explicit by Musa's senior advisor, Nabil Fahmy, who said that Egypt would seek Israel's agreement to place its nuclear weapons under international safeguards before engaging in economic cooperation with Israel.[48] Another report in the Arab press cited an Egyptian foreign ministry decision that Egypt would not implement the decisions of the October 1994 Casablanca Middle East Economic Conference "unless progress was made in controlling Israel's nuclear weapons."[49]

In January 1995 Musa further sharpened Egypt's rhetoric. In a speech to the Shura Council, he argued that "peace in the Middle East [is] under threat because Israel continues to accumulate weapons of mass destruction.... Israel possesses a nuclear arsenal the extent of which no one knows. The world must be told what is going on in this field so that it realizes the extent of the danger threatening the Middle East from weapons of mass destruction."[50] Musa continued this stream of militant statements in February, declaring that "Egypt would never accept a situation in which Israel is not an NPT signatory."[51]

This escalation of rhetoric was echoed by other senior Egyptian officials, including Defense Minister Muhammad al-Tantawi, who argued that "Israel's insistence on possessing a nuclear deterrent, in spite of our commitment to peace, does unacceptable strategic harm. The lack of balance would lead to irrational policies."[52] Al-Baz followed, warning that Israel's position might lead the Arab states to develop a countervailing nuclear capability: "If countries in the region think the possession [by] Israel of these weapons of mass destruction, especially nuclear, is a reality, then this might prompt them to follow suit.... For each action there is a reaction and ... we get into the syndrome of escalation and vicious circles."[53]

Egypt escalated its campaign to press Israel to sign and ratify the NPT despite Cairo's sensitivity to the importance of continued U.S. economic and military assistance and its awareness of the significance Washington attached to the treaty's indefinite extension. Mubarak signaled a willingness to confront Washington on this issue, despite the growing risks involved.

At the same time, there were some indications that Egypt was concerned that its NPT-focused campaign should not lead to a complete breakdown in Egyptian-Israeli relations. In a December 1994 meeting with Shimon Peres, 'Amru Musa reportedly said that while Egypt and Israel have some differences about the NPT, "they hope to deal with it in a quiet manner."[54] And, in a meeting in January 1995, Musa emphasized that "Egypt does not seek to push Israel to the corner" with respect to the NPT and does not raise the issue as Israel's enemy, but rather because "it is a problem concerning the regional order in the Middle East." He reportedly said that Egypt does not demand that Israel sign the NPT immediately, but rather that it "would take practical steps that would advance this matter." He also suggested that "Israel open a dialogue with Egypt on this issue" and proposed a number of "confidence building measures that could be adopted in this realm."[55] Meanwhile, al-Baz and other Egyptian officials continued to insist that their government did not want to spark a political crisis with Israel over the nuclear issue. They stressed that "Egypt wants to hear from Israel, at least in private, how and when Israel plans to open up its suspected nuclear program."[56]

Following increased U.S. efforts to gain Egypt's support for the indefinite extension of the NPT, and to lower tensions with Israel over this issue, Egyptian leaders and officials gave further indications that they were willing to consider a less dogmatic approach. President Mubarak was interpreted as "softening" Egypt's position when he noted that while Cairo remained adamant on linking its signature on an indefinitely extended treaty to that of Israel, "at least we should get Israel's promise to sign."[57] This opening for compromise was elaborated by Egypt's Ambassador to the UN, Nabil al-Arabi: "[Israel should] start working with us, give us a solid commitment that it would enter into the NPT. We are not telling the Israelis to forget about security because this would be nonsense. We are saying [that Israel] should take certain steps that would indicate that it is moving in that direction."[58]

In February 1995, Foreign Minister Musa repeated that "Egypt does not expect Israel to cancel or eliminate its nuclear program 'which it has developed with great talent.' Rather, Egypt expects Israel to become part of an international nuclear arms control regime."[59]

Four considerations seemed to have led Egypt to escalate its campaign to obtain Israel's signature and ratification of the NPT in late 1994. First, the April 1995 NPT Review and Extension Conference may have seemed to Egypt as the last opportunity to exert regional and international pressure on Israel to commit itself to rolling back its nuclear capabilities. President Mubarak may have believed that if the treaty were extended indefinitely without resolving the issue of Israel's nuclear potential, the international community would soon lose interest in the issue and the Arab states would be compelled to accept Israel's nuclear monopoly in the region indefinitely.

Second, by late 1994 it seemed that the Arab-Israeli peace process was progressing much more rapidly than had previously been expected. The September 1993 Israel-PLO Oslo Agreement and the October 1994 Israel-Jordan Peace Agreement were followed by increasing indications that a number of Gulf and Maghreb countries were willing to set the Arab-Israeli conflict aside. For the first time, Israeli-Syrian negotiations involved very high officials — the Chiefs of Staff of the Syrian and Israeli armed forces, General Hikmat Shihabi and General Ehud Barak. Another sign that Israel's efforts to gain acceptance in the region were succeeding was the November 1994 Middle East Economic Conference in Casablanca. Thus, Cairo faced what it viewed as the alarming prospect that Arab-Israeli peace would be resolved while leaving Israel's nuclear option intact. Not surprisingly, in early 1995 Egypt urged some Arab states to refrain from "rushing into peace."

Third, Egypt's campaign may have been an attempt to enhance its leadership role in the Arab world. By late 1994, attention in the Middle East peace process focused on the bilateral negotiations — primarily the Israeli-Syrian negotiations and Israeli-Palestinian efforts to implement the Oslo agreement; Cairo was no longer at the center of Middle East peace negotiations. At the same time, Egypt was also denied an important role in Gulf security affairs. The smaller Gulf Cooperation Council states humiliated Cairo when they did not adopt the post–Gulf War Damascus Declaration that proposed major roles for Egypt and Syria in ensuring Gulf security. In addition, Cairo was embarrassed by its inability to put an end to the recurrent acts of domestic terrorism by Muslim fundamentalist groups, which were devastating Egypt's tourism industry, further damaging its already ailing economy.

Leading the charge on the nuclear issue may have been an attempt to restore Egypt's leadership in the Arab world by making it appear as the guardian of the Arab states' security interests. Egypt's tough position also made Cairo a central address for appeals for indefinite extension of the NPT. Thus, Egypt's militant position may have been intended to compensate for its domestic troubles and diminished standing in regional affairs.[60] This became increasingly apparent as the NPT campaign evolved; Egypt's position evoked strong nationalist sentiments, increasing domestic support for the Mubarak government. Indeed, the advantages entailed in assuming such a role probably seemed to outweigh the potential risks to U.S.-Egypt relations.

Yet Egypt's grand-strategic motivations — its fourth consideration — may have been more important in inducing it to adopt a militant position with respect to the NPT. Two statements made by Egyptian leaders are particularly revealing. The first was directed by President Mubarak to Israelis and the U.S. public: "The fact that you do not sign and that the U.S. accepts this raises suspicions. What does it mean — that the U.S. wishes that Israel would control the entire area?"[61] The second was made by Foreign Minister Musa, explaining that for Egypt the core of the dispute regarding Israel's signature of the NPT is the future "regional order in the Middle East."[62] These statements indicate that Egypt was preparing itself for a post-peace Middle East, and that its primary concerns may have shifted to the future distribution of power and influence in the new regional environment. This may have been the prime motivation driving Egypt's policy regarding the NPT.

During the weeks immediately before the April Conference, Egypt's militancy began to collapse. By the end of the conference, Egypt and all other Arab parties to the treaty accepted the view of the majority of signatories supporting the indefinite extension of the NPT. In exchange, the United States agreed that the conference would adopt a "Resolution on the Middle East" that would not mention Israel by name but would urge non-parties to sign the NPT and to place their nuclear facilities under full-scope IAEA safeguards.

Egypt's position collapsed for two primary reasons: lack of Arab support and U.S. opposition. Most Arab states shared Egypt's objectives but did not actively support Cairo's efforts. There were three reasons for this reluctance: first, most Arab states probably judged that the odds of compelling Israel to join the NPT before comprehensive peace in the region is achieved were very low and that there were considerable costs and few benefits in launching a hopeless campaign. A number of Arab governments probably also expected that the United States — the only country that might influence Israel's policy in the nuclear realm — was most unlikely to exert any such pressures, particularly not at a delicate stage of Arab-Israeli peacemaking.

Second and closely related, most Arab states probably estimated that they would not be able to withstand the international pressure to sign the treaty. By late 1994, some two-thirds of the members of the Arab League had joined the Chemical Weapons Convention (CWC), despite their earlier resolution not to sign the convention until Israel joined the NPT. Based on this experience, most Arab governments preferred to avoid further humiliation. Recognizing this sentiment, Egypt refrained in 1995 from attempting to extract a similar Arab League decision.[63]

Third, most Arab states attributed far less urgency than did Egypt to the issue of incorporating Israel into the NPT regime. Implicitly, these states probably reasoned that they could endure a few more years alongside Israel's nuclear option, and that attempts to alter the nuclear asymmetry in the region immediately were not worth the political costs entailed. This was particularly so for the Gulf states, which may have been persuaded that they owed Washington some flexibility on this matter, especially in light of the massive effort undertaken by the United States in 1990–91 to save them from Saddam Hussein's ambitions.

The second and possibly more important reason why Egypt's position collapsed was the importance Washington attributed to the indefinite extension of the NPT, combined with its reluctance to apply any pressure on Israel with respect to the treaty. Instead, the administration and key members of Congress exerted substantial pressure on President Mubarak's government. As part of Washington's efforts, a large number of leaders and senior administration officials were sent to Cairo, most notably Vice President Gore. All impressed upon Egypt the importance attached by the Clinton administration to the indefinite extension of the NPT, hinting that Cairo's cooperation on this matter could affect the future of U.S. economic and military assistance to Egypt.[64]

U.S. pressure on Egypt reached its peak during Mubarak's April 1995 visit to Washington, when Clinton strongly urged Mubarak to adopt a more flexible approach to NPT extension. By then it became clear to Mubarak's advisors that Foreign Minister Musa's unyielding position on this matter might lead to a major clash with the United States. Complaints to this effect were already heard in both houses of Congress and among senior Congressional staffs, threatening the intimacy of U.S.-Egyptian bilateral relations. Consequently, Clinton and Mubarak seem to have reached an understanding: Egypt would not support the NPT's indefinite extension, but would avoid mobilizing other Arab states to support its position. Egypt is also said to have committed itself to remain an NPT signatory if a majority of member states voted to extend the treaty indefinitely.

Nevertheless, in a tough speech to the plenary session of the April NPT Review and Extension Conference, Musa left the impression that Egypt might seek the support of the 140-member nonaligned movement for a Syrian proposal to suspend the conference meeting until conditions allowing the Arab states to support the treaty's indefinite extension materialize. The Clinton administration felt that Musa's speech violated the understandings reached earlier with President Mubarak, leading State Department spokesman Nicholas Burns to note that "the U.S. has obtained certain assurances from the government of Egypt," and that Washington "intended to remind Cairo of these assurances." This uncharacteristically strong language was apparently followed by tough U.S.-Egyptian negotiations, resulting in the compromise mentioned earlier: Egypt joined the consensus recognizing that a majority of states supported the NPT's indefinite extension, and a "Resolution on the Middle East" urging all the region's states to join the treaty was adopted. (See Appendix 14.)

Nuclear-Weapon-Free Zone

In the mid-1970s, Egypt and Iran co-sponsored a resolution presented to the UN General Assembly, calling for the transformation of the Middle East into a nuclear-weapon-free zone (NWFZ).[65] After it ratified the NPT in 1980, Egypt began to present its own draft resolution for establishing such a zone. The UN General Assembly adopted the idea annually, approving by large majorities a version similar to the one proposed by Egypt. Later that year, Israel introduced its own draft resolution.

The main difference between the Israeli and Egyptian texts is the mechanism by which an NWFZ should be established in the Middle East. The Egyptian draft resolutions do not elaborate a mechanism for such establishment, or even suggest that a formal agreement to create such an NWFZ should be negotiated and signed by the region's states.[66] Rather, they implied that Middle East states should simply comply with the stipulations of the announced zone. Thus, the Egyptian approach did not envisage that a transformation of the political relations among the region's states must precede or accompany the creation of an NWFZ. Even when referring to the commitments undertaken by the region's states in establishing the zone, the proposal did not define the obligations that these states would be undertaking toward one another; instead, it referred to their "commitments toward the zone."[67]

Egypt did recognize that "efforts aimed at redressing the threats posed by the nuclear dimension of the arms race would without a doubt be facilitated by the resolution of the political problems in the region and vice versa." But it rejected the linkage between the two realms, arguing that arms control efforts cannot wait for peace. Thus, Egypt's approach was urgent, and it argued that "the situation in the

Middle East does not provide for the luxury of time. The ominous implications posed by the introduction of the nuclear dimension into the turmoil of the region must be addressed promptly."[68]

A second distinction between the Egyptian and Israeli proposals is their approaches to the NPT and to IAEA safeguards. The Egyptian proposal suggested that pending the establishment of an NWFZ in the Middle East, the region's states should adhere to the stipulations of the NPT and should subject all their nuclear facilities to IAEA safeguards. Elsewhere, Egypt argued that the "IAEA should play a useful role in verifying the veracity of the different declarations made prior to the zone, regarding the nuclear activities in the region through agreements reached with the concerned parties on an individual basis. The full-scope safeguard system now being implemented should be extended to cover all nuclear facilities in the Middle East as a confidence-building measure to facilitate the establishment of the zone. The IAEA should also serve as the kernel for the verification system to be implemented after the establishment of the zone, to be complemented by whatever additional measures are agreed upon by the concerned states."[69]

As a member of Egypt's delegation to the United Nations, Nabil Fahmy conceded that the NWFZ would have to be verified by intrusive measures:

Verification will, of course, have to be commensurate with the requirements for making the zone truly nuclear-weapons free. Consequently, they would by necessity have to involve measures more intrusive than those of the NPT regime, given the widely recognized Israeli nuclear capability as well as other extra-NPT prohibitions similar to those in other NWFZs.[70]

In 1991, Egypt suggested that the UN Secretary General distribute to members of the Arab League, Israel, and Iran a questionnaire to solicit their view regarding the modalities for a Middle East NWFZ, including its geographical extent; its basic prohibitions; the means of verifying compliance with these prohibitions; the commitments to the zone to be made by states outside the region; the duration of the arrangement; provisions regarding adjacent areas; the zone's relationship to similar zones; its relationship to other international agreements; and various technical clauses, such as verification and withdrawal provisions.[71]

On April 8, 1990, President Mubarak expanded Egypt's NWFZ proposal by calling for the transformation of the Middle East to a zone free of weapons of mass destruction (WMDFZ), thus adding a ban on biological and chemical weapons.[72] Egypt submitted this proposal to the United Nations on April 16, 1990 (see Appendix 4).[73] Informally, Egyptian officials presented the initiative as a concession to Israel's insistence that chemical and biological weapons are weapons of mass destruction.[74] Another Egyptian commentary said that the initiative was designed to encompass both "Iraq which possesses chemical weapons and Israel which possesses nuclear weapons," and noted that Iraq had rejected the Egyptian proposal in the 1990 Arab summit in Baghdad.[75] Similarly, the chief of staff of Egypt's Armed Forces, General Dhaffi al-Din Abu-Snaf, said that "Egypt is acting in international fora to place a complete ban on the use of chemical weapons. The best proof of this is Egypt's call for the transformation of the Middle East to zone free of weapons of mass destruction."[76] Similarly, Egyptian Defense Minister Yussuf Abu-Taleb said that the Gulf crisis confirmed the importance of President Mubarak's initiative, which represented an effort to devise "a formula which would create a linkage between the ban on nuclear weapons and a ban on chemical weapons."[77]

The Mubarak Initiative did not elaborate a mechanism for implementing a WMDFZ, but did emphasize certain points:

1. All weapons of mass destruction without exception should be prohibited in the Middle East, i.e., nuclear, chemical and biological, etc.

2. All states of the region, without exception, should make equal and reciprocal commitments in this regard.

3. Verification measures and modalities should be established to ascertain full compliance of all states of the region with the full scope of the prohibitions without exception.[78]

Mubarak's April plan was expanded in a paper submitted by Foreign Minister 'Amru Musa to the Conference on Disarmament in Geneva. It included the following stipulations:

1. Regional states are called upon to endorse the Zone in declarations

to the UN Security Council and to state their intention to refrain from actions which would impede the establishment of a zone.

2. Regional states should declare their readiness not to:

— use nuclear, chemical, or biological weapons;
— produce or acquire nuclear weapons; or
— produce or acquire nuclear weapons materials

. . . . 5. Regional states should support a future role for the UN or another international organization in verification of Middle East arms agreements.[79]

The formulation of the Mubarak Initiative as well as the wording of the July paper reveal that Egypt does not feel that the establishment of a WMDFZ in the Middle East must result from a process of negotiations by the region's states. Hence the transformation of the political relations among the region's states — which would allow such negotiations to take place   is not a prerequisite to the implementation of the Egyptian WMDFZ proposals.

This approach was also reflected in Egypt's 1991 call for the establishment of a WMDFZ in the Middle East, presented at the ACRS talks (see Appendix 8). The chairman of Egypt's delegation, Nabil Fahmy, proposed a political confidence-building measure:

The major arms-producing states and particularly the permanent members of the security council, as well as Israel, Iran and the Arab states, should deposit individual undertakings with the security council in which they clearly and unconditionally endorse the declaration of the Middle East as a region free of weapons of mass destruction and commit themselves not to take any steps or measures which would run counter to or impede the attainment of that objective.[80]

The papers submitted by Musa and Fahmy do not provide the region's states with a direct role in verifying the parties' compliance with the constraints imposed by the creation of the WMDFZ. Instead, Fahmy proposes that "the nations of the region should approve the assignment to an organ of the United Nations or another international organization a role in the verification of those nations' compliance with such agreements on arms reductions and disarmament as may be concluded between them."[81]

Fahmy's position on this issue was a slight variation on a similar statement made a year earlier by Egypt's Foreign Minister:

Egypt calls upon the states of the Middle East to announce their agreement to give a United Nations mechanism, a role to be agreed upon in the future, in regard to the verification of the states with arms control and disarmament agreements.[82]

As a member of Egypt's delegation to the UN, Fahmy had written that Israel's demand for reciprocal verification was an "unconventional verification approach." He wrote:

It is worth noting that Israel has consistently argued that it can only be assured of compliance if its own nationals participate in the verification process. One should not dismiss this condition lightly, particularly as Israel justified its attack against Iraq's nuclear reactor in 1981 by arguing that the safeguard system of the International Atomic Energy Agency, universally accepted as adequate to ascertain compliance with the provisions of the NPT, was not sufficient to assure Israel of the peaceful nature of Iraq's nuclear activities. While this position is not shared by any other state, and Israel's action was universally condemned, it does reflect Israel's unconventional verification approach.[83]

Fahmy added:

By any standard, [reciprocal participation in verifying compliance] appears a far-fetched expectation as long as the states of the region, or most of them, remain in a state of war. It is inconceivable that states at war would accept intrusive verification inspections by representatives of their enemies. It is even doubtful that states at war would allow for intrusive inspections by any state in the region, even one with which it was not at a state of war.[84]

Fahmy's discussion reveals that Egypt assumed that disarmament measures could be applied even if the region were still in a state of war. Thus, Egypt seems to have regarded the absence of peace as an obstacle to the application of intrusive verification measures, but not as a barrier to the conclusion and implementation of disarmament.

The Mubarak Initiative to transform the Middle East to a WMDFZ did not meet with universal enthusiasm in the Arab world. When Egypt presented the initiative at the June 1990 Baghdad Arab Summit meeting, Saddam Hussein objected to the proposal.[85] Concern was expressed that the initiative might damage Arab interests by allowing Israel to shift attention away from nuclear weapons to other weapons of mass destruction, and that the establishment of a WMDFZ might limit the access of the region's states to civilian technology.[86]

Nevertheless, by the end of 1994 Egypt obtained important support from Syria and Saudi Arabia for its position favoring the creation of a WMDFZ as an integral part of the peace process. This support proved to be a compromise between Cairo's desire that the two countries would refuse to support the indefinite extension of the NPT unless Israel signed the treaty, and Saudi Arabia's desire to avoid a confrontation with Washington over this issue. In the final statement of their late December 1994 Alexandria meeting, Mubarak, al-Asad, and Fahd announced:

The three states called on the international community, especially the cosponsors of the peace process, to work diligently to remove the obstacles created by the Israeli side to the peace process. In this context, the three leaders affirmed their demand for the establishment of a zone free of weapons of mass destruction, above all nuclear weapons.[87]

Although Egypt obtained the willingness of Syria and Saudi Arabia to view the creation of a WMDFZ as an integral part of Middle East peace, it was far from clear that President Asad and King Fahd believed that such a zone could be established without peace. Jordan's position was that the establishment of a comprehensive peace is a prerequisite for the creation of a WMDFZ. In a 1994 interview, the head of Jordan's delegation to the ACRS talks, Abdullah Toukan, emphasized: "You cannot have a weapons of mass destruction free zone without a comprehensive peace and vice versa. They go hand in hand."[88]

During the months preceding the April 1995 NPT Review and Extension conference, the Arab League instructed a group of Arab arms control experts to draft a WMDFZ treaty text. Anticipating likely Israeli concerns regarding the geographical extent of such a zone, the draft treaty acknowledged that a WMDFZ must incorporate Israel, Iran, and all twenty-two members of the Arab League. At the March 23, 1995, League meeting, the draft treaty was discussed but no decisions were made regarding its implementation.

Banning the Production of Weapons-Grade Material

Although Egypt officially welcomed the Middle East arms control initiative announced by President Bush in May 1991, it did not react specifically to his call for a freeze on the production of plutonium and enriched uranium. Nor did Egypt endorse the suggestions contained in the initiatives proposed by President Bush in July 1992 and by President Clinton in September 1993 that such production should be banned.

Informally, Egyptian officials expressed concern that the implementation of such a ban in the Middle East would make Israel's regional superiority in the nuclear realm permanent; it would not affect the products of Israel's alleged past nuclear activities but would prevent the Arab states from developing a countervailing capability. For example, Foreign Minister 'Amru Musa reportedly said that "the Bush initiative is unrealistic because it ignores Israel's possession of nuclear weapons."[89] This view seemed to be shared by other Arab states. For example, Syria's Foreign Minister Faruq al-Shar' stated that the Arabs would not accept U.S. proposals for arms control in the Middle East. He argued that these proposals favor Israel and damage vital Arab security interests.[90]

During 1994–95, as it seemed more likely that the Conference on Disarmament in Geneva might eventually negotiate a treaty banning the further production of fissile material, Egypt crystallized its position. It insisted that such a treaty must not only limit present and future activities, but must cover past activities as well by requiring signatories to place all their existing stockpiles of fissile material under international safeguards. Speaking at a CD meeting in September 1995, Egyptian Ambassador Mounir Zahran addressed "the need for a fissile material ban to prevent vertical as well as horizontal proliferation," and reiterated Egypt's view that such a ban should include "existing stockpiles of weapons-usable fissile material, both military and civilian."[91] Thus, to Egypt, a fissile material production ban treaty that would simply freeze the status quo is unacceptable.

Unofficially, a number of senior Egyptian scholars and former officials proposed their own versions of the production ban proposal. These proposals were first communicated informally to a number of Israeli analysts immediately after the Gulf War. Several of these "capping" proposals have been attributed to foreign sources by their Egyptian proponents.

The Egyptian versions of the production ban differed in four key respects from Bush's proposal. First, the Egyptian versions were not defined in global or region-wide terms; rather, they were specifically intended to cap Israel's nuclear capability. For example, a proposal by Salah Bassuni, former ambassador to the Soviet Union and then director of the National Center for Middle East Studies in Cairo, published in the newspaper *Al-Ahram* in April 1991, called for Israel "to discontinue its nuclear program," to commit itself to sign the NPT, and "to agree to place its nuclear stockpile and activities under international safeguards."[92]

Second, the proposals did not focus on dedicated facilities for plutonium separation and uranium enrichment; instead, they called for the closing of the Dimona nuclear reactor. Third, the proposals contained a transparency requirement: as a first step toward implementing the freeze, Israel would announce that it possesses a stockpile of weapons-grade material. Finally, the Egyptian versions elaborated a political timetable for moving from capping to disarmament; for example, Bassuni stipulated that "after a just and comprehensive peace is achieved, and during an agreed-upon schedule, the elimination of Israel's nuclear stockpile will be completed under international control."[93]

Bassuni explained that in exchange for Israel's consent, the Arab states would promise not to develop nuclear weapons and would remain committed to the NPT. He stressed that the purpose of the proposal was to avoid demanding that Israel rid itself of nuclear weapons, since no state had ever undertaken such a step and Israel would not be the first to do so.[94] The proposal would signal Arab acceptance of the fact that Israel possesses a nuclear arsenal and that this arsenal would be placed under international control.[95] Explaining the transparency clause in the proposal, Bassuni argued that it would not be possible to establish mutual confidence in the region as long as Israel resisted acknowledging its possession of nuclear weapons, and that any attempt to discuss regional disarmament of weapons of mass destruction was doomed to failure as long as Israel refused to place its nuclear stockpile on the negotiation table.[96]

Another version of this proposal was presented by Abd al-Monem

Sa'id 'Aly, Director of the Al-Ahram Center for Political and Strategic Studies. 'Aly endorsed a suggestion "to cap the Israeli nuclear capabilities by putting the Dimona reactor under the IAEA safeguards within the NPT system." He explained that this "would keep the Israeli nuclear deterrent intact until further political steps are taken on the road leading Israel to accept the provisions of a nuclear-weapon-free zone."[97] 'Aly did not explain how an Israeli nuclear deterrent would be incorporated in the NPT framework without amending the treaty. Like Bassuni, he envisaged a political timetable for progress from capping to disarmament:

Although certain asymmetries might be acceptable to facilitate agreements, symmetrical and reciprocal arrangements should be the norm at the end of the road. Therefore, if Israel keeps its nuclear weapons while safeguarding Dimona, these weapons should be phased out or reduced over a period of time as a confidence-building measure. Some of them could be eliminated as a result of international guarantees; others should be eliminated in a trade for peace treaties with Arab countries; the rest should be eliminated once full normalization of relations and different types of economic and functional cooperation are established. The same process should be applied to chemical weapons for both sides of the conflict. In this respect, arms control measures, along with other issues, should be part of the peace process, not separate from it.[98]

A third version of the capping proposal was presented by a retired Egyptian General, 'Ismaat A. 'Azz, who served as chairman of Egypt's delegation to the May 1994 plenary session of the ACRS talks held in Qatar. In a 1993 paper, 'Azz suggested a "freeze of the Israeli nuclear program." He explained that "this means that [the] Dimona reactor and separation facilities would be put under control," and argued that "this would not in any way hurt Israel strategically." 'Azz also suggested that:

Israel would retain, by Arab agreement, its strategic nuclear weapons, which are considered its final deterrent against any possible threat. These strategic nuclear weapons would be reconsidered for elimination after a period of 10–15 years *after* a peaceful atmosphere prevails in the region. In return, the Arab countries [would] commit themselves not to try to acquire nuclear weapons or any other weapons of mass destruction.[99]

In informal conversations, senior Egyptian officials have disassociated themselves from the Bassuni and Sa'id 'Aly capping proposals. Indeed, they rejected both pillars of the proposal; in their view, the capping dimension was unacceptable because it would make Israel's nuclear superiority permanent, and the transparency requirement would legitimize Israel's superiority.

Two additional proposals suggest a rollback of Israel's nuclear option, but do not insist that Israel disclose its alleged past activities. The first proposal, by Egypt's Ambassador to the UK, Muhammed Shaker, rejects the notion that Israel would continue to enjoy the status of "the sole nuclear power in the region" indefinitely, and reportedly recommends that Israel close down its nuclear reactor at Dimona, "as a first step demonstrating [its] good-will." Shaker emphasized, however, that Israel would be able to maintain ambiguity with respect to the products of its past activities, noting that even after such closing, "question marks would remain…. We know Israel has the capability, but we do not know with certainty whether Israel already assembled nuclear weapons, tested them or deployed them."[100]

The second proposal, by General Ahmed Abdul Halim, a senior member of Cairo's National Center for Middle East Studies, did not require Israel to close down Dimona but suggested that Israel abolish its nuclear weapons. In a presentation to the 1993 Second Ginosar Conference on Security and Arms Control in the Middle East, Halim emphasized that the proposal would allow Israel to retain a measure of nuclear deterrence: "Even if Israel accepts the elimination of its nuclear weapons, it will continue to possess the infrastructure as well as the know-how necessary for the reproduction of new nuclear weapons, should circumstances require it to do so. Thus Israel would retain an important leverage which constitutes an element of deterrence in its own standing."[101]

Conclusions

Egypt's approach to nuclear arms control in the Middle East continues to focus on attempts to limit and then roll back Israel's nuclear option. Egypt's formal position demands that Israel sign the NPT and subject all its nuclear installations to full-scope IAEA safeguards, and that it accept the stipulations involved in the transformation of the region to an NWFZ, a WMDFZ, or both. However, the priority of this issue relative to Egypt's other national interests and policy objectives remains unclear. Other Arab governments seem to regard Israel's nuclear disarmament as less urgent.

There are signs that Cairo may be prepared to support a treaty banning the production of fissile material, if the treaty requires that existing stockpiles of plutonium and enriched uranium be placed under international safeguards. This stance may indicate an Egyptian willingness to consider a more gradual approach to Israeli denuclearization. A number of Egyptian academics and former officials indicate a recognition that Israel is unlikely to roll back its nuclear option in the near future, and that capping Israel's nuclear potential is probably the most that could be hoped for until comprehensive peace in the Middle East is achieved.

Finally, consistent with its more general nuclear nonproliferation objectives, since early 1994 Egypt has taken an active part in the efforts conducted in the framework of the UN Conference on Disarmament to conclude a Comprehensive Test Ban Treaty (CTBT). In late July 1996, President Mubarak offered Egypt's support for the CTBT text drafted in Geneva.[102]

NOTES

1. *Al-Akhbar* (Egypt), June 16, 1991 (translated by HATZAV).

2. "Asad rejects arms control," *Ma'ariv* (Israel), June 3, 1991.

3. "*Al-Thawra* says peace conference aims to disarm Syria" (BBC, ME/1143, August 6, 1991, p. A/5).

4. "Syria: West trying to deprive Arabs of means for self-defense," *Jerusalem Post*, January 17, 1993, citing the Syrian newspaper *Al-Thawra.*

5. "China supports limiting arms transfers to the Middle East," *Hadashot* (Israel), June 6, 1991.

6. Egypt's Foreign Minister 'Amru Musa, quoted by MENA from Cairo January 28, 1993 (BBC, ME/1600, January 30, 1993, p. A/7).

7. "One on One," interview with 'Amru Musa, Egyptian Foreign Minister, *Defense News*, February 1–7, 1993. See also Aluf Ben, "Egypt demanding that Israel declare its willingness to place its nuclear facilities under international safeguards," *Ha'aretz* (Israel), February 5,

1993.

8. This consideration was echoed in Egyptian commentaries. For example, a mid-1991 editorial in *Al-Akhbar* asserts that "ignoring Israel's nuclear arsenal raises the possibility that other regional countries will try to produce or otherwise acquire similar weapons themselves at all costs." Cairo MENA in Arabic, July 6, 1991 (FBIS-NES-91-131, July 9, 1991).

9. Cairo MENA in Arabic, December 18, 1993 (FBIS-NES-93-242, December 20, 1993).

10. Interview with Abdullah Toukan, the head of Jordan's delegation to the ACRS talks, on Jordan Television, October 24, 1992 (translated by HATZAV).

11. " Asad: 'the North Korean ship did not transport Scud missiles to Syria'," *Hadashot*, March 13, 1992.

12. See statement by Syria's Foreign Minister Faruq al-Shar', cited by Syrian Arab Republic Radio January 28, 1993 (BBC, ME/1599, January 29, 1993, p. A/13).

13. Nabil Fahmy, "Regional Arms Control, CBM and Peacekeeping Requirements," paper presented at the Ninth Regional Security Conference of the International Institute for Strategic Studies, Istanbul, Turkey, June 7–10, 1992, p. 3.

14. "Egyptian Foreign Minister outlines policy on regional issues," MENA in Arabic, May 10, 1992 (BBC, ME/1379, May 13, 1992, p. A/3). A prominent Egyptian commentator, Muhammad Sayid Ahmad, expressed slightly more empathy when providing the context for this linkage: "Israel's siege mentality feeds on the hostility expressed towards it by its environment.... If it comes to be accepted by its immediate neighbors it will lose much of its sense of danger which fuels its belligerency." Muhammad Sayid Ahmad, "The Israeli epoch," *Al-Ahram Weekly* (Egypt), December 25, 1993–January 1, 1994.

15. "Egypt's ambassador to the UK: 'Israel should close down the nuclear reactor in Dimona as a sign of good-will'," *Ha'aretz*, May 8, 1991.

16. Fahmy, "Regional Arms Control, CBM and Peacekeeping Requirements," p. 3.

17. Ibid., p. 4.

18. "Report on Israeli nuclear arms agreement denied," Cairo MENA in Arabic, May 22, 1991 (FBIS-NES-91-100, May 23, 1991).

19. Dan Avidan, "Only by mutual recognition and not by military means" (Interview with Osama al-Baz), *Davar*, May 17, 1991.

20. Damascus Domestic Service in Arabic, January 8, 1989 (JPRS-TAC-89-003, January 27, 1989), cited by Peter Herby, *The Chemical Weapons Convention and Arms Control in the Middle East* (Oslo: PRIO, 1992), p. 55.

21. "'Israeli borders will not be immune to missiles,' warned a Syrian commentator," *Davar*, February 5, 1994.

22. "Asad: 'The North Korean ship did not transport Scud missiles to Syria'."

23. "*Tishrin* cited on reaction to Israeli armaments," Syrian Arab Republic Radio Network (Damascus), November 30, 1992 (FBIS-NES-92-231, December 1, 1992).

24. Statement by Ambassador 'Amru Musa, Permanent Representative of the Arab Republic of Egypt to the United Nations, on "Establishing a Nuclear Free Zone in the Region of the Middle East," First Committee, 45th Session of the General Assembly, November 9, 1990, p. 2.

25. Associated Press, September 14, 1992.

26. "Foreign minister of Qatar: Israel should sign treaty for the non-proliferation of nuclear weapons," *Ha'aretz*, May 4, 1994.

27. Cited in Musa, Statement on "Establishing a Nuclear Free Zone in the Region of the Middle East," p. 3.

28. Egypt's Reply to the Report of the Secretary General on "Establishment of a Nuclear Free Zone in the Region of the Middle East," UN Doc. A/46/150, June 1991, p. 14.

29. In a statement to the UN, Ambassador Musa said: "Let it be heard loud and clear, Israel must bring its commitments in the nuclear weapons field in line with those of the Arab states by adhering to the NPT. From that point on the states in the region can work together to develop more efficient and effective measures to ensure that nuclear weapons are not introduced into the region." See Musa, statement on "Establishing a Nuclear Free Zone in the Region of the Middle East," p. 5.

30. Egypt's Reply to the Report of the Secretary General on "Establishment of a Nuclear Free Zone in the Region of the Middle East," pp. 11–12.

31. Ibid., pp. 14–15.

32. Fahmy, "Regional Arms Control, CBM and Peacemaking Requirements." These demands were formulated a year earlier and were announced verbatim by Egypt's Foreign Minister in a press conference in Cairo on July 4, 1991.

33. Ibid. (emphasis in the original text).

34. See Nabil Fahmy, "Controlling Weapons of Mass Destruction in the Middle East," *American-Arab Affairs*, No. 35 (Winter 1990–91), pp. 127, 130. In Fahmy's words: "A case in point is the linkage drawn by the Arab states at the 1989 Paris conference between chemical and nuclear disarmament, because of their concerns regarding Israel's unsafeguarded nuclear program. The political message was clear and simple. The Arabs perceive Israel's nuclear program as a direct security threat. If adherence to future chemical agreements is to be assured, whether as part of a global process, or a regional initiative, this perception must be addressed" (p. 130).

35. Al-Ahram press agency in Arabic, January 3, 1993 (BBC, ME/1578 January 5, 1993, p. A/3). See also MENA from Damascus in Arabic, January 13, 1993 (BBC, ME/1587 January 15, 1993, p. A/13).

36. Speech by Foreign Minister 'Amru Musa to the 47th Session of the UN General Assembly, September 25, 1992.

37. 'Abd-al-Sattar Abu-Husayn, "U.S. Pressure on Egypt To Sign Treaty on Chemical Weapons," *Al-Sha'b*, November 25, 1992, p. 1 (FBIS-NES-92-231, December 1, 1992, p. 8). See also Ori Nir, "Pressure on Arab states to join treaty banning chemical weapons," *Ha'aretz*, December 9, 1992.

38. Voice of the Islamic Republic of Teheran, January 7, 1993 (BBC, ME/1582, January 9, 1993; p. A/9); and Voice of the Islamic Republic of Teheran, January 14, 1993 (BBC, ME/1588, January 16, 1993, p. A/14).

39. *Al-Ahali*, March 17, 1993 (FBIS-NES 93 055, March 24, 1993, p. 11).

40. MENA from Cairo, April 17, 1993 (FBIS-NES-93-073, April 19, 1993).

41. Amnon Barzilai, "Mubarak: 'If I knew that a visit to Israel would bring peace with Syria nearer, I would come tomorrow'." *Ha'aretz*, December 21, 1994. Similarly, Mubarak was later quoted in *Al-Ahram* as having told Israeli journalists: "If Israel doesn't sign this treaty, Egypt will not sign either." Addressing Israelis, he later repeated his position: "Regarding the dispute over signing the extension of the nuclear non-proliferation treaty, the issue is simply that [if] you will not sign — we will not sign," *Mideast Mirror*, January 4, 1995, p. 10. In a January 1995 meeting with Israel's Foreign Minister Shimon Peres, Mubarak again emphasized that "Egypt would not sign the NPT at the time of its renewal and will continue to refrain from signing the treaty as long as Israel does not join the NPT." Aluf Ben, "Egypt's foreign minister suggests opening bilateral nuclear talks with Israel," *Ha'aretz*, January 5, 1995.

42. Cited in *Al-Hayat*; see *Mideast Mirror*, December 21, 1994, p. 12.

43. "Egypt: Tripartite summit issues final communiqué," Cairo Arab Republic of Egypt Radio, December 29, 1994 (FBIS, December 30, 1994).

44. See Paris AFP in English, September 15, 1994 (FBIS-NES-94-180, September 16, 1994, p. 2). Indeed, by early 1995 the Arab League had yet to adopt the position advanced by Egypt and Syria, linking their support for the NPT's indefinite extension to Israel's signature of the treaty. For example, on January 9, 1995, the League's secretary general, Esmat Abdel-Meguid, confined himself to saying that the Middle East should be made a nuclear-free zone. But he hinted at his personal support for continuing to link the Arab states' joining the CWC to Israel's joining the NPT by suggesting that "any multilateral disarmament involving other weapons must be conducted on the basis of fairness and equality between the region's states." He added: "Otherwise the peace process will not be able to achieve its aims," a phrase close to that used by Egypt's foreign minister, 'Amru Musa. See "Arab League says Israeli nuclear arms imperil area," Reuters, January 10, 1995.

45. Mona Eltahawy, "Syria warns of nuclear race unless Israel signs NPT," Reuters (Cairo), February 6, 1995.

46. Yerach Tal, "Musa: 'Israel's refusal to disarms its nuclear weapons is an obstacle to comprehensive peace'," Ha'aretz, August 31, 1994.

47. See Mideast Mirror, December 20, 1994.

48. "Egypt sees safeguards on Israeli weapons as condition for economic cooperation," Davar, December 13, 1994.

49. "Egypt to increase pressure on Israel to agree to place its nuclear weapons under safeguards," Ha'aretz, December 9, 1994, citing Al-Sarq al-Awsat (London).

50. "Egypt says Israel's weapons a threat to peace," Reuters (Cairo), January 10, 1995.

51. Nitzan Hurewitz and Aluf Ben, "Musa: 'We will never accept that Israel does not join the treaty: Rabin is leading to a crisis'," Ha'aretz, February 2, 1995.

52. Samia Nakhoul, "Is long affair between Israel and Egypt on rocks?" Reuters (Cairo), January 16, 1995.

53. Samia Nakhoul, "Israel's nuclear stance may fuel tension — Egypt," Reuters (Cairo), January 22, 1995.

54. Peter Bale, "Peres and Egyptian minister meet, set new talks," Reuters, December 5, 1994.

55. Aluf Ben, "Mubarak: The summit of the leaders of Egypt, Syria, and Saudi Arabia was not directed against Israel," Ha'aretz, January 4, 1995.

56. Peter Waldman, "Egypt Confronts Israel on Nuclear Arms," Wall Street Journal, January 11, 1995.

57. Samia Nakhoul, "Egypt-Israel rift develops over anti-nuclear treaty," *Washington Times*, January 25, 1995.

58. Evelyn Leopold, "Still short votes on NPT, U.S. considers compromise," Reuters (United Nations), January 24, 1995.

59. See Akiva Eldar, Aluf Ben, and Gideon Alon, "Musa: Egypt does not expect Israel to give up its nuclear program, merely to accept controls," *Ha'aretz*, February 16, 1995.

60. See Mona Makram Obaid, "Towards a new strategic Egyptian role: The three new circles," *Al-Hayat*, November 27, 1994, in *Mideast Mirror*, November 28, 1994, p. 16.

61. Barzilai, "Mubarak: 'If I knew that a visit to Israel would bring peace'."

62. Ben, "Mubarak: The summit of the leaders of Egypt, Syria, and Saudi Arabia."

63. Ibid.

64. Akiva Eldar and Aluf Ben, "Mubarak was warned of a cut in U.S. aid if he refuses to support the NPT's extension," *Ha'aretz*, April 4, 1995.

65. See UN General Assembly Resolution 3263 in 1974 and 3472 in 1975 (approved December 11, 1975). Iran consistently supported the establishment of a NWFZ in the Middle East. For example, in late 1994, its deputy foreign minister for international affairs, Muhammad Javad Zarif, told a seminar in Teheran that Iran was committed to an NWFZ and wanted its opinion to be considered at the April 1995 NPT Review Conference. See "Iran wants Mideast as nuclear-free zone," *Washington Times*, December 19, 1994. Three weeks later, the chairman of Iran's atomic energy commission, Reza Amrollahi, told the Kuwaiti daily *Al-Watan* that "Iran would press ahead with plans to develop the peaceful use of nuclear power, while advocating the creation of a nuclear-weapon free zone throughout the Gulf and the Middle East." *Mideast Mirror*, January 10, 1995.

66. This deficiency was only slightly addressed by the draft NWFZ resolutions submitted by Egypt beginning in 1988. The new formulation called for authorizing the UN Secretary General to appoint a personal representative or group of experts to contact the states of the region with a view to formulating a model draft treaty for the creation of an NWFZ in the Middle East. It also called for inviting the IAEA to submit recommendations for verification and inspection measures that would be necessary in conjunction with the establishment of the zone. See Abdel Monem Said Aly, "Arms Control and the Arab-Israeli Conflict: An Arab Perspective," paper presented at the conference on Cooperative Security in the Middle East held by the Institute for Global Cooperation and Conflict of the University of California and the Institute of the USA and Canada, Moscow, October 21–24, 1994. Yet these suggestions merely call for studies, and can hardly be seen as modalities for the establishment of an NWFZ.

67. Egypt's Reply to the Report of the Secretary General on "Establishment of a Nuclear Free Zone in the Region of the Middle East," p. 17.

68. Ibid.

69. Ibid., pp. 15–16. This formulation does not exclude the possibility that the region's states would agree to apply additional safeguards, but it falls short of stipulating that such an agreement is necessary and it does not make clear whether "the concerned states" refers to the region's states or to outside powers.

70. Nabil Fahmy, "Middle East Arms Control: Bolder Nuclear Steps Needed," *Arms Control Today*, Vol 21, No. 4 (May 1991), p. 22.

71. Egypt's Reply to the Report of the Secretary General on "Establishment of a Nuclear Free Zone in the Region of the Middle East," p. 17.

72. *Al-Ahram* (Egypt), April 8, 1990. See also Nabil Fahmy, "Egypt's disarmament initiative," *Bulletin of the Atomic Scientists*, November 1990, pp. 9–10.

73. See letter dated April 16, 1990, from the Permanent Representative of Egypt to the United Nations addressed to the Secretary General transmitting the letter addressed to the Secretary General from Ahmad Ismat 'Abd al-Magid, Deputy Prime Minister and Minister of Foreign Affairs of Egypt (A/45/219-S/21252, April 18, 1990). See Appendix 4.

74. In more diplomatic terms, Nabil Fahmy noted that "Arab states, in supporting President Mubarak's initiative on weapons of mass destruction, expressed their readiness to deal with other weapons of mass destruction as a confidence building measure and incentive to Israel." Fahmy, "Middle East Arms Control," p. 22. Elsewhere, he presented the Mubarak Initiative as "the first disarmament proposal relating to the Middle East that touches upon weapons systems of concern to each of the traditional adversaries in the region." Fahmy, "Controlling Weapons of Mass Destruction in the Middle East," p. 132.

75. *Al-Jumhuriyya* (Egypt), December 13, 1990 (translated by HATZAV).

76. *Al-Difa'* (Egypt), October 1990 (translated by HATZAV).

77. Ibid.

78. Fahmy, "Controlling Weapons of Mass Destruction in the Middle East," p. 132.

79. Letter dated July 21, 1991, from Foreign Minister 'Amru Musa to the UN Secretary General, issued as Conference on Disarmament document CD/1098, and cited in Herby, *The Chemical Weapons Convention and Arms Control in the Middle East*, p. 66. See Appendix 8.

80. Fahmy, "Regional Arms Control, CBM and Peacemaking Requirements." This demand was formulated a year earlier and was announced verbatim by Egypt's Foreign Minister in a press conference in Cairo on July 4, 1991.

81. Ibid.

82. Egypt's Foreign Minister in a press conference in Cairo on July 4, 1991.

83. Fahmy, "Controlling Weapons of Mass Destruction in the Middle East," p. 130.

84. Ibid., p. 131.

85. Text of speech by President Husni Mubarak to a joint session of the People's Assembly and the Consultative Council at the People's Assembly Hall, Arabic Republic of Egypt Radio, Cairo, March 3, 1991 (BBC, ME/1012, March 5, 1991, p. A/5).

86. See also Fahmy, "Egypt's disarmament initiative," pp. 9–10.

87. "Egypt: Tripartite summit issues final communique."

88. Rana Sabbagh, "Israel, Arabs end talks on reducing war risks," Reuters, November 10, 1994.

89. "China supports limiting arms transfer to the Middle East," *Hadashot*, June 6, 1991 (citing *The New York Post*).

90. "'Israel's borders will not be immune to missiles,' warned a Syrian commentator."

91. *Nuclear Proliferation News*, No. 32, September 8, 1995, p. 3.

92. Ambassador Salah Bassuni, "Israel's Nuclear Option and the Issue of Peace," *Al-Ahram*, April 28, 1991.

93. Bassuni, "Israel's Nuclear Option and the Issue of Peace."

94. Bassuni wrote this three years before South Africa announced that it had unilaterally destroyed its nuclear arsenal.

95. Bassuni, "Israel's Nuclear Option and the Issue of Peace."

96. In informal communications, U.S. officials have rejected this notion, arguing that verifying a freeze requires only that the absence of further production is assured. Accordingly, they suggest that verification of such a freeze should focus on production facilities and should not require that present inventories and past activities be declared.

97. See Aly, "Arms Control and the Arab-Israeli Conflict: An Arab Perspective." The paper, originally presented at a conference, was subsequently published as Abdel Monem Said Aly, "Arms Control and the resolution of the Arab-Israeli Conflict," in Steven L. Spiegel, ed., *The Arab-Israeli Search for Peace* (Boulder, Colo.: Lynne Rienner, 1992), pp. 151–157. I heard a similar proposal by Osama al-Ghazala Harb, then acting director of the Al-Ahram Center for Political and Strategic Studies, at a conference held jointly by the Institut Français des Relations Internationales and the Fondation des Etudes le Defense Nationale in Paris, July 1991.

98. Aly, "*Arms Control and the Resolution of the Arab-Israeli Conflict,*" p. 156.

99. 'Ismaat A. 'Azz, paper submitted to a Pugwash conference, June, 1993.

100. "Egypt's ambassador to the UK: 'Israel should close down the nuclear reactor."

101. General Muhamed Ahmed Abdul Halim, "Middle East Regional Arms Control and Security," in Shai Feldman, ed., *Confidence Building and Verification: Prospects in the Middle East* (Tel Aviv: Jaffee Center for Strategic Studies, Tel Aviv University, 1994).

102. Steven Erlanger, "Back Land-for-Peace Stand, Egyptian Leader Urges U.S.," *New York Times*, July 31, 1996.

Chapter 8

Nuclear Arms Control:
Israel's Policies

This chapter attempts to portray Israel's approach to nuclear arms control. Israel has never provided an official and comprehensive definition of its arms control policy in a publicly available document; its position must be inferred from its behavior, public statements that address parts of the agenda, and less official attempts to define its approach.

The transformation of the Middle East security environment has caused Israel to crystallize its approach to arms control. Before the ACRS talks were launched in early 1992, Israel adopted positions toward specific items on the global arms control agenda on an *ad hoc* basis. The discussions and negotiations of the ACRS working group compelled Israel to enter into a governmental consultation process to allow adoption of a policy on the agenda and content of these talks. Starting in 1992, this more systematic approach has also defined Israel's positions with respect to the various facets of the global arms control agenda as they became increasingly salient. Thus, a pattern representing Israel's approach to the various issues involved can be identified.

Premises of Arms Control

Israel's approach to arms control comprises six principles and preferences. First, regional arms limitations should be applied only after the creation of an infrastructure of mutual confidence that reduces tensions and increases trust among the region's states. (See Appendix 6.) Hence, within the framework of the ACRS talks, Israel has repeatedly emphasized the importance of applying regional confidence and security building measures first.

Second, Israel insists that even *discussions* regarding the possibility of limiting sensitive arms — primarily in the nuclear realm — should begin only after comprehensive peace has been achieved and minimal degrees of confidence and mutual trust have been established. The Israeli government seems to believe that once discussions are initiated, it is difficult to ensure that they do not slip into negotiations. Israel insists that in order to avoid the pressures that premature negotiations are likely to produce, it is better to avoid discussions altogether.

Third, in Israel's eyes it is also futile to discuss nonproliferation until all major sources of proliferation concern can be brought into such discussions. For example, it is futile for the ACRS working group to discuss limits on weapons of mass destruction as long as Iraq and Iran — whose ballistic missile and WMD programs are regarded by Israel as a serious threat — remain outside the ACRS framework.

Fourth, Israel regards regional arms control arrangements as generally much preferable to the application of global arms control instruments in the Middle East. Many global instruments have proven deficient, primarily due to the inadequate means of verifying their signatories' compliance. For example, the Nuclear Non-Proliferation Treaty (NPT) and its associated (IAEA) safeguards are believed to have been repeatedly violated by Iraq and North Korea. The Biological Weapons Convention is widely regarded as unverifiable and there are also serious questions regarding whether compliance with the recently adopted Chemical Weapons Convention (CWC) can be ensured.

In Israel's judgment, regional arrangements such as the Tlatelolco treaty which transformed Latin America into a nuclear-weapon-free zone (NWFZ) are advantageous because they allow the parties to adopt a more robust verification regime in which international monitoring can be supplemented by regional compliance verification mechanisms, bilateral on-site inspections, and the reciprocal utilization of national technical means (NTMs). (See Appendix 2.)

Hence, Israeli leaders and senior officials have stated on more than one occasion that once peace is established, discussions should be conducted regarding the possible transformation of the Middle East to a mutually verifiable weapons of mass destruction–free zone (WMDFZ). Wording to this effect was also included in the text of the Israeli-Jordanian peace agreement in October 1994.

Fifth, in verifying arms control agreements, Israel demands no less than what was deemed by the U.S. and the Soviet Union as absolutely essential when they negotiated their bilateral agreements such as the Intermediate Nuclear Forces (INF), Conventional Forces in Europe (CFE), and START treaties: responsibility for the verification of arms control agreements must not be delegated to an international organization, but should be based on reciprocal on-site inspections and the use of NTMs.

Sixth and finally, Israel is determined that arms control cannot be allowed to undermine national security. Consequently, as long as deterrence needs to be maintained, arms control measures that might erode Israeli deterrence must be rejected. In the nuclear realm, therefore, Israel's perceived need to maintain an ambiguous deterrent led to its continued refusal to sign the NPT and to subject all its nuclear facilities to full-scope IAEA safeguards. Conversely, in the chemical weapons realm — where Israeli deterrence was not seen as being affected — Israel became an original signatory of the CWC in January 1993. These premises underlie Israel's stance on such issues as the NPT, NWFZ proposals, a fissile materials ban, and a CTBT.

The Nuclear Non-Proliferation Treaty

Israel's refusal to sign the Nuclear Non-Proliferation Treaty seems to have resulted from four considerations. Primarily, successive Israeli governments probably felt that such a signature would undermine their capacity to maintain Israel's ambiguous nuclear posture. For example, in a speech in Geneva on January 26, 1995, Israel's Foreign Minister Shimon Peres said that "ambiguity regarding the nuclear issue is part of Israel's national security concept. There is no reason for us to hurry in removing this ambiguity. This is particularly the case as neighboring countries, like Iran and Iraq, are calling for Israel's destruction."[1]

Peres has made a number of similar statements. For example, he has argued that "some people would like us to clarify where we stand. [But] if a fog is part of a deterrent, let's keep the fog."[2] He has also noted that "there are very hostile countries in the region, like Iraq and Iran, that regard Israel as a 'collective Salman Rushdie.' We have no reason to reassure the Iranians. If they are afraid — this is our best deterrence."[3] And elsewhere: "We see no reason to disperse the fog of

Iran's suspicions. Iran's suspicions [constitute] Israeli deterrence. If the Middle East would be without hostility and war, it would also be without unconventional weapons."[4]

This points to a second reason why Israel has not signed the NPT: until there is conclusive evidence that the region's states have reconciled themselves to Israel's existence and are willing to coexist peacefully with it, Israel must continue to enjoy whatever measure of "deterrence through uncertainty" can be derived from its ambiguous nuclear posture.[5] Characteristically, Israel's President Ezer Weizmann was most blunt about this, telling Egyptian reporters during a December 1994 visit to Cairo: "Israel will not sign the NPT until we have comprehensive peace.... You can forget about Israel signing the NPT now."[6] Later in Paris, Peres said more elegantly: "Israel has said it has no intention of introducing nuclear weapons into the Middle East ... but one must first introduce peace into the Middle East."[7] Peres later stressed: "The policy that we have adopted will remain in place until comprehensive peace is established."[8]

Third, while Israel supports the purposes of the NPT, it clearly considers the treaty a highly deficient instrument for arresting nuclear proliferation in the Middle East and elsewhere. Two related shortcomings of the NPT regime seem to have become the focus of Israeli concern: First, under the terms of the treaty, an NPT signatory can develop a full nuclear fuel cycle and stockpile large quantities of plutonium, as long as these stockpiles and facilities are subjected to periodic inspections by the IAEA. Second, Israel considered the NPT's verification system highly deficient,[9] as the case of Iraq proved conclusively. IAEA inspections were confined to declared facilities; prior notice of inspections was given to the inspected state; no provisions were made for surprise visits to suspected facilities; the inspected state could affect the national composition of the inspection team; and the IAEA lacked intelligence-gathering capabilities for identifying suspected facilities. In addition, inspectors' concerns about securing future access were perceived as limiting the rigor with which they inspected declared facilities. Thus, a country like Iraq could develop a full-scale military nuclear capability "right under the nose" of IAEA inspectors.[10]

Fourth, Israel considered itself at an inherent disadvantage with respect to the NPT-IAEA regime. First, the more numerous and vast

Arab countries are seen as far better positioned to hide large-scale forbidden nuclear facilities. Here, also, Iraq served as an excellent example. Second, soon after its establishment, Israel became uncomfortable with UN-related international organizations, primarily because the "one-state one-vote" rule adopted by such bodies meant that the more numerous Arab and Muslim states could always muster a majority against the Jewish state; hence Israel held long-standing skepticism with regard to IAEA safeguards.[11]

Shalheveth Freier, former head of Israel's Atomic Energy Commission, has summarized Israel's response to the various Arab pleas that it sign the NPT and place its nuclear facilities under full-scope IAEA safeguards:

It was the Israeli understanding that the Arab states wished Israel to be well controlled in the nuclear realm, and maintain the option of waging wars against it, at a time of their choosing, with nothing to worry about. Israelis saw further justification for their apprehensions, as time went along, when their concerns with the Iraqi nuclear enterprise were brushed aside by the supplier states on grounds that Iraq was a signatory to the NPT, and when Israel was roundly condemned and punished after it had put the Iraqi reactor out of action in 1981. Had it not been for the invasion of Kuwait and the subsequent acknowledgement of Iraq's military potential, Israel might still be left to contemplate its situation alone.[12]

THE NPT REVIEW AND EXTENSION CONFERENCE

The 1995 NPT Review Conference posed fewer dilemmas for Israel as a non-signatory of the treaty than for the Arab states. Clearly, it had no standing or direct role in the deliberations about the merits of the treaty's indefinite or limited extension. However, as the April 1995 Conference neared, Israel faced a serious campaign by Egypt to obtain Israeli signature on the NPT; Egypt threatened to oppose the indefinite extension of the treaty and block the consensus necessary to adopt the "Statement of Arms Control and Regional Security" by the ACRS plenary. While Israel adhered to its refusal to sign the treaty, its sensitivity to Egypt's concerns and its desire to see ACRS adopt the negotiated Statement eventually led it to soften its position with respect to the NPT.

This softening was also motivated by a desire to accommodate the Clinton administration, whose officials suggested that the chances of obtaining Egypt's support for the indefinite extension of the NPT and for an ACRS Statement might improve if Israel were to issue some "statement of intent" indicating its willingness to join the treaty in the future.[13] In late 1994 and early 1995, Israel made a number of statements and suggestions that indicated less than complete and indefinite rejection of the NPT. For example, after he listed Israel's concerns about the treaty, Foreign Minister Peres was asked in a December 1994 interview whether Israel "would be willing to say that we would consider it down the road." Peres replied: "Consider it, yes, once we have peace."[14]

Deputy Foreign Minister Yossi Beilin carried the same message to Cairo in January 1995. In his talks with President Mubarak's political advisor, Osama al-Baz, Beilin reportedly said that after regional peace is obtained, "one of the options we will consider would be to sign the NPT."[15] Elsewhere, Beilin was cited as saying: "Our view is that first we must have a comprehensive peace in our part of the world and only then will we have a nuclear free zone. Then, to complete [this step], one of the options is to join the [nuclear] nonproliferation treaty later on."[16]

More directly, the Israeli delegation to the December 1994 ACRS plenary meeting in Tunis floated a suggestion that the preamble to the ACRS "Statement" indicate the willingness of the region's states to consider joining the NPT as well as all other international treaties and instruments, after the establishment of comprehensive peace and the transformation of the region to a negotiated WMDFZ. The compromise formula was reportedly advocated by the co-chairman of Israel's delegation, Maj. Gen. (res.) David Ivri, and was approved by Prime Minister Itzhak Rabin.[17] While Egypt rejected the Israeli overture as "insufficient," the negotiations at Tunis signaled clearly that Israel's position with regard to the NPT was no longer an uncompromising and definite "no."

WOULD ISRAEL BECOME A DECLARED NUCLEAR POWER?

McGeorge Bundy, William Crowe, and Sidney Drell have suggested that the NPT, which now recognizes the existence of only five nuclear states, be amended to incorporate India, Pakistan, and Israel within its framework as new nuclear states.[18] (See Chapter 5.) The proposal would clearly change Israel's nuclear standing from an ambiguous to an explicit nuclear posture.

For Israel, the main question raised by this proposal is whether obtaining an official nuclear status would serve its interests. One Israeli concern would be that such a change might accelerate the proliferation of nuclear weapons in the Middle East by placing Arab governments under new domestic pressures to respond to Israel's now explicit nuclear capacity. Israel might also fear that its adoption of an overt nuclear posture would legitimize Arab efforts to acquire nuclear weapons, making it more difficult to dissuade nuclear suppliers from transferring sensitive materials and technology to Arab states. Israel would also be concerned that an official nuclear status might trigger the application of U.S. nonproliferation legislation nearly automatically, thus threatening important U.S. military, economic, and technological assistance to Israel.

So far, much of Israel's reluctance to adopt a more explicit nuclear posture seems to have been propelled by the desires not to encourage Arab nuclear efforts and to avoid a clash with U.S. nuclear nonproliferation policy. In the extremely unlikely event that the United States would regard the change proposed by Bundy, Crowe, and Drell as serving its nonproliferation objectives — and accordingly would be prepared to exempt Israel from the application of U.S. nonproliferation legislation — and that the Arab states were to drop their resistance to the legitimization of Israel's nuclear superiority, Israel might well find the option of joining the NPT as a new nuclear state attractive and might examine its long-standing opposition to the NPT.

The Nuclear-Weapons-Free Zone Proposals

The Israeli draft Nuclear-Weapon-Free Zone (NWFZ) resolution, first proposed to the UN on October 31, 1980, called upon "all states of the Middle East and non–nuclear-weapon states adjacent to the region, which are not signatories to any treaty providing for a nuclear-weapon-free zone, to convene at the earliest possible date a conference with a view to negotiating a multilateral treaty establishing a nuclear-weapon-free zone in the Middle East." (See Appendix 1.) Israel's proposal was motivated by the desire to state its position on nuclear arms control positively; since it supported the purposes of the NPT but found it impossible to join the treaty, Israel deemed it necessary to define an alternative avenue for obtaining the NPT's objectives in the Middle East.

In contrast to Egypt's NWFZ proposal, which merely requires the region's states to declare their willingness to adhere to the limitations and constraints stipulated by the statement creating the zone, the Israeli proposal emphasized the need to negotiate the terms of an NWFZ. Israel's focus on the negotiation mechanism was intentional, and primarily resulted from the conviction that Israel should not surrender the deterrent effect of its nuclear potential unless Arab acceptance of Israel's existence in the region is manifested in a willingness to negotiate with the Jewish state. Indeed, such willingness was regarded as a test of the Arab states' intentions, and the negotiation process was seen as an essential part of efforts to build mutual confidence among the region's states, without which an NWFZ could not be established.[19]

Some Israelis may originally have regarded Israel's proposal to establish an NWFZ as a bargaining chip designed to obtain Arab recognition and willingness to negotiate with Israel. That is, the Arab state's participation in direct negotiations with Israel would be the price they would have to pay for Israel to constrain its nuclear potential through the establishment of a nuclear-weapon-free zone. It is possible that some Israelis who supported the initiation of an NWFZ proposal insisted on this linkage because they assumed that the Arab states would never participate in such negotiations. Thus, the proposal may have been seen as a way for Israel to seem favorably disposed toward the establishment of an NWFZ, with very little danger that the dilemmas involved in the establishment of such a zone would ever have to be confronted.

Israel regards the establishment of a Middle East NWFZ as a substitute to its adherence to the NPT. At the very least, Israel insists that the establishment of an NWFZ in the region should precede its accession to the NPT.[20] This position is based on the view that the IAEA safeguard system is highly deficient. Consequently, Israel insists that credible and intrusive verification measures be negotiated by the region's states.[21]

Israel's preference for the establishment of a negotiated NWFZ over membership in the NPT thus seems to be based on three considerations. First, the establishment of an NWFZ negotiated directly by all relevant parties in the region — including Iraq, Iran, and Libya, which constitute the focus of Israel's nuclear proliferation concerns — requires the region's fundamental political transformation.[22] Only a basic change in its neighbors' approach will allow Israel to reconsider the role of its nuclear potential in its grand strategy.

Second, a mutually agreed NWFZ would allow the parties to adopt a verification system that is sufficiently intrusive to prevent further proliferation. Such a mechanism could avoid the two main deficiencies of current NPT and IAEA stipulations — allowing treaty members to accumulate weapons-grade material, and refraining from short notice and challenge inspections. An NWFZ could include a complete ban on the production and stockpiling of plutonium and enriched uranium and would allow a much more effective verification system.

Third, an NWFZ would allow the parties to assume the task of verification, rather than delegating the task to an international organization, in much the same manner that the United States and Russia currently monitor each other's compliance with the various arms control and confidence-building agreements concluded in recent years. Indeed, even if a third party — such as the IAEA or teams of U.S. and Russian inspectors — had a role in verification, the treaty could stipulate significant participation by inspectors from the region's states. In particular, it would be possible to ensure that challenge inspections to verify the NWFZ would include experts from the country presenting the challenge. The agreements concluded in recent years between Brazil and Argentina, which include bilateral arrangements as well as a mix of obligations assumed under the Tlatelolco NWFZ agreement, could provide useful precedents.

Officially, Israel has not addressed the relationship between the ongoing ACRS talks and its call for a negotiated NWFZ. In principle, the ACRS talks could eventually evolve into a framework for negotiating the establishment of such a zone if additional parties that have so far not taken part in the ACRS process — Syria, Iraq, Iran, and Libya — join the talks. However, Israel's view seems to be that much would have to be accomplished by the ACRS talks and the bilateral negotiations currently underway before the ACRS talks could focus on the establishment of an NWFZ in the Middle East.

Primarily, Israel seems to believe that the region's states ought first to create a political and strategic environment in which the application of an NWFZ in the region might be possible. This view is apparently shared by other regional parties. Syria, for example, is unlikely to agree to intrusive verification measures that would include the participation of Israeli inspectors without a prior resolution of its conflict with Israel. From Israel's standpoint, the various bilateral and multi-lateral negotiations currently underway must first mitigate the factors that have led it to develop a nuclear potential in the first place: the rejection of Israel by the region's states, and Israel's structural vulnerabilities in relation to its environment.

Israel's view seems to be that two strategic vulnerabilities would have to be addressed: The first is Israel's quantitative inferiority in standing conventional forces compared with those of the surrounding Arab states. Hence, effective security arrangements and confidence-building measures would have to be adopted in the framework of the bilateral and multi-lateral talks currently conducted to diminish Israel's fears of a surprise attack.

The second problem concerns the participation of a number of key states that currently remain outside the multi-lateral negotiating process. While in the conventional realm Israel could negotiate security and arms control agreements with each of its neighbors, Egypt, Jordan, Syria, and Lebanon, in the realm of nuclear weapons and ballistic missiles Israel's major concerns are the capabilities of more distant states: Iraq, Iran, Libya, and Algeria. In Israel's view, given appropriate delivery capabilities, the nuclear programs of these states pose a serious potential challenge to its security. Unless effective constraints are applied to these countries, nuclear proliferation in the Middle East would not be arrested. Thus, if an NWFZ is to be established, the participation of these states would have to be assured.

While the second of these conditions may seem self-evident, the first — linking the establishment of an NWFZ to the application of arms control and confidence building in the conventional realm — could be interpreted as a sign of reduced Israeli commitment to the establishment of such a zone. Paradoxically, such a linkage now arises from an otherwise positive development in the region's strategic environment: namely, the Madrid bilateral negotiating process designed to resolve the Arab-Israeli dispute. When Israel first proposed the establishment of an NWFZ, a comprehensive Middle East peace process involving the surrounding Arab states was considered highly unlikely. This process is now a reality, but understandably the focus of Arab demands in these negotiations is that Israel withdraw from all territories it has controlled since the 1967 War. If negotiations to establish a Middle East NWFZ were launched now, Israel would be asked to give up simultaneously both the deterrent effect of its nuclear potential and the defensive advantage of its control of the West Bank and the Golan Heights. It is extremely difficult to see how Israel could risk making such far-reaching concessions in both realms at once.

Nevertheless, by late 1992, following complex internal negotiations, the Israeli government adopted the central elements of the Mubarak Initiative calling for the transformation of the Middle East to a WMDFZ. This was done in a draft document defining Israel's approach to the goals of arms control in the Middle East. The essence of the approach was made public in a speech delivered by Foreign Minister Shimon Peres on January 13, 1993, to the international conference convened in Paris to sign the Chemical Weapons Convention (see Appendix 11). While it adopted the essence of the Mubarak Initiative, Israel indicated that the establishment of a WMDFZ in the Middle East requires the prior establishment of peace and the application of mutual verification measures.[23] Indeed, it was clear that the two conditions are closely related. For example, Israeli and Syrian inspectors are unlikely to be allowed to examine sensitive sites in each other's territory unless there is a stable contractual peace between the two countries.

Israel thus stressed an evolutionary approach, in which the materialization of the ultimate objectives is conditional upon the prior establishment of contractual peace and reconciliation among all the region's states. Israel's formulation differed from the Mubarak Initiative in two additional respects: first, it included ballistic missiles in the definition of mass destruction weapons; second, it stressed the importance of reducing the arsenals of conventional weapons in the region.

Israel's commitment to the eventual transformation of the Middle East to a WMDFZ was also reflected in the text of the agreed Israeli-Jordanian negotiations agenda concluded in Washington in September 1993. In their agenda, Israel and the Hashemite Kingdom of Jordan agreed to undertake a "mutual commitment, as a matter of priority and as soon as possible, to work towards a Middle East free from weapons of mass destruction — conventional and unconventional weapons." The agenda also states that "this goal is to be achieved in the context of a comprehensive, lasting and stable peace characterized by the renunciation of the use of force, reconciliation and openness." The formulation represented Jordan's willingness to meet Israeli concerns by agreeing to include conventional weapons within the definition of weapons of mass destruction. Similar language was inserted in the October 1994 Israel-Jordan Peace Agreement.

Another manifestation of Israel's endorsement of the transformation of the Middle East into a WMDFZ is found in the draft "Statement on Arms Control and Regional Security" discussed at the October 1994 ACRS conceptual basket meeting in Paris and at the December 1994 plenary meeting in Tunis. On those occasions, Israel proposed that the statement include a call for "establishing the Middle East as a mutually verifiable zone free of nuclear, chemical, biological weapons and ballistic missiles in view of their high destructive capacity and their potential to promote instability in the region."

Banning the Production of Fissile Material

In December 1993 Israel joined the consensus at the UN General Assembly that adopted Resolution 48/75, which stipulates that negotiations of an international treaty banning the production of fissile material shall be launched.[24] Until early 1996, however, Israel was not a member of the Conference on Disarmament that was authorized to negotiate the proposed treaty. Its participation, and that of twenty-one other states, was blocked by Washington's unwillingness to include Iraq among the states eligible for CD membership. Consequently, Israel had no formal standing in the CD's deliberations that led to the adoption of a "mandate" for negotiating the fissile material production ban treaty.

During the early 1990s, Israel refrained from official reactions to the proposals to cap the production of weapons-grade plutonium and enriched uranium contained in the May 1991 and July 1992 initiatives of President Bush and in President Clinton's September 1993 initiative. Hence, it is difficult to ascertain what position Israel may adopt once serious negotiations of a production ban treaty begin;

rather, its likely position must be inferred from Israel's general approach to nuclear arms control.

As long as Israel continues to perceive an imperative to maintain its nuclear potential and adhere to its ambiguous nuclear policy, these requirements will largely determine its views on the proposed treaty. Thus, Israel would have to be assured that the treaty would not lead to an erosion of its nuclear potential and that the text and associated verification mechanisms will not undermine Israel's ambiguous posture by imposing complete transparency on all past, present, and future nuclear activities by signatories.

The Bush "freeze" proposals (see Chapter 5), which made no reference to states' past nuclear activities, were designed to make it possible for Israel, India, and Pakistan to join the treaty. The Bush proposals contrast sharply with the position now adopted by Egypt, which insists that the production ban treaty impose limitations on existing stockpiles. They also contrast with the proposals advanced by a number of Egyptian scholars and former officials (see Chapter 7), which would require Israel to provide an account of its past activities and existing inventories of weapons-grade material.

Not surprisingly, some Israeli observers fear that the quest for nuclear transparency manifested in the Egyptian capping proposals might be designed merely to publicize Israel's nuclear potential, in the hope that the resulting international pressure might compel Israel to sign the NPT. In this view, the suggested freeze might prove merely a short transition to Israel's nuclear disarmament. Thus, the Bush initiatives, which avoid any erosion of the ambiguity surrounding a state's past nuclear activities, might prove a more realistic avenue for Israel than Egypt's official and unofficial approaches to the problem.

More broadly, Israel's view of a prospective fissile material production ban treaty is likely to be affected by three competing considerations. First, Israel's strategic interests would be served by a treaty freezing the present distribution of nuclear capabilities in the region. Israel is likely to examine carefully — but with a positive predisposition — whether the proposed treaty is likely to achieve this objective.

Second, Israel would probably also insist that all its neighbors — including Iraq and Iran — join the convention, and that the treaty be accompanied by intrusive verification measures to insure that all the region's signatories comply with a total ban on the production of fissile material. Clearly, Israel is also likely to prefer that the verification procedures include mutual inspections; however, it may accept a more flexible approach — similar to that adopted to insure compliance with the CWC — allowing the participation of its nationals in an international but intrusive inspection mechanism.

Above all, Israel would need to ascertain that the proposed treaty would not erode its nuclear option. Thus it would need to be assured that the proposed ban would apply only to present and future activities and that Israel's past activities — whatever their nature — would not be affected. This would insure that Israeli deterrence would remain intact until the political and strategic conditions in the region might allow progress beyond the capping of nuclear programs in the Middle East.

The Comprehensive Test Ban Treaty

Since 1994, Israel has taken an active role in the CTBT negotiations taking place in the framework of the Conference on Disarmament (CD) in Geneva. In early August 1996, Israel's new prime minister, Benjamin Netanyahu, approved the recommendation submitted by the ministries of defense and foreign affairs, as well by the Israeli Atomic Energy Commission, that Israel sign and ratify the CTBT.[25] On September 25, 1996, Israel signed the treaty.[26]

Israel's decision to sign the CTBT seems to be based on a number of considerations: first, the treaty allows Israel to express its general support for the purposes of the global nuclear nonproliferation regime. Second, it provides an opportunity for Israel to meet a priority of U.S. nuclear nonproliferation policy. Third, the treaty provisions are not seen as jeopardizing the ambiguity surrounding Israel's nuclear policy.

In this context an important Israeli concern was that the measures adopted to verify compliance with the CTBT might be abused in an effort to expose Israel's activities in the nuclear realm. It was particularly concerned that Arab states might demand on-site inspections of its Dimona nuclear complex and that the treaty's overflight provisions would allow the conduct of such flights over Dimona.[27]

While the possibility that such abuse may occur was not entirely eliminated during the long negotiations of the treaty, this danger was reduced through the adoption of enhanced "managed access" provisions that limit the obligations of a State Party "to provide access within the inspection area for the sole purpose of determining facts relevant to the purposes of the inspection."[28] Also important are the stipulations allowing the CTBTO Executive Council to punish a state party for demanding the conduct of an on-site inspection if such demand is later judged to have been "frivolous or abusive."[29]

Conclusions

Israel is likely to remain wary of the prospects for nuclear arms control in the Middle East. Generally, it is increasingly worried about the evolution of nuclear programs in remote states — Iraq, Iran, and to a lesser extent Libya and Algeria. Hence Israel will be reluctant to endorse any arms control regime that does not incorporate all states that comprise the focus of its proliferation concerns. It will also refrain from joining any regime that are not accompanied by intrusive verification measures — including reciprocal on-site inspections.

Israel would prefer the establishment of an NWFZ over the NPT because a region-based regime would allow the adoption of effective verification measures that go far beyond existing IAEA safeguards. Similarly, its approach to the proposed treaty banning the production of fissile material will also be determined by these twin considerations: whether all the region's states will join the treaty and whether the treaty will be accompanied by robust verification measures.

More broadly, Israel's approach to nuclear arms control will be affected by the extent to which it perceives that its original motivations to develop a nuclear option have been addressed — primarily that its continued existence is assured. Israel must gain confidence that its Arab neighbors have reconciled themselves to its permanence in the Middle East. Israel would also wish to ascertain that Arab capabilities to threaten its security and survival in the conventional realm — primarily the Arabs' capacity to translate their overall quantitative superiority to an ability to field and employ large standing conventional forces — have been adequately checked. Israel's view seems to be that nuclear arms control cannot be applied in the Middle East except in the context of a comprehensive peace that resolves the region's political disputes, and the implementation of a comprehensive arms control and confidence-building regime that will insure that the basic strategic asymmetries in the region are adequately and simultaneously addressed.

These priorities and predispositions have been reflected in Israel's approach to the ACRS talks. In these talks, Israel has emphasized political accommodation and the need to apply an evolutionary confidence-building approach. While Egypt stressed the need to implement nuclear disarmament, Israel emphasized the importance of conflict resolution and confidence building.[30] It also stressed the profound mistrust prevailing in the region and the importance of addressing the asymmetries of conventional force structures in the region.[31] Since all Middle East wars have been waged with conventional weapons at a considerable price in human lives and economic and social resources, Israel has stressed that conventional arms should also be considered weapons of mass destruction.

Israel's approach also implies that sensitive issues involving the various parties' central strategic systems should be addressed only after the region's states develop some measure of self-confidence and mutual trust.[32] Accordingly, Israel has proposed a wide range of regional confidence-building measures to prevent misperceptions and unintended escalation, and to reduce mutual fears of surprise attack.[33] Behind this approach is Israel's conviction that during the long and uncertain transition to reconciliation based on contractual peace, and until the stability of peace in the Middle East is assured, Israel should continue to maintain a credible deterrent.

In late 1995, the linkage between peace and nuclear arms control was underscored by Israel's then prime minister, Shimon Peres. In a conversation with newspaper editors, Peres reportedly said: "Give me peace and I will give up nuclear weapons."[34] While this statement was widely interpreted as signaling a change in Israel's nuclear policy, in fact it merely reflected a long-standing conviction that strategic deterrence must be maintained as long as Israel's security is challenged. Once peace is established and its stability is tested over time, nuclear disarmament would be both possible and desirable.

NOTES

1. Moti Basok, "Peres: 'Nuclear fog: part of our security concept'," *Davar* (Israel), January 27, 1995. Yuval Ne'eman, a former head of Israel's Atomic Energy Commission and former minister of science, has argued more explicitly that "Israel should not agree to any safeguards and controls which would deprive it of an option which may prove one day — if the Arabs would obtain nuclear weapons — essential for our continued survival." See Yuval Ne'eman, "1993: the balance of nuclear threats," *Ma'ariv* (Israel), January 4, 1993.

2. "Israel is not on Asad's Agenda," *Jerusalem Post*, International, December 31, 1994.

3. Aluf Ben, "Peres told Perry: 'As long as the Iranians are afraid of us, this is our best deterrent'," *Ha'aretz*, January 9, 1995.

4. Nitzan Hurewitz, "French press agencies: Peres met in Paris with Syrian personality," *Ha'aretz*, January 12, 1995.

5. In 1986, in a rare reference to this issue by an Israeli senior official, Israel's minister of economics, Gad Ya'acobi, said that Israel refrains from signing the NPT because its security is threatened. See Haim Handworker, "Nuclear energy will be too costly during the next decade, the minister of economics thinks," *Ha'aretz*, May 4, 1986.

6. Michal Goldberg, "Weizmann to Egyptian reporters: 'Israel will not sign the NPT'," *Yediot Aharonot* (Israel), December 21, 1994.

7. Doug Struck, "Israel continues to refuse to sign anti-proliferation treaty," *Baltimore Sun*, January 12, 1995. In December 1995, Peres returned to this theme: "Israel said that it would not be the first to introduce nuclear weapons into the Middle East. At the moment, there is only suspicion that Israel possesses nuclear weapons. Since nuclear weapons provide deterrence, why should I say that we do not possess such weapons?" See "Peres offers Arabs: Nuclear [weapons] in exchange for peace," *Yediot Aharonot*, December 12, 1995.

8. In the same interview Peres also said: "The [Egyptians] have no reason to approach us regarding the nuclear issue. A peace agreement was signed between Egypt and Israel when the distance between Egypt and Dimona was the same as it is today and the degree of transparency surrounding Dimona was the same as it is today. The Arabs adopted the slogan of 'territories for peace.' We gave all the territory; we can ask whether we received all the peace. But we cannot be presented with a new price [for peace] every time. They said: 'all right, we know that as long as there is a threat of war you do not wish to give up your ambiguity. But what will you do after [the threat of war is removed]?' We said: 'After [the threat of war is removed] we will be prepared [to give up ambiguity]'." See Aluf Ben, "Gaza is a compact entity" (interview with Foreign Minister Shimon Peres), *Ha'aretz*, April 20, 1995.

9. In late 1994, this was reported to be the view of Israel's Prime Minister Rabin. See Aluf Ben, "U.S. will not press Israel to join NPT," *Ha'aretz*, November 15, 1994. See also FBIS-NES-94-222, November 17, 1994, p. 39.

10. In 1991, Peres said: "The treaty proved itself as ineffective. Iraq signed the treaty, so what? The treaty became just a piece of paper. We should seek more serious agreements which will maintain balance and will prevent such weapons from falling into the hands of insane [individuals]." "To change the military doctrine," *Bemachane* (Israel), October 30, 1991. Similarly, in December 1994 President Ezer Weizmann told Egyptian reporters: "Iraq was a signatory to the treaty and [yet] Israel was compelled to destroy their reactor." Goldberg, "Weizmann to Egyptian reporters: 'We will not sign the NPT'."

11. See Shalheveth Freier, "A Nuclear-Weapon-Free Zone (NWFZ) in the Middle East and its Ambience," unpublished paper, July 14, 1993, p. 1.

12. Ibid., p. 3.

13. See "A spat in the nuclear family," *U.S. News and World Report*, January 9, 1995.

14. "Israel is not on Asad's Agenda."

15. Aluf Ben, "Beilin to al-Baz: After the establishment of regional peace — we will consider signing the NPT," *Ha'aretz*, January 23, 1995.

16. Samiah Nakhoul, "Israel's nuclear stand may fuel tension — Egypt," Reuters (Cairo), January 22, 1995.

17. Aluf Ben, "Israel declared its willingness to consider joining nuclear arms control treaties in the future," *Ha'aretz*, December 27, 1994.

18. McGeorge Bundy, William J. Crowe, Jr., and Sidney Drell, *Reducing Nuclear Danger: The Road Away from the Brink* (New York: Council on Foreign Relations Book, 1993), pp. 67–72.

19. See Freier, "A Nuclear-Weapon-Free Zone (NWFZ) in the Middle East and its Ambience," pp. 3, 6.

20. Ibid., p. 8.

21. Ibid., p. 3.

22. Ibid., p. 7.

23. David Makovsky, "Peres to seek mutual verification of arms Ban with Arabs," *Jerusalem Post*, January 13, 1993; Nitzan Hurewitz, "Peres proposes to the Arab states to establish a WMD-free zone in the Middle East," *Ha'aretz*, January 14, 1993; and Aluf Ben, "Cornerstone for building trust," *Ha'aretz*, January 26, 1993. On the imperative of establishing peace in the Middle East before an NWFZ can be implemented, see Freier, "A Nuclear-Weapon-Free Zone (NWFZ) in the Middle East and its Ambience," p. 7.

24. UN General Assembly Resolution 48/75 was adopted without a vote on December 16, 1993. The draft resolution was approved by the UN First Committee in early November. See UN General Assembly, 48th session, First Committee, Agenda item 71(c), Document A/C.1/48/L.44, November 4, 1993.

25. Aluf Ben, "Israel accepts test ban treaty draft," *Ha'aretz*, July 29, 1996.

26. "Israel signs nuclear test ban treaty," *Baltimore Sun*, September 26, 1996.

27. Ibid. See also Rebecca Johnson, "CTB Negotiations — Geneva Update No. 29," *Disarmament Diplomacy*, No. 6 (June 1996), p. 22.

28. *Trust and Verify*, No. 67 (July 1996), p. 2.

29. Johnson, "CTB Negotiations — Geneva Update," p. 22.

30. Aluf Ben, "Agreement in the arms control talks on establishing regional communication center for the Middle East," *Ha'aretz*, November 9, 1993.

31. See Freier, "A Nuclear-Weapon-Free Zone (NWFZ) in the Middle East and its Ambience," p. 7.

32. Aluf Ben, "Jerusalem's priorities in demilitarizing the Middle East: Nuclear weapons last," *Ha'aretz*, November 29, 1993. It is interesting that a year before the ACRS talks were launched, Nabil Fahmy, the head of Egypt's delegation to these talks, adhered to a position quite similar to Israel's priorities. He wrote: "The conflicts in the Middle East are highly political, and over the years have generated a heightened degree of suspicion among the states of the region. As long as these conflicts remain unresolved, the already intricate and complex process of negotiating disarmament agreements between adversaries, will be encumbered with a burden of enmity, suspicion and bad faith, making a traditional independent weapons-system-disarmament approach unworkable." See Nabil Fahmy, "Controlling Weapons of Mass Destruction in the Middle East," *American-Arab Affairs*, No. 35 (Winter 1990–91), p. 129.

33. See Freier, "A Nuclear-Weapon-Free Zone (NWFZ) in the Middle East and its Ambience," p. 2.

34. In the same conversation, Peres also said: "If there will be peace, we would be able to give up nuclear weapons in the entire Middle East." See "Peres offers Arabs: Nuclear [weapons] in exchange for peace"; Gideon Alon, "Peres: 'If there will be peace, we can give up the nuclear option'." *Ha'aretz*, December 24, 1995. Another report cited Peres as having said: "If there will be regional peace, I think we can free the Middle East from nuclear weapons." Hanna Kim, "In the end of days," *Ha'aretz*, December 29, 1995; see also Amir Oren, "The dance of chairs," *Ha'aretz*, December 29, 1995.

Chapter 9

Is Linkage to Conventional Arms Control Feasible?

This chapter explores the utility of linking nuclear arms control with conventional arms control in the Middle East, examining Arab and Israeli perceptions of one another's conventional capabilities and the extent to which they view these capabilities as threatening. The problems inherent in any effort to control the proliferation of conventional weapons and force structures in the Middle East are detailed. [1]

First, however, linkage of nuclear arms control with conventional arms control is contrasted with the linkage between nuclear weapons control and the control of chemical and biological weapons. In the Middle East, the links among the needs to control nuclear, chemical, and biological weapons in the region seem almost self-evident. Despite the very different physical properties of these three weapons, Israel and key Arab states have come to regard them all as "strategic." Moreover, the linkage among these weapons has been accepted by all the parties to the ACRS talks; the texts proposed for the ACRS "Statement on Arms Control and Regional Security" by Egypt and Israel both contained similar commitments to transforming the region into a zone free of all weapons of mass destruction (WMDFZ).

These formulas reaffirmed the April 1990 proposal by Egypt's President Mubarak to create a WMDFZ in the Middle East. [2] They also confirmed the commitments made by Israel and Jordan, in a speech delivered by Foreign Minister Peres in January 1993 and in the October 1994 Israel-Jordan peace treaty, to the eventual establishment of such a zone. All of these commitments and proposals linked nuclear, chemical, and biological arms. (See Chapters 7 and 8.)

More important, the close connection between the three types of unconventional weapons is dictated by the strategic imperatives of Israel and the Arab states. In Israel, chemical and biological weapons have come to be regarded in near-nuclear terms. Given its small and dense population, Israel sees itself as especially vulnerable to a high level of fatalities if attacked by such weapons. Indeed, Israelis see themselves as more vulnerable than any other nation in the region to the possible use of weapons of mass destruction; this perception is not only due to Israel's relative size and the density of its population, but also because a substantial part of its population is composed of first and second-generation victims of the Holocaust. The fact that Nazi Germany used gas to exterminate millions of Jews during the Second World War has created a unique Israeli sensitivity to the possible use of chemical weapons against its larger cities. This sensitivity was clearly evident during the 1990–91 Gulf War, when Iraqi attacks using chemical warheads against Israeli cities were feared.

Some Israelis also see Arab leaders as less inhibited by moral principles from using unconventional weapons. Israelis cite Egypt's use of chemical weapons during the Yemen War of the mid-1960s and Iraq's use of such weapons during the later stages of the 1980–88 Iraq-Iran War as evidence.[3] Consequently, as long as its neighbors continue to possess chemical and biological weapons, Israel is unlikely to accept any significant erosion of its capacity to deter their use.

The linkage between nuclear nonproliferation and the disarmament of other unconventional arms seems to be equally espoused by some of the Arab states. The late 1992 decision of the Arab League not to sign the Chemical Weapons Convention (CWC) until Israel joins the Nuclear Non-Proliferation Treaty (NPT) provides clear evidence of this linkage. Some Arab observers argue that giving up the option of possessing chemical arms while Israel remains outside the global nuclear nonproliferation regime would expose the Arab states to an Israeli monopoly in "strategic weapons." Other Arab officials stress that if the Arab states are to accept the limitations stipulated by the CWC, Israel should reciprocate by accepting the constraints entailed by the NPT, or the establishment of a Middle East nuclear-weapon-free zone (NWFZ) or weapons of mass destruction–free zone (WMDFZ).

CONVENTIONAL/NUCLEAR LINKAGE

While efforts to arrest the spread of nuclear weapons in the region cannot be separated from the need to address the proliferation of chemical and biological arms, however, the logic that links nuclear and conventional arms control in the Middle East appears much weaker. In the ACRS talks, Israel has stressed the need to discuss conventional arms, and it seems to have adopted the position that the proliferation of conventional weapons should be arrested and the size of the standing conventional forces should be reduced before the region takes on the task of nuclear disarmament. Israelis see themselves as vulnerable to the Arab states' quantitative advantage in conventional weapons and argue that it is with these weapons that all Middle East wars have been waged. Israel is therefore reluctant to accept nuclear arms control measures that might reduce its existential deterrent before the dangers it perceives in the conventional realm are fully addressed. This linkage between conventional and nuclear arms control is embedded in Israel's original rationale for developing a nuclear option as a hedge against the vast preponderance of Arab conventional forces. However, by the mid-1990s this linkage appears increasingly problematic: the quality of Israel's conventional capabilities seems as threatening to some Arab states as the size of Arab conventional forces are to Israel. Indeed, Israel and its neighbors have equally long lists of concerns regarding one another's conventional weapons, military doctrines, and force structures. Hence they are likely to discover that neither would lose more than the other from separating nuclear nonproliferation and conventional arms control.

Israeli Perceptions of the Regional Environment

Israel's long-standing threat perceptions stem from the many ways in which it is quantitatively inferior to the surrounding Arab states. Its small territory means that it has no strategic depth. Its small population means that it can only field small standing forces. The limits on its natural and financial resources mean that its Arab neighbors have superior access to the commercial global arms markets. The greater number of Arab states wield a greater combined influence in international forums.

The absence of strategic depth makes many Israelis feel enormously vulnerable. It primarily implies an inability to trade space for time in slowing a surprise attack. With some 80 percent of its population and industrial infrastructure concentrated in a strip of land only 60 miles long and in some places only 15 miles wide, Israel regards itself as vulnerable to an Arab assault centered on its narrow pre-1967 territory, which could destroy its central strategic assets with a single thrust. Accordingly, Israelis viewed Arab moves and preparations on the eve of the 1967 War as representing an existential threat. Hence, Israelis perceive an imperative to avoid waging war on their own territory.

The vast asymmetry in the size of populations has compelled Israel to place the majority of its military forces in reserves rather than active forces. Thus there is a dramatic imbalance in standing forces between Israel and the Arab states. The Syrian and Egyptian standing forces are seen as vastly larger than the IDF until all its reserves are mobilized. Israelis view the success of the Egyptian and Syrian armed forces during the opening phases of the 1973 war as illustrating the risks. Israel feels extremely vulnerable to surprise attack because it fears that attacking Arab forces would be able to exploit such an opportunity and fortify their initial gains, making the IDF's efforts to overcome these gains very costly.

More generally, many Israelis are concerned that the dramatic quantitative advantage of the Arab states' regular conventional forces may allow them to overcome Israel's qualitative edge or at least to extract heavy costs from the IDF in time of war.[4] In order to withstand the large Arab conventional forces, Israel would have to mobilize a very large part of its population to active reserve service. Yet extended mobilization for war results in considerable economic dislocations, perhaps even the complete paralysis of Israel's industry and trade. Thus, Israel also sees itself as very vulnerable to the effects of a protracted general war.

The asymmetry in populations also causes Israel to regard itself as much more sensitive to casualties than its Arab neighbors. In turn, this sensitivity causes it to view itself as threatened by any form of warfare that involves a high toll in human lives — from attrition at the front, to the possible use of ballistic missiles and chemical or biological weapons against its rear. Thus, in addition to fearing defeat, Israel also fears any victory won at a very high cost.

In addition, the tight-knit nature of Israel's very small population implies that substantial social and psychological costs are attached to each casualty. In wartime, most Israeli citizens will know an extended family member, close friend, or neighbor who has died or was seriously injured as a result of the war. This was particularly evident in the immediate aftermath of the 1973 War. Israel believes that larger populations provide Arab leaders with the possibility to pursue policies that may require considerable human sacrifice, but most Israeli leaders do not see themselves as enjoying such flexibility.

The superior natural and financial resources of some of the Arab states are seen by Israel as providing them nearly unlimited access to the world's arms markets. In the past, Israel believed that Iraq, Saudi Arabia, and Libya were acquiring arms at a rate that surpassed their capacity to absorb the weapons. Moreover, the volume of commercial interactions taking place between the region's states and western Europe were seen as permitting these states to overcome any resistance to their quest for advanced arms and sensitive technologies.

As a consequence of the basic strategic asymmetries in the Middle East, Israelis perceive a number of specific threats in the realm of conventional warfare. First, Israel's vulnerability to surprise attack is particularly acute on the Golan Heights, where a large part of Syria's armed forces is positioned very close to the front lines. Syria's forces could begin hostilities with relatively little prior movement or preparations that could be detected and interpreted in time.

Second, Israel is worried about the size of Egypt's armed forces and their continued improvement.[5] Egypt has made enormous defense expenditures despite its mounting economic problems. Because the 1979 Egypt-Israel peace agreement leaves only Libya and Sudan, which have very marginal military power, capable of posing threats to Egypt, some Israelis interpret the ongoing Egyptian buildup as an indication that Cairo still regards Israel as a potential adversary and that Egypt might one day join or lead a new Arab war coalition.

Third, Israelis fear that cooperation among a number of Arab states — even if confined to the opening stages of the war — might produce a preponderant coalition. While in the past such cooperation tended to break down soon after the outbreak of hostilities, Israel fears that a well-coordinated and well-rehearsed attack — modeled on the opening phases of the 1973 war — could achieve substantial initial gains. Arab states would be able to devote all their forces to one adversary, while Israel would have to combat a number of Arab states simultaneously.[6]

A related Israeli fear is that Arab expeditionary forces would be sent to support the capabilities of one of Israel's more immediate neighbors. This was experienced during the 1948, 1967, and 1973 wars, when Iraqi forces supported Syria and Jordan.[7]

Finally, as a consequence of Israel's extreme sensitivity to costs, Israelis fear possible efforts to exploit the Arabs' quantitative advantage by engaging Israel in static attrition warfare. For this and other reasons, some Israelis are not content with a favorable balance of power that promises ultimate triumph; instead, they emphasize the importance of maintaining a robust deterrent for effective war prevention. On more than one occasion, the resulting concern to avoid any possible loss of deterrence credibility has created a perceived imperative to avoid yielding ground. This outlook has conditioned much of the IDF's behavior throughout Israel's history — from the struggle over the demilitarized zones in the 1950s to the "forward defense" exercised on the Golan Heights and along the Suez Canal after the 1967 war.

Arab Perceptions of the Israeli Conventional Threat

Israel's concerns in the conventional realm are matched by a long list of Arab worries about Israel's perceived conventional capabilities.[8] Most of these worries stem from the Arab states' view that Israel enjoys an overall scientific-technological superiority. Arab observers tend to view the Israeli society as immersed in a general "culture of science and industry," allowing it complete control of specific cutting-edge technologies. This perception explains the uneasiness expressed in various Arab quarters regarding the destruction of Iraq's military-industrial infrastructure during and after the 1991 war. In contrast, Israel is seen as being permitted to develop a sophisticated military industry, producing state-of-the-art weapon platforms and sophisticated systems and sub-systems.

Arab observers have paid particular attention to the fact that Israel's indigenous arms production has become so advanced as to allow the export of some of its products to NATO countries. For example, Israel has sold remotely piloted vehicles (RPVs) to U.S. armed services. Israel was also the only Middle East state invited by the United States to take part in a cutting-edge research and development program — the Strategic Defense Initiative (SDI).[9] The product of Israel's involvement in the program — the development of the "Arrow"

Anti-Tactical Ballistic Missile (ATBM) system — is a particular focus of Arab concern. By contrast, Arab arms industries are far less sophisticated, making the Arab states entirely dependent on external suppliers for all essential components of their force structures.

In recent years, Arab observers have often expressed their apprehension about Israel's projection of its capabilities into space. In particular, Egyptian observers noted their concern about Israel's activities in what they regard as "the fourth dimension of warfare." In their view, this involves not only Israel's role in the SDI program, but also its indigenous development of intelligence and communication satellites.

SPECIFIC THREATS PERCEIVED BY ARABS

These general Arab perceptions are reflected in specific concerns regarding Israel's conventional capabilities. First, Israel is seen as enjoying an extremely potent conventional military force. Arab observers point out that its potency has been demonstrated repeatedly in the wars of 1948, 1956, and 1967, as well as during the 1973 War, notwithstanding the gains made by Egyptian and Syrian armed forces during the opening stages of the latter engagement.

Second, some Arab officials dismiss the notion that Israel suffers a quantitative inferiority. They argue that Israel's military forces are larger than any of the Arab armed forces; Israel's forces appear small only when compared with the combined strength of all key Arab states. These officials claim that wall-to-wall Arab cooperation never existed and even smaller combinations of Arab states never managed to cooperate for more than a few days. They describe the willingness of Arab states to cooperate as "pathetic."

These officials emphasize that in the few instances when Arab states cooperated in preparing and launching a joint attack against Israel, cooperation broke down soon after the opening stages of the campaign, with each Arab state pursuing its narrow national interests. In their eyes, the records of the 1948 and 1973 wars and the pre-1967 Arab coalition illustrate that each member of the Arab "coalition" conducted its affairs without regard to the fate of other members, allowing Israel to exploit their disunity.[10] Hence, they regard estimates of the over all Arab-Israeli military balance as irrelevant.

Third, Arab observers view Israel as enjoying a clear qualitative edge over all Arab force structures: its highly potent military force, which is equipped with state-of-the-art weapons, employs imaginative tactics, demonstrates high mobility, and is capable of effective combat management. Its well-trained personnel are of high quality, and possess expertise and dedication. In particular, Arab observers regard Israel as equipped with force multipliers such as highly sophisticated command, control, communication, and intelligence systems. In their eyes, Israel deploys and employs the most advanced weapon systems available, so that even when Arab states purchase platforms that are as advanced as those possessed by Israel, Israel is seen as capable of further upgrading its platforms with new and improved subsystems, often produced endogenously. Together, these advantages are seen by Arabs as allowing Israel to extract the maximum output from its military machine.

Fourth, Arab observers believe that Israel has a superior capacity to mobilize reserve forces. Some estimate that Israel can mobilize its entire order-of-battle within 72 hours; in contrast, most Arab armies require up to two weeks to call up their reserves. These observers explain that the asymmetry is caused by the imperfect discipline of Arab publics and the inferior internal communication and transportation systems of the Arab states.

Fifth, Arab observers and officials express concern about Israel's offensive strategy and military doctrine. A number of Arab observers appreciate that the defensive purposes and the circumstances that motivate this strategy and doctrine (Israel's territorial and demographic vulnerability) create for Israel the imperative to transfer the battle to the adversary's territory and to bring the war to an early conclusion, but nonetheless they regard the doctrine and the force structure it necessitates as an enduring threat.

Concern is also expressed that an offensive doctrine and force structure designed for defensive purposes will eventually serve offensive designs as well. Israel's 1982 invasion of Lebanon is often cited as evidence of this possibility. Since the war was presented as designed to secure the defense of Israel's north from Palestinian terrorism, the IDF's prolonged and deep involvement in Lebanon — during which Israel found itself controlling a large civilian population — is seen by Arab observers as proving that Israel's use of the term "defense" may be applied in ways that can threaten the Arab states' national security.

A related facet of this threat involves Arab alarm about the IDF's emphasis on preemptive action. Arabs suspect that the preemptive aspect of Israel's military doctrine is simply another dimension of the defensive ethos that coats Israeli aggression. Thus, when in early 1989 the IDF Chief of Staff, Lt. General Dan Shomron, stated his preference for preemptive action, this was interpreted in the Arab world as an indication that Israel harbored offensive designs.[11]

Sixth, Arab observers and officials emphasize that Israel enjoys the advantage of internal lines, which allows the IDF to attack a number of Arab states serially by shifting emphasis rapidly from front to front. The advantage of internal lines is seen as complemented by the high mobility of the IDF's ground forces, which are based on armor, self-propelled artillery, and an entirely mechanized and heliborne infantry force.

Seventh, the superiority of the Israeli Air Force (IAF) is seen as particularly important — allowing the IDF to shift its "flying artillery" from one theater of operations to another within minutes. More generally, the complete command of the skies exercised by the IAF is, for Arab observers, the most salient manifestation of Israel's overall qualitative edge in the conventional realm. Arabs see this command in the IAF's ability to fly unhindered anytime and anywhere in the Arab world, in contrast to the inability of Arab airforces to penetrate Israel's airspace, as well as in the one-sided outcome of almost all air-to-air encounters between the IAF and the air forces of the Arab states.[12]

This concern about Israel's superiority in the air explains why Arabs feel particularly threatened by the development of the Arrow Anti-Tactical Ballistic Missiles. Arab observers stress that Arab states began to acquire ballistic missiles beginning in the early 1970s solely to offset Israel's absolute air superiority and the inability of Arab air forces to penetrate Israel's airspace. These observers argue that in any case, the ballistic missiles acquired by Arab countries provide only partial compensation for Israel's superior air power and that Israel's acquisition of the Arrow will negate even this partial response, and will restore Israel's first-strike capacity: its ability to employ its air force unconstrained by fear of Arab retaliation.

Finally, Arab states seem particularly alarmed by the IDF's ability to operate at great distances. This capability has been demonstrated repeatedly: in a number of operations in Beirut in the early 1970s; the 1976 rescue operation at Entebbe; the 1981 bombing of the Osiraq nuclear reactor near Baghdad; the October 1985 raid on terrorist headquarters and training bases in Tunisia; the April 1988 delivery and extraction of the force that assassinated PLO leader Abu Jihad in Tunisia; and in "Operation Exodus," which brought thousands of Ethiopian Jews from Addis Ababa to Israel in April 1991.

Thus, the Arab states seem threatened by many features of what they view as Israel's robust conventional capabilities. If the parties ever reach the point of negotiating conventional arms reductions, Arab states will surely present a long list of concerns for these negotiations to address.

Obstacles to Conventional Arms Control

Efforts to link nuclear and conventional arms control are bound to prove futile not only because Israel and the Arab states have equally long lists of concerns in the conventional realm, but also because the task of arresting proliferation and reducing the arsenals of conventional weapons in the Middle East is nearly intractable. First, the conventional capabilities and military doctrines of the region's states are very dissimilar. While the Arab states enjoy an enormous quantitative superiority, particularly in the size of their regular forces, Israel enjoys an impressive qualitative edge in weapon systems, force multipliers, and the conduct of military operations. While some Arab states have very large standing forces, most of Israel's military forces are in reserves, thus making the state vulnerable to surprise attack. While some Arab states possess superior financial resources, allowing them to import large quantities of military hardware, Israel is far more able to produce arms endogenously. While a number of Arab states have a preponderance of surface-to-surface missiles, the Israeli Air Force enjoys complete command of the skies. These vast differences would make it very difficult to compare such forces and capabilities to create criteria for force reductions.[13]

Second, these asymmetries would lead the region's states to condition each concession in any realm in which they possess an advantage on concessions by their adversaries in their own realms of strength. This introduces the problem of "linkages" within the conventional realm; restraints or reductions in each category of weapons become hostage to progress achieved in all other areas.

Third, while the existence of NATO and the Warsaw Pact made the successful negotiations of the CFE Treaty possible, such neat divisions do not exist in the Middle East. The two-bloc division of Europe was exceedingly important; it provided a single point of reference for each of the member states. Each state was a part of one of the blocs and the combined strength of each bloc could be compared with the total strength of the other. By contrast, the Arab states reject any suggestion that they belong to a bloc and insist that the strength of each state should be compared with Israel's power separately. Even more important, each of Israel's neighbors has more than one context within which its military power must be considered. For example, Egypt feels threatened by potential developments in Sudan and Libya; Jordan's relations with Syria led to open hostilities in the early 1970s and its relations with Saudi Arabia are tense; and Syria feels threatened by Turkey, a NATO member equipped with a robust military force. Syria's relations with Iraq and Jordan have also been tense, and its preoccupation in Lebanon continues to place demands on its armed forces. Saudi Arabia is simultaneously threatened by Iraq and Iran, as well as by developments in Yemen. These multiple threats allow the Arab states to argue that they cannot reduce their forces relative to those of Israel without exposing themselves on other fronts.

Fourth, many of the region's states are likely to be wary of suggestions that they reduce the size of their armed forces or that they transform some of their regular units to reserves. In particular, Egyptian and Syrian observers argue that such changes can only be made incrementally, because the sudden release of tens of thousands of soldiers and officers to national economies that already suffer high unemployment would fuel domestic instability and increase the appeal of extremist movements.

Efforts to negotiate limits on imports of conventional arms to the Middle East will encounter equally perplexing problems. First, Arab states will argue that such limitations would place them at a disadvantage to Israel, with its advanced indigenous arms production capability. But controls on indigenous production are difficult to apply and must be extremely intrusive to be effective. Moreover, as a result of diminished demand in the international arms market and real reductions in its own defense expenditures, Israel has been applying painful cutbacks in its defense industries since the mid-1980s. These cutbacks have increased unemployment among both skilled and unskilled labor, so further restrictions on Israel's indigenous arms production could be an explosive domestic political issue.

In addition, negotiators would find it difficult to decide what to control and how such limitations should be applied. A complete ban on arms imports might be easy to apply and to verify; any observed arms transfer would be clear evidence of noncompliance. But such a ban is likely to be dismissed by the region's states as violating their legitimate right to possess the means for adequate defense and deterrence. Conversely, selective limitations involve the need to decide what types of systems are more dangerous than others and should be controlled. Such decisions require judgments about the effects of each weapon system — whether it provides an advantage to the offense or the defense, whether it does or does not create incentives for a first strike, and thus whether it might prove stabilizing or destabilizing. Moreover, verification measures to insure compliance with selective import restraints would have to be very complex. A large number of systems and subsystems would have to be traced and multiple points of entry would need to be observed. In addition, determining noncompliance on the basis of the data collected would require detailed agreements on elaborate counting procedures.

Third, it is unlikely that arms import restraints will be effective without the cooperation of actual and potential suppliers. While some of these suppliers might be interested in preventing weapons proliferation, their desire to support their friends and allies often induces them to favor specific arms sales to some of the region's states. For example, U.S. arms transfers to Egypt and Israel, and U.S. arms sales to Saudi Arabia are often presented as supporting the Middle East peace process and as securing a stable military balance in the region, and — since the Gulf War — as helping to deter Saddam Hussein. These interests propelled the United States to overcome its interest in restraining arms transfers to the region.[14]

Even more important, the competing interest of these suppliers in earning hard currency often induces them to prefer arms exports. For example, since the Gulf War, Western arms suppliers — particularly the United States, Britain, and France — have competed aggressively to win lucrative contracts for arms sales to Saudi Arabia and the smaller Gulf states.

The desire to gain hard currency is particularly central to the Third World arms suppliers that have entered the Middle East market in recent years, such as Brazil, Argentina, China, and North Korea. Given this imperative, it would be very difficult to obtain their cooperation with limitations on arms exports to the region. The best reflection of this was North Korea's tenacity in transferring Scud-C ballistic missiles and launchers to Syria and Iran in the early 1990s.

The breakup of the former Soviet empire and the end of the Cold War further compounds these difficulties. The defense industries of the former Soviet Union and former Warsaw Pact countries have lost their primary customers but have been unable to convert rapidly to civilian production. These countries and their respective industries have been forced to regard arms exports as an absolute imperative; hence in Czechoslovakia in 1991–92, the Havel government felt compelled to sell T-72 tanks to Syria.

Negotiating conventional arms control among the Middle East states is likely to prove complex, and the world's suppliers of conventional arms are unlikely to cooperate in this endeavor. Therefore, the chances that effective limitations on conventional arms in the Middle East will be negotiated and implemented any time soon do not appear very high.

Conclusions

A strong linkage exists among efforts to limit the spread of the three principal weapons of mass destruction: chemical, biological, and nuclear arms. Since Israel regards chemical and biological weapons as near-nuclear, it is unlikely to accept any erosion of its ambiguous nuclear deterrence as long as it faces the danger of chemical and biological attacks. Conversely, key Arab states view chemical weapons as a strategic counterweight to Israel's nuclear option and are therefore unlikely to sign the Chemical Weapons Convention until Israel signs the NPT.

By contrast, there is a far weaker linkage between the ability to advance arms control measures in the nuclear and conventional realms. Israel and the Arab states perceive equally significant sources of concern regarding the other's conventional capabilities and conduct. Thus, neither Israel nor the Arab states stand to gain from linking nuclear nonproliferation to conventional arms control. Moreover, the problems entailed in trying to implement conventional arms control in the Middle East are nearly intractable. Under such conditions, linking nuclear nonproliferation to progress in arresting the spread of conventional weapons and in reducing the force structures of the region's states would merely insure complete paralysis of all efforts at arms control.

NOTES

1. Israel's perceptions regarding each of the Arab states are not elaborated in this chapter except as illustrations of more general propositions; similarly, variations in Arab states' views of Israel are not detailed.

2. Indeed, Egyptian officials argue that the 1990 Mubarak Initiative — proposing the transformation of the Middle East to a WMDFZ — was a response to the linkage Israel made earlier among nuclear, chemical, and biological weapons when it argued that nuclear weapons are not the only weapons of mass destruction and that therefore nuclear weapons should not be singled out.

3. When Saddam Hussein warned in April 1990 that if Iraq were attacked he would annihilate "half of Israel" using binary chemical weapons, Israeli Prime Minister Itzhak Shamir noted that "the Iraqi regime is known for its brutality, internally and externally, and in the past it has already made use of [chemical] weapons more than once." Akiva Eldar, "Saddam Hussein: If attacked we will destroy half of Israel; Rabin: Let him not provoke us," *Ha'aretz* (Israel), April 3, 1990. Indeed, Saddam's 'clarifications' that his threats would be activated only if Israel first attacked Iraq did not calm Israeli concerns. Defense Minister Moshe Arens expressed Israel's reaction in mid-1990: "I wish to warn of Iraqi aggression which is being expressed without Israeli provocation. Saddam Hussein has no [reason to] fear an Israeli attack on Iraq. We do not even have a common border with Iraq and Saddam Hussein's statements certainly do not advance the cause of peace. We have had occasion to get to know him over a relatively long period and we regard his statements as hostile. Sometimes these statements seem moderate because he threatens us [only] if we attack an Arab country. But we know that there are Iraqis and Iraqi officials who claim that the very existence of the state of Israel comprises an act of aggression against the Arab nation." Eitan Rabin, "The prime minister hopes that an international effort would fold the chemical plant constructed in Libya," *Ha'aretz*, June 20, 1990.

4. In April 1990, Prime Minister Itzhak Shamir noted: "Israel is threatened not only by atomic, chemical and bacteriological weapons. Conventional arms also endanger Israel, as the quantities [of weapons and military personnel] at the adversaries' disposal become 'quality'." See Amos Ben Vered, "Shamir to the Knesset committee on foreign and defense affairs: The

danger of Iraqi weapons can be addressed through diplomatic means," *Ha'aretz*, April 24, 1990.

5. In July 1990, Defense Minister Arens told the Knesset Committee on Foreign and Defense Affairs: "Israel is also worried by the 700 tanks given to Egypt free of charge." See Dan Margalit, "Arens: 'The likelihood of war is now greater than in past years'." *Ha'aretz*, July 25, 1990.

6. Israel is worried that in a wider Arab-Israeli war, Saudi Arabia's weakness might cause it to capitulate to external pressures to place its small but modern military in the service of the Arab coalition or to transfer weapons and ammunition to other members of the coalition. Such worries provide the context for Israel's residual concern about the continuous strengthening of the Saudi armed forces. For example, Defense Minister Arens told the Knesset Committee on Foreign and Defense Affairs in July 1990: "There is justification for worry about the U.S.-Saudi arms deals in the framework of which the Saudis are to receive a 'TOW' missile of a generation not yet seen in the Middle East." See Margalit, "Arens: 'The likelihood of war is now greater than in past years'."

7. In February 1990, then–Defense Minister Rabin stated: "Israel will not remain indifferent to signs of military cooperation between Jordan and Iraq.... The Jordanian threat to Israel does not involve the fear of a direct confrontation between the two countries, but rather evolves from Jordan's weakness in the region." See "Rabin warns Jordan: 'We shall not remain indifferent'." *Ma'ariv* (Israel), February 21, 1990. See also David Makovsky, "Rabin: Iraqi-Jordanian move is no surprise," *Jerusalem Post*, February 21, 1990.

8. An effort was made to provide open-source references to the propositions advanced here regarding the Arab states' threat perceptions; however, much of this discussion — like the earlier discussion of Arab perceptions in the nuclear realm — is based on numerous conversations with officials and scholars in Arab states. Due to the obvious sensitivities involved, I must refrain from identifying these officials by name.

9. The program was later transformed into the Ballistic Missile Defense Organization (BMDO).

10. Some Arab observers further point out that during the 1948 war, the attacking Arab states were totally uncoordinated, allowing Israel to defeat their armies separately. Similarly in the 1956 and 1967 wars, Syria and Jordan failed to launch a full-scale attack when Israel attacked Egypt. In 1967 this allowed Israel to follow its defeat of the Egyptian forces and the conquest of the Sinai with the defeat of the Arab Legion and the Syrian Forces in sequence. Syrian-Egyptian strategic cooperation during the 1973 war did not endure beyond the initial attack; thereafter, Egypt's forces in the Sinai were brought to a halt, allowing Israel to devote all its remaining forces and energy to defeating the Syrian army. Iraqi support of Syria during the war is sometimes described as "pathetic."

11. Shomron argued that "as a means for gaining the initiative ... a preemptive strike is both moral and legitimate if it is clear that Israel is on the brink of war." See *JCSS Bulletin*, Jaffee Center for Strategic Studies, Tel Aviv University, No. 6 (June 1989), p. 1.

12. Arab observers often cite a T-shirt sold in Israel carrying the words: "Visit Israel before Israel visits you."

13. The observation that states' conventional forces are very dissimilar and the argument that this presents a serious obstacle to conventional arms control is made by Barry R. Posen, "Military Lessons of the Gulf War — Implications for Middle East Arms Control," in Shai Feldman and Ariel Levite, eds., *Arms Control and the New Middle East Security Environment*, JCSS Study No. 23 (Tel Aviv: Tel Aviv University, Jaffee Center for Strategic Studies, 1994), pp. 61–78.

14. This partially explains the contradiction between President Bush's post–Gulf War statement that "it would be tragic if the nations of the Middle East and the Persian Gulf were now, in the wake of the war, to embark on a new arms race," and the fact that during a one-year period after the statement was made, the Bush administration approved $8.6 billion in new arms sales to the region, the highest one-year total ever. See "Delay the F-15 Sale," *International Herald Tribune*, March 9, 1992.

Chapter 10

Interim Measures

The political environment in the Middle East seems increasingly favorable for consideration of nuclear arms control in the region. Following fifteen years of Egyptian-Israeli peace, substantial progress has been made by the mid-1990s in widening the scope of the Israeli-Arab peace process. The October 1994 Israel-Jordan peace treaty and the milestones reached in the Palestinian-Israeli peace process may pave the way to further breakthroughs, notably in the Syrian-Israeli and Lebanese-Israeli negotiations. In turn, these breakthroughs may allow further progress in the multi-lateral talks launched by the 1992 Moscow conference in an effort to address the region-wide problems of the Middle East.

These developments are likely to diminish the extent to which the states taking part in the peace process perceive their security and survival as threatened. In turn, perceptions of reduced threat would diminish the degree to which these states see an imperative to acquire ever-greater stockpiles of conventional and unconventional arms. With less motivation to possess weapons of all kinds, these states are likely to become more willing to consider the adoption of arms control measures.

In fact, by the mid-1990s much progress was made in laying the foundations for an arms control process in the region. This progress has occurred largely in the framework of the ACRS talks, which produced initial gains in conceptualizing and defining the political context in which regional security and confidence-building measures could be applied. Thus, by the mid-1990s, the prospect for some form of arms control — at least in the Arab-Israeli part of the Middle East — have improved.

Moreover, the current state of the region's nuclear programs make this a particularly opportune time for considering measures to arrest the spread of nuclear arms. At least in the short term, the region seems relatively unlikely to undergo rapid proliferation. While Israel is widely considered to have acquired a nuclear potential years ago, Iraq's ambitious nuclear program has been arrested by a combination of Israeli preventive action, coalition bombings during the 1990–91 Gulf War, and the dismantling of Iraq's nuclear facilities and the continued monitoring of its activities by UN Special Commission and International Atomic Energy Agency (IAEA) teams in the framework of implementing UN Security Council Resolutions 687 and 715.

Iran and Algeria are devoting significant assets to the construction of a nuclear infrastructure with potential military applications, but both are still years away from possessing nuclear bombs. There are no signs that Egypt has changed or is about to change the strategic decision it made in the late 1970s not to develop a military nuclear capability. Libya's nuclear program seems largely dormant and Syria's nuclear efforts are at the embryonic stage. Jordan, Saudi Arabia, Yemen, and the Gulf States remain outside the nuclear realm. Barring the possibility that a state might obtain significant amounts of fissile material smuggled from the former Soviet Union, the near-term odds of nuclear proliferation in the region are low. The static nature of the region's nuclear programs suggest that an opportunity now exists to freeze current nuclear activities in the Middle East until conditions for a rollback of nuclear capabilities in the region are created.

Unfortunately, however, political conditions in the Persian Gulf region seem far from ripe for the adoption of nuclear nonproliferation measures. The odds of incorporating the subregion's pariah states — Iran and Iraq — in the new Arab-Israeli "arc of hope" seem low. This is likely to continue to limit the feasibility of nonproliferation measures in the Arab-Israeli conflict area as well: the range of some of the systems acquired or developed in the Gulf region extends to states in the western part of the Middle East, as illustrated during the 1991 Gulf War. Moreover, some Middle East states remain outside the regional arms control process. By late 1995, Syria and Lebanon continued to resist joining the ACRS talks, while Libya had not even been invited to take part. Thus, the positive developments in the Middle East during the early 1990s are confined to some of the region's states; their impact on other parts of the region is still uncertain.

Israeli and Arab Perspectives

From Israel's standpoint, the prospects for nuclear arms control in the Middle East are likely to be tied to the three conditions that seem to have led it to develop a nuclear option in the first place: Arab rejection of its existence; the quantitative asymmetry characterizing its overall strategic relations with its neighbors; and the need to hedge against the possibility that one or more of the region's states might acquire nuclear weapons or other weapons of mass destruction.

Clearly, Israel would entertain the dismantling of its nuclear option only under extremely favorable circumstances. Most important, Israel must perceive that its neighbors accept its existence. Israel is likely to measure such acceptance not only by the conclusion of peace agreements that will be tested over time but also by its neighbors' willingness to allow Israel to become fully integrated into regional security frameworks and other institutions that might be created to address problems such as economic development, water and land utilization, refugee resettlement, and the environment. Irrespective of the direct contribution of such institutions to its security, their political significance — as indications that the Arab states no longer consider Israel an anathema — is considerable.

Israel would also require that it need no longer worry about its ability to hedge against the acquisition of nuclear, chemical, and biological weapons by other states in the region. Israel will attach increasing importance to this imperative given the nuclear, chemical, and biological programs evolving in the Middle East at large. This prerequisite could be satisfied only by the implementation of a complete and verifiable ban on the development, production, acquisition, and possession of these weapons, preferably by transforming the region into a weapons of mass destruction–free zone (WMDFZ).

For a Middle East WMDFZ to be meaningful, all of the region's states must accept the limitations it creates, and compliance must be verified by a regional verification mechanism similar in scope and intrusiveness to the Organization for the Prohibition of Chemical Weapons (OPCW). The highly imperfect IAEA verification of NPT compliance, the still-nonexistent verification mechanisms of the Biological Weapons Convention (BWC), and the impressive verification procedures attached to the Chemical Weapons Convention (CWC) must be reinforced by special on-site inspection procedures tailored to the particular characteristics of the Middle East environment. This multi-lateral verification mechanism should be supplemented by bilateral inspection agreements that would stipulate additional on-site inspections to be conducted on a reciprocal basis.

However, a verifiable agreement among all the region's states to transform the Middle East into a WMDFZ is unlikely except in the context of a comprehensive peace: not only do such far-reaching arms control measures require a high degree of mutual trust, but intrusive verification mechanisms also imply a high level of transparency and interaction.

In contrast, a number of Arab states led by Egypt seem eager to place some limits on the spread of nuclear capabilities in the region, and particularly on Israel's nuclear potential, before a comprehensive peace in the Middle East is achieved. These Arab states are also likely to continue to demand that Israel sign the NPT and place all its nuclear installations under IAEA full-scope safeguards. Until political circumstances allow Israel to meet this demand or to join a Middle East nuclear-weapon-free zone, these states are likely to urge that Israel at least agree to take some initial steps toward nuclear disarmament.

Israel would be reluctant to adopt measures that might erode its strategic deterrence prematurely. However, given the importance it attaches to the peace process, Israel might seek to accommodate its neighbors' concerns if this could be done while leaving Israel's ambiguous deterrent intact. Therefore, the near-term challenge is to define steps that might begin to address Arab concerns in the nuclear realm without damaging Israeli deterrence.

This task will become all the more important once the web of Middle East peace agreements expands to include Syria and Lebanon. In these new circumstances, Arab states are likely to argue that while the conclusion of peace with all its immediate neighbors will not have eliminated all threats perceived by Israel, it will have removed the existential threats. They are likely to urge that such a fundamental change in Israel's security environment justifies a relaxation of its reliance on the deterrence provided by its ambiguous nuclear posture.

Once Arab-Israeli peace is expanded, these Arab suggestions may be seconded by outside powers, primarily the United States. Washington's willingness to tolerate Israel's nuclear potential stems from its recognition that Israel deserves the right to retain an existential deterrent. Once a growing number of Arab states sign peace agreements with Israel, some voices within Congress and the executive branch may argue that the rationale for continuing to treat Israel as a "special case" in U.S. nuclear nonproliferation policy is no longer valid. In such circumstances, Washington might add its weight to Arab demands that Israel make some concessions in the nuclear realm.

Interim Nuclear Arms Control Measures

Until circumstances become ripe for implementing far-reaching nuclear arms control measures in the Middle East, three interim efforts could be made to meet Arab priorities and concerns in the nuclear realm without eroding Israel's strategic deterrence. First, an informal discussion might be held among Israel, Egypt, and Jordan regarding the implications of nuclear proliferation and deterrence in the Middle East. Second, a discussion might be conducted regarding the modalities and conditions for implementing a ban on the production of weapons-grade fissile material in the region. Third, talks aimed at reaching a consensus on the requirements and prerequisites for the denuclearization of the Middle East might be attempted.

NUCLEAR PROLIFERATION AND DETERRENCE

An informal discussion of the implications of nuclear proliferation and deterrence in the Middle East should initially include three principal ACRS participants: Israel, Egypt, and Jordan. Egypt's participation is essential given its concern about the implications of Israel's nuclear potential and the stated interest of Egyptian officials in being engaged in such a dialogue. The inclusion of Egypt is also justified by its full compliance with its peace agreement with Israel over many years and through many trials and tribulations. Jordan should be included because of the commitments contained in the 1994 Israel-Jordan peace treaty to negotiate a WMDFZ, and because of Jordan's leading positive role in the ACRS talks.

Details of these discussions — if not their conduct — should remain confined to the participants. Their purpose would be to enable Egypt and Jordan to discuss their concerns regarding the implications of Israel's nuclear potential and to allow Israel a chance to alleviate these concerns. In addition, the talks would provide both parties an opportunity to analyze the potential ramifications of nuclear proliferation in the region's states.

The talks could be held without specific reference to any particular nuclear program, but would be limited to a general discussion of the issues involved. This would allow the role of nuclear deterrence and nuclear proliferation in the Middle East to be elaborated in an atmosphere free of the media limelight and the presence of other regional and extraregional parties.

Before such a discussion could take place, the three parties would need to conduct some pre-discussions regarding the modalities of the suggested talks. In these pre-discussions, the parties should agree on the boundaries within which the envisaged talks will take place. The purpose of such limitations would be to allow the parties to address each other's concerns without diminishing the formal ambiguity currently surrounding nuclear capabilities in the region. In addition, such boundaries would prevent the parties from becoming accomplices to the nuclear activities of any of the region's states. Thus, none would be compelled to pass judgment on the nuclear activities of any particular party, and none could be accused of having provided legitimacy to a specific nuclear program.

IMPLEMENTING A BAN ON THE PRODUCTION OF FISSILE MATERIAL

A quiet dialogue on nuclear arms in the Middle East could eventually pave the way for a second interim measure: a wider discussion among ACRS participants regarding the conditions and modalities of implementing a ban on the production of nuclear weapons–grade material in the Middle East. The relevant clauses of the arms control initiatives announced by President Bush in May 1991 and in July 1992 and by President Clinton in September 1993 could serve as the basis for the suggested discussions. Thus, the talks would seek to create the conceptual framework for the implementation of a nuclear freeze in the Middle East.

Specifically, the discussions should focus on three issues. First, what specific activities should be prohibited by the freeze to make it effective, and what activities should be ignored so that capabilities are frozen but do not deteriorate? Second, what are the political prerequisites for the application of a ban on the production of fissile material? Could such a freeze be feasible without the participation of all the region's states? If a subset of these states suffice, which states must participate for the freeze to be effective and meaningful? Third, what reassurances could be provided to reduce fears that the implementation of such a fissile material ban would produce immediate pressures to adopt more far-reaching measures of nuclear disarmament?

A critically important task would be for the parties to explore whether compliance with such a fissile material ban could be verified without exposing the parties' possible past activities. That is, could the region's countries maintain existing ambiguities regarding their past nuclear activities? The answer might affect responses to the next question: Should the proposed ban be implemented in the Middle East in the form of unilateral commitments, as envisaged by President Bush, or should it be institutionalized and formalized in the form of a regional or global treaty, as President Clinton suggested? Finally, if the contractual option is adopted, what institutional procedures and modalities should be adopted for verifying compliance with the obligations undertaken in the framework of the freeze? What would be the role of international organizations in verification, and what complementary or alternative regional institutions should be created? What bilateral inspection agreements might be concluded to strengthen the regional verification mechanism? Who would determine noncompliance? What sanctions could be applied, and how, if states are found to be violating their obligations?

Reaching agreement among ACRS participants on these complex issues would be difficult. If a formal or informal consensus could be reached, it could serve as the basis for future negotiations on establishing the proposed freeze once the requisite states that currently remain outside the ACRS process join it.

DENUCLEARIZATION OF THE MIDDLE EAST

The third suggested interim nuclear arms control measure is that the ACRS talks become a forum for Arab-Israeli discussions regarding the prospects and conditions for the denuclearization of the Middle East. Since it seems that such denuclearization could only happen as part of the transformation of the region into a WMDFZ, the discussions would be designed to explore the implications and to elaborate the modalities of creating such a zone in the Middle East.

The purpose of the talks would be to prepare the conceptual framework for establishing a WMDFZ in the region, for the time when conditions for implementation materialize. In addition, the talks would serve as an important confidence-building measure; they would meet Egypt's request that the issue be discussed. At the same time, the talks would sensitize the region's states to the conditions that must be fulfilled before a WMDFZ could be created.

To alleviate Israeli sensitivities, this discussion would need to be preceded by a detailed agreement among ACRS participants regarding the parameters of the proposed talks. For example, the parties would agree to refrain from efforts to transcend the suggested talks by pressing for premature implementation, and would agree to avoid unintended consequences, such as altering the ambiguous nature of nuclear potentials in the region.

The agenda should include the following five sets of issues: First, what are the implications of establishing such a zone? How would the transformation of the region into a WMDFZ affect the likelihood of war and the costs of war in the region? What weapons of mass destruction would be banned? What limitations on the possession of other types of weapons should be adopted to enable the creation of a WMDFZ? What conventional arms control measures, and what limitations on the possession of development and acquisition of ballistic missiles, would need to be adopted?

Second, once the region's states agree to establish a WMDFZ, what actions would facilitate and what actions would undermine its creation? Specifically, what confidence building measures might these states adopt in order to facilitate the establishment of a WMDFZ?

Third, what are likely to be the political prerequisites — the relations among the region's states and the involvement of outside powers — for establishing a WMDFZ in the Middle East? What states should it encompass?

A fourth set of issues concerns the specific obligations that external powers should be asked to undertake toward the zone and its members. What actions should such powers refrain from taking in order to avoid violating the stipulations of the zone or otherwise undermining its purposes? More specifically, what negative security assurances should outside powers be asked to provide to members of the zone? And conversely, what positive security assurances in the form of commitments or guarantees should outside powers be asked to provide members of the zone against violations of its provisions?

A fifth topic for discussion is the verification procedures that would ensure compliance with the zone's stipulations. What inspection procedures should be implemented in order to ensure compliance? What would be the responsibilities of the IAEA and the OPCW in helping to verify compliance with a Middle East WMDFZ? What special regional organizations would need to be created to supplement international verification mechanisms? What complementary bilateral inspections procedures could the member states adopt in order to ensure compliance with the WMDFZ? Who would be responsible for resolving compliance disputes, and what sanctions could be applied if a state were found to be violating the zone's stipulations?

By 1995, the ACRS process has gained ground as the first valid framework for discussing security, arms control, and confidence building in the Middle East. While Syria resists joining the talks, insisting that greater progress in Israeli-Syrian bilateral talks must first be achieved, and some of the region's key proliferation concerns — Iraq, Iran, and Libya — remain completely outside the ACRS framework, these limitations should not invalidate the use of the ACRS talks as a setting for discussions of interim nuclear arms control measures in the Middle East. Given the wide gap between the Arab and Israeli approaches to nuclear arms control described in this book, such discussions are the most realistic arena for potential progress.

Appendices

Appendix 1

Israel's Draft Resolution Proposing the
Establishment of a Nuclear-Weapon-Free Zone
in the Region of the Middle East,
Presented to the UN General Assembly,
October 31, 1980

The General Assembly,

Reaffirming paragraph 60 of the Final Document of the tenth special session of the General Assembly, which reads as follows: "The establishment of nuclear-weapon-free zones on the basis of arrangements freely arrived at among the States of the region concerned constitutes an important disarmament measure,"

Aware of the urgent need to establish such a zone in the Middle East, in view of conflict situations which threaten the peace of that region,

Convinced that the effective way to prevent the proliferation of nuclear weapons in the Middle East is through negotiations leading to the establishment of a system of mutually-binding obligations which would provide each state in the region with a contractual assurance of others' compliance with the commitment to abstain from introducing nuclear weapons into the region,

Recalling its resolution 31/70 on the comprehensive study of the question of nuclear-weapon-free zones in all its aspects, particularly paragraph 3, which reiterates the conviction that the establishment of nuclear-weapon-free zones can contribute to the security of members of such zones, to the prevention of proliferation of nuclear weapons and to the goals of general and complete disarmament,

Recalling further its resolution 33/91 B of 16 December 1979 on confidence-building measures and convinced that the adherence of all Member States of the Middle East region to a treaty establishing a nuclear-weapon-free zone in the Middle East would in itself serve to reduce tensions and pave the way for the introduction of further confidence-building measures,

1. *Calls upon* all States of the Middle East and non-nuclear-weapon States adjacent to the region, which are not signatories to any treaty providing for a nuclear-weapon-free zone, to convene at the earliest possible date a conference with a view to negotiating a multilateral treaty establishing a nuclear-weapon-free zone in the Middle East;

2. *Urges* all States of the region to state by 1 May 1981 their willingness to participate in the conference;

3. *Requests* the Secretary-General to provide the necessary facilities for the convening of such a conference.

Appendix 2

Excerpts from the Address of
Prime Minister Itzhak Shamir to the
UN General Assembly,
June 7, 1988

The agreements concluded between the United States of America and the Union of Soviet Socialist Republics and the further reductions now being negotiated between them should serve as our example. Those agreements are of course important in themselves; they are even more important as testimony to a political will to resolve conflicts through negotiations and to renounce the use of arms. Israel has taken two initiatives in the same direction.

As early as 1980 we proposed in the General Assembly of the United Nations the establishment of a nuclear-weapon-free zone in the Middle East, based on free and direct negotiations between the States of the region. We did so in addition to our repeated declaration that Israel would not be the first country to introduce nuclear weapons into the Middle East. Such zones have been established in Latin America by direct negotiations among the countries of the region. And recently the States of the South Pacific reached a similar agreement in the same manner. The mode of negotiating those agreements and the mutual assurances built into them are vital components in establishing and maintaining such nuclear-weapon-free zones. This has been expressly stated by the Commission headed by the late Prime Minister of Sweden, Mr. Palme.

We made that proposal because we assumed that the process of reaching those agreements and their successful conclusion would in effect serve to reduce not only the risk of nuclear war but also the more real and immediate danger in the region — the prospect of conventional war.

Many have urged us to sign the Treaty on the Non-Proliferation of Nuclear Weapons (NPT), but we have seen that the Treaty has in no way prevented wars between its signatories. It is our view that, if establishing and maintaining a nuclear-weapon-free zone can make conventional wars less likely, then its benefits will far outweigh anything that can be gained from a non-proliferation treaty.

We have repeatedly invited the Arab States to negotiate the establishment of a nuclear-weapon-free zone, but they have rejected the idea. They have refused to sit down with us. They have refused to negotiate with us. They have refused to apply the procedures of Latin America and the South Pacific. And they have refused to adopt the recommendations of the Palme Commission on the manner of creating such a zone in the Middle East.

We do not understand this blanket refusal. It reflects a consistent attitude of rejection of any kind of dealings with Israel, even on matters of vital concern to the security and future of the peoples of our region. Nevertheless, our offer stands. It is testimony to our faith that common sense, logic and the yearning for peace by the peoples of the Middle East will in time induce the Arab Governments to come to terms with Israel's existence.

From this rostrum, I should like to address an appeal to the leaders of the Arab States in the Middle East. We are entering an era of greater openness and understanding between former rivals, of accommodation between the great Powers, and of unprecedented steps in nuclear disarmament. Let us join this wave of goodwill and seek together a new path that will lead us away from past hostilities and belligerence and from barren and futile options that are imported from outside. Let us meet and reason together. Let us listen to each other directly. Let us negotiate even in the present rough seas, and not relent until we reach the shores of mutual accommodation, understanding and peace.

Appendix 3

Excerpts from the Address of
Egyptian Foreign Minister Ismat Abdel Meguid to the
UN General Assembly,
June 13, 1988

It may be appropriate for me to dwell first upon the issue of halting the arms race and achieving nuclear disarmament. Despite the repetition, I find it essential to emphasize that the most serious threat to humanity is that of a nuclear war. There are various military and scientific theories and research with conflicting purposes and philosophies. However, they all agree on the impossibility of controlling any military conflict in which one party started to use nuclear weapons. That would be a situation which could destroy the entire world. Moreover, the political declaration of the leaders of the two superpowers at their meeting at Geneva in November 1985 stressed that in a nuclear war there are no victors. Is all that not enough to question the logic behind retaining such weapons? Should that not lead us to eliminate them once and for all?

In that regard, Egypt appeals to the two superpowers and other parties concerned to finalize the comprehensive nuclear test ban treaty at the earliest possible date. That would be an important step towards halting the nuclear arms race and the proliferation of those weapons.

Egypt firmly believes that the problems of security and related disarmament measures are indivisible. They encompass both the international and the regional level. Stability can never be achieved unless we work simultaneously on those two levels, particularly in the fields of disarmament and nuclear arms limitations. While genuine security against the nuclear menace cannot be attained unless comprehensive global measures to halt the nuclear arms race and its vertical proliferation are taken, we would be contradicting ourselves if we restricted our endeavors in this domain to global measures while overlooking the regional dimensions. In this context I wish to highlight the following points.

First, the nuclear Powers should attach more importance to

finding a suitable and just formula for an agreement on arrangements that would ensure the non-use or threat of the use of nuclear weapons against non-nuclear-weapon States. It is neither fair nor logical that non-nuclear-weapon States should remain threatened by nuclear weapons while at the same time they are called upon not to acquire such weapons. We wish here to reiterate what we have stated before, that Security Council resolution 255 (1968) of 19 June 1968 and the unilateral declarations by nuclear States are not, in our opinion, a sufficient guarantee to retain the confidence and trust of the non-nuclear weapon States and to induce them to give up their attempts to acquire such weapons.

Honesty and security concerns call upon us to face this issue clearly and squarely. It is not acceptable to put in the same basket all the non-nuclear-weapon States without distinction between those which are party to security arrangements within military and political alliances, which provide a nuclear umbrella to protect them, and those countries that have refused to enter into such arrangements, namely, the nonaligned and neutral countries. If we are serious and sincere in our endeavor to prevent the emergence of new nuclear-weapon States and to reach our declared objective of developing a broader and more effective international non-proliferation regime, we have no alternative but to tackle the obvious contradictions in dealing with this issue and to provide genuine and effective guarantees to non-nuclear States in order to prevent the use or threat of the use of nuclear weapons against them.

Secondly, the nuclear-weapon States, and indeed the whole world, should make sincere efforts to insulate more regions from nuclear threats.

Egypt has spared no effort at the international level to protect its people and the neighboring areas against the threat of nuclear annihilation. Egypt has acceded to the Non-Proliferation Treaty and has adopted constructive positions in the various international forums to curb that threat. The world testifies to Egypt's persistent efforts to safeguard Africa and the Middle East from nuclear threats. In 1964 Cairo was host to the African summit conference which issued the call for the denuclearization of Africa. On this occasion I cannot but express our grave concern about the policies of the racist regime in South Africa which hinder the implementation of the Declaration on the Denuclearization of Africa. This forum must face such policies squarely and not allow that continuous defiance of the will of the international community by South Africa.

Since 1974 Egypt has sponsored an initiative aimed at the establishment of a nuclear-weapon-free zone in the Middle East. That initiative has in recent years been consistently endorsed by the General Assembly, by consensus. Such a consensus should be maintained and should not be impaired as a result of the military nature of the nuclear programmes of a country in the region. The introduction of nuclear weapons into the Middle East or the threat of their introduction would lead to grave and complex consequences and create a very delicate situation.

At a time when we are striving sincerely to ease international tension and attain disarmament, I wish to state before the Assembly in all frankness that Egypt will never allow a nuclear race in the Middle East in which one state would become superior to another, a situation which would jeopardize security in the area and in the world at large. Nuclear technology is not the monopoly of a few; it has become accessible to all. Egypt will not remain complacent but will take all necessary measures to ensure its own security and that of the region once it is evident that nuclear weapons are being introduced into the region.

From this rostrum I wish to call on Israel to accede to the Non-Proliferation Treaty and to place all its nuclear facilities under the system of IAEA surveillance and inspection, so that the peoples of the region may be sure that its nuclear programmes are not oriented towards military purposes. We reject the argument that the Non-Proliferation Treaty does not contribute to the prevention of conventional wars, nor is that argument an acceptable excuse for a State's not becoming a party to the treaty. I must caution against the danger of a nuclear arms race in the Middle East, which would constitute a threat to the peace and security of the whole world. I wish to call on the nuclear States in particular to shoulder their responsibilities in this regard.

Although the consensus on the proposal to establish a nuclear-weapon-free zone in the Middle East represents an important step, we shall continue to pursue the proposal actively until it receives tangible expression. In this regard, Egypt would make the following proposals.

First, all States of the region, as well as nuclear-weapon States beyond the region, should declare that they will not introduce nuclear weapons into the Middle East. Secondly, the Secretary-General should be authorized to appoint a personal representative or a group of experts to contact the States of the region with a view to formulating a model draft of a treaty and to evolve specific practical measures capable of creating the necessary conditions for the establishment of a nuclear-weapon-free zone in the Middle East. Thirdly, IAEA should be invited to do a study and submit specific proposals related to the necessary verification and inspection measures which would be implemented in connection with the establishment of a nuclear-weapon-free zone in the Middle East.

Appendix 4

The "Mubarak Initiative"
(Letter from the Deputy Prime Minister and
Minister of Foreign Affairs of Egypt to the
UN Secretary-General,
April 16, 1990)

The Middle East, as you are well aware, continues to be a highly volatile conflict-torn region. Even in these times, when a rising tide of peace seems to be emerging in different regions of the world, as you so succinctly remarked in your report to the General Assembly at its forty-fourth session on the work of the United Nations (A/44/1), "the situation of the Middle East remains a source of profound and intense concern."

Recent developments in the region have further underscored the importance and urgency of safeguarding the Middle East from the ominous implications associated with nuclear weapons and other weapons of mass destruction.

Egypt has, for over 15 years, called for the establishment of a nuclear-weapon-free zone in the Middle East. This position emanated from our unwavering commitment to nuclear disarmament, as well as nuclear weapons non-proliferation, and our deep conviction that the introduction of nuclear weapons into the Middle East would have devastating consequences on the prospects for stability and security in the region, and for the maintenance of international peace and security in general.

At the forty-third session of the General Assembly, the international community once again reiterated its support for the establishment of a nuclear-weapon-free zone in the Middle East. In its resolution 43/65 of 7 December 1988, the General Assembly adopted without a vote, *inter alia*, highlighted certain measures and steps to be considered by States of the region pending the establishment of such a zone, foremost amongst which were adherence to the Treaty on the Non-Proliferation of Nuclear Weapons and the application of International Atomic Energy Agency (IAEA) safeguards to the nuclear facilities in the States of the region.

It is worthy of note that Egypt and the other Arab States that have significant nuclear programmes have undertaken these measures. They have met the standard, universally acknowledged to be a legally binding determination, not to acquire nuclear weapons, as well as the verification procedures imperative to assure compliance. Now it is of paramount importance that all States of the region adhere to the said treaty, and accept the application of full IAEA safeguards to their nuclear facilities.

Egypt has also taken an equally forthcoming position and active role in disarmament efforts relating to other weapons of mass destruction, including in particular chemical weapons. It is Egypt's considered opinion that chemical weapons should be dealt with in a comprehensive and global context involving all types of weapons of mass destruction, whether nuclear, chemical or biological, in order to ensure international and regional security.

President Hosni Mubarak, on 8 April 1990, categorically declared Egypt's support for ensuring that the Middle East become a zone free from all types of weapons of mass destruction. President Mubarak emphasized the following:

(1) All weapons of mass destruction, without exception, should be prohibited in the Middle East, i.e. nuclear, chemical, biological, etc.

(2) All States of the region, without exception, should make equal and reciprocal commitments in this regard.

(3) Verification measures and modalities should be established to ascertain full compliance by all States of the region with the full scope of the prohibitions without exception.

Egypt shall continue to work with States in the region, and beyond, towards declaring the Middle East a zone free from all weapons of mass destruction, and the establishment of the requisite international verification measures, applicable to all the States of the region on an equal basis. It is our sincere hope that the other States of the region will be equally forthcoming in this regard, as we strive to enhance the prospects for a just, lasting peace in the Middle East.

Appendix 5

Excerpts from General Assembly Resolution 45/52,
"Establishment of a nuclear-weapon-free zone
in the region of the Middle East,"
December 4, 1990

The General Assembly,

1. *Urges* all parties directly concerned to consider seriously taking
the practical and urgent steps required for the implementation of the
proposal to establish a nuclear-weapon-free zone in the region of the
Middle East in accordance with the relevant resolutions of the General
Assembly, and, as a means of promoting this objective, invites the
countries concerned to adhere to the Treaty on the Non-Proliferation
of Nuclear Weapons;

2. *Calls upon* all countries of the region that have not done so,
pending the establishment of the zone, to agree to place all their
nuclear activities under International Atomic Energy Agency safeguards;

3. *Takes note* of the report of the Director General of the International Atomic Energy Agency on the implementation of paragraph 2 of
resolution GC(XXXIII)/RES/506, which is contained in document GC
(XXXIV)/926;

4. *Also takes note* of the request made by the General Conference
of the International Atomic Energy Agency to the Director General in
paragraph 2 of resolution GC(XXXIV)/RES/526 "to deploy further
efforts in continuing the consultation with the States concerned in the
Middle East area with a view to applying Agency safeguards to all
nuclear installations in the area, keeping in mind the relevant
recommendations contained in paragraph 75 of the report attached to
document GC(XXXIII)/687, as well as various proposals and opinions
referred to in the Governments' replies contained in document
GC(XXXIV)/926 and the situation in the area of the Middle East";

5. *Invites* all countries of the region, pending the establishment of
a nuclear-weapon-free zone in the region of the Middle East, to declare
their support for establishing such a zone, consistent with paragraph

63 (d) of the final Document of the Tenth Special Session of the General Assembly, and to deposit those declarations with the Security Council;

6. *Also invites* those countries, pending the establishment of the zone, not to develop, produce, test or otherwise acquire nuclear weapons or permit the stationing on their territories, or territories under their control, of nuclear weapons or nuclear explosive devices;

7. *Invites* the nuclear-weapon States and all other States to render their assistance in the establishment of the zone and at the same time to refrain from any action that runs counter to both the letter and the spirit of the present resolutions;

8. *Welcomes* the completion of the study undertaken by the Secretary-General in accordance with paragraph 8 of resolution 43/65 and contained in his report, on effective and verifiable measures which would facilitate the establishment of a nuclear-weapon-free zone in the Middle East;

9. *Requests* all parties of the region and other parties concerned, in particular the nuclear-weapon States, to submit to the Secretary-General their views and suggestions with respect to the above-mentioned study, as well as on follow-up measures which would facilitate the establishment of a nuclear-weapon-free zone in the Middle East;

10. *Requests* the Secretary-General to submit to the General Assembly at its forty-sixth session a report on the implementation of the present resolution;

11. *Decides* to include in the provisional agenda of its forty-sixth session the item entitled "Establishment of a nuclear-weapon-free zone in the region of the Middle East."

Appendix 6

Excerpts from an Address by Yitzhak Shamir,
Prime Minister of Israel, to the
American Enterprise Institute,
December 12, 1990

. . . . We have been asked by many, particularly the press, if we were bringing new initiatives and proposals on this visit. Peace plans, ladies and gentlemen, are neither fashions nor automobiles. We cannot and we must not produce a new, improved model every year. We believe that our four-point plan of May 1989, which was endorsed by the administration at the time, is a good, viable plan.

. . . . One of the points calls for the implementation of confidence-building measures between Israel and its neighbors. Such measures proved helpful in cracking the wall of enmity between East and West in Europe. Such steps have helped develop tacit understandings between Israel and Jordan. These steps can range from direct telephone communications between opposing military leaders in order to avoid dangerous misunderstandings, to something as simple and natural as tourism. Today, Arabs can freely cross back and forth to our territory over the bridges of the Jordan. There is no reason why Israeli Jews should not move with equal freedom in and out of Arab countries.

. . . .

MS. KIRKPATRICK: Prime Minister, we have several questions on Israeli participation in a Middle East arms control process. One, for example, says: "Would Israel be supportive of a Middle East arms control regime, including a nuclear-free zone, if other countries of the region agreed and proper verification could be put in place?"

PRIME MINISTER SHAMIR: Our answer is positive in principle. And this idea is not new to us. We have proposed it ten years ago, I think. I personally have proposed it in the United Nations. And we are ready to start a serious study of all these problems of disarmament and a nuclear-free zone and all the arrangements in order to limit and annihilate any possibility of the use of unconventional arms in our area.

Of course, it's a very serious and complicated issue. And there are necessary — there is a need for many preconditions for it. It has to come with a complete change of all relations between the various countries in the Middle East. But, all that is very desirable and we are ready to participate in this work.

Appendix 7

Bush "Freeze Proposal"
(Excerpts from a Press Release, White House
Office of the Press Secretary, Kennebunkport, Maine:
"Fact Sheet on Middle East Arms Control Initiative,"
Wednesday, May 29, 1991)

Fulfilling the pledge he made in his March 6 address to a joint session
of Congress, the President announced today a series of proposals
intended to curb the spread of nuclear, chemical and biological
weapons in the Middle East, as well as the missiles that can deliver
them. The proposals also seek to restrain destabilizing conventional
arms build-ups in the region.

The proposals would apply to the entire Middle East, including
Iraq, Iran, Libya, Syria, Egypt, Lebanon, Israel, Jordan, Saudi Arabia,
and the other states of the Maghreb and the Gulf Cooperation Council.
They reflect our consultations with allies, governments in the region,
and key suppliers of arms and technology.

The support of both arms exporters and importers will be essential
to the success of the initiative. Since proliferation is a global problem,
it must find a global solution. At the same time, the current situation
in the Middle East poses unique dangers and opportunities.

Thus, the President's proposal will concentrate on the Middle East
as its starting point, while complementing other initiatives such as
those taken by Prime Ministers John Major and Brian Mulroney. It
includes the following elements:

Nuclear Weapons

The initiative builds on existing institutions and focuses on activities
directly related to nuclear weapons capability. The initiative would call
on regional states to implement a verifiable ban on the production and
acquisition of weapons-usable nuclear material (enriched uranium or
separated plutonium); reiterate our call on all states in the region that
have not already done so to accede to the Non-Proliferation Treaty;
reiterate our call to place all nuclear facilities in the region under

International Atomic Energy Agency safeguards; and continue to support the eventual creation of a regional nuclear-weapons-free zone.

This initiative complements our continuing support for the continuation of the UN Security Council embargo against arms transfers to Iraq, as well as the efforts of the UN Special Commission to eliminate Iraq's remaining capabilities to use or produce nuclear, chemical, and biological weapons and the missiles to deliver them.

Appendix 8

Excerpts from Letter from the
Minister for Foreign Affairs of Egypt to the
UN Secretary-General,
July 21, 1991

I am pleased to inform you that, on 5 July 1991, Egypt announced a series of additional ideas and proposals designed to contribute to the ongoing dialogue on efforts to reduce armaments in our region and, in particular, to accelerate the establishment of the Middle East as a zone free of weapons of mass destruction.

These proposals are as follows:

(a) Egypt calls on the major arms-producing States — and particularly the permanent members of the Security Council — as well as Israel, Iran and the Arab States to deposit undertakings with the Security Council in which they clearly and unconditionally endorse the declaration of the Middle East as a region free of weapons of mass destruction and commit themselves not to take any steps or measures which would run counter to or impede the attainment of that objective.

(b) Egypt calls on the arms-producing States and the parties to the Treaty on the Non-Proliferation of Nuclear Weapons to step up their efforts to ensure that all Middle East nations which have not yet done so adhere to the Treaty, in recognition of the fact that this is a step of the utmost importance and urgency.

(c) Egypt calls on nations of the Middle East region which have not yet done so to declare their commitment:

(i) Not to use nuclear, chemical or biological weapons;

(ii) Not to produce or acquire any nuclear weapons;

(iii) Not to produce or acquire any nuclear materials susceptible to military use and to dispose of any existing stocks of such materials;

(iv) To accept the International Atomic Energy Agency safeguards regime whereby all their nuclear facilities become subject to international inspection.

(d) Egypt calls on those nations of the region which have not yet done so to declare their commitment to adhere to the Treaty on the Non-Proliferation of Nuclear Weapons, as well as to the Convention concerning the prohibition of biological weapons of 1972, no later than the conclusion of the negotiations on the prohibition of chemical weapons being conducted by the Conference on Disarmament in Geneva.

(e) Egypt calls on Middle East States to declare their commitment actively and fairly to address measures relating to all forms of delivery systems for weapons of mass destruction.

(f) Egypt calls on nations of the region to approve the assignment to an organ of the United Nations or another international organization of a role, to be agreed upon at a future date, in the verification of those nations' compliance with such agreements on arms reduction and disarmament as may be concluded between them.

In order to give added impetus to the negotiations between all the parties concerned with these matters, Egypt intends to make direct contact with the major parties concerned — both internationally and in the Middle East region — by dispatching envoys and through the use of conventional diplomatic channels, with a view to discussing these various ideas and means for their implementation in both the bilateral and multilateral contexts at the regional and international levels.

Appendix 9

Excerpts from Israel's reply to the UN Study on the
"Establishment of a Nuclear-Weapons-Free Zone
in the Region of the Middle East,"
October 22, 1991

1. Since the submission of the study contained in the Secretary-General's report (A/45/435, annex), the Gulf war has intervened. Consequently, the comments of the Government of Israel on the report pertain to the situation as it appears at present. A few prefatory references to the present circumstances are therefore in order.

2. The Gulf war has borne out Israel's contention that it faces an existential problem, which is separate and apart from the Palestinian problem. Yet, it is only the latter which has been recognized, because it is amenable to compromise. The existential problem was disregarded, because there is no compromise between existence and the denial of it. Others could disregard this, but Israel could not.

3. Iraq's threats to obliterate Israel by non-conventional means and its gratuitous launching of over 30 missiles against Israel, as well as the international deployment of half a million troops to confront the Iraqi forces, are stark evidence of what Israel would have had to face all alone from Iraq had it not been for the invasion of Kuwait.

4. Israel had maintained throughout the years that Iraq's threats were backed up by a nuclear programme designed to give substance to them. But Israel was condemned for putting the Osiraq nuclear reactor out of action, and the item is still on the agenda of the General Assembly. During the Gulf war, however, Iraqi nuclear installations were specifically targeted by the coalition forces, and the scope of the Iraqi enterprise now stands revealed as a declared threat to Israel and a potential threat to Iraq's neighbors. Had it not been for the invasion of Kuwait, it is doubtful that the international community would have taken note of the resoluteness of the Iraqi nuclear programme any more than it had in the past.

5. Iraq profited from its status as a signatory to the Treaty on the Non-Proliferation of Nuclear Weapons (NPT) even as it stood in flagrant violation of its commitments. The concept of a nuclear-weapon-free

zone, based solely on all-round adherence to NPT as it is embodied in United Nations resolutions, could not have prevented this development. The concept of a nuclear-weapon-free zone as proposed by Israel these last 11 years, which is based on direct negotiations and includes mutually reassuring arrangements, could most probably have prevented Iraq's menacing enterprise and also might have prevented a Middle East war altogether.

6. On all these topics, on Israel's existential problems, on Iraq's military nuclear multibillion dollar projects in fulfillment of their threats and on Israel's views of a credible nuclear-weapon-free zone, it is regrettable that Israel's voice was a lonely one and that so much effort was instead expended on arraigning and pressuring Israel, from which no threat emanated at any time.

7. This experience fortifies Israel in its belief that it need follow its own counsel, as long as its affairs are not judged on their merits by others.

8. These observations invite some general conclusions.

9. There are regional circumstances and issues, especially in matters of security, which can only be settled if the States of the region feel inclined to settle them. These circumstances pertain to one's immediate neighbors, and they cannot be settled by bland international dispositions. A case in point is Europe, as are the treaties of Tlatelolco and Raratonga in the nuclear context. It should be noted in this regard that Iraq presented no military threat to any country outside this region.

10. Weapons of mass destruction are, in the view of the Government of Israel, all those weapons that can kill civilians indiscriminately. Superior quantities of conventional weapons are as much a part of this category as are weapons traditionally classified as weapons of mass destruction. Given Israel's situation, it is obvious that arms control need include all these types of weapons.

11. Confidence is the basis for any agreement. And unlike technical dispositions, confidence can only be built over time. The Helsinki Accords took many years to mature, and recent upheavals in Europe illustrate how cautious one need be.

12. In order to reassure Israel, confidence-building measures are a most essential beginning to any credible peace process. Such measures would include, *inter alia*:

(a) A public declaration on the part of all States of the region that they will not resort to force in the settlement of their differences. Israel, for its part, is ready to reaffirm its repeated pledges to this effect;

(b) A public renunciation on the part of all States of the region of attempts to enforce a boycott of any of them or to delegitimize the international standing of any of them. Israel, for its part, has never employed such measures and undertakes never to resort to them in the future.

13. The recurrent wars in the Middle East, as well as most of the present problems in the region, need not have arisen if these simple modes of conduct had ben accepted and observed.

14. The building of confidence, moreover, requires progress on outstanding political problems. For when tensions abate, the likelihood of a promising attempt at arms control grows proportionately. It is far too early to tell if the Middle East is finally emerging from a past fraught with wars. But Israel cannot contemplate its situation with equanimity as long as its existence is still questioned by any of its neighbors.

15. All that which has been said above is pertinent to the comments of the Government of Israel on the thoughtful report of the Secretary-General. The Government of Israel appreciates the careful analysis contained in the Secretary-General's report and especially of the difficult situation which Israel has faced and continues to face.

16. While a good number of the confidence-building measures of a general nature proposed in the report are acceptable to the Government of Israel, the more substantive proposals make unrequited demands on Israel which are not consistent with the analysis contained in the report itself. These demands would only aggravate Israel's situation rather than alleviate it.

17. The following juxtaposition of the report's analyses and proposals will bear out the concerns of which Israel cannot divest itself.

18. In paragraphs 97 and 98, the report spells out the precariousness of Israel's situation. Yet, no mention is made of express and unconditional threats to Israel's existence nor of the fact that Israel has never threatened any country. In this "sustained hostility between itself [Israel] and the great majority of the States of the region,"

mentioned in paragraph 98, there is no symmetry. Israel has no *a priori* hostility towards any state.

19. Paragraph 81 of the report makes a nuclear-weapon-free zone dependent on all-round adherence to NPT or International Atomic Energy Agency (IAEA) safeguards. Ample reference to this suggestion has already been made above, and experience has borne out Israel's contentions. It is regrettable that the report makes no reference to Israel's concept of a nuclear-weapon-free zone and its confidence-building modalities.

20. The Government of Israel fully supports the references in paragraph 110 to the need for confidence, and the "linkage" among all the elements which affect security as set out in paragraph 151. The Government of Israel especially subscribes to paragraph 153, which says clearly that technical-military confidence-building measures cannot substitute for the political process.

21. In paragraphs 112 to 115, 120, 180 and 181, the report dwells on putting all Israeli nuclear facilities under IAEA inspection. This suggestion is disturbing, because it proposes that Israel abandon its policy of making safeguards dependent on the prior negotiation of a nuclear-weapon-free zone and the confidence-building modalities leading towards it. As has been said repeatedly, the Israeli concept need lead to a cessation of wars altogether and the nuclear-weapon-free zone will be credible once all parties have confidence that outstanding disputes will no longer be settled by force.

22. The pressure on Israel to put its nuclear installations under full-scope safeguards ignores, for the sake of principle, Israel's special concerns which were recently illustrated by the Gulf war. In particular, the Arabs' refusal to negotiate a nuclear-weapon-free zone with Israel, and their insistence on keeping up international pressure for Israel to accept full-scope safeguards, does not bode well. Israel views this as an attempt to keep it well controlled in the nuclear realm while retaining the option of waging war against it. Israel needs a sustained climate of confidence in order to see things differently.

23. Israel needs to be reassured, above all, that there is a will to redress its precarious situation, as described in the report. Confidence building by way of direct negotiations and advances in the political process must precede confidence-building measures of a technical nature. The latter feed on the former.

Appendix 10

President George Bush's
Nonproliferation Initiative,
July 13, 1992

Guiding Principles

First, the United States will build on existing global norms against proliferation and, where possible, strengthen and broaden them.

Second, the United States will focus special efforts on those areas where the dangers of proliferation remain acute, notably the Middle East, the Persian Gulf, South Asia, and the Korean Peninsula.

Third, U.S. nonproliferation policy will seek the broadest possible multilateral support, while continuing to show leadership on critical issues.

Fourth, the United States will address the proliferation issue through the entire range of political, diplomatic, economic, intelligence, regional security, export controls, and other tools available.

Policy Objectives

NUCLEAR MATERIALS

Nuclear materials production. The United States shall not produce plutonium or highly enriched uranium for nuclear explosive purposes. This step is intended to encourage countries in regions of tension such as the Middle East and South Asia to take similar actions, such as those proposed in the May 1991 Middle East Arms Control Initiative. The United States will seek further multilateral support for concrete measures to discourage production or acquisition of weapons-usable nuclear materials in South Asia, the Korean Peninsula, or other areas where they would increase the risk of proliferation.

MULTILATERAL ACTIONS

Compliance with international nonproliferation norms. The United States will take into account other countries' performance on key international nonproliferation norms in developing its cooperation and technology transfer relationships, and will consult with friends and allies on similar approaches.

Enforcement of international nonproliferation norms. The United States will consult with friends and allies on international actions to be taken against serious violations of nonproliferation norms, e.g., the transfer of any weapon of mass destruction or key weapon facilities, violation of safeguards agreements, or confirmed use of nuclear, chemical, or biological weapons. Actions could include United Nations Security Council embargoes or inspections, assistance to victims of attacks by such weapons, extradition agreements, or immigration restrictions against individuals who have knowingly contributed to proliferation.

Support for special inspections and weapon destruction. The United States will examine, in consultation with friends and allies, establishment of multilateral funding efforts to support special inspection regimes where necessary and to help states destroy existing weapon stockpiles.

Harmonization of export controls. The United States will promote harmonized nonproliferation export control lists and enforcement, including an agreement among suppliers not to undercut one another's export restraint decisions.

REGIONAL EFFORTS

Targeted Approaches. The United States will continue to focus special efforts on the dangers of proliferation in South Asia, the Persian Gulf, the Middle East, and on the Korean peninsula, including efforts to achieve confidence-building measures, inspection regimes, and other economic, political, and security-related measures.

Former Soviet Union. The United States will continue to work with authorities from Russia and the other new states toward the following objectives:

Implementation of all relevant international agreements, such as the Non-Proliferation Treaty, Biological Weapons Convention and, when opened for signature, the Chemical Weapons Convention.

Effective internal accounting and physical protection against theft or diversion of nuclear-related materials and equipment.

Effective export controls on chemical, biological, nuclear, and missile technologies consistent with existing multilateral regimes, including appropriate laws and regulations, as well as education of exporters and customs and enforcement officials.

Safe and secure dismantlement of nuclear warheads, and effective controls over nuclear-weapon material.

Consideration of requests for assistance in dismantling or destroying Russian biological weapons facilities or in converting these facilities to production of vaccines and other pharmaceutical products, provided Russia is in full compliance with the Biological Weapons Convention.

GLOBAL NORMS

Chemical Weapons Convention. The United States reaffirms its commitment to see a CWC concluded this year, and calls on all nations to commit to become original signatories.

NPT and Tlatelolco. The United States will seek the indefinite extension of the NPT in 1995 and full entry into force of the Treaty of Tlatelolco by 1993.

International Atomic Energy Agency. The United States will work with other nations to strengthen the International Atomic Energy Agency (IAEA), and will support needed increases in the safeguards budget.

Biological Weapons Convention. The United States will continue to urge universal adherence to the Biological Weapons Convention and increased support for the confidence-building measures agreed by the parties at the 1991 Review conference.

Missile Technology Control Regime. The United States reiterates the call of the MTCR Partners for all governments to adopt the MTCR Guidelines as part of their national policy.

INTELLIGENCE

Nonproliferation Center. The intelligence community, including the newly created Nonproliferation Center, will increase support to international nonproliferation regimes and seek to enlarge the pool of experienced, well-trained experts committed to the nonproliferation mission.

Appendix 11

Excerpts from an Address by the
Foreign Minister of Israel, Mr. Shimon Peres,
at the Signing Ceremony of the
Chemical Weapons Convention, Paris,
January 13, 1993

In the spirit of the global pursuit of general and complete disarmament, and the establishment of regional and global arms control regimes, Israel suggests to all the countries of the region to construct a mutually verifiable zone, free of surface-to-surface missiles and of chemical, biological and nuclear weapons.

Arms control negotiations and arrangements should be mutually agreed upon and include all states in the region. Implementation and verification mechanisms, the establishment of comprehensive and durable peace, should be region-wide in their application. Priority in this process ought to be assigned to systems whose destabilizing potential and effects have been proven through their use in wars and have inflicted mass casualties.

Appendix 12

Excerpts from
"U.S. Nonproliferation and Export Control Policy,"
White House fact sheet issued on the occasion of
President Clinton's address to the
UN General Assembly,
September 27, 1993

The president today established a framework for U.S. efforts to prevent the proliferation of weapons of mass destruction and the missiles that deliver them. He outlined three major principles to guide our nonproliferation and export control policy:

> Our national security requires us to accord higher priority to nonproliferation, and to make it an integral element of our relations with other countries.

> To strengthen U.S. economic growth, democratization abroad and international stability, we actively seek expanded trade and technology exchange with nations, including former adversaries, that abide by global international norms.

> We need to build a new consensus — embracing the executive and legislative branches, industry and public, and friends abroad — to promote effective nonproliferation efforts and integrate our nonproliferation and economic goals.

The president reaffirmed U.S. support for a strong, effective nonproliferation regime that enjoys broad multilateral support and employs all the means at our disposal to advance our objectives.

Key elements of the policy follow.

Fissile Material

The United States will undertake a comprehensive approach to the growing accumulation of fissile material from dismantled nuclear weapons and within civil nuclear programs. Under this approach, the United States will:

Seek to eliminate where possible the accumulation of stockpiles of highly-enriched uranium or plutonium, and to ensure that where these materials exist they are subject to the highest standards of safety, security, and international accountability.

Propose a multilateral convention prohibiting the production of highly-enriched uranium or plutonium for nuclear explosive purposes or outside of international safeguards.

Encourage more restrictive regional arrangements to constrain fissile material production in regions of instability and high proliferation risks.

Submit U.S. fissile material no longer needed for our deterrent to inspection by the International Atomic Energy Agency.

Pursue the purchase of highly-enriched uranium from the former Soviet Union and other countries and its conversion to peaceful uses as reactor fuel.

Explore means to limit the stockpiling of plutonium from civil nuclear programs, and seek to minimize the civil use of highly-enriched uranium.

Initiate a comprehensive review of long-range options for plutonium disposition, taking into account technical, nonproliferation, environmental, budgetary, and economic considerations. Russia and other nations with relevant interests and experiences will be invited to participate in this study.

The United States does not encourage the civil use of plutonium and, accordingly, does not itself engage in plutonium reprocessing for either nuclear power or nuclear explosive purposes. The United States, however, will maintain its existing commitments regarding the use of plutonium in civil nuclear programs in Western Europe and Japan.

Export Controls

To be truly effective, export control should be applied uniformly by all suppliers. The United States will harmonize domestic and multilateral controls to the greatest extent possible. At the same time, the need to lead the international community or overriding national security or foreign policy interests may justify unilateral export controls in specific cases. We will review our unilateral dual-use export controls and policies, and eliminate them unless such controls are essential to national security and foreign policy interests.

We will streamline the implementation of U.S. export controls. Our system must be more responsive and efficient, and not inhibit legitimate exports that play a key role in American economic strength while preventing exports that would make a material contribution to the proliferation of weapons of mass destruction and the missiles that deliver them.

Nuclear Proliferation

The United States will make every effort to secure the indefinite extension of the Non-Proliferation Treaty in 1995. We will seek to ensure that the International Atomic Energy Agency has the resources needed to implement its vital safeguards responsibilities, and will work to strengthen the IAEA's ability to detect clandestine nuclear activities.

. . . .

Regional Nonproliferation Initiatives

Nonproliferation will receive greater priority in our diplomacy, and will be taken into account in our relations with countries around the world. We will make special efforts to address the proliferation threat in regions of tension such as the Korean peninsula, the Middle East and South Asia, including efforts to address the underlying motivations for weapons acquisition and to promote regional confidence-building steps.

In Korea our goal remains a non-nuclear peninsula. We will make every effort to secure North Korea's full compliance with its nonproliferation commitments and effective implementation of the North-South denuclearization agreement.

In parallel with our efforts to obtain a secure, just and lasting peace in the Middle East, we will promote dialogue and confidence-building steps to create the basis for a Middle East free of weapons of mass destruction. In the Persian Gulf, we will work with other suppliers to contain Iran's nuclear, missile and CBW ambitions, while preventing reconstruction of Iraq's activities in these areas. In South Asia, we will encourage India and Pakistan to proceed with multilateral discussions on nonproliferation and security issues, with the goal of capping and eventually rolling back their nuclear and missile capabilities.

. . . .

Military Planning and Doctrine

We will give proliferation a higher profile in our intelligence collection and analysis and defense planning and ensure that our own force structure and military planning address the potential threat from weapons of mass destruction and missiles around the world.

. . . .

Appendix 13

Draft "Statement on Arms Control and
Regional Security," ACRS, Tunis,
December 1994

Preamble

The regional participants in the Arms Control and Regional Security
working group,

Reaffirming their respect for the Charter of the United Nations,

Bearing in mind the urgent necessity of achieving a just, lasting
and comprehensive peace settlement in the Middle East based on
United Nations Security Council Resolutions 242 and 338, and
conscious of the historic breakthroughs towards such a settlement
since the 1991 Madrid Middle East Peace Conference, particularly the
Israeli-Palestinian Declaration of Principles and the subsequent
Agreement on the Gaza and Jericho Area, and the Jordan-Israel peace
treaty of October 26, 1994,

Agreeing that all regional parties should pursue the common
purpose of achieving full and lasting relations of peace, openness,
mutual confidence, security, stability and cooperation throughout the
region,

Recognizing that the multilateral working groups, including the
Arms Control and Regional Security working group, should continue
to complement the bilateral negotiations and help improve the climate
for resolving the core issues at the heart of the Middle East peace
process, and that the peace process also created the opportunity to
cooperate in addressing additional issues of region-wide concern,

Embarking in this context on a process through the Arms Control
and Regional Security working group to establish arms control and
regional security arrangements aimed at safeguarding the region from

the dangers and ominous consequences of future wars and the horrors of mass destruction, and enabling all possible resources to be devoted to the welfare of the peoples of the region, including such areas as economic and social development,

Recognizing the importance of preventing the proliferation of nuclear, chemical, and biological weapons and of preventing the excessive accumulation of conventional arms in enhancing international and regional peace and security,

Conscious that the arms control and regional security process seeks to achieve a stable balance among military capabilities in the region that takes into account quantitative and qualitative factors, and also recognizes the significance of structural factors, and that provides for equal security for all,

Welcoming the special role of the United States and Russia as active co-sponsors of the Middle East peace process and calling on them and other extra-regional states to provide continuing support for the objectives and arrangements of the arms control and regional security process,

Recognizing that the full realization of the objectives contained in this Statement would be facilitated by the involvement in the arms control and regional security process of all regional parties, and calling on all such parties to support the principles contained in this Statement and, in this connection, to join the arms control and regional security process at an early date,

Have adopted the following:

I. FUNDAMENTAL PRINCIPLES GOVERNING SECURITY RELATIONS AMONG REGIONAL PARTICIPANTS IN THE ARMS CONTROL AND REGIONAL SECURITY WORKING GROUP

In their pursuit of a just, lasting and comprehensive peace in the Middle East, the regional participants will be governed in their security policies by the following fundamental principles, among others:

— The participants reaffirm their commitment to the principles of the Charter of the United Nations;

— Participants must refrain from the threat or use of force and from acts of terrorism and subversion;

— Security requires that participants fulfill in good faith obligations under international law;

— Security must be based on respect for and acknowledgment of sovereignty, territorial integrity, and political independence, non-interference in internal affairs, and reconciliation and cooperation among participants;

— Arms control and regional security arrangements should be aimed at achieving equal security for all at the lowest possible level of armaments and military forces;

— Military means, while needed to fulfill the inherent right of self-defense, and to discourage aggression, cannot by themselves provide security.

Enduring security requires the peaceful resolution of conflicts in the region and the promotion of good neighborly relations and common interests.

II. GUIDELINES FOR THE MIDDLE EAST ARMS CONTROL AND REGIONAL SECURITY PROCESS

The regional participants recognize the following as guidelines for the arms control and regional security process:

—The arms control and regional security process, as an integral part of the Middle East peace process, should create a favorable climate for progress in the bilateral negotiations and complement them by developing tangible measures in parallel with progress in the bilateral talks.

— The arms control and regional security process should strive to enhance security and general stability on a region-wide basis, even beyond the scope of the Arab-Israeli conflict, by pursuing regional security and arms control measures that reduce tension or the risk of war;

— The scope of the process must be comprehensive, covering a broad range of regional security, confidence and security building and arms control measures that address all threats to security and all categories of arms and weapons systems;

— The arms control and regional security process should not at any stage diminish the security of any individual state or give a state a military advantage over any other;

— The basic framework of the process is to pursue a determined, step-by-step approach which sets ambitious goals and proceeds toward them in a realistic way;

— The basis for decision-making on each issue in the arms control and regional security process should be consensus by the regional participants directly concerned;

— Each regional arrangement adopted in the arms control and regional security process should be the result of direct regional negotiations and should be implemented by all those regional parties relevant to the arrangement;

— Strict compliance with arms control and disarmament measures adopted within the framework of the arms control and regional security process is essential to the integrity of that process and for building confidence among the regional participants;

— All arms control and disarmament measures adopted by regional participants within the framework of the arms control and regional security process will be effectively verifiable by the regional parties themselves and should include, where appropriate, mutual on-site inspection and other rigorous monitoring techniques and mechanisms, and such verification could be complementary with verification measures in international arrangements.

III. STATEMENT OF INTENT ON OBJECTIVES FOR THE ARMS CONTROL AND REGIONAL SECURITY PROCESS

In the context of achieving a just, secure, comprehensive and lasting peace and reconciliation, the regional participants agree to pursue, *inter alia,* the following arms control and regional security objectives:

— preventing conflicts from occurring through misunderstanding or miscalculation by adopting confidence and security building measures that increase transparency and openness and reduce the risk of surprise attack and by developing regional institutional arrangements that enhance security and the process of arms control;

— limiting military spending in the region so that additional resources can be made available to other areas such as economic and social development;

— reducing stockpiles of conventional arms and preventing a conventional arms race in the region as part of an effort to provide enhanced security at lower levels of armaments and militarization, to reduce the threat of large-scale destruction posed by such weapons, and to move towards force structures that do not exceed legitimate defense requirements;

— promoting cooperation among regional participants in the peaceful uses of outer space, including the pursuit of appropriate means of sharing the benefits from satellite systems, of ensuring that outer space and other environments will not be used for acts of aggression by regional participants, and of enhancing the security of regional participants; and

[LANGUAGE PROPOSED BY ISRAEL:

— *establishing the Middle East as a mutually verifiable zone free of nuclear, chemical, biological weapons and ballistic missiles in view of their high destructive capacity and their potential to promote instability in the region.*]

[LANGUAGE PROPOSED BY THE UNITED STATES:

— *establishing the Middle East as a zone free of all weapons of mass destruction, including nuclear, chemical, and biological weapons and their delivery systems — since such weapons, with their high destructive capacity and their potential to promote instability in the region, pose a grave threat to security — through a combination of regional arrangements, such as weapons-free zones, and international arrangements, such as the BWC, the NPT, and the CWC.*]

[LANGUAGE PROPOSED BY EGYPT:

— *establishing a zone free of all weapons of mass destruction, including nuclear, chemical and biological weapons and their delivery systems, since such weapons, with their high destructive capacity and their potential to exacerbate the arms race in the region, pose the greatest threat to its security.*

— *that all parties of the region will adhere to the NPT in the near future.*]

Regional participants will be guided in their conduct by the principles embodied in this Statement and will refrain from actions or activities that are inconsistent with its guidelines or principles and that preclude the attainment of its objectives.

Appendix 14

Resolution on the Middle East of the
Conference of the State Parties to the Treaty on the
Non-Proliferation of Nuclear Weapons, New York,
May 11, 1995

Reaffirming the purpose and provisions of the Treaty on the Non-Proliferation of Nuclear Weapons,

Recognizing that, pursuant to article VII of the Treaty on the Non-Proliferation of Nuclear Weapons, the establishment of nuclear-weapon-free zones contributes to strengthening the international non-proliferation regime,

Recalling that the Security Council, in its statement of 31 January 1992, affirmed that the proliferation of nuclear and all other weapons of mass destruction constituted a threat to international peace and security,

Recalling also General Assembly resolutions adopted by consensus supporting the establishment of a nuclear-weapon-free zone in the Middle East, the latest of which is resolution 49/71 of 15 December 1994,

Recalling further the relevant resolutions adopted by the General Conference of the International Atomic Energy Agency concerning the application of Agency safeguards in the Middle East, the latest of which is GC(XXXVIII)/RES/21 of 23 September 1994, and noting the danger of nuclear proliferation, especially in areas of tension,

Bearing in mind Security Council resolution 687 (1991) and in particular paragraph 14 thereof,

Noting Security Council resolution 984 (1995) and paragraph 8 of the Decisions on Principles and Objectives for Nuclear Non-Proliferation and Disarmament adopted by the Conference on 11 May 1995,

Bearing in mind the other Decisions adopted by the Conference on 11 May 1995,

1. *Endorses* the aims and objectives of the Middle East peace process and recognizes that efforts in this regard, as well as other efforts, contribute to, *inter alia*, a Middle East zone free of nuclear weapons as well as other weapons of mass destruction;

2. *Notes with satisfaction* that in its report Main Committee III of the Conference (NPT/CONF.1995/MC.III/1) recommended that the Conference "call on those remaining States not parties to the Treaty to accede to it, thereby accepting an international legally binding commitment not to acquire nuclear weapons or nuclear explosive devices and to accept International Atomic Energy Agency safeguards on all their nuclear activities";

3. *Notes with concern*, the continued existence in the Middle East of unsafeguarded nuclear facilities, and reaffirms in this connection the recommendation contained in paragraph VI/3 of the report of Main Committee III urging those non-parties to the Treaty which operate unsafeguarded nuclear facilities to accept full scope International Atomic Energy Agency safeguards;

4. *Reaffirms* the importance of the early realization of universal adherence to the Treaty on the Non-Proliferation of Nuclear Weapons, and *calls upon* all States of the Middle East that have not yet done so, without exception, to accede to the Treaty as soon as possible and to place their nuclear facilities under full-scope International Atomic Energy Agency safeguards;

5. *Calls upon* all States in the Middle East to take practical steps in appropriate forums aimed at making progress towards, *inter alia*, the establishment of an effectively verifiable Middle East zone free of weapons of mass destruction, nuclear, chemical, and biological, and their delivery systems, and to refrain from taking any measures that preclude the achievement of this objective;

6. *Calls upon* all States party to the Treaty on the Non-Proliferation

of Nuclear Weapons, and in particular the nuclear-weapon States, to extend their cooperation and to exert their utmost efforts with a view to ensuring the early establishment by regional parties of a Middle East zone free of nuclear and all other weapons of mass destruction and their delivery systems.

Center for Science and International Affairs

Graham T. Allison, Director
John F. Kennedy School of Government
Harvard University
79 JFK Street, Cambridge MA 02138
(617) 495-1400

The Center for Science and International Affairs (CSIA) is the hub of research and teaching on international relations at Harvard's John F. Kennedy School of Government. CSIA seeks to advance the understanding of international security and environmental problems with special emphasis on the role of science and technology in the analysis and design of public policy. The Center seeks to anticipate emerging international problems, identify practical solutions, and encourage policymakers to act. These goals animate work in each of the Center's four major programs:

- The International Security Program (ISP) is the home of the Center's core concern with international security issues.

- The Strengthening Democratic Institutions (SDI) project works to catalyze international support for political and economic transformations in the former Soviet Union.

- The Science, Technology, and Public Policy (STPP) program emphasizes public policy issues in which understanding of science, technology, and systems of innovation are crucial.

- The Environment and Natural Resources Program (ENRP) is the locus of interdisciplinary research on environmental policy issues.

Each year CSIA hosts a multinational group of approximately 25 scholars from the social, behavioral, and natural sciences. Dozens of Harvard faculty members and adjunct research fellows from the greater Boston area also participate in CSIA activities. CSIA also sponsors seminars and conferences, many open to the public; maintains a substantial specialized library; and publishes a monograph series and discussion papers. The Center's International Security Program, directed by Steven E. Miller, publishes the CSIA Studies in International Security, and sponsors and edits the quarterly journal *International Security*.

The Center is supported by an endowment established with funds from the Ford Foundation and Harvard University, by foundation grants, by individual gifts, and by occasional government contracts.